MAILING ADDRESS
Maritime Studies Research Unit
Memorial University of Newfoundland
St. John's, Newfoundland A1C 5S7, Canada

RESEARCH IN MARITIME HISTORY
NO. 46

NEW DIRECTIONS IN NORWEGIAN MARITIME HISTORY

Edited by
Lewis R. Fischer and Even Lange

International Maritime Economic History Association

St. John's, Newfoundland
2011

ISSN 1188-3928
ISBN 978-0-9864973-6-0

Research in Maritime History is available free of charge to members of the International Maritime Economic History Association. The price to others is US $25 per copy, plus US $5 postage and handling.

Back issues of *Research in Maritime History* are available:

No. 1 (1991) David M. Williams and Andrew P. White (comps.), *A Select Bibliography of British and Irish University Theses about Maritime History, 1792-1990*

No. 2 (1992) Lewis R. Fischer (ed.), *From Wheel House to Counting House: Essays in Maritime Business History in Honour of Professor Peter Neville Davies*

No. 3 (1992) Lewis R. Fischer and Walter Minchinton (eds.), *People of the Northern Seas*

No. 4 (1993) Simon Ville (ed.), *Shipbuilding in the United Kingdom in the Nineteenth Century: A Regional Approach*

No. 5 (1993) Peter N. Davies (ed.), *The Diary of John Holt*

No. 6 (1994) Simon P. Ville and David M. Williams (eds.), *Management, Finance and Industrial Relations in Maritime Industries: Essays in International Maritime and Business History*

No. 7 (1994) Lewis R. Fischer (ed.), *The Market for Seamen in the Age of Sail*

No. 8 (1995) Gordon Read and Michael Stammers (comps.), *Guide to the Records of Merseyside Maritime Museum, Volume 1*

No. 9 (1995) Frank Broeze (ed.), *Maritime History at the Crossroads: A Critical Review of Recent Historiography*

No. 10 (1996) Nancy Redmayne Ross (ed.), *The Diary of a Maritimer, 1816-1901: The Life and Times of Joseph Salter*

No. 11 (1997) Faye Margaret Kert, *Prize and Prejudice: Privateering and Naval Prize in Atlantic Canada in the War of 1812*

No. 12 (1997) Malcolm Tull, *A Community Enterprise: The History of the Port of Fremantle, 1897 to 1997*

No. 13 (1997) Paul C. van Royen, Jaap R. Bruijn and Jan Lucassen (eds.), *"Those Emblems of Hell"? European Sailors and the Maritime Labour Market, 1570-1870*

No. 14 (1998) David J. Starkey and Gelina Harlaftis (eds.), *Global Markets: The Internationalization of The Sea Transport Industries Since 1850*

No. 15 (1998) Olaf Uwe Janzen (ed.), *Merchant Organization and Maritime Trade in the North Atlantic, 1660-1815*

No. 16 (1999) Lewis R. Fischer and Adrian Jarvis (eds.), *Harbours and Havens: Essays in Port History in Honour of Gordon Jackson*

No. 17 (1999) Dawn Littler, *Guide to the Records of Merseyside Maritime Museum, Volume 2*

No. 18 (2000) Lars U. Scholl (comp.), *Merchants and Mariners: Selected Maritime Writings of David M. Williams*

No. 19 (2000) Peter N. Davies, *The Trade Makers: Elder Dempster in West Africa, 1852-1972, 1973-1989*

No. 20 (2001) Anthony B. Dickinson and Chesley W. Sanger, *Norwegian Whaling in Newfoundland: The Aquaforte Station and the Ellefsen Family, 1902-1908*

No. 21 (2001) Poul Holm, Tim D. Smith and David J. Starkey (eds.), *The Exploited Seas: New Directions for Marine Environmental History*

No. 22 (2002) Gordon Boyce and Richard Gorski (eds.), *Resources and Infrastructures in the Maritime Economy, 1500-2000*

No. 23 (2002) Frank Broeze, *The Globalisation of the Oceans: Containerisation from the 1950s to the Present*

No. 24 (2003) Robin Craig, *British Tramp Shipping, 1750-1914*

No. 25 (2003) James Reveley, *Registering Interest: Waterfront Labour Relations in New Zealand, 1953 to 2000*

No. 26 (2003) Adrian Jarvis, *In Troubled Times: The Port of Liverpool, 1905-1938*

No. 27 (2004) Lars U. Scholl and Merja-Liisa Hinkkanen (comps.), *Sail and Steam: Selected Maritime Writings of Yrjö Kaukiainen*

No. 28 (2004) Gelina Harlaftis and Carmel Vassallo (eds.), *New Directions in Mediterranean Maritime History*

No. 29 (2005) Gordon Jackson, *The British Whaling Trade*

No. 30 (2005) Lewis Johnman and Hugh Murphy, *Scott Lithgow: Déjà vu All Over Again! The Rise and Fall of a Shipbuilding Company*

No. 31 (2006) David Gleicher, *The Rescue of the Third Class on the Titanic: A Revisionist History*

No. 32 (2006) Stig Tenold, *Tankers in Trouble: Norwegian Shipping and the Crisis of the 1970s and 1980s*

No. 33 (2007) Torsten Feys, Lewis R. Fischer, Stéphane Hoste and Stephan Vanfraechem (eds.), *Maritime Transport and Migration: The Connections between Maritime and Migration Networks*

No. 34 (2007) A.B. Dickinson, *Seal Fisheries of the Falkland Islands and Dependencies: An Historical Review*

No. 35 (2007) Tapio Bergholm, Lewis R. Fischer and M. Elisabetta Tonizzi (eds.), *Making Global and Local Connections: Historical Perspectives on Ports*

No. 36 (2008) Mark C. Hunter, *Policing the Seas: Anglo-American Relations and the Equatorial Atlantic, 1819-1865*

No. 37 (2008) Lewis R. Fischer and Even Lange (eds.), *International Merchant Shipping in the Nineteenth and Twentieth Centuries: The Comparative Dimension*

No. 38 (2008) Adrian Jarvis and Robert Lee (eds.), *Trade, Migration and Urban Networks in Port Cities, c.1640-1940*

No. 39 (2009) Henry T. Chen, *Taiwanese Distant-Water Fisheries in Southeast Asia, 1936-1977*

No. 40 (2009) John Armstrong, *The Vital Spark: The British Coastal Trade, 1700-1930*

No. 41 (2009) Carina E. Ray and Jeremy Rich (eds.), *Navigating African Maritime History*

No. 42 (2010) S.G. Sturmey, *British Shipping and World Competition*

No. 43 (2010) Maria Fusaro and Amélia Polónia (eds.), *Maritime History as Global History*

No. 44 (2010) Silvia Marzagalli, James R. Sofka and John J. McCusker (eds.), *Rough Waters: American Involvement with the Mediterranean in the Eighteenth and Nineteenth Centuries*

No. 45 (2011) Jaap R. Bruijn, *The Dutch Navy of the Seventeenth and Eighteenth Centuries*

Research in Maritime History would like to thank Memorial University of Newfoundland for its generous financial assistance in support of this volume.

Table of Contents

About the Editors / iii

Contributors' Notes / v

Introduction / 1

Global Integration

Jan Tore Klovland, "A Great Hundred Years of Timber Freights, 1757-1876" / 7

Camilla Brautaset, "When Distance Matters: The Output of the Norwegian Merchant Fleet, 1830-1865" / 37

Dag Hundstad, "The Silver Schooner" / 57

Political Issues

Elisabeth Solvang Koren, "In a Peculiar Position: Merchant Seamen in Norwegian Health Policy, 1890-1940" / 83

Per Kristian Sebak, "The Norwegian-American Line: State Incentives and Mediations with Dominant Market Players" / 101

Eivind Merok, "After the Boom: The Political Economy of Shipping in Norway in the Interwar Period" / 125

Andreas Nybø, "International Maritime Trade Politics and the Case of Norway, 1948-1990" / 151

Success and Failure

Morten Hammerborg, "Inheriting Strategies: Understanding Different Approaches to Shipping during the World War I Boom in Haugesund, Norway" / 177

Trygve Gulbrandsen, "Why Did They Fail? Business Exits among Norwegian Shipping Companies since 1970" / 199

Stig Tenold and Karl Ove Aarbu, "Little Man, What Now? Company Deaths in Norwegian Shipping, 1960-1980" / 233

Espen Ekberg, "The Growth of the Deep-Sea Car-Carrying Industry, 1960-2008" / 253

ABOUT THE EDITORS

LEWIS R. FISCHER <lfischer@mun.ca> is Professor of History at Memorial University of Newfoundland, Editor-in-Chief of the *International Journal of Maritime History* and Series Editor of *Research in Maritime History*. His research interests focus on the history of merchant shipping, the operation of maritime labour markets and the history of ports. His recent publications include "The International Merchant Marine in Comparative Perspective: An Analysis of Canada and Norway, 1870-1900," in Erik Hoops (ed.), *Aspects of Research on the History of Navigation in Honour of Prof. dr. Lars U. Scholl* (Bremerhaven, 2012), forthcoming; "Are We in Danger of Being Left with Our Journals and Not Much Else: The Future of Maritime History?" *Mariner's Mirror*, XCVII, No. 1 (2011), 366-381; "A Mixed Record: Naval Shipbuilding in the United States and Canada in World Wars I and II," in Dominique Barjot (ed.), *Deux guerres mondiales, 1914/1918-1939/1945: La mobilisation de la nation* (Paris, 2011, with Robert L. Davison); *International Merchant Shipping in the Nineteenth and Twentieth Centuries: The Comparative Dimension* (St. John's, 2008, edited with Even Lange); and *Making Global and Local Connections: Historical Perspectives on Ports* (St. John's, 2007, edited with Tapio Bergholm and M. Elisabetta Tonizzi). His current book project is a history of Norwegian merchant shipping between 1750 and the First World War.

EVEN LANGE <even.lange@iakh.uio.no> is Professor of Modern History at the University of Oslo. He is the founder and former director of the Centre for Business History at the Norwegian School of Business. While his previous research concentrated on industrial development, banking consumer co-operatives and economic policy in nineteenth-century Norway, he is currently directing a research project on the history of Norwegian merchant shipping, 1814-2014. His most recent publications include *Centres and Peripheries in Banking. The Historical Development of Financial Markets* (Aldershot, 2007, edited with Philip L. Cottrell and Ulf Olsson); *International Merchant Shipping in the Nineteenth and Twentieth Centuries: The Comparative Dimension* (St. John's, 2008, edited with Lewis R. Fischer); "Have Your Cake and Eat It Too: National Policy and Private Interest in a Small Open Economy: The Case of Norway," in Margit Müller and Timo Myllyntaus (eds.), *Path-*

breakers: Small European Countries Responding to Globalisation and Deglobalisation (Bern, 2008), 151-174 (with Helge Pharo); "The Survival of Family Dynasties in Shipping," *International Journal of Maritime History*, XXI, No. 1 (2009), 175-200 (with Trygve Gulbrandsen); *Vendepunker i norsk utenrikspolitikk. Nye internasjonale vilkår etter den kalde krigen* (Oslo, 2009, edited with Øyvind Østerud and Helge Pharo; and *Global Shipping in Small Nations: Nordic Experiences after 1960* (Basingstoke, 2012, edited with Stig Tenold and Martin Jes Iversen).

CONTRIBUTORS

KARL OVE AARBU <karl.ove.aarbu@tryg.no> is Adjunct Associate Professor at the Norwegian School of Economics and Business Administration and Chief Analyst for Tryg Forsikring, a Nordic insurance company. He holds a PhD in Economics from the Norwegian School of Economics in 2010. His field of specialization is micro-econometric modelling, and he has conducted empirical research in public economics, insurance economics and personnel economics.

CAMILLA BRAUTASET <Camilla.Brautaset@ahkr.uib.no> is an Associate Professor at the Department of Archaeology, History, Cultural Studies and Religion at the University of Bergen and a visitor at the Business History Unit of the London School of Economics and Political Science. Her main research interests are fish and ships. During 2011-2014 she is heading the project "Merchants and Missionaries: Norwegian Encounters with China in a Transnational Perspective, 1890-1937" which is funded by a major grant from the Norwegian Research Council.

ESPEN EKBERG <Espen.Ekberg@iakh.uio.no> is a postdoctoral fellow at the University of Agder, Norway. He has published books and articles on the history of the consumer co-operative movement in Norway and internationally, as well as on the contemporary history of Norwegian banking. He is currently working on a research project on the history of Norwegian merchant shipping.

TRYGVE GULBRANDSEN <trygve.gulbrandsen@samfunnsforskning.no> is a senior researcher at the Institute for Social Research in Oslo and Professor of Sociology at the Department of Sociology and Human Geography in the University of Oslo. His research interests include elites and power, trust, ownership and family businesses.

MORTEN HAMMERBORG <Morten.Hammerborg@uni.no> is a senior researcher at the Uni Rokkan Centre in Bergen, Norway. He holds a doctorate in the history of medicine. His previous publications include *Skipsfartsbyen: Haugesunds skipsfartshistorie 1850-2000* (Bergen, 2003), the shipping history of Haugesund, Norway.

DAG HUNDSTAD <Dag.Hundstad@ahkr.uib.no> is a PhD student in history at the University of Bergen. His first publication, *Klevefolk: Historien om en havn* (Mandal, 1996), won first prize in the Norwegian Contest for Young Scientists, while his MA thesis, "Sørlandske uthavnssamfunn – fra maritime monokulturer til fritidssamfunn" (University of Bergen, 2004), led to scholarships from the Fritt Ord Foundation and the Norwegian Historical Association. His other publications include "The Norwegian Term 'Coastal Culture' and the Movement Associated with It," *Deutsches Schiffartsarchiv*, XXX (2008), 421-426; and "A 'Norwegian Riviera' in the Making: The Development of Coastal Tourism and Recreation in Southern Norway in the Interwar Period," *Journal of Tourism History*, III, No. 2 (2011), 109-128.

JAN TORE KLOVLAND <Jan.Klovland@nhh.no> is Professor of Economics at the Norwegian School of Economics. His principal research interests include macroeconomic maritime and financial history. His recent publications include "The Construction of Ocean Freight Rate Indices for the Mid-Nineteenth Century," *International Journal of Maritime History*, XX, No. 2 (2008), 1-26; "New Evidence on the Fluctuations in Ocean Freight Rates in the 1850s," *Explorations in Economic History*, XLVI, No. 2 (2009), 266-284; and "New Series for Agricultural Prices in London, 1770-1914," LXIV, No. 1 (2011), 72-87 (with Peter Solar).

ELISABETH SOLVANG KOREN <Elisabeth.S.Koren@marmuseum.no> wrote a PhD thesis on the history of seamen's health. She is currently a Senior Curator at the Norwegian Maritime Museum in Oslo. Her main research interest is the social and cultural history of seamen.

EIVIND MEROK <eivind.merok@iakh.uio.no> is a PhD student at the University of Oslo, where he is writing a thesis on the Norwegian shipping industry in the interwar period. Before entering the doctoral programme, he was a research fellow at the Institute for Social Research in Oslo, where he co-authored a monograph on Norwegian retail history.

ANDREAS NYBØ <Andreas.Nybo@iakh.uio.no> is doctoral research fellow in history at the University of Oslo. He is currently working on a PhD thesis on Norwegian actors in international maritime trade politics, 1965-1995.

PER KRISTIAN SEBAK <Per.Sebak@ahkr.uib.no> is a specialist in nineteenth- and early twentieth-century European and transatlantic maritime and migration history. He has recently completed a PhD in the Department of Archeology, History, Cultural Studies and Religion at the University of Bergen.

STIG TENOLD <Stig.Tenold@nhh.no> is Professor of Economic History at the Norwegian School of Economics and Business Administration. He has published extensively on Norwegian maritime history and East Asian economic development. Among his current research areas are nineteenth-century voyage patterns, postwar innovation in the maritime industries and the concept of "scenes" in popular music.

Introduction: New Directions in Norwegian Maritime History

Even Lange and Lewis R. Fischer

A comprehension of the maritime sector is central to an understanding of Norwegian economic development and cultural identity during the last two centuries. Indeed, it is difficult to find any other nation where maritime activity has consistently played a more important role since the early nineteenth century. But the establishment of maritime history as a scholarly discipline in this country has been very long in the making. Until recently, few professional historians ventured into the sub-discipline, and those who did for the most part only stayed in the field for a short period of time. As a result, the writing of Norwegian maritime history was for a long time left to amateurs and journalists. When Helge W. Nordvik, an outstanding exception to this generalization, surveyed the state of the field at the beginning of the 1990s, his conclusion expressed a profound ambivalence: while important progress had been made in the preceding couple of decades, Norwegian maritime history still focused on fishing and the associated spheres of whaling and sealing. Despite public fascination with the sea and most things maritime, Norwegian scholarly literature, in Nordvik's view tended "to neglect the actual operations of maritime firms and the economics and policies of maritime transport" which constitute the dominant part of the modern maritime sector.[1]

This disjunction between the nature and importance of Norwegian maritime activity on the one hand, and the scholarly literature on the other, is now much less of a problem. Professional maritime history has developed as one of the attractive sub-disciplines in the expanding field of Norwegian economic history during the last few decades. At schools of business and economics in Oslo and Bergen, and at universities in several parts of the country, historical research has increasingly been directed towards modern economic and business activities, including those in the maritime sector. The rapid growth and regional spread of higher education, fuelled by rich oil revenues since the 1970s, is obviously among the driving forces behind this development. The relatively backward state of economic and maritime history at the outset motivated important efforts to improve our knowledge in these fields. A small, but growing, circle of research groups dedicated to the professionalization of business

[1]Helge W. Nordvik, "Norwegian Maritime Historical Research during the Past Twenty Years: A Critical Survey," *Sjøfartshistorisk Arbok* (Bergen, 1991), 241.

and commercial history was established from the 1980s and has in the interim made important contributions to changing the landscape of maritime history.

In the last couple of decades, this increased scholarly interest in maritime activity has fostered a new generation of professional historians who are trying to integrate the shipping experience into a more comprehensive, general historical framework. A project at the University of Oslo on Norwegian shipping history between 1814 and 2014 has in the last few years endeavoured to bring several of these scholars - and some newcomers - together in a collaborative effort to stimulate studies on the impact of international shipping during Norway's 200 years as an independent nation. This volume presents some results from this and related research. It is organized around three themes which reflect different, but equally important, aspects of the new scholarly efforts to understand and interpret the Norwegian maritime experience in a wider context.

The first three articles deal with the impact of international economic integration on Norwegian maritime activity. This, of course, is an old theme, but here it is approached in new ways by modern scholars. Jan Tore Klovland and Camilla Brautaset analyze different aspects of international freight patterns essential to the early growth of Norwegian shipping. Klovland's painstaking work on timber freight rates establishes a new framework for assessing the background of Norway's spectacular rise to a prominent position in the timber trade from the first half of the nineteenth century and provides a more solid basis for estimating freight income. Brautaset approaches the question of Norwegian shipping development in this period from a different quantitative perspective. She focuses on the spatial distribution of maritime services through a variety of new statistical analyses of the output of the merchant fleet. Rather than the traditional emphasis on volume (tonnage) as the most important indicator of production in the mid-1800s, Brautaset establishes a basis for the calculation of output in ton-miles, thus explaining the vital growth of the volume of shipping in the newly emerging cross-trades through changes in trading patterns that involved rapidly increasing distances. Finally, Dag Hundstad provides an interesting example of the local impact of international shipping activity. His essay highlights the interesting interaction between local and global culture associated with an American schooner engaged in the opium trade which arrived at a small community outside Mandal in southern Norway in 1816. The story of the "Silver Schooner," which had been the victim of mutiny in the Atlantic, lived on in the popular imagination until the end of the twentieth century as an example of the exotic aspects of intercontinental maritime activity in the era of the sailing ship.

The second batch of articles in this volume addresses an altogether different subject: the political dimensions of international shipping. This theme has surfaced as an important part of the new developments in maritime history,[2] and it is approached here from different angles: One article discuses the spin-offs from general social policy on the group of people who manned the merchant fleet; two essays examine the role of the central government in the development of various aspects of shipping activity before and after World War I; while a final contribution investigates the role of a small state like Norway in international maritime trade politics.

In the 1890s, seamen began to appear on the public health agenda. The issue was linked not only to the disturbingly high losses of Norwegian ships and crew in this period but also to concerns over the safety and social conditions of working people more generally, thus paralleling similar concerns in industrial societies elsewhere in Europe. Elisabeth Solvang Koren traces the development of the seamen's health issue in national policy until World War II and analyzes the intimate relation between this field and changes in general attitudes toward public health in Norway. The policies implemented seem to have been more complex than indicated by similar studies in Britain, mainly because the state bore some of the costs for seamen who became ill.

Per Kristian Sebak's study of the establishment of the Norwegian-American Line, 1908-1913, examines another aspect of extended government involvement in Norwegian shipping affairs. Norway's entry into the capital-intensive, highly organized transatlantic passenger liner business marked a symbolic step in the country's development of modern shipping services. State intervention, incentives and support were instrumental in achieving a positive result. The twin imperatives of nation building and animosity against Sweden shortly after the dissolution of the union between the two countries motivated strong political action and shaped the outcome in fundamental ways.

Government support in a somewhat different form played an even more important role in Norway's participation in international shipping in the following decades. During the interwar years, Norwegian shipping performed amazingly well. From the mid-1920s onwards, a large-scale technological modernization took place, with a special emphasis on the tanker business, and the country's merchant fleet grew more rapidly than that of any other leading maritime nation. Eivind Merok examines the background of this development in his contribution to the volume. His findings strongly suggest that a favourable tax regime, originating in 1916 and extended after the war, goes a long way toward explaining this extraordinary expansion.

Andreas Nybø approaches the interplay of government and private interests in the shipping arena at another level. His study of international shipping politics during the last half of the twentieth century focuses on the formation of new international organizations and their attendant networks. Nybø explains how a small nation like Norway adapted to the changes in this field

---

[2]Camilla Brautaset and Stig Tenold, "Globalisation and Norwegian Shipping Policy 1850-2000," *Business History*, L, No. 5 (2008), 565-582.

and sought to promote the interests of its shipping community through close cooperation between the national shipowners' association and government agencies. Civil servants and representatives of the shipping industry worked together in substantial efforts - mostly in vain, albeit also with some success - to influence the direction of international maritime policy.

Four articles on the failures and successes of Norwegian shipping ventures since the early 1900s comprise the final section of the book. In the business history literature, studies of successful firms dominate, mainly because they survived long enough to have their histories written. To understand the development of a highly dynamic industry like shipping, however, we also need to examine what we might think of as "creative destruction." A particular emphasis on failed business strategies and other factors that have led shipping companies to fold seem appropriate in periods of strong turbulence. Accordingly, the articles on bankruptcies are situated in the contexts of the First World War and the crises of the 1970s and 1980s. But those turbulent years also offered new opportunities, and two of the articles investigate the ways in which some Norwegians tried to grasp them.

Morten Hammerborg actually handles *both* failure and success in his contribution on business strategies during World War I. Tracing the parallel, but often divergent careers of a pair of twin brothers - each in charge of a shipping company into which they had married in Haugesund on the southwest coast of Norway - he analyzes the main factors behind their radically different business trajectories, ending in fabulous wealth for one and bankruptcy for the other. The difference in outcome - riches or ruin - can in Hammerborg's view be attributed to strategies that were deeply rooted in the past experience of each firm. Without stretching the point too far, it seems safe to conclude that this is a strong case for affirming the truism that history matters!

During the prolonged depression in the freight markets during large parts of the 1970s and 1980s, more than sixty percent of Norwegian shipping firms went out of business. In two articles, Trygve Gulbrandsen and Stig Tenold and Karl Ove Aarbu examine this phenomenon from different angles. Gulbrandsen's essay is a detailed study of how four mid-size firms failed, focusing on factors related to ownership and other company-specific features. Each of them had been operating for fifty years or more and seems to have failed to weather the difficult economic times mainly for endogenous reasons, such as inadequate strategic decisions, poor governance and conflicts within the owning family, but some were also victims of unforeseen disasters.

Tenold and Aarbu have chosen a different approach to the question of why companies left the industry. They include both the peaks and nadirs of the business cycle and concentrate on statistical data. Through a quantitative analysis of the population of Norwegian shipping companies in the 1960s and 1970s, Tenold and Aarbu map central business characteristics to examine the relationship between variables like the size of firms at the outset, their geographic origins, the composition and age of their fleets and their subsequent fate. The salient feature of their conclusion on the mortality rates from 1960 to 1980 is that "company size was by far the most important factor" in explaining which shipping firms survived and which went out of business. Only one-quarter of small companies survived, for example.

As Tenold and Aarbu point out, the cycles of boom and bust are not, however, adequately described in terms of company exits alone. Equally important to gaining a complete answer is the expanding side of development characterized by technological innovation and changing structures of trade, both of which offered new possibilities. An accelerated specialization of the world fleet has transformed the shipping industry since the 1960s. The share of specialized tonnage grew from less than five percent to nearly half of total tonnage during the last half-century. Norwegian shipowners found a way to expand out of the tanker crises through increased specialization. In the last article in this volume, Espen Ekberg investigates how the successful transformation of shipping services came about in the case of the car-carrying business. Focusing on the participation of a small number of Norwegian shipowners, he underlines the importance of studying small actors to understand the origin and nature of wide-ranging changes.

Throughout the last few decades, the Norwegian shipping sector has been battling serious difficulties. At the same time, booming offshore petroleum activities have drastically reduced the importance of the traditional merchant marine to the national economy. Oil and gas production has replaced shipping as the jewel in Norway's economic crown. Ironically, our understanding of the historic value of shipping as the mother industry of Norwegian economic development appears to be increasing. We hope that this collection of articles will contribute to bringing the study of international shipping in a small nation to the level it deserves.

A Great Hundred Years of Timber Freights, 1757-1876[1]

Jan Tore Klovland

Introduction

The timber trade was the backbone of Norwegian shipping in the nineteenth century. Norwegian vessels participated in all the major trades involving timber and wood - pine, spruce and oak from the Baltic, Canada and the White Sea; pitch pine from the southern US; mahogany and logwood from Central America; and teak from the East Indies. But it all began with the flourishing exports of Norwegian timber and wood to the United Kingdom and northern Europe in the preceding century. In the first half of the eighteenth century, the timber trade to Britain was dominated by British vessels due to the heavy losses suffered by the Norwegian merchant fleet during the Great Northern War. Norwegian shipping prospered again in the last quarter of the eighteenth century, and much of the timber exported to the UK was carried by Norwegian ships.[2] In 1771-1773, as much as seventy-one percent of the tonnage entering from Norway and Denmark was accounted for by foreign vessels, which was significantly more than in any other trade.[3] Not all the foreign vessels were Scandinavian, though. Dutch participation in the trade, which had been considerable in the first part of the seventeenth century, was still important around 1770, as witnessed by the fact that timber exports from Drammen, the largest shipping port for timber at the time, was carried chiefly by Dutch vessels.[4]

---

[1]I would like to thank Lewis R. Fischer and Stig Tenold for helpful suggestions.

[2]H.S.K. Kent, "The Anglo-Norwegian Timber Trade in the Eighteenth Century," *Economic History Review,* New ser., VIII, No. 1 (1955), 62-74; A.N. Kiær, "Historical Sketch of the Development of Scandinavian Shipping," *Journal of Political Economy*, I, No. 3 (1893), 329-364; and Ralph Davis, *The Rise of the English Shipping Industry in the Seventeenth and Eighteenth Centuries* (London, 1962; reprint, Newton Abbot, 1972).

[3]Davis, *Rise of the English Shipping Industry*, 215.

[4]Kiær, "Historical Sketch," 333-334. This was also true for timber exports to the Continent.

The tonnage of the Norwegian fleet trebled between 1777 and 1806. This was a splendid period for owners of Norwegian vessels carrying hewn timber and sawn wood, as well as a diminishing proportion of older staple products, masts and spars. Two factors then caused a halt and even significant reduction in the tonnage of timber ships from Norway. First, the depletion of Norwegian forests meant that there was little room for the expansion of timber exports. Second, and of far greater immediate consequence, was the destruction of much of the Norwegian fleet during the Napoleonic wars.

The timber export trade was the main source of expansion as the Norwegian shipping industry recovered after the destructive Napoleonic war years. Exports to the three main markets - the United Kingdom, France and Holland/Belgium - accounted for eighty-two percent of total exports of timber and wood in the years 1826-1830. The proportions carried in Norwegian vessels to these three countries in this period have been estimated at eighty-two, ninety-five and sixty-four percent, respectively.[5]

The volume of timber and wood exports from Norway did show some expansion in the 1830s and 1840s, and even more so in the 1850s, but the limits to domestic forest resources entailed a marked reduction in Norway's share of world exports of these products.[6] Hence, a further expansion of Norwegian shipping emanating from the timber trade was crucially dependent upon access to foreign export markets. In the early 1820s, trade acts generally prohibited ships from third countries carrying goods to the main European markets. Two fortuitous changes to these principles were to open the British market for timber and wood to Norwegian shipowners, however. First, in 1825, the restriction that prohibited Norwegian vessels from carrying goods between Sweden and foreign countries (and *vice versa*) was abolished. As the English (and other nations') navigation laws did not distinguish between Norwegian and Swedish vessels, this allowed Norwegian ships to take part in the growing timber export trade from Sweden.[7] At first, this trade took place from western North Sea ports, mainly Gothenburg, but from the 1840s more and more also from the Baltic.[8] The second event was the repeal of the British Navigation Acts in 1850. Thereafter, Norwegian shipping expanded rapidly, particularly in the cross-trades in timber and wood. Because Norwegian shipowners had em-

[5]Oskar Kristiansen, *Penge og Kapital, Næringsveie* (Oslo, 1925), 178 and 293-298.

[6]Camilla Brautaset, "Norsk eksport, 1830-1865: I perspektiv av historiske nasjonalregnskaper" (Unpublished PhD thesis, Norwegian School of Economics and Business Administration, 2002).

[7]Kiær, "Historical Sketch," 342-343.

[8]Ernst Söderlund, *Svensk trävaruexport under hundra år* (Stockholm, 1951).

ployed their vessels in the timber trade for a century or more, a large part of their fleet was eminently suitable for this trade.

The literature on Norwegian shipping and its involvement in the timber trade is voluminous, but little systematic research on timber freight rates has been published so far. This essay presents new annual time series of timber freights for a number of trade routes all over the world from the late 1830s to the late 1870s. The bulk of the freight rate data that has been available previously in published sources only starts in 1869 and is based on the Angier circulars published in *Fairplay* in 1920. As a result, the new freight rate series will shed some light on freight rate markets in preceding decades for which the quantitative basis previously has been rather patchy.[9] A further motivation for presenting these time series is that they may provide a firmer basis for estimating the gross freight earnings of the Norwegian shipping industry prior to the publication of "official" figures beginning in 1866.[10]

I then go on to link these series to the existing data on timber freights from the Baltic and Norway extending back to the 1760s, thus covering more than a century of timber freights. I will also examine how well integrated the various timber trade routes were from the perspective of how freight rates developed over time.

Norwegian Shipping in the Nineteenth Century: Cargoes and Deployment

In the early 1830s, the gross freight earnings of the Norwegian merchant fleet were dominated by revenue from carrying domestic goods to foreign countries. Revenue from this source has been estimated at ten million Norwegian *kroner* (NOK), while the corresponding figure derived from the involvement of Nor-

---

[9]The Angier data are presented in L. Isserlis, "Tramp Shipping Cargoes, and Freights," *Journal of the Royal Statistical Society,* CI, No. 1 (1938), 53-146. This is also the source of the well-known Isserlis Freight Rate index, which is still a benchmark for post-1869 developments. A revised freight rate index, based on a somewhat expanded data set, can be found in Saif I. Shah Mohammed and Jeffrey G. Williamson, "Freight Rates and Productivity Gains in British Tramp Shipping, 1869-1950," *Explorations in Economic History,* XLI, No. 2 (2004), 172-203. Some useful data on freight rates before 1869 can be found in C. Knick Harley, "Ocean Freight Rates and Productivity, 1740-1913: The Primacy of Mechanical Invention Reaffirmed," *Journal of Economic History,* XLVIII, No. 4 (1988), 851-876; Harley, "Coal Exports and British Shipping, 1850-1913," *Explorations in Economic History*, XXVI, No. 2 (1989), 311-338; and Jan Tore Klovland, "The Construction of Ocean Freight Rate Indices for the Mid-Nineteenth Century," *International Journal of Maritime History,* XX, No. 2, 2008, 1-26.

[10]Brautaset, "Norsk eksport," provides a careful set of estimates of Norwegian gross freight earnings for the period 1830-1865 using the "British" freight rate index constructed by Harley, "Ocean Freight Rates."

wegian shipping in the cross-trades only amounted to about two million NOK.[11] The latter grew much faster over the ensuing decades, however, surpassing the traditional export trade in terms of gross revenue in 1860, and it expanded rapidly thereafter, making the Norwegian merchant fleet the leading foreign carrier of goods to and from Britain by 1870.[12]

Table 1
Gross Freight Earnings of Norwegian Sailing and Steam Ships in 1873
(percentage distribution by country of entry and clearance)

Country	Inward	Outward
United Kingdom	44.9	9.0
United States	3.8	20.0
Sweden	1.9	18.2
Russia and Finland	3.0	9.5
France	12.6	1.4
Germany	6.4	2.3
Other North European Countries	12.6	0.8
British North America	0.3	9.7
Spain and Portugal	2.3	2.2
Other European Mediterranean Countries	1.4	1.1
South America	2.0	2.2
West Indies and Central America	1.0	2.6
Asia	0.4	2.9
Africa	1.1	0.5
Australia	0.2	0.2
Norway	6.1	17.2
Total	100.0	100.0

Source: Norway, *Tabeller vedkommende Norges Skibsfart i Aaret 1873* (Christiania, 1875).

Table 1 gives an overview of the gross freight earnings of the Norwegian shipping industry in 1873. Although the United Kingdom and continental northern Europe accounted for about three-quarters of the revenue from inward shipments, these figures show clearly how well diversified the activities of the Norwegian fleet were. Norwegian vessels carried goods to all parts of

[11]Brautaset, "Norsk eksport," 259.

[12]John Glover, "Tonnage Statistics of the Decade 1860-70," *Journal of the Royal Statistical Society*, XXXV, No. 2 (1872), 218-230. See also Helge W. Nordvik, "The Shipping Industries of the Scandinavian Countries, 1850-1914," in Lewis R. Fischer and Gerald E. Panting (eds.), *Change and Adaptation in Maritime History: The North Atlantic Fleets in the Nineteenth Century* (St. John's, 1985), 119-148.

the world; only 6.1 percent of earnings were produced by carrying imports to Norway.

The global orientation of Norwegian shipping is even more clearly reflected in the figures for outward-bound cargoes where the United States and Canada (British North America) were the most important, accounting for almost thirty percent of earnings, while Sweden and Norway each contributed about eighteen percent. The fact that outbound earnings were relatively larger than inward ones from countries such as Canada, Russia and Finland, Sweden and Norway is certainly an indication that a large proportion of gross freight revenues must have been derived from timber freights. From the United Kingdom and the European continent in particular, it appears that many Norwegian vessels must have departed in ballast.

With respect to domestic exports, we know that about two-thirds of the tonnage clearing Norwegian ports in the early 1870s comprised timber. The share of timber freights from individual countries is difficult to determine exactly from the published statistics, but for 1873 we have an estimate of the distribution of total freight earnings of Norwegian sailing ships by types of cargo. These data are shown in table 2, which clearly underscores the dominant position of the timber trade in Norwegian shipping. This trade accounted for fifty-three percent of the total earnings of sailing vessels, outstripping by far the contributions of grain, petroleum, coal and colonial goods trades.[13]

Table 2
Gross Freight Earnings of Norwegian Sailing Ships in 1873
(percent distribution by trade)

Trade	Percent
Timber and Wood	53.2
Grain and Seeds	8.7
Petroleum and Petroleum Products	8.1
Coal	6.4
Cotton (North America only)	3.5
Rice and Other Cargoes from Asia and Australia (other than timber)	2.5
Guano, Nitrates and Wheat via Cape Horn	0.7
Other Cross-Trades Not Listed Above (sugar, coffee, iron, general cargo, etc.)	11.5
Fish, Ice and Other Domestic Trades	5.4
Total	100.0

Source: See table 1.

Two rather obvious conclusions can be drawn from this brief survey of the Norwegian shipping industry in the early 1870s. First, timber freights were the single most important trade in which the Norwegian merchant fleet participated. Although data for previous periods are less precise, this conclu-

[13]Sailing vessels produced 92.4 percent of total gross earnings in 1873.

sion is presumably valid for much of the middle part of the nineteenth century. Second, the estimates of timber freight rates relevant to Norwegian shipping may also form the basis for a world timber freight index because Norwegian ships were sailing from all of the world's major timber ports.

Freight Rate Series

The annual freight rate series presented in the following tables cover the main timber trade routes in the middle of the nineteenth century. These include freights to the UK and France from Christiania; Gothenburg; the German, Russian and Swedish Baltic; the White Sea; Canada; the southern United States; Central America; and the East Indies. The data are annual averages of all quotations found for a specific trade route in each year. This implies that more weight is given to freight rates prevailing during the peak season of the year and less to months of low activity. In northern waters, most shipments took place in the spring and summer months, but it should be noted that there was often a significant chartering activity in the winter months, quoting rates on a "first open water" basis. Because the data series comprise both London brokers' quotations, which commenced early in the year, and spot fixtures during the shipment season, the resulting time series will usually reflect market conditions during much of the year, but with a lower implicit weight attached to late autumn charters.

This way of averaging seems to be the best way to produce true annual averages and is much preferable to the average of the year's high and low quotes on which all estimates from the Angier data are based. But it is not without its shortcomings. When the number of underlying quotations for a particular trade route in any year is small, the resulting figure may turn out to be unrepresentative of the true annual level for a number of reasons. These include strong short-term cycles, seasonal patterns, acts of war and various ephemeral factors affecting freight rate quotations. For this reason, the annual average data tabulated here will not be ideal as the basis for computing freight rate indices for the various routes – it is preferable to use monthly observations for this purpose.

The data presented here are computed from a large sample of monthly freight rate quotations covering the years 1835-1876. The sources include a number of British, Norwegian, American and Finnish contemporary newspapers and periodicals as well as British and Norwegian consular reports and parliamentary papers. As noted above, both quotations from the London brokers' lists, which can be found in the newspapers, and actual fixtures from the various markets, were used. It is my impression from scrutinizing many brokers' quotations that these in general did not deviate in any systematic way from the actual fixtures. The former were mostly indicative, although some reflected actual offers made by merchants. The most common cause of any significant deviation between these two sources was the spot versus forward dimension; a broker's quotation usually referred to a sailing taking place some weeks into the future because the vessel needed some time to proceed to the port of loading. This feature was more prevalent before communications were greatly improved by the telegraph.

Western Scandinavia

Timber freights from Gothenburg played a vital role during the reconstruction period of the Norwegian merchant fleet from the 1830s. The timber export trade from Norwegian ports stagnated in this period, one source describing it as being essentially reduced to a subsidiary cargo that helped finance the transition to foreign timber markets.[14] This seems to be a slight exaggeration, though, because the number of deals and battens imported into London was still larger from Christiania and Drammen than from Gothenburg around 1840. In the five-year period 1838-1842, Norwegian wood accounted for fifteen percent and Gothenburg for twelve percent of total imports of deals and battens into London.[15] It is nevertheless fair to say that the Gothenburg trade became a springboard to further expansion abroad, providing a quantitatively important and reliable source of employment for Norwegian vessels in the transition period from the Napoleonic wars to the repeal of the British Navigation Acts. During the 1840s, the tonnage employed in this trade accounted for about half of the total Norwegian shipping capacity engaged in the cross-trades. Norwegian vessels dominated the wood trade from Gothenburg in these years; in 1841, for example, Norwegian vessels carried 181 cargoes of wood from this port, of which eighty-eight went to the UK, sixty to France, twenty-five to Belgium, three apiece to Denmark and North Africa and two to North America.[16] The relative importance of the Gothenburg trade diminished after the 1850s as the centre of gravity of Swedish timber exports moved to Baltic ports. Timber freights from Christiania and Gothenburg are presented in appendix table 1. The bulk of timber and wood shipments from these ports went to UK and French ports, which are both represented in the table. Some cargoes of planed wood were also sent to Belgian, Dutch, Spanish and North African

---

[14]Fredrik Scheel, "Fra Napoleonskrigene til navigasjonsaktens opphevelse," in Jacob S. Worm-Müller (ed.), *Den norske sjøfarts historie* (6 vols., Oslo, 1923-1951), II, part 1, 181-204.

[15]Statistics on London timber imports in *Morgenbladet* (Christiania), 19 February 1844. It should be added that the French market was of even greater importance to Norwegian and Swedish timber exporters in the decades before 1850.

[16]*Morgenbladet* (Christiania), 12 February 1842.

ports and, from the 1870s, to Australia. Freight rate quotations for such ports can also be found in my sample, but are less complete than those listed here.

Baltic

Appendix table 2 presents timber and deal freights from the lower Baltic, Russian and Swedish Baltic ports. The timber trade from the Lower Baltic ports of Danzig, Memel, Stettin and Riga, as well as the trade in deals and battens from Kronstadt/St. Petersburg and Vyborg, were well established in the eighteenth century. While the vast timber resources of the Swedish Baltic were not exploited on a large scale until the middle of the nineteenth century, the growth of timber and deal exports from Swedish Baltic ports from the 1840s was spectacular. The year 1843 marked the first year in which more deals were imported into London from Sundsvall and adjacent Baltic ports than from Gothenburg, and from the 1850s it rapidly outstripped the Gothenburg trade with respect to the volume of exports.[17] Before the repeal of the British Navigation Acts in 1850, the Swedish Baltic timber trade was therefore of particular importance to Norwegian shipowners.

The White Sea

Around 1840, the wood trade from Archangel and Onega was much less important than those from the Baltic and Scandinavia, representing only about three percent of London's imports of sawn wood (see appendix table 3 for the freight rates).[18] It grew considerably in importance in the coming decades, and Norwegians were major participants.[19] In 1871, a total of 140 Norwegian vessels entered Archangel, a number surpassed only by the 161 British ships that visited. In most cases the vessels carried sawn wood to the United Kingdom as a return cargo, with the addition of some oats, linseed and tar.[20]

Canada

In the late eighteenth century, Baltic and Scandinavia were the main sources of timber supply to Britain, but wartime difficulties and a one hundred percent

[17]*Ibid.*, 19 February 1844; and Söderlund, "Svensk trävaruexport."

[18]*Morgenbladet* (Christiania), 19 February 1844.

[19]Jacob S. Worm-Müller, "Fra klipperen til motorskibet," in Worm-Müller (ed.), *Den norske sjøfarts historie*, II, part 2, 189.

[20]*Uddrag af Consulatberetninger vedkommende Norges Handel og Skibsfart i Aaret 1871* (Christiania, 1872), Consular Report for Archangel, 1871.

increase in the duty on foreign (non-colonial) timber in 1811 "changed the pattern of the timber trade towards a heavy dependence on Canada, which lasted for more than thirty years."[21] It is unfortunate that the data on Canadian timber freight rates in appendix table 4 only begins in 1839. It appears that there are no easily accessible and rich sources of such data before the early 1850s, after which there are frequent market reports in British, American and Norwegian newspapers. Before the mid-1850s, some of the annual average freight rates, in particular from Saint John, New Brunswick, are based on a single or a very limited number of quotations and must be used with caution.

Norwegian shipowners responded quickly to the new opportunities that the liberalized regulatory regime presented after 1850 with respect to carrying timber and wood from Canada to the UK. In October 1849, even before the Navigation Laws ceased to be effective, the Norwegian ship *Flora* was reported to be on its way from Québec to London with timber, deals and staves, having been chartered in New York in September.[22] The report from New York that contained this news further stated that this was a new and advantageous opportunity for Norwegian and Swedish vessels arriving at ports on the northeastern seaboard of America with emigrants. The sustained flow of emigrants from Scandinavia during the ensuing decades, for which Québec for many years was the main port of entry, laid the foundation for a strong Norwegian participation in the Canadian wood trade. British and Norwegian vessels dominated this trade; in 1872, 80.9 percent of foreign vessels arriving at the port of Québec were British, while 15.6 percent were Norwegian.[23]

Southern United States, Central America and the East Indies

The pitch pine trade from US ports on the Gulf of Mexico only began on a large scale in the 1860s, but it grew rapidly in importance thereafter. The trade in expensive furnishing timber, such as teak from the East Indies and mahogany from the Caribbean and Central America, had a much longer history. Its share of total timber imports in the UK declined relative to the imports of constructional softwoods, from about twenty percent in 1780 to five percent in 1850.[24] These trades were somewhat more peripheral to Norwegian shipowners than the other timber trades discussed above, but from the consular reports

---

[21]Ralph Davis, *The Industrial Revolution and British Overseas Trade* (Leicester, 1979), 48.

[22]*Morgenbladet* (Christiania), 17 October 1849.

[23]*Uddrag af Consulatberetninger vedkommende Norges Handel og Skibsfart I Aaret 1872* (Christiania, 1873), Consular Report for Québec, 1872.

[24]Davis, *British Overseas Trade*, 46.

we know that Norwegian vessels participated regularly in, for example, the Belize mahogany trade (see the freight rates in appendix table 5).

Freight Rate Indices

To see how freight rates evolved on the various routes, I calculated a set of annual indices. These were constructed from monthly rates for seven regions: Scandinavia (Norway and western Sweden, chiefly Gothenburg); Baltic (including Swedish and German Baltic, Finnish and Russian ports); White Sea (Archangel, Onega); Canada (Canadian and northern US ports on the eastern seaboard as far south as New York); Gulf (US pitch pine ports in the Gulf and ports as far north as Wilmington, NC); Central America (from Mexico to Belize); and Burma (Moulmein). The method was the chain price index frequently used in the housing market where it is known as a "repeat sales" index. This type of index was developed for markets where the price of each object is quoted infrequently and at irregular intervals. I have discussed this index elsewhere and referred to it as a "repeat sailings index" because it uses a "sailing" as the unit of measurement (corresponding to one particular property in the real estate market). A sailing is defined as a passage between two ports with a specific cargo, distinguishing between sail and steam, and in some cases whether the freight rate was fixed on the spot or was a broker quotation.[25]

In this way, a very large number of freight rate observations, corresponding to precisely defined sailings, can be utilized to compute an accurate index. In the sample underlying the Baltic index, for example, there are 19,407 timber freight rate observations for the period from 1837 to 1876.[26] There are ninety-three different specifications of wood and timber cargoes that can be applied to characterize any single observation, 175 different potential ports of clearance in the Baltic, and many hundreds of ports where the cargoes were unloaded in the UK and continental Europe. Only a subset of these "sailings" will be quoted in a specific month or year, however. Even for the most common ones, such as Danzig or Memel to London with balks, listed in appendix table 2, quotations are missing for some years. The appealing feature of this type of index is that it automatically handles such gaps in the time series. In essence, this type of index is a common chain index (and would be identical to an ordinary chain index if there were no gaps in the time series), using simple regression procedures for handling gaps in the data.

[25]Klovland, "Construction of Ocean Freight Rate Indices;" and Klovland, "New Evidence on the Fluctuations in Ocean Freight Rates in the 1850s," *Explorations in Economic History*, XLVI, No. 2 (2009), 266-284.

[26]The calculations use the percentage change from a point in time to the next occurrence of a specific sailing, so only those which are repeated are used. In large samples, about ninety percent of all observations are useful in this sense.

Table 3
Timber Freight Rates Indices, 1835-1876

Year	Scandinavia	Baltic	White Sea	North America	Southern US	Central America	East India
1835	110.8						
1836	122.7						
1837	129.3	136.4					
1838	131.5	125.4					
1839	128.8	132.1	142.0	148.2			
1840	117.6	124.5	132.4	141.2			
1841	111.3	106.6	109.0	113.3			
1842	107.0	94.4	98.9	97.9			
1843	102.4	93.4	98.6				
1844	105.3	106.7		132.5			
1845	114.0	118.0					
1846	118.3	119.2					
1847	120.0	139.5	136.2	150.8			
1848	106.1	112.7	112.0	117.0		117.6	117.9
1849	99.8	104.3	110.7	110.9		118.6	103.7
1850	100.0	100.0	100.0	100.0		100.0	100.0
1851	101.3	96.7	97.4	99.7		93.4	91.8
1852	102.6	95.9	101.0	105.8		99.6	87.5
1853	147.1	163.3	160.3	145.4		129.4	106.6
1854	149.6	157.9	197.8	147.1		140.0	124.8
1855	125.3	126.6		114.5		122.6	120.7
1856	123.5	120.8	131.0	126.8		120.0	121.8
1857	111.1	111.8	118.6	110.4	119.5	108.1	119.7
1858	96.0	94.9	97.8	100.8	113.5	94.6	88.9
1859	103.8	97.1	100.6	105.2	105.9	96.5	70.8
1860	109.7	113.1	109.2	118.6	109.4	93.2	91.9
1861	110.4	112.5	112.6	118.0	121.0	102.8	108.1
1862	104.7	107.3	111.6	123.5		99.3	101.6
1863	107.5	113.6	111.8	121.7		91.3	103.3
1864	115.8	121.7	118.3	112.8		95.6	104.5
1865	106.6	109.9	113.1	101.9	102.0	94.2	93.9
1866	98.4	96.8	106.0	102.6	96.4	95.2	84.3
1867	92.7	92.5	96.9	100.5	95.0	93.0	78.5
1868	88.8	92.8	100.5	107.4	96.0	95.3	87.4
1869	85.2	86.2	96.7	105.4	100.0	97.0	74.4
1870	94.0	93.9	97.3	103.9	96.5	94.9	70.2
1871	89.6	89.3	96.0	107.6	98.8	96.8	90.1
1872	92.2	90.3	99.3	115.7	102.5	89.7	91.4
1873	103.0	111.7	109.4	149.6	140.4	104.5	100.1
1874	95.1	100.6	108.0	125.0	126.0	111.1	93.7
1875	86.2	83.0	91.9	107.0	117.3	99.5	79.6
1876	86.0	88.6	93.4	108.2	113.2	96.5	80.5

Notes: 1850=100, except for southern US, where 1869=100.

Sources: See text.

The problems of interpolating and splicing individual time series, which pose great difficulties in traditional, simple index calculations, are thus overcome. In addition, subtle differences with respect to ports and cargoes can be taken into account - for example, freights from Kronstadt were always marginally lower than from St. Petersburg, freights to Hull a little higher than to Newcastle and round sleepers were more expensive per load to transport than square sleepers. Using a fine grid of specifications of ports, cargoes and ships, this method ensures a high degree of accuracy in computing changes over time in the index. The annual index values are shown in table 3.

Northern Europe

Figure 1 shows the computed indices for northern European waters, aggregated to annual averages, with 1850 set equal to 100. A striking feature is the very close correlation between the (western) Scandinavian and the Baltic index. The long-run trends are virtually identical, and although fluctuations in the Baltic index are somewhat larger during the 1840s, the cyclical features are very similar even here; thereafter, the cycles are extremely well synchronized. The two freight rate markets were obviously well integrated.[27] This result seems to make sense; a Norwegian shipowner would probably often first contemplate sailing through the Sound and seeking employment in the Baltic if freights were scarce or less remunerative in Norway or Gothenburg than in the Baltic, thus equilibrating the freight rates.

The White Sea index shares the cyclical movements with the other two north European timber freight indices, but deviates from these in two respects. The surge in freight rates was significantly stronger during the Crimean War years (1854-1856), which is easily explained by the increased risk factors associated with this trade during the conflict. The second notable feature is the upward drift in the White Sea index relative to the others from about 1860 onwards. Timber freight rates were more stationary in the Archangel trade, although the reasons are not clear. Although steam had made its entry in all three trade routes by the mid-1870s, the north European timber trade was still largely dominated by sailing vessels. In this regard, there was probably no great difference between these regions. In the Baltic grain trade, steam had a greater impact, thus possibly putting some pressure on timber freights as well.

---

[27]This result is in some contrast to the findings of Lewis R. Fischer and Helge W. Nordvik, "Myth and Reality in Baltic Shipping: The Wood Trade to Britain, 1863-1908," *Scandinavian Journal of History*, XII, No. 2 (1987), 99-116, who claimed that they found "no particular relationships" between freight rates from the various ports in the Baltic. If markets were highly integrated across western Scandinavia and the Baltic, it seems implausible that there was little synchronization of freight rate movements within the Baltic itself.

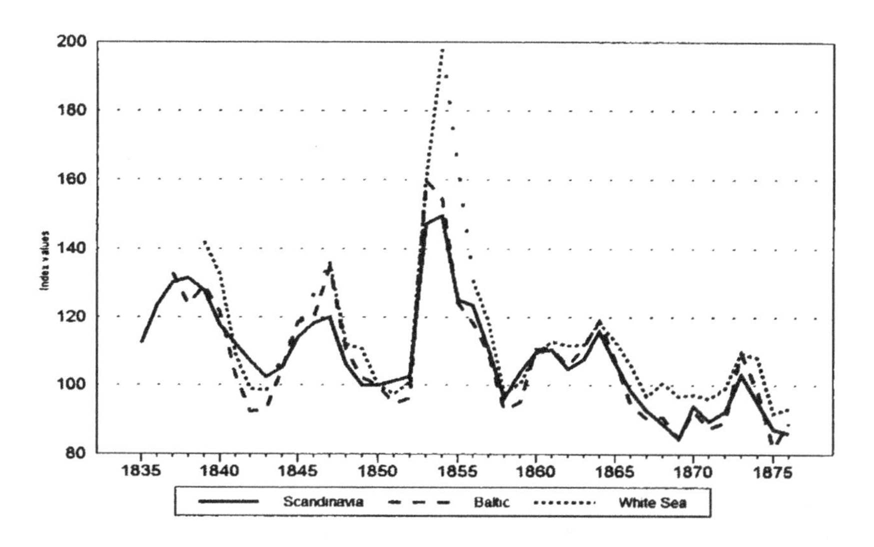

Figure 1: North European Timber Freight Indices, 1835-1876 (1850=100)

Sources: See text.

America and East India

Figure 2 presents indices for the three American and the East Indian trades. It shows a more diversified pattern of development over time than was the case in the European trades. Some features are common to these indices, particularly in the 1850s: the cyclical low in the early 1850s, the steeply rising freight rates in 1853-1854, followed by a more moderately high level until timber freight markets collapsed after 1857. The great business cycle boom of 1872-1874 is also reflected in all four trades, but as most pronounced in the North American and Gulf trades.

Although a common cyclical picture is still discernible to some extent after 1860, more persistent gaps opened up between the North American, Central American and East Indian timber freights. The long-run level of the North American freight rates did not show any decline from 1850 to 1876; if anything, it exhibited perhaps a slight tendency to rise. The sample period is shorter for the pitch pine trade from the Gulf ports, but the similarity with the North American trade is clearly marked; in fact, the tendency toward increasing freights in the last decade was even more pronounced here. In the East Indian teak trade, however, freight rates were established at a much lower level after the late 1850s; only in the very best years did they attain the level in 1850. The Central American trade with mahogany and logwood occupied a middle position and was characterized by more stability, particularly from the late 1850s onwards.

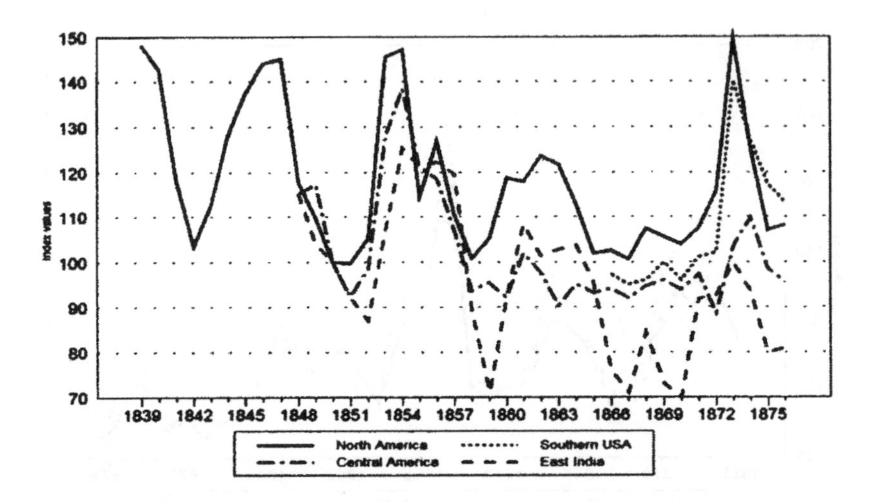

Figure 2: American and Asian Timber Freight Indices, 1839-1876 (1850=100; 1869=100 for Southern US)

Sources: See text.

A Comparison of European and North American Timber Freight Rates

In Figure 3, where the Baltic and the North American indices are compared, a decoupling of the two indices after the American Civil War is clearly visible.[28] Why did the North American rates show no tendency to fall, in contrast to the Baltic rates? First, it should be noted that it does not seem to be a statistical aberration due to the way the indices are constructed. As noted above, the sample underlying these regional indices comprises many more freight routes than those listed in appendix tables 1-5. In the North American case, the sample from which the index is computed contains 15,617 observations; from the 1860s there are typically between 400 and 800 observations per year. One might perhaps surmise that freight rates from or to outports behaved differently from the main timber trade routes from Québec and Saint John to London, Liverpool and the Bristol Channel. Furthermore, as the North American index also comprises some quotations of lumber freights to the West Indies, Brazil and the River Plate, particularly from the mid-1860s, this may have affected the index.[29]

[28]The Baltic index is taken as representative of the European trade here since figure 1 shows that it was so well synchronized with Scandinavian trade.

[29]Timber freights to the West Indies and South America typically originated from Montréal rather than Québec, as well as from Saint John, Norfolk and New York. Freight rates were stipulated in US dollars, but the common practice seems to have

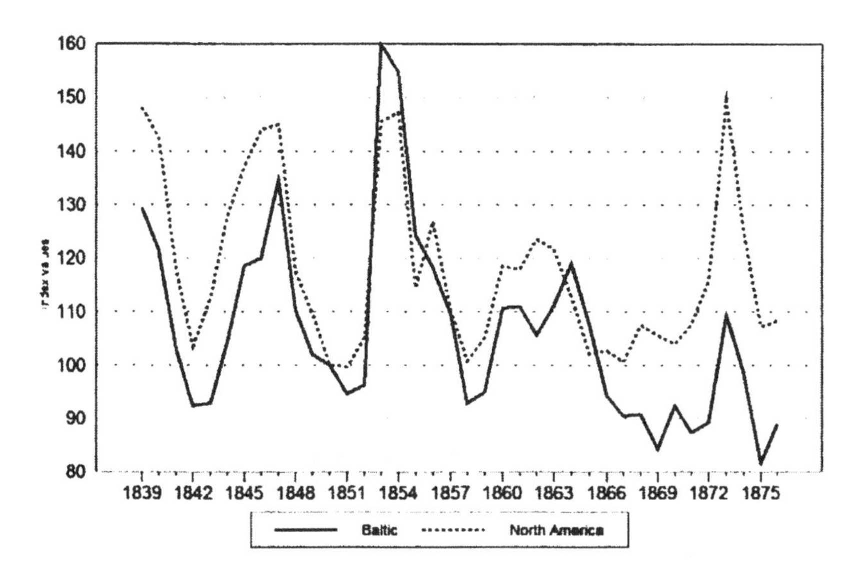

Figure 3: Baltic and North American Timber Freight Indices, 1839-1876 (1850=100)

Sources: See text.

A rough test for all these factors can be performed using the seven main Baltic and North American freight rates series listed in appendix tables 2 and 5 as a benchmark. The American data are confined to Québec and Saint John quotations to the main UK timber ports. The average ratios of the 1875 freight rates to the 1865 levels for each of the two groups have been chosen for this purpose. If these ratios are roughly in line with the corresponding ratios from the index calculations, we should feel more confident that the indices do not give a distorted picture of the course of freight rates. The calculation for the Baltic route gives very close results: a decline of 24.0 percent from 1865 to 1875 according to the index and 21.8 according to the average of the seven key freight rate series. In the North American case, the deviations are larger: an increase of five percent according to the index, compared to a rise of 20.7 percent from the seven key time series, perhaps indicating that the South American trade or freights from or to outports had a dampening effect. If anything, then, the mystery of the diverging European and North American freight rate developments becomes larger using only the key freight rate series.[30]

---

been that they contained a gold clause or were in Mexican silver dollars; therefore, fluctuations in the dollar-sterling exchange rate should not affect the rates.

[30]Using the same procedure to see whether the long-run trend of the index values and the key series are roughly in line, the ratio of 1875 to 1851 figures were

The relative rise of North American timber freights may be due to several factors. If, for example, it could be shown that costs associated with shipping timber from Canadian ports increased relative to North European ports, this might go some way towards explaining this feature. These costs may refer to, for instance, port charges and expenses associated with loading. There are scattered pieces of evidence regarding costs for various ports in this period, but the lack of systematic information makes this hypothesis speculative. The available information is often contradictory, as exemplified by the report for 1875 of the Norwegian consul in Québec. He reported that in Saint John, the vessel's crew had now been given permission to participate in loading or unloading, calling on hired workers only if needed. Together with increased competition in the supply of port services, this had reduced loading costs in this port. On the other hand, there were massive complaints from Miramichi that port expenses were excessive and turnaround time was long.[31] A number of other hypotheses may be put forward, but none of them seem to be the most likely explanation. During the American Civil War, North American freight rates rose relative to North European rates, but this tendency was reversed as the war ended, so permanent effects from this source must be ruled out. Many vessels carrying emigrants from Norway to North America went to Québec or New York each year, but the ebbs and flows of emigration are not obviously synchronized with the increase of North American freights after 1865. In addition, the number of emigrant ships was so small relative to the total of the westbound fleet that any significant influence on market freight rates is unlikely.

In the decades following the American Civil War the exports of American grain, provisions and petroleum to Europe increased enormously, exerting pressure on the carrying capacity of the merchant fleet. Large volumes of grain and provisions went by the regular Liverpool and London steamers, but petroleum cargoes were almost exclusively the domain of tramp sailing vessels through the 1870s. Moreover, during periods of high grain exports, sailing ships still accounted for a substantial part of the transport work. From this perspective, it might be possible that the ever-increasing eastbound transport requirements led to higher freight rates from North America. But if this was so, and there was a permanent upward shift in earnings from this trade, why did not European shipowners transfer more vessels to the North Atlantic trade? This argument runs counter to the view that freight markets

---

computed. In the case of the Baltic, the time series fell less (5.0 percent) than the index (13.7 percent); for North America, the average of the time series increased by 7.0 percent, whereas the index indicated an increase of 7.4 percent.

[31] *Uddrag af Consulatberetninger vedkommende Norges Handel og Skibsfart i Aaret 1875* (Christiania, 1877), 92.

were fairly well integrated in this period, and many would be reluctant to accept this reasoning.

I still believe, however, that the increasing eastbound traffic from North America holds the key to an explanation. Cargo volumes carried eastbound always exceeded what was carried west by a considerable margin.[32] The tonnage entering UK ports with cargoes from the eastern seaboard of the United States and British North America (Canada) almost doubled from 1859 to 1875; the ratio of westbound to eastbound tonnage decreased from 0.79 in 1859 to 0.60 in 1875.[33] Knick Harley has repeatedly drawn attention to the importance of the joint nature of production in shipping, aptly noting that in Atlantic shipping, eastbound shipments created westbound capacity.[34] W. Arthur Lewis, who published an early study focusing on the relation between inward and outward freight rates, concluded that "there is a tendency for inward and outward rates to move inversely on any one route when the general conditions elsewhere are stable."[35]

Figure 4 shows two time series ratios of North American and Baltic freight rate indices. One is the ratio of North American to Baltic timber freight rates discussed above. The graph shows that after an initial decline from the early 1840s to the middle of the 1850s, the ratio increases, at first temporarily during the American Civil War and then more strongly after the mid-1860s. The second curve shows the ratio of outward coal freight rates from the UK to the Baltic relative to North American ports. This time series shows that coal freights to the Baltic increased by about twenty percent relative to the North Atlantic from 1850 to the end of the American Civil War; thereafter, there was a dramatic decline in coal freight rates to North America, resulting in relative

---

[32]C. Knick Harley, "North Atlantic Shipping in the Late Nineteenth Century Freight Rates and the Interrelationship of Cargoes," in Lewis R. Fischer and Helge W. Nordvik (eds.), *Shipping and Trade, 1750-1950: Essays in International Maritime History* (Pontefract, 1990), 147-171.

[33]*Annual Statement of the Trade and Navigation of the United Kingdom in the Year 1859* (London, 1860); and *Annual Statement of the Trade and Navigation of the United Kingdom in the Year 1875* (London, 1876).

[34]Harley, "North Atlantic Shipping;" and C. Knick Harley, "Coal Exports and British Shipping, 1850-1913," *Explorations in Economic History*, XXVI, No. 2 (1989), 311-338.

[35]W. Arthur Lewis, "The Inter-Relations of Shipping Freights," *Economica*, New ser., VIII, No. 1 (1941), 62. For a contrary position based on the experience of a British tramp shipping firm in the early 1900s, see Gordon Boyce, "Edward Bates and Sons, 1897-1915: Tramping Operations in Recession and Recovery, *International Journal of Maritime History*, XXIII, No. 1 (2011), 13-50.

rates increasing from a factor of 1.2 in 1866 to almost two at the end of our period.

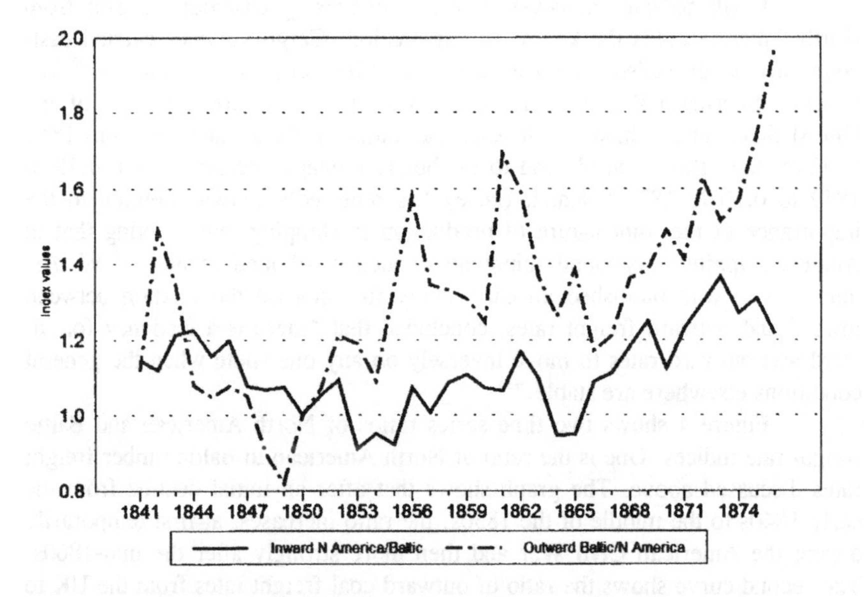

Figure 4: Ratios between Baltic and North American Inward and Outward Freight Indices, 1841-1876 (1850=100)

Sources: See text.

Noting the reversal of the regions in the two ratios, the Lewis-Harley hypothesis corresponds to a positive relationship between the two relative freight rate series. After 1865, this is exactly what we observe here. As the volume of eastbound traffic soared, westbound capacity outstripped the demand, and outward freight rates plummeted. To compensate for this, eastbound grain, petroleum and timber rates had to increase relative to those in the North European trade, which they truly did according to the graph.

Timber Freight Rates before 1835

The new data on freight rates presented here go back to 1835 for western Scandinavia, 1837 for the Baltic and 1839 for the Canadian timber trade. It is possible to extend the annual northern timber freight rate series back to 1757 using published sources, although not for the entire period for all trade routes.[36] The Baltic data go back to 1757 and end in 1833, with some gaps between 1767 and 1777, as well as during the Napoleonic wars. Data from the Norway trade begin in 1761, ending in 1824. Canadian time series start in 1810 and can be extended to be spliced with our new data beginning in 1839. With the exception of 1768, we are thus able to compute a continuous yearly index of timber freights for the period 1757-1876. The data are presented in figure 5. The indices are constructed by piecing together a number of shorter time series from the Baltic and the Norway trade to London. From 1810 onwards, the Canadian index is shown together with the somewhat patchier Baltic and Norwegian index. The same chain-type index, the repeat sailings index described above, has been used to compute the index numbers.

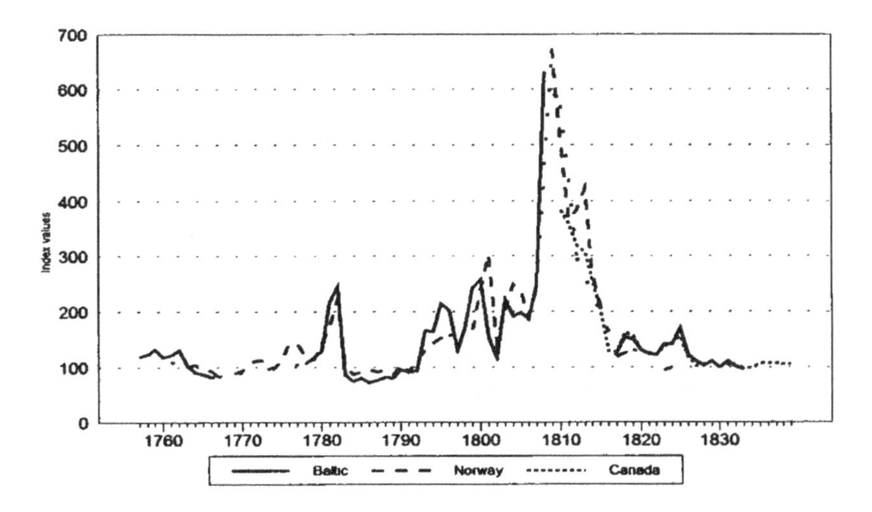

Figure 5: North European and Canadian Timber Freight Indices, 1757-1839 (Baltic and Canada, 1830=100; Norway, 1763=100)

Sources: See text.

---

[36]The main sources are Great Britain, Parliament, *Parliamentary Papers (BPP)*, 1833, VI, No. 690, "Report from the Select Committee on Manufactures, Commerce, and Shipping;" "Report from the Select Committee on Timber Duties," 1835, XIX, No. 519; and "Report from the Select Committee on British Shipping," 1844, VIII, No. 545. These were supplemented by Douglass C. North, "Ocean Freight Rates and Economic Development 1750-1913," *Journal of Economic History*, XVIII, No. 4 (1958), 537-555; Steinar Kjærheim, "Norwegian Timber Exports in the 18th Century: A Comparison of Port Books and Private Accounts," *Scandinavian Economic History Review*, V, Nos. 1-2 (1957), 188-201; Scheel, "Fra Napoleonskrigene til navigasjonsaktens opphevelse," 1-64 and 98-231; and Jacob S. Worm-Müller, "Licensfart," in Worm-Müller (ed.), *Den norske sjøfarts historie*, II, part 1, 65-97.

Fluctuations in freights in these years were considerable, with rates during the peak of the blockade years 1808 to 1812 being almost unquotable. Henry Warburton, giving evidence to the Select Committee on Timber Duties in 1835, stated that

> [d]uring the disastrous period for the trade with the North of Europe, subsequently to 1807, it was in obtaining freight for the timber, not in purchasing the timber in the foreign market, that the principal source of expense and difficulty lay....in 1811, I gave my correspondent at Riga an order for shipping goods, unlimited as to freight; but was disappointed in obtaining ships.[37]

The estimates for these years, derived from various sources, are therefore more uncertain than in other periods and must be considered as tentative only.

Apart from the turbulent years of the Napoleonic wars, however, there is a remarkably close correspondence between the Baltic index, on the one hand, and the Norwegian index prior to 1824, and with the Canadian index, beginning in 1810, on the other. Except for a steep rise during the American war years (1778-1782), when British vessels disappeared from the northern timber trades, it appears that timber freight rates were reasonably stable until 1793.[38] Both the Baltic and Norwegian data support this. After 1816, freight rates showed a long-run tendency to decline, interrupted by shorter cycles, peaking in 1818 and 1825. Again, the evidence from both sources provides almost exactly the same picture. By the 1830s, nominal freight rates were back at the level of the 1760s.

A Great Hundred Years of Timber Freights

It is now time to put the indices for the various trades and time periods together to construct an annual index from 1757 to 1876. Up to 1839, it is based on the Baltic, Norwegian and Canadian data; thereafter, the White Sea, Central American, southern US and East Indian index data are included as well. It is pieced together using the same repeat sailings procedure described above.

The world index is reproduced in table 4. Figure 6 shows the new world timber index along with Harley's British index.[39] The latter index was constructed by splicing a set of overlapping freight rate series, including coal

[37] *BPP*, "Select Committee Report, 1833," 346.

[38] Kjærheim, "Norwegian Timber Exports," 199.

[39] Harley, "Ocean Freight Rates."

from the Tyne to London, timber from the Baltic and Canada, grain from the Black Sea and New York, and cotton from the United States. It should be noted that between 1807 and 1816, the Harley index is based on the coastal coal freights to London only; hence, it does not show the same large fluctuations during the war years as does the timber index.

Table 4
World Timber Freight Rate Index, 1757-1876
(Index Values, 1850 = 100)

Decade	0	1	2	3	4	5	6	7	8	9
1750s								157.4	164.2	175.5
1760s	156.9	161.0	178.7	144.2	136.9	130.7	123.3	110.4		117.0
1770s	123.4	143.1	149.6	146.4	128.8	148.5	192.0	189.7	160.1	161.8
1780s	192.8	275.5	330.9	132.1	114.5	120.8	117.6	117.9	123.4	116.8
1790s	142.0	192.2	145.1	206.7	217.3	257.1	253.0	159.2	198.9	276.4
1800s	341.5	297.7	178.0	292.0	300.8	296.2	259.0	337.3	838.9	957.5
1810s	736.0	544.2	474.2	504.4	380.1	311.9	192.7	190.5	223.2	221.6
1820s	197.6	195.9	174.4	179.7	186.3	212.7	155.5	138.7	134.3	143.1
1830s	130.1	139.9	131.7	125.2	121.4	127.6	133.9	137.5	134.5	135.3
1840s	126.9	109.3	99.3	100.4	111.0	122.8	127.9	135.1	112.7	107.2
1850s	100.0	96.2	98.3	139.9	150.6	123.5	119.7	109.1	93.7	92.3
1860s	101.6	107.8	105.0	104.2	106.1	98.8	91.5	87.3	90.8	87.3
1870s	88.4	92.0	93.0	110.6	103.3	90.4	90.9			

Notes: The column numbers in the heading designate the last digit of the year in each decade, i.e., for the 1750s the index value for 1757 is equal to 157.4; for the 1870s, the index value for 1876 is 90.9.

Sources: See text.

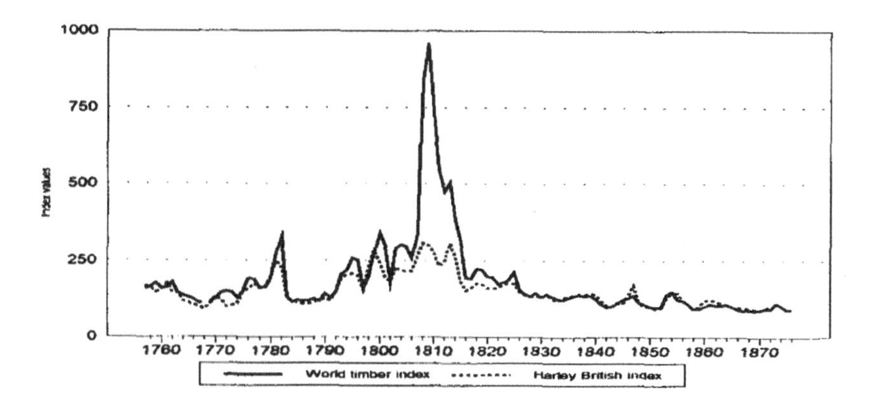

Figure 6: World Timber Index and Harley's British Index, 1757-1876 (1850=100)

Sources: See text.

The similarity between the two indices, apart from the years of the Napoleonic wars, is remarkable. The long-run course of freight rates derived from these two indices is virtually identical. The Harley index is at exactly the same level in 1767 and 1850, while the timber index falls by 10.4 percent over the same period. There is a slight decline in the trend level of freight rates between 1760 and the end of our sample period in the 1870s. On the other hand, if observations for the years before 1757 had been available, the Harley index, which goes back to 1741, indicates that an earlier starting point might have reversed that conclusion. A general conclusion may be that although there were large cyclical fluctuations in timber freight rates, in peacetime periods as well as in war years, the nominal reward for carrying timber did not change much over the 120 years considered here.

The new data on *nominal* timber freight rates presented here may also be used as points of departure to shed some light on how *real* freight rates developed over time. The issues of real freight rates and productivity gains in merchant shipping are crucial to our understanding of the shipping world of the nineteenth century, but estimating them is extremely difficult for various reasons.[40] In addition to the uncertainty of the nominal freight rate index, there are many troublesome features associated with price indices as well. In particular, there are the vexing issues associated with defining a relevant price concept and finding an index that is measured consistently over a long time span. Although obviously imperfect in several respects, standard wholesale price indices may nevertheless give a rough idea of what is implied by the new freight rate data.

To cover the entire sample period, three separate British price indices were spliced to provide a real timber freight rate index extending back to 1757.[41] It is difficult to select a time period that is representative of the normal cost of carrying goods in the early years of the sample due to the many wars, but the late 1760s and early 1770s were a relatively tranquil period. Depending

[40]The seminal contributions are North, "Ocean Freight Rates;" and Harley, "Ocean Freight Rates." For an excellent review of some recent contributions, see Yrjö Kaukiainen, "Growth, Diversification and Globalization: Main Trends in International Shipping since 1850," in Lewis R. Fischer and Even Lange (eds.), *International Merchant Shipping in the Nineteenth and Twentieth Centuries: The Comparative Dimension* (St. John's, 2008), 1-56.

[41]For the years before 1890, I used the Schumpeter-Gilboy price index with a weight of seventy percent for consumers' goods and thirty percent for producers' goods, while for the period 1790-1845 the Gayer, Rostow and Schwartz index was used; both are reproduced in B.R. Mitchell, *British Historical Statistics* (London, 1988), 719-721. These were spliced to the revised and expanded Sauerbeck price index in Jan Tore Klovland, "Zooming in on Sauerbeck: Monthly Wholesale Prices in Britain 1845-1890," *Explorations in Economic History*, XXX, No. 2 (1993), 195-228.

on the exact year chosen, the calculations indicate an annual rate of decline in real freight rates of 0.3 to 0.5 percent on average for the century to 1876. Between 1840 and 1876, the annual rate of decline of real freights is estimated at 0.4 percent. These estimates are decidedly lower than the productivity figures based on real freight rates suggested by Yrjö Kaukiainen for the years from 1870 to World War I (on the order of one to one and a half percent per year).[42] It is also lower than the one percent annual productivity growth in Dutch shipping in the three centuries before 1800 estimated by Jan Luiten van Zanden and Milja van Tielhof, although their data seem to suggest that productivity growth fell below the long-run average after 1700.[43]

Although the tentative nature of these estimates should be underscored once again, the rather low productivity gains in the timber trade in the period covered here do not seem unreasonable. The vessels employed in this trade in general did not embody the most advanced technology. In the 1870s, wood cargoes were still largely carried by wooden sailing vessels. Steam penetration was generally low, but in the Baltic it started to rise during the 1870s, from eight percent in 1873 to twenty-nine percent in 1878, nearly all accounted for by the expanding fleet of British steamships.[44] In the Canadian timber trade, sail still dominated the trade at the end of the 1870s, and Norwegian shipowners often employed second-hand Nova Scotia-built vessels in this trade.[45] On the other hand, the comparison with the Harley index above showed that the new timber freight index moved more-or-less in line with the general course of freight rates. Hence, these results may be indicative of a fairly low rate of productivity growth in shipping at least until the late 1870s.

---

[42]Kaukiainen, "Growth, Diversification and Globalization."

[43]Jan Luiten van Zanden and Milja van Tielhof, "Roots of Growth and Productivity Change in Dutch Shipping Industry," *Explorations in Economic History*, XLVI, No. 2 (2009), 389-482.

[44]Fischer and Nordvik, "Myth and Reality in Baltic Shipping," 12.

[45]Worm-Müller, "Fra klipperen til motorskibet," 202. It would appear that Worm-Müller used the term "Nova Scotia" in the generic sense to refer to all vessels built in the eastern part of British North America, since many second-hand Canadian-built vessels used by Norwegians to carry wood were in fact constructed in New Brunswick, Prince Edward Island and Québec. See Clement W. Crowell, *Novascotiaman* (Halifax, 1979).

Appendix Table 1
Wood Freights from Christiania and Gothenburg, 1835-1876

A: 1835-1870

	Christiania			Gothenburg			
Year	**London dbb KS**	**London Firewood Cub.fath.**	**Havre dbb KS**	**London dbb PS**	**Hull dbb PS**	**Calais dbb PS**	**Bordeaux dbb PS**
1835	23.6	42.0	38.1				
1836	27.5	52.5	41.2				
1837	29.0	50.4	44.2	47.3	42.2	69.8	83.8
1838	28.3	51.1	45.4	46.8	41.2	71.8	82.1
1839	29.6	52.5	45.5	45.9	39.2	70.0	80.1
1840	25.8	45.8	39.3	40.4	38.9	62.4	75.0
1841	25.0	39.6	37.1	38.6	35.3	59.2	66.1
1842	23.4	40.5	35.6	38.4	33.7	57.8	61.5
1843	23.2	36.9	34.5	37.3	31.0	55.4	56.3
1844	20.8	36.7	37.4	39.4	33.4	55.9	59.7
1845	24.5	45.0	38.6	39.6	35.8	59.2	67.6
1846	25.9	46.9	39.1	40.0	35.2	59.9	74.8
1847	25.7	48.0	39.7	42.6	38.9	59.9	74.8
1848	23.8	44.1	37.6	36.3	31.3	55.6	64.0
1849	20.6	36.3	34.9	33.4	30.6	51.7	56.4
1850	20.3	36.7	34.5	35.4	30.5	52.0	60.9
1851	20.7	36.4	34.6	35.3	31.6	53.4	62.9
1852	20.4	35.9	35.6	34.9	32.5	53.8	62.1
1853	35.3	58.1	48.4	54.3	45.6	87.2	82.3
1854	31.3	59.8	50.8	48.6	40.4	84.0	105.0
1855	25.3	45.8	40.2	40.9	40.1	61.7	81.1
1856	26.3	50.3	41.4	39.3	36.8	62.4	81.8
1857	23.6	41.0	37.5	31.5	30.0	59.2	79.0
1858	19.9	39.9		31.9	25.2	52.4	66.9
1859	25.3	42.5	38.5	31.1	28.2	58.3	75.0
1860	22.3	40.7	34.6	38.8	30.3	54.5	77.1
1861	22.1	42.0		35.3	31.7	57.8	76.3
1862	22.1	42.0		36.6	31.0	55.7	78.7
1863			36.8	36.1	31.4	56.8	77.9
1864				42.9	31.3	59.3	81.6
1865	23.5	42.8	35.2	36.2	30.9	51.7	70.9
1866	21.5	39.9	31.9	31.8	29.3	46.4	60.2
1867				30.8	28.1	43.5	55.2
1868	21.8		29.4	29.0	26.5	42.2	55.0
1869	19.4		29.4	25.0	29.0	40.0	52.5
1870	20.5	36.8	28.4	29.5	30.0	40.0	54.6

B: 1870-1876

	Christiania				Gothenburg		
Year	**London dbb KS**	**London Firewood Cub.fath.**	**ECUK Props PS**	**Liverpool dbb PS**	**London dbb PS**	**ECUK Props PS**	**Bordeaux dbb PS**
1870	20.5	36.8	25.1	45.0	29.5	25.1	54.6
1871	21.4	42.5	27.6	42.0	28.9	23.7	57.8
1872	19.7	46.1	27.9	43.8		28.5	
1873	18.9	39.3	33.9	37.8	27.5		68.2
1874	22.5	42.5	27.5	35.0	30.9		
1875	19.7	32.0	21.8	30.0			
1876	16.9	33.0	25.5	34.1			

Notes: dbb = deals, battens and boards; KS = Christiania Standard (103.125 cubic feet); PS = Petersburg Standard (165 cubic feet). ECUK refers to coal ports (Newcastle, Sunderland, Hartlepool) on the east coast of UK. Quotations for English ports are in shillings, for French ports in French francs, inclusive of any known primage. A five percent primage was invariably given for French ports from both Christiania and Gothenburg; for UK ports, the same procedure applied to many (but not all) fixtures from Christiania; from Gothenburg, the standard was to quote in full.

Sources: See text.

Appendix Table 2
Wood Freights from Baltic Ports to London, 1837-1876

Year	Danzig Balks Load	Memel Balks Load	Stettin fir timber load	Riga Deals PS	Kronstadt Deals PS	Lower Bothnia Deals PS	Upper Bothnia Deals PS
1837	22.0	20.9					
1838	21.5	22.0				62.0	
1839	22.3	205		74.1	73.8		
1840	20.0	19.6					
1841	17.3	16.7		54.2		52.0	
1842	16.0	14.8		45.0		52.5	
1843	16.8	14.8		50.0		47.3	
1844	17.1	16.9	20.0	66.0		52.5	
1845	18.9	18.0	17.0	74.0		48.5	58.0
1846	18.9		17.0			54.8	67.8
1847	24.7	23.2	20.4	75.0		64.0	
1848	18.3	18.2			50.0		62.0
1849	16.8	16.0		54.0	45.4	46.7	
1850	15.1	14.8	12.3		36.4	45.0	50.0
1851	15.9		12.0		36.5	52.3	55.8
1852	16.0	15.0	10.0		37.8	50.7	57.5
1853	20.0		22.6	81.3	93.9	85.8	92.6
1854	28.0		18.0	138.7		96.2	112.9
1855			16.5			65.8	78.7
1856			14.2	73.6	64.3	68.5	75.5
1857	18.5		13.0	64.0	50.0	61.3	69.4
1858	14.0	14.9		47.5	38.4	47.9	54.6
1859	15.7	15.9		58.9	44.7	51.0	58.6
1860	17.4	22.0	12.6	66.0	43.0	56.8	67.5
1861	18.6	17.5			42.6	60.3	66.9
1862	16.8	16.4	13.5		44.3	57.8	63.4
1863	18.5	18.3	12.6	59.8	42.8	59.6	69.3
1864	21.9	21.6	20.0	77.5	57.2	62.2	77.3
1865	17.4	17.5	13.4	61.9	52.8	59.0	72.8
1866	16.1	16.6	11.0	60.0	49.0	51.2	58.1
1867	15.0	14.3		52.1	44.4	48.9	56.7
1868	13.3	14.5		50.0	43.5	49.8	
1869	12.9	14.1			35.1	44.9	52.5
1870	14.5	15.1	11.6	52.0	43.5	52.6	61.3
1871	15.0	15.0		48.8	42.5	47.3	53.3
1872	12.5	13.3	13.7	47.7	45.3	55.0	61.3
1873	18.9	19.3		58.6	61.6	63.8	65.0
1874	16.9	17.0		53.0	50.4	52.0	56.3
1875	13.1	14.6	12.0	45.0	41.9	45.6	50.8
1876			12.1	46.3	44.6	42.6	52.8

Notes: Quotations are in shillings per load for timber and in shillings by Petersburg Standard for deals. Lower Bothnia ports include those as far north as Husum; Upper Bothnia ports are those farther north as well as Finnish ports.

Sources: See text.

Appendix Table 3
Wood Freights from Archangel and Onega, 1847-1876

Year	Archangel		Onega	
	London or East Coast	Bristol Channel	Marseilles	London or East Coast
1847			160.1	
1848	79.2			80.0
1849	78.0			
1850	71.2	85.0	120.0	71.9
1851	70.7			72.2
1852	69.9	90.0		75.0
1853	118.2	136.9		109.5
1854	156.4	160.6		150.1
1855				
1856	93.8	97.5		92.7
1857	82.5	99.4		81.6
1858	71.1	75.0		70.9
1859	70.5	86.3		73.1
1860	81.3	79.2	133.1	75.2
1861	83.6	91.6		84.0
1862	76.8	87.2		76.4
1863	82.1	90.0		75.6
1864	87.8	96.9	162.8	84.6
1865	82.8	90.9	154.9	77.3
1866	79.0	90.0	148.3	71.3
1867	73.6	80.4	131.3	67.0
1868	75.7	80.0	130.0	70.0
1869	74.2	82.5	124.3	66.9
1870	75.2	80.2	121.5	65.5
1871	73.8	77.6	123.9	66.3
1872	72.5	79.6		66.1
1873	78.9	97.5	146.7	76.6
1874	78.0	92.6	144.8	73.6
1875	68.6	75.1		60.6
1876	70.4	75.2		62.8

Notes: Freight rates are for deals per Petersburg Standard, in shillings to UK ports and in French *francs* to Marseilles. London or East Coast figures include cargoes both directly to London or the East Coast ports of Hull and Grimsby and those on "London and East Coast" terms. Bristol Channel comprises Liverpool, Bristol and Gloucester direct as well as "Bristol Channel" contracts.

Sources: See text.

Appendix Table 4
Wood Freights from Canadian Ports to the UK, 1839-1876

	Québec					Saint John, NB	
Year	London Timber Load	Liverpool Timber Load	Bristol Timber Load	London Deals PS	Liverpool Deals PS	London Deals PS	Liverpool Deals PS
1839	44.9	41.7	43.3	133.3	126.0		
1840	42.0	38.0	43.0	126.0			
1841	32.8	32.0		101.3			
1842	28.3	28.3	28.3				
1843							
1844	39.0						
1845							
1846							
1847						119.0	
1848	35.3	32.0				92.5	
1849	31.0			93.0			
1850	30.9	28.0				85.0	60.0
1851	30.0	29.8	30.4	95.0	86.7	74.3	60.0
1852	31.0	33.0	36.0	97.7	90.0		68.8
1853	44.8	43.4	42.4	136.3		116.4	112.1
1854	48.6	44.1	50.2	150.4		117.5	84.6
1855	34.2	40.8	32.7	91.8	77.5	80.3	72.4
1856	38.7	36.4	36.1	112.9		99.7	95.6
1857	34.8	31.6	32.8	99.5		77.1	63.7
1858	28.3	26.2	27.3	81.2	75.5	72.8	71.9
1859	30.3	29.3	28.8	90.0		73.4	64.7
1860	33.2	32.4	31.8	102.5	99.6	86.0	88.2
1861	33.4	31.3	32.2	92.4	82.0	80.5	81.7
1862	32.9	33.0	31.5	99.9	88.2	84.8	73.9
1863	33.7	32.4	32.9	95.0	89.8	83.3	82.6
1864	32.9	29.4	29.6	93.3	79.4	68.0	58.7
1865	28.9	24.0	24.2	77.6	64.1	73.8	70.3
1866	28.6	26.1	27.5	79.7	73.9	65.0	70.0
1867	27.8	26.1	26.0	75.4	74.5	66.0	66.0
1868	30.3	27.9	28.0	79.2	76.3	74.2	76.0
1869	29.0	27.4	25.0	77.3	81.3	67.3	67.7
1870	29.0	26.8	26.8	76.1	75.1	66.6	67.8
1871	30.1	29.1	29.2	78.2	78.6	63.8	67.9
1872	31.8	31.6	30.0	81.2	81.4	73.9	77.2
1873	42.5	41.5	40.3	106.1	105.5	102.6	106.9
1874	36.1	30.8	34.2	82.1	81.8	85.3	82.8
1875	35.0	32.0	33.9	84.0	85.0	76.1	74.9
1876	32.9	31.3	31.5	80.3	81.4	72.3	74.1

Notes : PS = Petersburg Standard. Quotations are in shillings.

Sources: See text.

Appendix Table 5
Wood Freights to the UK from the United States, Central and South America, The Caribbean and the East Indies, 1848-1876

Year	Belize Mahogany	Mexico Mahogany	Cuba and Haiti Mahogany	Honduras-Guayana Mahogany	Jamaica Logwood	Southern US Pitch Pine	Moulmein Teak
1848	62.5			79.2			106.7
1849	59.9						93.8
1850	53.6						90.4
1851	52.1		59.5				83.0
1852	54.1		61.7				79.7
1853	77.9		73.7	91.6			98.2
1854	82.4	88.5	86.5	106.7			111.4
1855	69.5	88.1	74.3	77.1			108.7
1856	65.7	80.6	79.7	80.2			114.8
1857	57.5	74.0	69.2	75.0		52.5	112.5
1858	52.9	60.8	58.1	59.5		35.1	84.7
1859	53.1	70.3	59.4	62.0		35.0	65.1
1860	56.2	64.7	58.4	62.1		40.6	80.6
1861	60.5	68.9	61.6	70.6			100.9
1862	58.9	72.5		61.7			94.5
1863	40.0	60.0					96.3
1864	52.5		55.0				100.0
1865	48.8				30.0		88.1
1866	48.8	74.1	57.2	51.3	36.3	39.0	70.6
1867	47.8	67.5	57.0	56.9	31.4	35.8	70.1
1868	47.5	72.5			33.0	36.5	82.3
1869	48.2	67.9	60.0	51.3	39.1	37.5	70.9
1870	44.2	60.0	55.0	50.0	36.8	37.0	66.0
1871	45.0	63.8	57.5	60.0	38.5		80.8
1872	51.3	62.8			36.1	41.1	88.2
1873	58.8	74.0	45.0		41.9	55.8	92.0
1874	60.2	72.0		66.4	42.8	47.7	85.9
1875	52.5	65.9		61.3	38.9	44.4	72.9
1876	51.7	66.9		62.5	36.7	42.0	72.4

Notes: Freight rates are in shillings per ton, except for pitch pine, which are in shillings per load. Mexican ports include Minatitlan, Tabasco, Laguna, Frontera, Coatzacoalcos and Bay of Mexico. Mahogany ports in Cuba are Nuevitas, Cardenas, Cayo Frances, Manzanilla, Santa Cruz de Cuba, while the Haitian port is Aux Cayes. Ports between Honduras and Guyana (other than Belize) comprise Honduras Bay, Waux River, Woonta River, Roman River and Patook. Pitch pine ports in the southern US include Pensacola, Mobile, Pascagoula, Darien and Doboy.

Sources: See text.

When Distance Matters: The Output of the Norwegian Merchant Fleet, 1830-1865

Camilla Brautaset

Introduction

In their reflections on the state of maritime history[1] in Norway, both Atle Thowsen and Helge Nordvik bemoaned the lack of interest by academic historians which, they argued, had left maritime history in the hands of laymen and as a marginal topic in the scholarly community.[2] Slightly more than two decades after Nordvik's article, however, there are signs that this is finally starting to change. This shift can be seen in at least three areas. First, the number of master's and doctoral theses on maritime topics has been rising over the past decade.[3] Second, notable research projects have been anchored within aca-

[1]Over the past few decades, it has become commonplace to apply Frank Broeze's definition of maritime history as humankind's relationship with the sea. See Frank Broeze, "From the Periphery to the Mainstream: The Challenge of Australia's Maritime History," *The Great Circle*, XI, No. 1 (1989), 1-13. In this essay, however, the discussion is limited to merchant shipping.

[2]Atle Thowsen, "Norsk sjøfartshistorie - periferi eller sentrum i norsk historieforskning?" *Sjøfartshistorisk Årbok 1972* (Bergen, 1973), 9-38; and Helge W. Nordvik, "Norwegian Maritime Historical Research during the Past Twenty Years: A Critical Survey," *Sjøfartshistorisk Årbok 1990* (Bergen, 1991), 240-278. For a further discussion, see also Camilla Brautaset and Stig Tenold, "Lost in Calculation? Norwegian Merchant Shipping in Asia, 1870-1914," in Maria Fusaro and Amélia Polónia (eds.), *Maritime History as Global History* (St. John's, 2010), 203-221.

[3]Examples of recent doctoral theses include Stig Tenold, "The Shipping Crisis of the 1970s: Causes, Effects and Implications for Norwegian Shipping" (Unpublished PhD thesis, Norwegian School of Economics and Business Administration, 2001); Camilla Brautaset, "Norsk eksport, 1830-1865: I perspektiv av historiske nasjonalregnskaper" (Unpublished PhD thesis, Norwegian School of Economics and Business Administration, 2002); and Elisabeth S. Koren, "Beskytte, forme, styrke: helsefremmende arbeid overfor norske sjøfolk i utenriksfart med hovedvekt på perioden, 1890-1940" (Unpublished PhD thesis, University of Bergen, 2008). There are also several theses in progress, including those by Knut M. Nygaard, Per Kristian Sebak, Andreas Nybø and

demic institutions.[4] Finally, a new generation of maritime historians has been employed in academic positions at universities and other research institutions.

The extent to which this long-awaited institutional integration of maritime history will be coupled with a historiographical shift to produce a different kind of scholarship remains to be seen. Internationally, the rise of econometrics in general and the globalization debate in particular has attracted a group of scholars with a newfound interest in shipping: the maritime historical economists. While these economists can easily find a home among economic historians, traditional maritime historians tend to prefer the company of their own herd, although they do enjoy an occasional flirtation with business historians. The Norwegian community of maritime historians, though, has yet to experience the same antagonism. Maritime history in Norway is still dominated by qualitative, actor- and micro-orientated approaches. Nonetheless, there are a few outliers with an eye for quantitative sources and methods.[5] Thus, rather than taking history out of the equation, new perspectives and increased methodological complexity are brought to the genre through the utilization of new sources, analytical tools and research questions.

This is also the aspiration of this essay. My ambition is to enhance our understanding of the development of Norwegian shipping in the nineteenth century by approaching it from a macro-level and quantitative perspective. More specifically, I ask how Norway's merchant marine was transformed from being based on the domestic economy to becoming a carrier of freights worldwide. Thus, the focus of the analysis will be on the production and spatial distribution of shipping services. This requires establishing new series of historical statistics on the output of the merchant fleet. In existing works on nineteenth-century Norwegian maritime history, output has implicitly been defined simply as the volume of goods carried in the hulls of vessels. Yet in shipping economics and modern shipping, it is usual to define output in terms of ton-

---

Eivind Merok. In temporal terms, the majority of these works have been firmly rooted in the twentieth century.

[4]The most important example is the project led by Even Lange at the University of Oslo on "Norwegian Shipping History, 1814-2014." Moreover, Stig Tenold at the Norwegian School of Economics has been involved in a multitude of large research projects, including "Specialization Strategies and Structural Transformation in Twentieth-Century Norwegian Shipping." More recently, a new project led by the current author focussing on Norwegian shipping in China, 1890-1937, has been awarded a large grant (Ref: 205553/V20) by the Norwegian Research Council.

[5]The most prominent scholar in this respect is Professor Jan Tore Klovland of the Norwegian School of Economics. See, for instance, Klovland's article in this volume; and "New Evidence on the Causes of the Fluctuations in Ocean Freight Rates in the 1850s," *Explorations in Economic History,* XLVI (2009), 266-284.

miles, taking both weight and distance into account.[6] Mapping the production of such an "invisible" factor of production in the nineteenth century requires a rigorous, yet simplified, framework of assumptions. My ambition, however, is for the analysis to be based as far as possible on empirical observations.

The temporal parameters of this study are the years 1830 to 1865. This is largely a reflection of the state of the sources, existing official statistics and shifting technological regimes. The starting point has been determined by access to systematic contemporary sources; annual official shipping statistics are only available from 1830 onwards.[7] The most important source in this respect is *Statistiske Tabeller*, a publication that is of immense value to maritime research but which also imposes some important restrictions. The information in these tables came from Swedish-Norwegian consuls posted around the world. As a result, shipping in ports where no consul or vice-consul was present was less likely to be captured. By ending the study in 1865, we can ensure that it is limited to one technological regime, since in Norway steam was at best a curiosity among vessel owners before that date.[8]

The merchant fleet underwent a significant expansion throughout the period (see figure 1). The growth in tonnage was especially strong from 1838 to 1844 and from 1850 to 1857, with annual compound growth rates of 5.5 and 7.1 percent, respectively.It should also be noted that even though the total fleet increased consistently, the average size of vessels appears to have dipped in the early 1840s, before rising again after 1845.[9]

---

[6]Even in the international literature, few studies have adopted the ton-mile approach for the nineteenth century. For examples, see Edwin Horlings, *The Economic Development of the Dutch Service Sector, 1800-1850: Trade and Transport in a Premodern Economy* (Amsterdam, 1995); and Yrjö Kaukianen, "Journey Costs, Terminal Costs and Ocean Tramp Freights: How the Price of Distance Declined from the 1870s to 2000," *International Journal of Maritime History*, XVIII, No. 2 (2006), 17-64.

[7]For a further discussion, see Brautaset and Tenold, "Lost in Calculation," esp. 208-211.

[8]The choice of 1865 as an end date also reflects the fact that the construction of these series was originally part of a larger project attempting to revise historical national accounts in Norway using public statistics starting in that year.

[9]In 1841, the average vessel was ninety-eight net registered tons (nrt), an insignificant increase from ninety-five nrt in 1830. Thereafter, average tonnage fell to eighty-two nrt in 1844 before rising to 147 nrt in 1865. There are no obvious explanations for the decline in the 1840s. An examination of new additions to the fleet shows a slight decrease in the average size of new vessels, still the prime source of new tonnage. Second-hand vessels from abroad, however, increased in average capacity but were nevertheless anomalies, accounting for a mere nine percent of new vessels and twenty-two percent of new tonnage in 1844. Still, the number of newly built vessels is

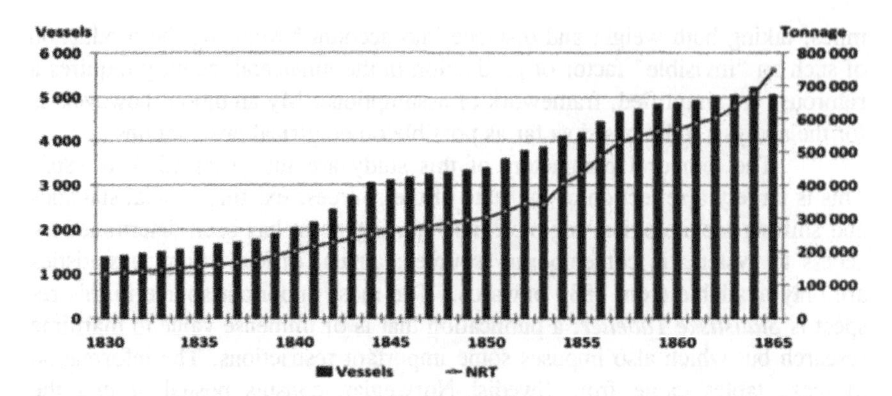

Figure 1: Norwegian Merchant Fleet, 1830-1865

Source: Camilla Brautaset, "Norsk eksport, 1830-1865: I perspektiv av historiske nasjonalregnskaper" (Unpublished PhD thesis, Norwegian School of Economics and Business Administration, 2002), 258.

In addition to the growth of the fleet, three salient features characterized Norwegian merchant shipping between 1830 and 1865, namely a reliance on sail, the carriage of bulk cargoes and the predominance of tramp shipping. While these characteristics were as valid for 1865 as they were for 1830, the market base for these services changed dramatically during this period. From being primarily limited to bilateral services through domestic-based shipping (i.e., the use of Norwegian ports for both departures and arrivals), the focus after mid-century increasingly became multilateral voyages as Norwegian owners entered the cross-trades.

This essay is organized into three main parts. First, I will map the cargo transported, before moving on to the actual output. The third and final section of the paper will discuss the implications of the findings.

Cargo Transported by Domestic-based Shipping, 1830-1865

As mentioned above, *Statistiske Tabeller* is the single most important quantitative source for the nineteenth-century merchant fleet. From 1835, it offers detailed figures on ports of departure and arrival and the volume of cargo car-

---

not sufficient to explain the entire decrease. A closer examination of how the sources were constructed reveals that from 1841 onwards information on previously non-registered vessels (*ikke-registrerte skip*), which were generally smaller, were included in the official statistics. Thus, changes in statistical procedures appear to be the most likely explanation for what on the surface appears to be a phenomenon of smaller ships in a period marked by increases in supply (tonnage) and demand.

ried between them.[10] While *Statistiske Tabeller* reported all registered foreign exchanges in goods and shipping, the contemporary publication *Amtmenns-beretningene* provided detailed analysis of the state of affairs in the regional administrative units, referred to as "amts." This division was not fixed from the start, since the first issues of *Amtmennsberetningene* (1829 and 1835) also offered statistical data on foreign trade and shipping. But this information was sketchy prior to 1838.[11] It has thus been necessary to estimate the figures for 1830-1837 using other sources and statistical interpolation.[12]

A key source for constructing my time series is Martin Braun Tvethe's figures for domestic-based shipping in 1836, which were based on unpublished sources.[13] For one year, 1837, my efforts to find figures for domestic-based shipping have been unsuccessful. But because during the century both exports and imports were dutiable, customs revenues ought to mirror the volume of foreign trade. Consequently, it seems reasonable to assume that the volume of cargo carried in Norwegian hulls should correlate well with customs revenues from foreign trade. Fortunately, Tvethe provided annual figures for these from 1815 to 1847. I have thus used the relationship between the average customs revenues between 1838 and 1843 and domestic shipping in 1836 and 1838 to estimate the figures for domestic-based shipping in 1837.[14]

---

[10]Norway, Det kongelige Finants-, Handel og Told-departementet, *Statistiske Tabeller for Kongeriget Norge. Femte Rœkke, indeholdene Tabller, vedkommende Norges Handel og Skibsfart i Aaret 1838* (Christiania, 1840). The publication continued as *Norges Handel og Skipsfart* from 1861, and from the 1870s under two separate titles, *Norges Handel* and *Norges Skipsfart*. It was published every three years until 1850, after which it appeared annually. The publications for 1841, 1844, 1847 and 1850, however, also provide data for the intervening years.

[11]Official sources only provide figures for 1830-1834 on the most aggregate level in terms of the number and capacity of vessels arriving and departing from Norwegian ports. The sources for 1835 are more descriptive, but still do not differentiate between vessels carrying cargo and those sailing in ballast.

[12]Martin Tvethe's figures for domestic-based shipping in 1836 have been a key source in creating these series. See Martin Braun Tvethe, *Norges Statistik* (Christiania, 1848). For further discussion on methodology, please see Brautaset, "Norsk eksport," 131-136.

[13]Martin Braun Tvethe, *Norges Statistik* (Christiania, 1848). Efforts to locate these sources in various Norwegian archives have unfortunately been unsuccessful.

[14]This exercise reveals a slight growth over 1836 and a marginal decline in the following year (1838). This corresponds with other observations regarding developments in the Norwegian economy in the 1830s. See Ola Honningdal Grytten, "The Gross Domestic Product for Norway 1830-2003," in Jan Øyvind Eitrheim, Jan Tore

Not all vessels, however, carried cargo. Thus, the preliminary figures must be adjusted to prevent overestimates of the shipping volume. As figure 2 shows, Norwegian vessels had a strong market position in the shipping of domestic goods. Moreover, it is clear that multilateral trade in shipping services was limited in this period, despite non-discriminatory port charges for most foreign vessels. Based on observations for 1838-1843, more than ninety-five percent of Norwegian vessels clearing domestic ports carried cargo.

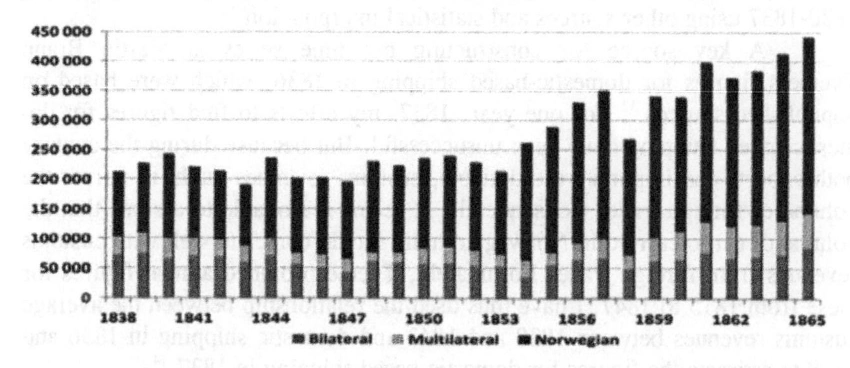

Figure 2: Vessels Departing Norwegian Ports with Cargo, 1838-1865 (net register tons [nrt])

Note: "Bilateral" is defined as vessels from the country where the cargo was bound, while other foreign vessels carrying cargo are categorized as "multilateral." The distribution between vessels carrying cargo and those in ballast between 1830 and 1837 is based on averages for the successive five-year period.

Sources: *Statistiske Tabeller* (Christiania, 1838-1859); and *Norges Handel og Skibsfart* (Christiania, 1860-1865).

The competition for homebound cargo seems to have been far greater, as on average only fifty percent of vessels returned with cargoes. But figure 3 demonstrates that over time Norwegian vessels increasingly gained a stronger foothold in these trades, just as they did in the export of Norwegian staples. In outbound services, multilateral trade was limited both nominally and relatively. Consequently, the shipping of goods to and from Norwegian ports remained a bilateral affair for the entire period analyzed here. The development of Norway's foreign trade is in sharp contrast to how its merchant marine capitalized in both scale and scope on the expanding demand for shipping services.

Klovland and Jan F. Qvigstadt (eds.), *Historical Monetary Statistics for Norway, 1819-2003* (Oslo, 2004), 272.

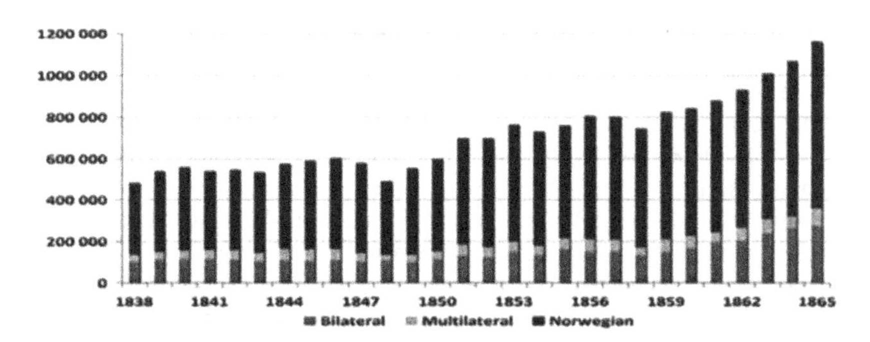

Figure 3: Domestic and Foreign Vessels Arriving at Norwegian Ports with Cargo, 1838-1865 (nrt)

Note: See figure 2.

Source: See figure 2.

Cargo Transported in the Cross-Trades, 1830-1865

The nature of the sources makes it somewhat more challenging to establish comprehensive series on the engagement of Norwegian vessels in the cross-trades. *Statistiske Tabeller* published its first systematic data on Norwegian vessels in the cross-trades in 1838, followed by similar information for 1841 and 1844; from 1847, this information appeared annually. *Statistiske Tabeller* offers two sets of tables, one on Swedish ports and the other for journeys between international harbours.[15] Both provide information on the number and tonnage of the vessels, and whether the ship was carrying cargo. Though it is clear that the records refer to the cross-trades, neither link the ports of call. In other words, the source does not tell us from where the vessels came or where they were bound. Because vessels were recorded upon both arrival and departure in foreign ports, the same voyage is recorded twice. In principle, though, these should correspond, but a comparison shows that this was not the case. The discrepancies are minor, though in no particular direction. To remedy this situation, I have used the arithmetic average of arrivals and departures.

What about the years not covered by the sources? *Amtmennsberetningene, 1846-1850*, provides information on Norwegian vessels abroad departing with cargo for another foreign port.[16] Schweigaard, Tvethe and Jacob S.

[15]The figures for Sweden include vessels sailing between Norwegian and Swedish ports, i.e., domestic-based shipping, as well as Norwegian vessels travelling between Swedish and international ports.

[16]Norway, *Amtmannsberetningene, 1846-50* (Christiania, 1853), 91 ff.

Worm-Müller offer sporadic information regarding the extent of shipping in the cross-trades.[17] Though these sources are valuable, they are not sufficient to provide coherent, annual series for the entire time span 1830-1865 because it has not been possible to locate empirical sources for this type of shipping for the years 1830-1836 or 1839-1840. For a historian, interpolation and extrapolation are the last resort in establishing historical statistics, but this approach has been necessary for a limited number of years in the 1830s. Luckily, the decade is not entirely without traces of information. The figures for 1837 and 1838 are well documented, and it is also possible to draw upon the data on trade-based shipping. This opens up the possibility of providing informed indicators for shipping in the cross-trades in the 1830s by applying the relative proportions between domestic-based and third-country shipping in 1837-1838. In line with this, shipping in the cross-trades in 1830-1836 and 1839-1840 is estimated to be ten percent of domestic-based shipping, as was the case in 1837 and 1838.

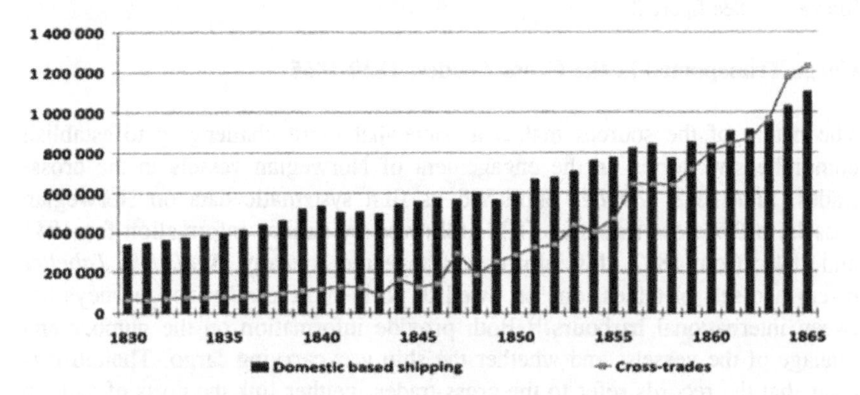

Figure 4: Cargo Transported in Domestic-based Shipping and the Cross-Trades, 1830-1865 (nrt)

Source: See figure 2.

[17]Anton Martin Schweigaard, *Norges Statistik* (Christiania, 1840), offers figures for 1837 and 1838, and Tvethe, *Norges Statistik*, does so for 1837-1838, 1841-1844 and 1846. Jacob Worm-Müller, "Forutsetningene for ekspansionen," in Worm-Müller (ed.), *Den norske sjøfarts historie* (6 vols., Oslo, 1923-1951), II, part 1, 304. As the authors claim that they are based on the same sources, it is not surprising that they correspond well, with the exception of Tvethe's data for the 1840s. Cross-referencing the data reveal that Tvethe most likely did not consider that the data for Swedish ports were reported in Swedish units of measurement (*svenske læster*) rather than the corresponding Norwegian measure, the *commercelæster*.

Figure 4 captures two of the most striking features of the development of Norwegian shipping 1830-1865. First, it indicates the rapid expansion of both domestic based and third-country shipping. Secondly, it also shows a dramatic change where vessels going between foreign ports presumably for the first time became the dominant source of business for Norwegian vessel owners in terms of cargo. Still, as argued previously, further information is required to get a broader picture of the composition of output.

Distances and Trade Routes for Domestic-based Shipping

In his doctoral thesis, "Økonomi, teknologi og historie: Analyser av skipsfart og økonomi 1866-1913," Ole Gjølberg explained why matching cargo and distances between each port in historical studies is difficult.[18] As a result, he chose to assume that all vessels departed from a single port in Norway (Oslo) and called only at Hamburg, London or New York.[19]

Of course, some kinds of simplifications when matching cargoes and ports are unavoidable. As the borders of political units were frequently in flux, I have been guided by the seas and their ports rather than nation-states. The main challenge in deriving series of produced output in ton-miles is to establish representative routes and reliable measures between the ports involved. Yet this is less straightforward than it might appear. Economists, economic historians and social scientists studying globalization and space have argued that distance is "dead, abolished and annihilated."[20] To the maritime historian, though, distance is never unimportant. On the contrary, in the nineteenth-century context of an emerging world economy and the intensification of global relations, distance is especially important. Still, distances at sea are elusive measures. Distance calculations are relatively complex, and the approach to measuring them has changed over time. Indeed, various sources often provide different distance figures for the same routes.[21]

---

[18]Ole Gjølberg, "Økonomi, teknologi og historie: Analyser av skipsfart og økonomi, 1866-1913" (Unpublished PhD thesis, Norwegian School of Economics and Business Administration, 1979), 45.

[19]Gjølberg argued that his study was directed towards the structure of the statistics and not the nitty-gritty of individual observations. *Ibid.*, 49-53.

[20]See, for instance, Martin Heidegger, "The Thing," in Heidegger, *Poetry, Language, Thought* (New York, 1971); Niall Fergusson, "Sinking Globalization," *Foreign Affairs*, LXXXIV, No. 2 (2005), 64-77; and Frances Cairncross, *The Death of Distance: How the Communications Revolution Will Change Our Lives* (Boston, 1997).

[21]For an introduction to the technicalities and various standards of such calculations, see, for instance, Charles H. Cotter, *A History of Nautical Astronomy* (London, 1968). The cross-referencing was done using various sources published over a rela-

Sources containing systematic information on distances at sea began to appear in the nineteenth century. Over time, these measurements began to reflect the shifting technological regimes, where references to steamers were replaced by motor vessels and later supplemented with separate tables for tankers. Since the Norwegian fleet between 1830 and 1865 consisted almost entirely of sailing vessels, this presents a challenge in applying these figures. Yet the biggest cause for concern is that the distances do not match. The proportions of the discrepancies vary and do not seem to be systematic. This leads to the conclusion that the disparities cannot be explained by technological or methodological changes. Nonetheless, technology did have a major influence on how far the vessels actually travelled. A sailing vessel steered by wind and currents would necessarily travel a greater distance on the same route than would steam- or motor-powered ships.

Since no published source appears to be substantially more correct than the others, I have based the distance calculations in this study on information previously available at the internet site "World Sea Ports" and currently on-line at "PortWorld."[22] There are two main reasons for this decision. First, these sources offered the greatest selection of ports.[23] Second, the distances in these two databases tend to be slightly higher than in the Lloyd's tables. Paradoxically, this ought to make them more compatible with the age of sail.

Two factors have been considered when selecting routes for domestic-based shipping. First, the departures and destinations had to represent major trade routes for exports and/or imports. Second, Norwegian vessels had to play an active role in this transport. In short, I have selected established routes that were both representative of certain trades and for the distance estimates.

For trade with Nordic, Baltic and Russian ports, I have therefore chosen Bergen-Königsberg.[24] As a former Hanseatic port located in the heart of the Baltic coastline and linked to its hinterland through the river Pregel (Pre-

---

tively long time span. These included *Lloyd's Calendar 1910* (London, 1910); John William Noire, *Brown's Nautical Almanac* (London, 1924); Ernest W. Blocksidge, *Merchant Ships and Shipping* (London, 1933); Edward F. Stevens, *Shipping Practice* (London, 1947); *Lloyd's Maritime Atlas* (London, 1966); Norsk Rederforbund, *Distansetabeller* (Oslo, 1978).

[22]http://www.world-ports.com, accessed May 2001; and http://www.portworld.com, accessed January 2011.

[23]The World Sea Ports database comprises 2865 ports in 133 countries.

[24]Today called Kaliningrad oblast. Prussia was the most important destination for Norwegian vessels in the Baltic in this period. The sources, however, only list "Prussia," rather than specific ports, as a destination. An alternative port in this region could have been Danzig, but in terms of distance, this choice would have had only a marginal impact.

golya), Königsberg had long traditions as a regional trade hub.[25] During the period studied here, Königsberg was a prominent naval base and the capital of the Kingdom of Prussia between 1824 and 1878. The city underwent rapid changes during the nineteenth century, with the extension of the railway network of particular importance. The construction of the Prussian Eastern Railway opened up new markets, including Berlin and St. Petersburg from 1860. While grain was the most sought-after import commodity from the Baltic, the most important Norwegian export was fish in general and herring in particular.[26] While Norwegian herring catches were notoriously volatile, from around 1808 until the last quarter of the nineteenth century, herring swarmed the western coast of Norway. Rogaland dominated herring exports in general, and Bergen was the centre of this trade. These factors explain the selection of the ports to represent this route.

Measured by both tonnage and the number of ships, Prussia was the sixth largest destination/departure point for Norwegian vessels during the period studied here.[27] Yet as Helge Nordvik convincingly argued, shipping with Prussia is likely underestimated, and that with Sweden overestimated, in the Norwegian statistics for fiscal reasons.[28] The export tax on fish products was lower for Swedish than other foreign ports due to a customs arrangement between Norway and Sweden in the form of *Mellomrikslovene*.[29] Thus, skippers going to the Baltic with herring had every incentive to state that they were bound for Sweden for tax purposes. Still, there obviously was a trade in fish with the ports along the strait of Helsingør and elsewhere in Scandinavia. This

---

[25]Königsberg is also connected to the river Vistula through the Vistula lagoon.

[26]The role of Königsberg and Danzig in the herring trade, the challenge of finding return cargo and the consequences for Holland and England is beautifully described by Daniel Defoe, *An Humble Proposal to the People of England, For the Increase of Their Trade, And Encouragement of their Manufactures; Whether The Present Uncertainty of Affairs Issues in Peace or War* (London, 1729), 19 ff.

[27]Tests for individual years show that the UK, France, Holland, Denmark and Sweden had all more Norwegian tonnage arriving and departing their ports than did Prussia.

[28]Helge Wallum Nordvik, "Sildehandelens struktur og utvikling i Stavanger, 1820-1860," *Stavanger Museums Årbok* (Stavanger, 1982), esp. 22-27.

[29]*Mellomrikslovene* was a general trade agreement between Norway and Sweden which was revised periodically between 1825/1827 and 1895/1897. The historian Harald Hamre, "Med havets sølv på Planke-Kina: Sildefarten på Østersjøen på 1800-tallet," *Stavanger Museums Årbok* (Stavanger, 1992), 23, has suggested that between 1841 and 1850 more than half of the herring exported from Stavanger with Sweden as the stated destination was in fact discharged in foreign ports.

means that by basing the distance calculation on trade between western Norway and the Prussian coast we may be overestimating the output of shipping services. Balancing this, however, the trade in fish and grain also took place with more distant ports, such as Kronstadt.

The second trade route selected for domestic-based shipping is Christiania-London. The most frequently visited foreign ports were British, and London was unparalleled in its importance. The main Norwegian export to the UK was timber, but there were a diverse selection of return cargoes, including coal, cotton and linen products, exotic foodstuffs like coffee, sugar and spices, metals, bricks and chemicals. Christiania was one of the major export ports for Norwegian timber to the UK, while exporters in Drammen, Fredrikstad, Sarpsborg and Langesund were orientated more towards ports in France and Holland. Because the single most important continental port for Norwegian timber was Le Havre, the third route chosen is Drammen-Le Havre. Return cargoes from France were textiles, wines, vinegar, spirits and cheese.[30]

Figure 2 depicts the distribution of Norwegian exports carried by domestic and foreign vessels. The largest part of exports carried by overseas vessels comprised salted and dried cod (*bacalao*) from Sunnmøre and Nordmøre to ports along the Atlantic coasts of Portugal and Spain.[31] Part of the explanation for why foreign vessels had a stronghold on this trade can be found in the tariff systems in the main markets. Up to the 1850s, domestic vessels were charged lower import duties in Spanish and Portuguese ports. But Norwegian vessels were calling at Mediterranean ports in the 1830s, and the importance of this market was growing. As Norwegian shipowners gained an increasing foothold in the transport of *bacalao*, tramp shipping in the Mediterranean and the Black Sea increased. From the 1850s onwards, trade with Black Sea ports attracted vessels from Stavanger and Bergen in particular. Traditionally, salt and fruit from Spain and Portugal had been return cargoes, but these were increasingly supplemented by grain from the Black Sea. With these changes in trade and a relatively broad range of distances, it is a challenge to identify a single, representative port for the entire period. However, I have chosen Bergen-Barcelona both because of the prominence of fish as the largest export commodity and the location of the latter near large supplies of quality salt.

---

[30]The bilateral trade between Norway and France was an uneven affair during these decades, with Norwegian bulk goods far outstripping French exports, a fact that contributed to the difficulties in negotiating a trade treaty between Sweden-Norway and France. In fact, it took nearly twenty years of talks before a treaty was signed in 1865. Øyvind Laastad is investigating these negotiations with a special emphasis on the shipping sector in his forthcoming MA thesis at the Department of Archaeology, History, Culture and Religion at the University of Bergen.

[31]Customers in ports farther south had a preference for Newfoundland cod.

Throughout the period 1830-1865, European ports were the prime destinations for Norwegian vessels departing and arriving from domestic ports, but transcontinental trades were also on the rise. In order to capture these sailings, I have examined three routes; Christiania-Québec (North America), Bergen-Rio de Janeiro (Caribbean and South America) and Christiania-Port Adelaide (Asia/Australia).[32] These routes and distances are summarized in table 1.

Table 1
Routes and Distances for Domestic-based Shipping

Domestic Ports	Foreign Ports	Regions	Nautical Miles
Bergen	Königsberg	North Sea and Baltic	1066
Christiania	London	UK and Ireland	819
Drammen	Le Havre	Continent	874
Bergen	Barcelona	Mediterranean	2833
Christiania	Québec	North America	4457
Bergen	Rio de Janeiro	South America	6030
Christiania	Port Adelaide	Asia and Oceania	19378

Source: See text.

Distances and Trade Routes for the Cross-Trades

As indicated earlier, the nature of the sources requires the application of a rather rigorous set of assumptions in order to establish indicators for the output volume in the cross-trades. During the nineteenth century, the position of the UK in world trade was unrivalled.[33] Its hegemonic power was also felt at sea: most British exports were transported in British hulls. But throughout the period the UK had a surplus of imports, and foreign vessels carried an increasing share after the repeal of the Navigation Acts in 1850.

[32]Rio de Janeiro was developing rapidly in this period as a hub for trade in sugar, coffee, cotton and rubber. I also considered using a route involving sub-Saharan ports in Africa, but direct trade with this region was only marginal, with several years often elapsing between Norwegian voyages to or from Cape Town.

[33]Paul Bairoch, "Geographical Structure and Trade Balance of European Foreign Trade from 1800-1970," *Journal of European Economic History*, III, No. 3 (1978), 583, indicates that the UK had thirty-one percent of world imports in 1860.

Norwegian vessels took an active role in this trade.[34] Until the 1850s, timber was the main cargo in the third-country trade of Norwegian shipping. There were two main sources of supply, Sweden and the Baltic. While Britain was the principal market for Swedish timber, timber from the Baltic was chiefly sold on the continent. According to Schweigaard, transport to and from Sweden constituted around two-thirds of total third-country shipping in 1837 and 1838, and arrivals at British, Belgian, French and Dutch ports accounted for seventy-eight percent of all arrivals in this trade.[35] Corresponding figures from Tvethe indicate that this pattern remained stable a decade later in terms of arrival ports, while Baltic export ports had gained importance relative to Swedish harbours for departures.[36] Both quantitative and qualitative sources strongly suggest that Norwegian shipping in the cross-trades up to the 1850s was limited to trade between European ports. As the most important destinations were clustered around the English Channel, London will serve as a representative indicator in terms of distance calculations prior to 1850.

The single most important change in Norwegian third-country shipping between 1830 and 1865 was institutional. The repeal of the Navigation Acts not only opened up the market to and from Britain but also led to similar changes elsewhere and to a liberalization of the international shipping market.

In the following, I have assumed that Norwegian ships were firmly enmeshed in the British web of worldwide trade. A rough indication of the validity of this assumption can be found through comparing the amount of cargo carried by Norwegian vessels in the cross-trades and the tonnage of imported goods into the UK. Figure 5 suggests that these two trends tracked each other closely until the late 1850s. Then, however, the tonnage carried by Norwegian third-country shipping outstripped British imports, which was still rising after the Crimean war. It therefore appears that the assumption is reasonable given that the two trends were broadly similar throughout the period. Applied to the calculations, I have chosen London as the departing/arriving port for trade with Europe, Asia and South Africa, while Liverpool will be used for trade with the Americas. A total of twelve trades have been selected to estimate distances and thus output in the cross-trades prior to 1865 (see table 2).

---

[34]The economic historian Edgar Hovland argued that the Norwegian cross-trades up to the late 1860s were dominated by Europe, with the UK as the focus. See Hovland, "Gjenreising og vekst - norsk økonomi, 1815-1875," in Rolf Danielsen, *et al.*, *Grunntrekk i norsk historie* (Oslo, 1992), 200.

[35]Schweigaard, *Norges Statistik*, 177 ff.

[36]Tvethe, *Norges Statistik*, 153 ff. For a further discussion, see Fredrik Scheel, "Østersjøfart," in Worm-Müller (ed.), *Den norske sjøfarts historie*, II, part 1, 183 ff.

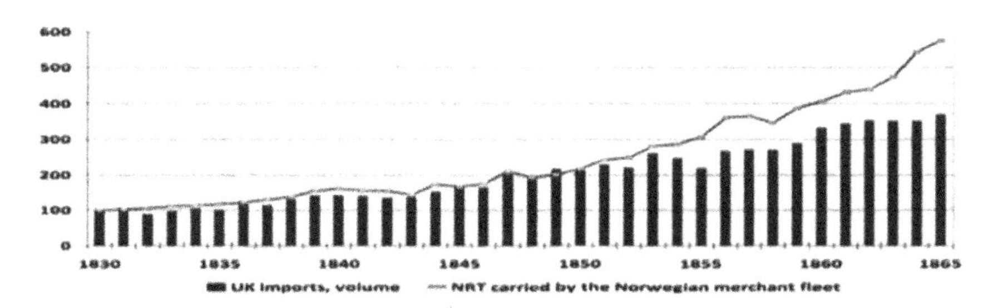

Figure 5: British Imports and Tonnage Carried by the Norwegian Merchant Fleet in the Cross-Trades, Volume Indices, 1830-1865 (1830 = 100)

Sources: Brautaset, "Norsk eksport, 1830-1865," 143; and Albert H. Imlah, *Economic Elements in the Pax Britannica: Studies in British Foreign Trade in the Nineteenth Century* (Cambridge, MA, 1958), 94-96.

Table 2
Routes and Distances for Third-Country Shipping

	Ports	**Macro Regions**	**Nautical Miles**
London	Antwerp	From Hamburg to Belgium	268
	Le Havre	French Ports	124
	Königsberg	From Russia to Mecklenburg	1461
	Gothenburg	Sweden, Denmark, Lübeck	848
	Porto	Portugal and Gibraltar	878
	Barcelona	Spanish Ports	2011
	Naples	Italian, Austrian and Greek Ports	2672
	Alexandria	Eastern and Southern Med. Ports	3783
	Cape Town	Sub-Saharan Africa	6135
	Hong Kong	East Asian Ports	13441
	Bombay	West Asia Ports	10846
Liverpool	Québec	North American Ports	4127
	Rio de Janeiro	South American Ports	5176

Source: See text.

When Distance Matters

Looking first at the output of domestic-based shipping, we can see a strong upward trend (see figure 6). But there are also signs that the transport of imports and exports responded differently to swings in the business cycle. In boom years, as during the Crimean War, the carriage of exports expanded substantially, while trade in imports was stagnant or declining. For other years, however, especially the crisis years of 1848 and 1858, the shipping of domestic produce declined, while homeward cargoes expanded slightly. While inbound and outbound freights had similar growth rates, domestic exports remained the predominant source of output for domestic-based shipping. In effect, international market conditions for Norwegian staples had a binary effect on the balance of trade and hence on overall economic development during this period.

The differences between homeward and outbound freights were naturally subject to the possibility of joint production for vessel owners. The most important Norwegian exports, timber and fish, posed substantially different demands for tonnage. Vessels carrying herring were generally smaller than those carrying bulky shipments of timber. The ports importing herring were frequently exporters of grain, which was the most important Norwegian import throughout this period. Thus, the herring vessels enjoyed a higher rate of return cargo than those specializing in the timber trade. Similarly, vessels carrying dried and salted cod were destined for ports on the Atlantic and Mediterranean coasts, where salt, wines and fruit were valuable return cargoes.

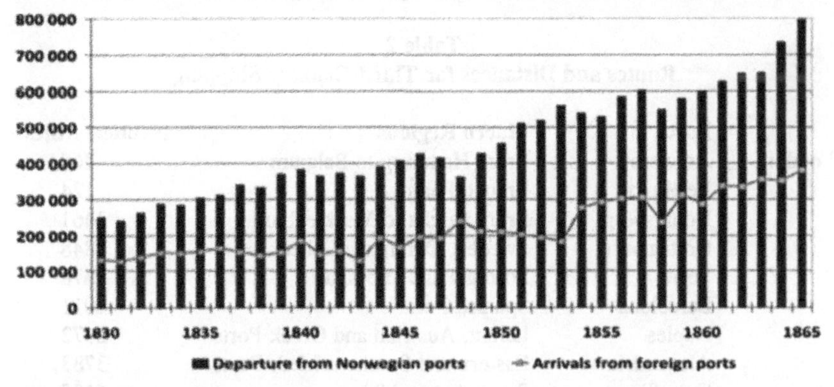

Figure 6: Output of Domestic-based Shipping, 1830-1865 (ton-miles)

Source: See figure 2 and text.

Because of the way these series were constructed, there are two potential sources behind this expansion: a surge in transported tonnage and/or longer voyages in terms of distance. Through a very simple Laspeyres index it is possible to get an idea of which factor was the driving force behind the growth in output. Such a comparison can be seen in figure 7.

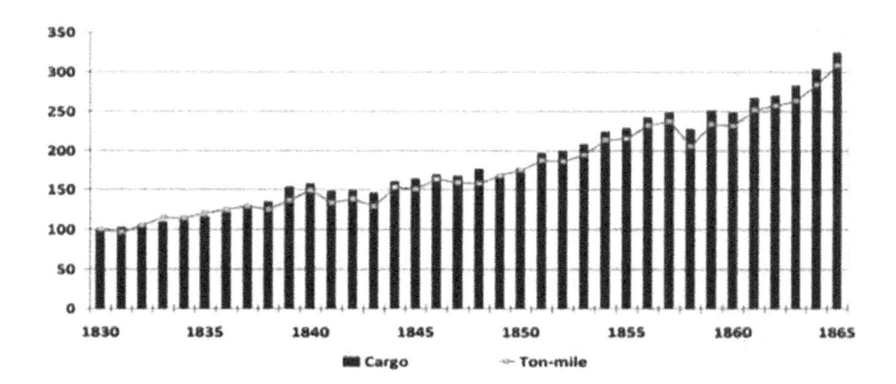

Figure 7: Transported Cargo and Ton-Miles of Domestic-based Shipping, 1830-1865 (1830 = 100)

Source: Based on figure 6.

At first glance, it might be easy to forget that these units are not separate entities and that tonnage and distance were thus equally important to the growth in output. Indeed, the striking correspondence between the two units of observation strengthens the perception that the expansion of domestic-based shipping reflected an increase in trade, a larger market share and a relatively stable trading pattern.

For Norwegian vessel owners, domestic-based shipping implied a deepening and strengthening of their position in existing markets. The story of the cross-trades, however, was an entirely different story. This type of shipping was based on new and rapidly expanding tramp markets. Due to institutional restraints through bilateral trade arrangements, third-country shipping was not widespread prior to the 1850s; instead, the transport of timber from Sweden and the Baltic was the main niche for Norwegian vessels in the 1830s and 1840s. But from mid-century the increase in output was staggering. From being a lesser companion to domestic-based shipping, the cross-trades became the most important source of output growth in Norwegian merchant shipping (see figure 8). This signalled a dramatic change for both the shipping industry and the Norwegian economy as a whole. Within a relatively short period of time, one of the country's main export earners increased both the scale and scope of its business through reaping the benefits of the rapid growth in multilateral trade. This would soon change the dynamics of foreign trade as well as accelerate the pace at which the Norwegian economy became integrated into the emerging world economy.

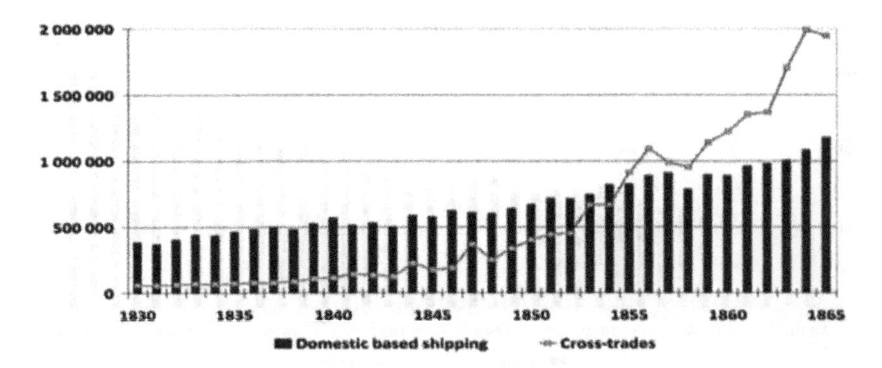

Figure 8: Output of Norwegian Shipping, 1830-1865, Measured in Ton-Miles

Source: See figure 2 and text.

Figure 9 and table 3 suggest that there was a striking difference in the basis of growth between domestic-based shipping and the cross-trades. As we have seen earlier, domestic-based shipping expanded primarily on the basis of the carriage of increased quantities of goods. The growth of output in the cross-trades, however, was due to momentous changes in trading patterns that entailed increased distances. Not only did foreign ports and trades become the main channels for the growing production of shipping services, these ports also increasingly were further apart. Hence, Norwegian merchant shipping's increasing engagement with global markets implied that distance mattered more than ever before.

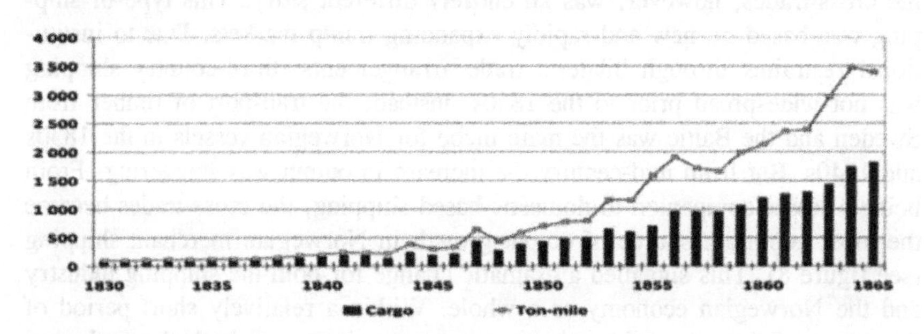

Figure 9: Transported Cargo and Ton-Miles of Shipping in the Cross-Trades, 1830-1865 (1830=100)

Source: Based on figure 8.

Table 3
Output of the Norwegian Merchant Fleet, 1830-1865

	Carried Tonnage, NRT		Output, Ton-miles	
Year	Domestic-based Shipping	Cross-Trades	Domestic-based Shipping	Cross-Trades
1830	339,481	67,414	382,167	57,325
1831	347,495	64,985	368,392	55,259
1832	359,095	70,815	401,450	60,217
1833	370,695	77,462	439,128	65,869
1834	382,295	76,707	434,847	65,227
1835	393,895	81,180	460,207	69,031
1836	410,864	84,293	477,850	71,678
1837	439,299	86,945	492,889	73,933
1838	456,627	96,959	477,404	83,822
1839	520,418	109,858	523,133	104,627
1840	534,204	119,078	567,040	113,408
1841	501,732	131,611	511,470	138,710
1842	504,290	124,732	527,969	131,992
1843	494,338	90,811	494,212	123,553
1844	542,011	162,345	583,494	221,678
1845	554,174	126,329	572,921	171,876
1846	571,426	141,027	621,812	186,544
1847	566,142	293,509	607,225	366,507
1848	598,366	185,063	601,913	246,460
1849	565,482	253,646	638,784	335,318
1850	600,316	285,041	666,202	399,802
1851	668,023	321,850	715,214	441,154
1852	675,627	334,612	712,311	449,916
1853	706,941	434,914	743,306	663,746
1854	760,048	402,240	816,580	663,374
1855	776,360	468,252	822,316	913,143
1856	823,068	643,358	886,833	1,093,314
1857	843,635	639,935	907,223	987,603
1858	772,049	638,003	785,373	952,113
1859	852,273	717,116	892,675	1,139,447
1860	843,660	807,345	884,951	1,220,614
1861	905,867	847,785	963,209	1,353,361
1862	915,054	870,773	982,267	1,368,145
1863	960,399	965,011	1,005,514	1,702,306
1864	1,030,993	1,175,061	1,084,718	1,990,844
1865	1,101,591	1,227,857	1,177,338	1,944,068

Source: Based on figures 7-9.

Conclusion

The focus of this paper has been on the output of the Norwegian merchant fleet between 1830 and 1865. As any historian working with numbers would acknowledge, the creation and use of time series is not an exact science. The series in this essay have been constructed for a specific purpose and should not be regarded as the final word. What they do represent, however, is a new set of data offering informed and empirically verifiable indicators of the volume of production of one of the main engines of growth in the nineteenth-century Norwegian economy. Consequently, what has been referred to as "invisible foreign trade" is made available for economic analysis. As a result, shipping is placed on more equal terms with industries that produce material end products in examining macroeconomic development over time.

The analyses of the various output series have paid particular attention to the way the Norwegian merchant marine enhanced and transformed its market base in the shift from domestically based foreign trade to the cross-trades. The new data not only make it possible for us to place this development in time but also offer empirical images of the speed and scale of the transition. The findings indicate that the output of Norwegian merchant shipping expanded more than seven-fold during the thirty-five-year period from 1830 to 1865. This strong growth reflected both an increase in Norwegian merchandise exports and, more importantly, the development of tramp cross-trades between foreign ports. In both segments, Norwegian sailing vessels gained an increasing share of a steadily increasing market. Growing participation in the cross-trades is a clear indication of the increased importance of long-distance, multilateral trade - and thus of the increasing significance of distance to the shipping output after 1850. The point is underscored when comparing the development in transported cargo with that of ton-miles in the cross-trades as shown in figure 9. For the Norwegian merchant fleet, this was a trend that would be strengthened further in the coming decades as sailing vessels were increasingly displaced in the European trades by steamships. In short, the main finding of the essay is to accentuate the argument that distance is of crucial importance when analyzing what has been referred to as the most international of all trades - especially within the context of an emerging world economy.

Norwegian maritime history today provides a home for laymen, enthusiasts and scholars alike. Though their interests are diffuse, their methodological approaches are not. This essay has approached nineteenth-century Norwegian maritime history from a quantitative, macro-oriented perspective. In historiographical terms, this is not new. But the introduction of new scholars with new questions makes me optimistic that we are now about to witness increased methodological diversity. This will hopefully be a welcome complement to existing knowledge and research traditions and hence lead to a strengthening of Norwegian maritime history as a field of study.

The Silver Schooner

Dag Hundstad

Mutiny. Even today the word has a menacing sound. When a master's power is in dispute, the ship's social system becomes unstable; if he is overthrown, the crew is temporarily without norms, a condition in which anything can happen. It is no wonder that narratives about mutinies have proven so popular in maritime sea lore.[1]

In the harbour of Kleven, near Mandal in southern Norway, tales of the mutiny of the so-called "Silver Schooner" can still be heard. It is a bloody story that contains some of the classic elements of the narratives of sea lore - mutiny, smuggling and hidden treasure. Because of its dramatic nature, it was used by Thorbjørn Egner in his primary school textbook, and through this, generations of Norwegian school children came to know it.[2]

The story concerns an American schooner which arrived in Kleven with a cargo of coffee. There was nothing extraordinary about that, but the vessel's crew soon attracted attention because of their odd behaviour. When the authorities began to make inquiries, they discovered that the seamen had mutinied on the Atlantic, killing their officers and sailing to Norway to seek refuge. It turned out that the real cargo was not coffee, but a huge number of silver coins. When this came to light, the crew attempted to escape but were caught, transferred to the United States and hanged on a pier. Although the authorities never recovered all the silver coins, many believed that one of the barrels was hidden on the island of Gismerøya, and people have been searching for this "hidden treasure" ever since. What makes this narrative so significant is that most of the events are "true" in the sense that they can be confirmed by contemporary written sources.

Putting the Pieces Together

While working in the 1920s on a history of Mandal, Christian A. Bugge used the oral tale of the "Silver Schooner" as a starting point. With the assistance of

[1]For a comprehensive collection of sea lore, see Horace Beck, *Folklore and the Sea* (Middletown, CT, 1973; reprint, Mystic, CT, 1996).

[2]Thorbjørn Egner, *Thorbjørn Egners lesebøker* (16 vols., Oslo, 1950-1972), V, 73-75 and 85-86.

the distinguished Norwegian historian, Professor Jacob S. Worm-Müller, Bugge unearthed some archival sources which seemingly corroborated some of the story's basic elements. It turned out that the name of the "Silver Schooner" was *Plattsburg* and that the incident occurred in 1816.[3] The records Bugge found were from a comprehensive description of a trial concerning the smuggling of coffee in the schooner.[4] These documents tell us a good deal about maritime adaptation and illegal trade in the port of Kleven, and I therefore used the story in a monograph I wrote about the port in 1996.[5] Yet because the mutiny did not interest Norwegian authorities, some of the basic questions about the narrative remained unresolved: Who owned the ship? Why did it contain this particular cargo? Were the mutineers really executed?

It was not until 2009 that I began to resolve this puzzle. There turned out to be several useful American sources, including a little booklet entitled *Narrative of the Mutiny on Board the Schooner Plattsburg, William Hackett, Master, in Consequence of which John Williams, Francis Frederick, Nils Peterson, and John P. Rog Suffered Death on the 18th March 1819*.[6] There was also a book on the trial of the mutineers, as well as stories in American newspapers.[7] P.R. Hamblin's *United States Criminal History* devoted twenty pages to the mutiny.[8] An account of the incident was also written by the American

---

[3]Christian August Bugge, *En Sørlandsby: Erindringer og skildringer fra Mandal i gammel og nyere tid* (Christiania, 1924), 94-100.

[4]Regional State Archives, Kristiansand, Archives of the County Governor, Commission regarding the schooner *Platzburg*.

[5]Dag Hundstad [Johannesen], *Klevefolk: Historien om en havn* (Mandal, 1996), 70-78.

[6]Stephen B. Onion, *Narrative of the Mutiny on Board the Schooner Plattsburg, William Hackett, Master, in Consequence of which John Williams, Francis Frederick, Nils Peterson, and John P. Rog Suffered Death on the 18th March 1819* (Boston, 1819).

[7]*The Trial of John Williams, Francis Frederick, John P. Rog, Nils Peterson, and Nathaniel White, on an Indictment for Murder on the High Seas, before the Circuit Court of the United States, Holden for the District of Massachusetts at Boston, on the 28th of December, 1818* (Boston, 1819); *A Concise Sketch of the Execution of John Williams, Peter Peterson (alias Nils Peterson), Francis Frederick and John P. Rog, Who Were Executed on the 18th of February, 1819, for Murder and Piracy, Prefaced with Moral Reflections, to which is Added a Solemn Address* (Boston, 1819); and *An Address to the Spectator of the Awful Execution of the Pirates in Boston, February 18, 1819* (Boston, 1819).

[8]P.R. Hamblin, *United States Criminal History; Being a True Account of the Most Horrid Murders, Piracies, High-Way Robberies, &c., Together with the Lives,*

sailor, journalist, politician and author John Sherburne Sleeper in his autobiography, *Jack in the Forecastle*.[9] In 1817, Sleeper was employed in a vessel which carried one of the mutineers from Gothenburg to Boston for trial. The Boston-based maritime historian Fred Hopkins also wrote about the mutiny in the journal *American Neptune*,[10] using US primary sources to show how the repatriation of the mutineers created diplomatic problems.

In this essay, I will use both Norwegian and American sources to provide a new version of the "Silver Schooner." What was the purpose of the ship's voyage? What happened to the mutineers? In what way did the incident influence the various Norwegian actors concerned? Was the smuggling in *Plattsburg* representative of what went on in the ports of southern Norway? To answer these and other related questions, the starting point will be *Plattsburg*'s owner, Isaac McKim of Baltimore.

A New Trade for Isaac McKim

Isaac McKim is remembered today as a congressman from Maryland. He served in the War of 1812 as adjutant to General Samuel Smith; as a member of a powerful business family, he was, according to his congressional biography, also "engaged in mercantile pursuits."[11] After the conclusion of the War of 1812, Baltimore's commercial life underwent a crisis. During the postwar depression, many of the old merchant families encountered severe financial problems, and some teetered on the brink of bankruptcy. During the war, Maryland's economy had prospered because of its trade with neutrals, a pursuit which was now ended. Trade with the West Indies was slow to revive, and at any rate the merchants did not have many local products to export.[12]

The McKims began in flour milling. During the War of 1812, they opened the Baltimore Steam Works Factory, which used steam power to grind wheat into flour, which was then exported to Brazil where it was exchanged for coffee. While most of the coffee was re-exported at a profit, McKim

---

Trials, Confessions and Executions of the Criminals, Compiled from the Criminal Records of the Counties (Fayetteville, NC, 1836), 381-400.

[9]John Sherburne Sleeper, *Jack in the Forecastle or, Incidents in the Early Life of Hawser Martingale* (Boston, 1860; reprint, Lenox, MA, 2010), 421-428.

[10]Fred Hopkins, "The *Plattsburg* Mutiny, 1816," *American Neptune*, LV, No. 2 (1995), 135-141.

[11]http://bioguide.congress.gov/scripts/biodisplay.pl?index=M000516.

[12]Geoffrey M. Footner, *Tidewater Triumph: The Development and Worldwide Success of the Chesapeake Bay Pilot Schooner* (Mystic, CT, 1998), 132.

wanted more than coffee from South America; he also wanted copper, a commodity that was much in demand and which increasingly was being processed in Baltimore by entrepreneurs such as McKim.[13]

Unfortunately, McKim needed more than just flour in order to procure enough copper for his new industry. He eventually developed what the historian Geoffrey Footner has called "an ingenious plan." He would import Turkish opium from Smyrna, which he would sell to other merchants, who in turn would export it to China. McKim would use the profits from the trade to purchase copper and other products.[14]

Although technically illegal, the opium trade with China attracted both British and American merchants. Chinese goods were quite popular in the West, and opium was one of the very few commodities, along with specie, that the Chinese wanted in return. In the 1770s, the British East India Company was granted a monopoly to grow poppies in India and to produce opium for sale in China. When McKim started his business, Chinese consumption of opium was increasing dramatically among all strata of society. Although most of the opium consumed in China was produced in India, American-owned vessels were not permitted by the British to carry the product from India to China until 1838. Before this, Americans involved in the China trade were forced instead to buy lower-quality opium in Turkey. Before the Limitation Law of 1933, Turkey produced opium almost everywhere west of the Euphrates, with Smyrna the major port of export. It was not illegal in the US to engage in the opium trade, but the trade was banned by the Chinese. At this time, however, the emperor turned a blind eye to opium imports. His subsequent change of heart on this issue would later result in the First Opium War (1839-1842) between Britain and China.

Some of Baltimore's leading mercantile families owed their fortunes to this trade. This was not a heritage of which their descendants would be proud, and there have been attempts to paper over this part of the city's past.[15] McKim was a man of discretion, and without the incident involving *Plattsburg*, there would have been no records of his involvement in this trade.

Plattsburg of Baltimore

In 1815 and 1816, McKim purchased three new schooners - *Rossie II*, *Tropic* and *Plattsburg*, all built by Thomas Kemp and George Gardner in Baltimore. Kemp was a well-known, established Chesapeake Bay shipbuilder. His part-

---

[13]*Ibid.*, 132-133.

[14]*Ibid.*, 133.

[15]Thomas N. Layton, *The Voyage of the Frolic: New England Merchants and the Opium Trade* (Stanford, 1997), 157.

nership with Gardner lasted only a year before Kemp retired. Through Kemp, Gardner received an established network of customers, most of whom, including Isaac McKim, were Baltimore businessmen who had personal bonds with each other and with Kemp.[16]

The name *Plattsburg* reflected the patriotism of its owner. The Battle of Plattsburg (sometimes called the Battle of Lake Champlain) in 1814 was a great victory for the Americans and blunted the final British invasion during the war. Shortly thereafter, the Treaty of Ghent brought the conflict to a close.

Plattsburg was a fore-and-aft schooner built in 1815 and measuring 101 feet 5 inches (30.9 metres) in length and 23 feet 8 inches (7.2 metres) in breadth, with a carrying capacity of 237 tons. Although relatively small, vessels of this type were often called the "Great Baltimore Schooners" and had good reputations despite the fact that they were difficult to handle. Because of their ability to sail close to the wind, many were used as pilot boats.[17] The ships built by Gardner and his successors (Gardner Brothers) were also used as privateers and slavers.[18] Due to their low freeboards, single flush decks, light spars and standing riggings, they were "easily able to evade capture on the open sea."[19] Of the three ships McKim purchased, the destinies of *Rossie II* and *Tropic* are unknown, but the dramatic incidents onboard *Plattsburg* mean that we know much more about this vessel.

A Fatal Maiden Voyage

On 29 June 1816, *Plattsburg* departed from Fells Point in Baltimore on its maiden voyage with a cargo of 600 bags and 71 barrels of coffee, valued at US $30,000, and various bags and boxes of silver and gold coins valued at US $50,000. The captain was instructed to sell the coffee at Smyrna and to use the proceeds to purchase opium.[20] The coins were Spanish dollars, the principal currency in the region that was also widely used in Europe, the Americas and

---

[16]Footner, *Tidewater Triumph*, 132; and Layton, *Voyage of the Frolic*, 45.

[17]Hopkins, "*Plattsburg* Mutiny," 135; Footner, *Tidewater Triumph*, 103; and Layton, *Voyage of the Frolic*, 44.

[18]Some year later, an ex-slave wrote about his work at Gardner Brothers. The author was Frederick Douglass, who later gained his freedom and became an important abolitionist writer. For the rest of his life, Douglass carried a scar on his cheek from an attack by white apprentices at Gardner Brothers. Layton, *Voyage of the Frolic*, 48.

[19]Footner, *Tidewater Triumph*, 102.

[20]Hopkins, "*Plattsburg* Mutiny," 135.

East Asia.[21] The opium was to be brought home to Baltimore for an "East-India voyage."[22] In all probability, it was to be sold to middlemen in India who would smuggle it into China.

William Hackett was the captain of *Plattsburg*.[23] The first mate was Frederick Engelhardt Yeizer, a veteran of the War of 1812, and the second mate was Stephen Barriet Onion, of unknown origin. Thomas Baynard of Baltimore was the supercargo, with a special responsibility for the precious cargo. The crew of ten was comprised mainly of foreigners. We know their names, but not all their nationalities; they were the American John Williams (b. 1789) of Chazy, New York, who was brought up in Canada; the Dane Jens (or Jon) Petersen Raag (b. 1789);[24] the Swede Nils Peterson Fogelgreen (b. 1799) of Gothenburg; the Englishman Nathaniel White; the Prussian John Stürmer; Johan Johannsen (likely Swedish); the Spaniard Frank Frederick (or Frederick Frank) of Minorca; Daniel Wendt (unknown nationality); the Frenchman Jean Armand Lemolgat (probably Le Molgat) of Brittany; and the Afro-American Edward Sauberson (Sammerson, Samuel), who served as the steward.[25] Sauberson's ethnicity is also mentioned in the Norwegian sources. It was not uncommon for American shipowners to employ an ethnically mixed crew.[26]

There are several accounts of the sailors exhibiting deviant behaviour during the voyage. According to Sleeper, some members of the crew were "desperate, hardened ruffians" who had learned lessons in villainy as priva-

---

[21]In the Norwegian sources, the coins were referred to as *piastres*.

[22]*Niles Weekly Register* (Baltimore), 16 November 1816.

[23]Probably the same W.H. as the captain of the sloop *Nancy* of Maine, which was seized by French privateers in the West Indies in 1799; Greg H. Williams, *The French Assault on American Shipping, 1793-1813: A History and Comprehensive Record of Merchant Marine Losses* (Jefferson, NC, 2009), 255.

[24]According to Hamblin, *United States Criminal History*, Raag (or Rog) was born "at Christiansand in Denmark." As the city of Christiansand, in southern Norway, is mentioned in other places in the text, this is probably a misunderstanding or a misprint. All the other accounts of the incident state that Raag was Danish.

[25]Hopkins, "*Plattsburg* Mutiny;" and Hamblin, *United States Criminal History*. Hopkins must have been mistaken when he treated Edward Sauberson (or Samberson) and Edward Samuel as two different people, since from the sources they appear to be the same person. The names of the crew are spelled in several different ways in the various sources.

[26]Hundstad, *Klevefolk*, 61; Erling Eriksen, "Vår gamle sjøfartskultur," in Olav Bø (ed.), *Norsk kulturarv* (Oslo, 1968), 105.

teers during the war.[27] It is hard, however, to see these characteristics of the men apart from the deeds they were about to commit. McKim was known as a hard businessman, and he probably hired the least costly crew available.[28]

Mutiny on the Open Sea

The tales of the mutiny on *Plattsburg* vary somewhat, which is not surprising because some are oral transmissions which have been altered in the re-telling.[29] There is a consensus, however, about the main events. The most comprehensive version was provided by the second mate, Onion, and the steward, Sauberson, during their trial in Boston in 1819.[30] Although both tended to underestimate their own participation in the crime, the outline seems reliable. The ship cleared the Chesapeake for Gibraltar on 1 July 1816. As it passed the Virginia Capes, a dispute occurred between the master and crew member John Williams. Although this was "soon quieted," a desire to get their hands on the precious cargo was brewing among the crew. Tensions were also rising between the crew and the officers, who allegedly were rude and violent toward the able-bodied seamen (ABs).[31]

By 22 July, when *Plattsburg* was off Madeira, Williams took the lead in an attempt to murder the master, mates and supercargo by poisoning their coffee. This failed only because the poison was not strong enough. Instead, the officers blamed the steward for the poor quality of the coffee. A day or two later, as the vessel approached the Azores, the crew plotted to attack the officers as they were taking observations of the sun and to disembark them into a small boat, which might enable them to reach one of the islands. According to Sleeper, the mutineers got the idea for this plan from the mutiny on HMS

---

[27]Sleeper, *Jack in the Forecastle*, 422.

[28]Footner, *Tidewater Triumph*, 134.

[29]Apart from the literature already mentioned, see also *Aftenposten* (Oslo), 30 June 1921 and 19 April 1930; and Carl August Olsen, *Guldgraverliv og Sjømandsfærd: Oplevelser og Meddelelser* (Christiania, 1880), 4-6.

[30]The testimony appeared in print in 1820 in *Trial of John Williams*, which is the source for the following events.

[31]Hamblin, *United States Criminal History*, 385, states that the captain was "a man of irritable temper and violent passions" and that Hackett was the master of the schooner *Swift* before he was appointed to command *Plattsburg*. Williams was also a member of the crew on *Swift* where from time to time tensions between the captain and the crew arose.

Bounty,[32] although this might be a *post hoc* rationalization. Sleeper wrote his book in 1860, and despite the fact he had spoken to one of the mutineers, this was more than forty years earlier. Williams carried a rope to bind the captain, but according to the witnesses, "the hearts of his associates failing them," the plan was abandoned. But the intention to mutiny was not forsaken.

At midnight on 24 July, about 100 miles (160 km) from land, either Raag or Williams made a loud cry of "Sail, ho!" The first and second mates ran forward, but the first mate, Yeizer, was knocked down and thrown overboard by the crew. As he fell, the mate caught a rope, but it was cut by Stürmer. The second mate, Onion, was struck down with an axe and captured by Williams, who shouted "here is one of the damned rascals." When the captain arrived, Williams loosened his hold on Onion, who crept away and hid in the bread locker. The captain was struck with a handspike; he fell across the railing and was immediately thrown over the side. Onion then heard the mutineers call for the supercargo in an angry tone.

Sauberson, who until this time had been below in his cabin, was ordered on deck, where he saw the supercargo, Baynard, lying on his back. The Dane, Raag, later bragged that he had struck "the son of a bitch" with a stone in his stocking. Baynard was thrown overboard, and Sauberson heard him screaming for help. Then Onion appeared from the locker and begged for his life, and the crew determined that he should be spared. He was asked to take an oath of fidelity and was admitted as a member of the "fraternity." Stürmer was appointed the new master, with Williams as first mate and Onion continuing as second mate. The next morning, the money being carried was brought on deck and divided, with each crew member receiving $3000. Onion and Sauberson, who had not taken part in the uprising, accepted shares as well.

The mutineers then held a meeting where it was decided that they should set sail for Norway and that Onion should alter the ship's documents. After he accomplished this, the manifest showed that the coffee was destined for a "Mr. Myers" of Hamburg. Williams changed the logbook to correspond with this, writing that the ship was bound for Bremen.

A question which yet has to be solved is why the mutineers chose to sail for Norway. The Norwegian author Carl A. Olsen, who heard the tale of the mutiny from his father, claimed that the vessel reached Norway more or less by chance when heading northwards. They chose to hide in a harbour in this "mountain land" where they thought only bears and wolves roamed.[33] This tale cannot be correct, since three members of the crew were Scandinavians who undoubtedly had rounded Cape Lindesnes before and knew that the coast was populated and that the harbours were frequently visited by foreign ships.

---

[32]Sleeper, *Jack in the Forecastle*, 422.

[33]Olsen, *Guldgraverliv og Sjømandsfærd*, 6.

Sleeper claims that by entering "some obscure port of Norway," they believed there would probably not be a rigorous inquisition about the vessel or its crew, and that they could use a Norwegian port as a starting point from which to proceed to another part of Europe.[34] According to Hamblin, Stürmer insisted on heading for Norway, "having traded there before." On the coast of Norway, he could run the ship "among the rocks" and smuggle the cargo safely ashore. A suggestion to sail to South America was rejected.[35] If this is true, it reflects an interesting image of Norway in the sailors' mental maps.

In any case, in late August 1816, with the help of two local pilots, *Plattsburg* entered the harbour of Kleven on the southernmost coast of Norway.[36] Was this really the peripheral place the mutineers hoped for?

Kleven[37]

Kleven has a good natural harbour and is situated two kilometres from the small city of Mandal. The name originally referred to the Dutch seamark, *clof-fuen*, the cleavage between two hills overlooking the harbour. The seamark was possible to spot from a great distance. It was mentioned in Dutch maps from the sixteenth century, and the port was described for the first time by Peder Claussøn Friis around 1613. It has deep water and two different fairways. The harbour is protected by the island of Gismerøya.[38]

Because of its good harbour, Kleven was one of the most frequented ports on the south coast of Norway. The archipelago along this coast has many treacherous stretches, but crews sailing between the North Sea and the Baltic still considered this route to be safer than sailing along the coast of Jutland, where the risk of running ashore was greater. In addition, the currents tended to carry the ships towards the Norwegian coast near Cape Lindesnes ("the Naze of Norway"). It was sometimes difficult to round the cape, and ships often moored in nearby harbours for weeks awaiting the right wind.[39] The

---

[34]Sleeper, *Jack in the Forecastle*, 424.

[35]Hamblin, *United States Criminal History*, 392.

[36]In the trial, Kleven was called Cleveland.

[37]For a monograph on Kleven, see Hundstad, *Klevefolk*.

[38]*Ibid.*, 16; and Jacob S. Worm-Müller, *Den norske sjøfarts historie* (3 vols., Oslo, 1923-1951), II, book 2, 131.

[39]Jarle Bjørklund, "Søllingbåter i kaperfart: Små, hurtige og lett manøvrerlige," *Kysten*, XC, No. 2 (1990), 10; and Johannes Balle, "Fra de gamle grønlandsfareres tid," *Handels- og Søfartsmuseet paa Kronborg Aarbøger*, XIII (1954), 23; reprinted in *Grønland*, No. 7 (1959), 260.

natural conditions made the main channel between the Baltic and the North Sea run near Kleven and the other outports; in addition, ships sailing along the Norwegian coastline made use of it.[40] Sailing vessels needing repairs, supplies or water moored in these safe harbours when the winds were unfavourable.[41]

There was a repair yard in Kleven at least from the beginning of the eighteenth century.[42] Its business expanded during the second half of the century, as did trade and shipping in general. Accounts from the Øresund customs house show that about 5000 ships passed Øresund each year in the 1750s; by 1790, the number had doubled.[43] The main repair yards were situated on the island of Gismerøya. The need for repairs often resulted in a large number of foreign sailors being "stranded" in Kleven, where they found an inn and other recreations. When weather conditions were particularly bad, the number of foreign sailors visiting the outports could be very high. On 2 August 1803, for example, seventy-eight ships arrived in Kleven. Since there were only about two hundred inhabitants in the community at this time, the presence of 1000 sailors would certainly have strained local resources.[44]

Among the outports on the southern Norwegian coast in the nineteenth century, Kleven was likely the one most frequented.[45] The ships that entered the harbour were of various nationalities, but the vast majority came from northern Europe. According to the journals of the custom officers, which are preserved from 1848, growth peaked in 1855, when 853 ships passed in

---

[40]Sverre Steen, *Ferd og fest: Reiseliv i norsk sagatid og middelalder* (Oslo 1929; reprint, Oslo, 1942), 243; and Steen, "Veiene og leden i Norge," in Johannes Brøndstæd and Adolf Schück (eds.), *Nordisk kultur: Samlingsværk, Vol. XVI: Handel og samferdsel* (Oslo, 1934), 220.

[41]For a synthesis of the history of the outports of southern Norway, see Dag Hundstad, "Uthavnssamfunnene på sørlandskysten: Fra maritime monokulturer til fritidssamfunn" (Unpublished MA thesis, University of Bergen, 2004). See also Hundstad, "Det sørlandske uthavnssamfunnet - en maritim monokultur," *Heimen* XLII, No. 1 (2005), 3-19; and Hundstad, "Sørlandske uthavnssamfunn - rendyrkede sjøfartskulturer," *Sjøfartshistorisk årbok 2004* (Bergen, 2005), 7-141.

[42]Jarle G. Bjørklund, "Gismerøyarkivet," *Norsk Sjøfartsmuseums Årbok 1974*, 63-72. Hundstad, *Klevefolk*, 20, and 25-39; and Michael Bessesen Sars, "Gismerø Verft gjennom 200 år" (Unpublished MA thesis, University of Oslo, 1946).

[43]Henning Henningsen, "Skippere, Klarere og Toldere: Livet omkring Øresunds Toldkammer og Helsingørs havn i 1800-tallet," *Frederiksborgs Amts Historiske Samfund Årbog 1968-1969*, 15.

[44]Hundstad, *Klevefolk*, 54.

[45]Worm-Müller, *Den norske sjøfarts historie*, II, book 2, 130-135.

and out of the port. From the 1870s, the gradual transition to steam ships, which did not need the outports, led to a rapid decrease in the number of vessels entering the harbour of Kleven.[46]

Most of the ships calling at Kleven were in need of services the town could provide. Kleven seems to have been the outport community on this stretch of coastline which adapted most successfully to the needs of visiting ships and crews.[47] Townspeople operated taverns and ship chandleries, and some worked as pilots, but the residents were also involved in a broad spectrum of other trades which served visiting seamen. While the largest part of the adult male population worked as sailors or pilots, women, children and the elderly provided services for the visiting sailors. Hence, the maritime environment pervaded the entire community. Children rowed between the vessels and the pier, bringing seamen ashore or handling the mooring lines to earn a valuable extra income. Craftsmen served both the needs of the local populace and the visiting sailors. Women washed clothes for foreign seamen and ironed the captain's wardrobe. At the bottom of the social ladder were the manual laborers, quite a few of whom were women. Most of them were employed on a day-to-day basis as dock workers.[48]

There was a sharp competition between the various service providers, and the most entrepreneurial often boarded vessels as they approached the harbour to attract potential customers. The so-called "boarding culture" which developed resembled those in larger ports like Helsingør.[49] Like other outports, Kleven was also a regional centre for owling and smuggling,[50] a subject to which we will turn later. But first, we will return to *Plattsburg* and to the activities of its crew in Kleven harbour.

---

[46]Hundstad, *Klevefolk*, 114; and Hundstad, "Uthavnssamfunnene på sørlandskysten," 79-81.

[47]Hundstad, "Uthavnssamfunnene på sørlandskysten," 52 and 153.

[48]Hundstad, *Klevefolk*; and Hundstad, "Uthavnssamfunnene på sørlandskysten," 42-56.

[49]Henningsen, "Skippere, Klarere og Toldere;" Hundstad, "Uthavnssamfunnene på sørlandskysten," 52; and Dag Hundstad, "Kapringslosene i Mandal Losoldermannskap," *Agder Historielags Årsskrift*, LXXVII (2002).

[50]Hundstad, *Klevefolk*, 106. "Owling" was a common term for the smuggling of sheep or wool out of England at the start of the industrial revolution. It was often used by contemporaries, however, as a synonym for smuggling in general.

Extravagant Sailors

When it first arrived in Kleven, there did not appear to be anything suspicious about *Plattsburg*. The schooner appeared to need repairs because, according to testimony at the American trial, the crew had carried away the main boom to make the vessel look as though it was in distress.[51] The ship's documents were examined by the quarantine commission and the commissioner for maritime casualties, Giert Tørrissen Giertsen. The papers seemed to be in order, but the list of the crew, which was harder to falsify, was not inspected.[52] Giertsen, who also acted as the British vice-consul, was the head of the dominant merchant family of Mandal, the Nedeneses, a clan which had dominated both trade and power in the little city since the late seventeenth century. In addition to the ship and repair yards in Kleven, as well as various other enterprises, the family also owned the ground on which all the houses in Mandal were built.[53]

When he met with Giertsen, Stürmer played the role of the master, but he identified himself as the original captain, William Hackett. He explained that the ship was on its way to sell its cargo of coffee in Germany, but damage to the vessel forced the crew to seek assistance in Kleven. Stürmer also reported that *Plattsburg* had encountered another ship in the North Sea whose master advised that the market for coffee in Germany was unfavourable. As a result, the crew began to sell the cargo at low prices to many of the locals, including Giertsen. The coffee was smuggled inland and sold for low prices; some of the valuable goods were even given away.[54] We will return to this aspect of the incident later.

After some days, the behaviour of the seamen began to attract attention.[55] The many inns in the harbour were strictly divided between the simple establishments which catered to everyone and the so-called "captain's houses" where only the masters and perhaps select mates were granted access. Such inns often had a "ballroom" on the upper floor where the captains could play

---

[51]Hamblin, *United States Criminal History*, 399.

[52]Bugge, *En Sørlandsby*, 94-95 and 97.

[53]Finn-Einar Eliassen, *Mandal bys historie* (2 vols., Mandal, 1995), I, 190-191 and II, 288.

[54]Bugge, *En Sørlandsby*, 94-95; and Hopkins, "*Plattsburg* Mutiny," 135. Sleeper, *Jack in the Forecastle*, 424, also claims that Stürmer wanted to sell the ship, without being very specific about the price. Frederick and Raag, he suggests, revealed some of the secrets when they had too much to drink. These details would certainly have raised suspicion, but they are not mentioned in any of the other sources.

[55]Hundstad, *Klevefolk*, 74.

billiards, drink toddies and dance. While the parties went on, ABs had to sit in a little room next door waiting to escort the officers back to their ship. ABs went to simpler inns. From time to time, fights could occur when inebriated ABs were denied access to the captain's houses.[56] Socially as well as economically, there were also strict divisions between the families of the officers and those of the ABs living in Kleven. A large proportion of the sailors in the outports were captains, and they had the opportunity to establish and maintain a local culture where their set of values dominated.[57] Having no experience of the *habitus* of the officers, Stürmer probably embarrassed himself in an environment which placed a great deal of emphasis on accepted social roles.

What appeared most suspicious, however, was that the members of the crew had a seemingly unlimited supply of Spanish silver dollars. The various services they procured in the town, regardless of their importance, were paid for in an offhand fashion that was highly unusual, even in an environment used to big-spending sailors.[58] Although the decision at sea to divide the money among the mutineers was probably regarded as a good way to avoid later confrontations, it certainly did not promote discretion. The profligate use of currency was even more suspicious in Norway, which after gaining its independence from Denmark in 1814 had a serious shortage of specie. Indeed, in the same year as the *Plattsburg* incident, this situation caused the Norwegian government to levy a hefty tax on its citizens in order to build up the supply of silver in the new national bank. This so-called "silver tax" was supposed to be paid only in silver and gold, but since these precious metals were hard to obtain, it could also be paid in paper money. A few years later, the Norwegian viceroy had to procure a loan of one million *speciedalers* to avoid national bankruptcy. In these conditions, it was virtually certain that Plattsburg's free-spending crew members would attract the attention of the authorities.

Unmasking

After only four or five days in the harbour, Onion, Williams and Sauberson left Kleven for Denmark with the local captain Marsilius Rolfsen, who later received a heavy fine for shipping persons without passports out of the country. Shortly after the first three fled, they were followed by Raag. Before they left, they had divided the clothes of the deceased officers. When Consul Giertsen confronted the master about the peculiar behaviour of his crew, his expla-

---

[56]*Ibid.*, 123-125 and 419-420; and Hundstad, "Uthavnssamfunnene på sørlandskysten," 51.

[57]Hundstad, "Uthavnssamfunnene på sørlandskysten," 64-66.

[58]Olsen, *Guldgraverliv og Sjømandsfærd*, 4; and Bugge, *En Sørlandsby*, 95.

nation was that the sailors were morally degenerative privateers who during earlier escapades had accumulated considerable sums of money, which they now spent in careless ways. Even as the master, he claimed, he lacked the authority to punish them. He told Giertsen that he had let some of the worst go, referring to those who had decamped for Denmark. On 21 August, two more crew members (probably Johannsen and Wendt) left in another local ship for Holland, travelling under pseudonyms.[59]

The next day, the American consul in the nearby city of Kristiansand, the wealthy merchant Peder Isaachsen, arrived in Mandal to represent the interests of the shipowner. He met Consul Giertsen, and even had a meeting with Stürmer at Giertsen's house. There were no signs that the vessel was preparing to leave, despite favourable winds, which added to Isaachsen's growing suspicions. Stürmer must have felt that it was only a matter of time before the masquerade ended. He managed to convince Giertsen that one of the crew who had left for Denmark had stolen a very important document and that in order to reclaim it he needed to go to Denmark himself.[60]

Giertsen helped the master by providing the necessary travel documents which had to be issued by the tax collector. One of his captains and two local pilots then escorted Stürmer to Fladstrand (present-day Frederikshavn) in Denmark on 23 August. The remaining sailors (likely Fogelgreen, Lemolgat and Frederick) escaped in the brig *Ma Belle Marie* for Scotland after Giertsen also arranged their travel documents.[61] Before this, Frederick had given his belongings to Jon Olsen, one of the pilots who had brought the vessel into the harbour. By the time that Isaachsen felt he had sufficient evidence to arrest the master, it was too late: he and most of his crew had left Norway and were now scattered throughout northern Europe, often travelling under pseudonyms.[62]

Tracking down the Mutineers

According to Hopkins, when Onion, Williams and Sauberson arrived in Copenhagen, they immediately went to see US Consul Hans Rudolph Saabye to obtain passports to Christiania, the Norwegian capital, where they were to

---

[59]*The National Register* (Washington), 9 January 1819; Hundstad, *Klevefolk*, 72. Bugge, *En Sørlandsby*, 95-96; and Hopkins, "*Plattsburg* Mutiny," 135.

[60]Bugge, *En Sørlandsby*, 96-97; and Hopkins, "*Plattsburg* Mutiny," 135.

[61]Bugge, *En Sørlandsby*, 26. The precise chronology of these escapes is a bit unclear, and the sources are contradictory about which mutineers left exactly when and where.

[62]Hamblin, *United States Criminal History*, 395. Hopkins, "*Plattsburg* Mutiny," 135; Bugge, *En Sørlandsby*, 96-97; and Hundstad, *Klevefolk*, 77.

meet a Danish ship loaded with sugar and rum they had purchased for 1400 Spanish dollars.[63] The consul had several reasons to be sceptical about this story. The amount of money involved, the condition of their travel documents and the scant resemblance between Onion and Yeizer, the murdered mate whom he was impersonating, made the consul suspicious. In addition, Sauberson thought that the commissioner of police had heard rumours of an abandoned ship in Mandal. The three mutineers, along with Raag, were arrested on 7 September 1816. After first denying that they had committed a crime, Sauberson, Onion and Williams confessed to what had transpired on *Plattsburg*.[64] The following January, however, Onion recanted his confession and wrote a letter asserting his innocence. This statement even appeared in American newspapers.[65]

By the time Consul Isaachsen in Kristiansand was warned of this, all but one of the seamen had escaped from Kleven. The remaining mutineer was Nathanael White, who claimed to be a Norwegian citizen and had therefore been freed. Before the news of the confessions reached Norway, he had fled the country. White was later arrested in Hamburg and sent to Copenhagen.[66]

After his eight-day expedition to Scotland, Frank Frederick returned to Mandal to collect his belongings. He was immediately arrested, shackled and jailed in Kristiansand. When questioned, he pretended to understand nothing, but he confessed to some people how and where he had disposed of portions of his plunder. He was then sent to Copenhagen in shackles. According to his version, he was chained to an anchor during the voyage without any protective cover; this caused his feet to freeze.[67]

Johann Johannsen probably managed to escape the Gothenburg police, who reportedly were on his trail.[68] Nils Petersson Fogelgreen, also of Gothenburg, was less fortunate. He was arrested after moving into his father's house, having concocted a believable narrative to explain his suddenly improved financial condition.[69] Armand Lemolgat and Daniel Wendt both tried to evade

---

[63]Hopkins, "*Plattsburg Mutiny*," 135-136.

[64]*Ibid.*, 136; and Hamblin, *United States Criminal History*, 395.

[65]*The Baltimore Patriot and Mercantile Adviser*, 10 May 1819.

[66]Hopkins, "*Plattsburg* Mutiny," 136.

[67]Hamblin, *United States Criminal History*, 395; and Hundstad, *Klevefolk*, 77.

[68]Hopkins, "*Plattsburg* Mutiny," 136.

[69]Sleeeper, *Jack in the Forecastle*, 36; and Hamblin, *United States Criminal History*, 395.

the authorities in France. While Wendt appears to have had some success, Lemolgat was arrested in Vannes. The leader of the mutineers, John Stürmer, was taken into custody in Danzig on 1 September 1816, still travelling under the name of his murdered master, William Hackett.[70]

Diplomatic Complications

After Consul Saabye died in 1817, John M. Forbes, the new consul, took charge of the matters regarding *Plattsburg*. Before his death, Saabye had done impressive work in tracking down the mutineers. In addition, he had managed to recover a fair amount of the money and goods from the ship. Although this might suggest that most of the case was now solved, as Hopkins showed, there were diplomatic difficulties in returning the prisoners to the US to stand trial. The main problem was that the incident occurred before the United States had signed extradition treaties with European nations. In addition, American captains were reluctant to transport men who they regarded as dangerous. The diplomatic intrigues reached the highest levels of government.[71]

The prisoners in Sweden and Denmark did not object to being returned to the US, apparently because they believed that the worst that could happen was a period in jail. After his arrest in Gothenburg, Fogelgreen was shackled in a dungeon for nearly a year. Following several complications, he was transferred to the brig *Joseph*, bound for the US, at the beginning of September 1817.[72] John Sleeper, a member of *Joseph*'s crew, recalled that the prisoner did not resemble "the ferocious, ill-looking, big-whiskered ruffian, whose image is conjured up by the mention of the word *pirate*." Instead, Fogelgreen proved to be only nineteen years old, polite and intelligent; as a result, he was unshackled and allowed to assist the crew. Fogelgreen denied being a mutineer, and *Joseph*'s crew believed him. Ironically, evidence at the trial showed that he had been one of the most cold-blooded participants.[73]

The six mutineers in Copenhagen (Raag, Sauberson, Onion, Williams, White and Frederick) were regarded as too dangerous to be returned to America in a merchant vessel. Because of this, President James Monroe or-

---

[70]Hopkins, "*Plattsburg* Mutiny," 136.

[71]*Ibid.*

[72]*Ibid.*, 137; Hamblin, *United States Criminal History*, 395-396; and Sleeper, *Jack in the Forecastle*, 426.

[73]Sleeper, *Jack in the Forecastle*, 426-427.

dered the sloop-of-war *Hornet* to collect this group.[74] But the case of the ringleader, Stürmer, proved particularly delicate. The Prussian Minister of Foreign Affairs claimed that under Prussian law, Stürmer had to confess his guilt before he could be surrendered to a foreign power. This triggered a good deal of pressure from the Americans, but the Prussian king decided that no Prussian citizen could be turned over to a foreign state for trial. While Stürmer could be punished in Prussia, he had to be identified by the mutineers in jail in Copenhagen. After several delays, *Hornet*, with the prisoners on board, sailed into Helsingør, where Stürmer was also brought. During the subsequent examination in the Hall of Magistrates, all the mutineers identified Stürmer and accused him of planning the entire scheme.[75]

Stürmer knew, though, that under Prussian law he had to confess before he could be executed, despite the fact that he had in his possession when apprehended the belongings of the murdered officers. He even mocked the proceedings by demanding to be sent to the United States for trial, knowing full well that this would be rejected by the Prussian authorities. He returned to Prussia, tried and given a life sentence. On 5 September 1818, *Hornet* set sail for Boston without the main suspect in the case.[76]

Lemolgat's case proved even more difficult. Secretary of State John Quincy Adams's offer to the French Prime Minister, the Duke de Richelieu, to have Lemolgat tried in French courts was rejected on the grounds that Lemolgat could not be punished in France because his crime was committed outside the country. Nor could he be surrendered to the United States, since the Americans referred to "evidence" about his guilt *before* he was put on trial. Hopkins, who wrote a detailed account of the negotiations, claimed that Lemolgat indeed seemed to have "gotten away with murder."[77]

The Trial in Boston

In November 1818, *Hornet* arrived in Boston with the six mutineers; Fogelgreen had arrived on 24 October in *Joseph*. The trial of Williams, Raag, Frederick, Fogelgreen and White was conducted in the Circuit Court from 14 to 29 December, with the well-known Justice Joseph Story presiding. Despite their involvement in the crime, Sauberson and Onion were admitted as prosecution witnesses. The other five mutineers were accused of the murder of Hackett, Yeizer and Baynard, as well as piracy and revolt. The defence

[74] *The National Register* (Washington), 9 January 1819; and Hopkins, "*Plattsburg* Mutiny," 138-139.

[75] Hopkins, "*Plattsburg* Mutiny," 138-139.

[76] *Ibid.*, 139-140.

[77] *Ibid.*, 137-138.

claimed that there was no proof of the murderers' identity and that the Court should not rely solely on the testimony of persons who had been involved in the crime. Nonetheless, the district attorney "moved the court in a very impressive manner," arguing that the five should be executed for the murder of Thomas Baynard. The other murder charges were not ruled on.[78]

In the end, four of the five were found guilty of murder. Although White was acquitted, he was convicted of receiving stolen goods, sentenced to two years in jail and fined one dollar. Another charge against him was postponed until May, when Onion and Sauberson were to be tried; according to Hopkins, however, the documents relating to this later trial have been lost.[79] The author of *United States Criminal History* seemed surprised that Onion and Sauberson were regarded more as victims than accomplices. At sea they had to play along with the pirates, but they did not take the opportunity to speak about the mutiny in either Kleven or Copenhagen. Indeed, Onion even engaged in business transactions with Williams. In his defence, Onion claimed that he had been constantly intoxicated from the time *Plattsburg* entered Kleven until his arrest in Copenhagen. Sauberson appears to have engaged Hamblin's sympathy. The steward was not implicated in the plotting of the mutiny. According to his testimony, he had tried to inform the consul in Mandal but failed because some of the crew were present. Still, he had had the opportunity to inform the police in Copenhagen.[80]

After the guilty verdict was announced, the prisoners were given the opportunity to speak. Williams, Frederick and Fogelgreen maintained their innocence, blaming their shipmates instead. Raag was not fluent enough in English to speak. After hearing their speeches, Justice Story pronounced "that they be hanged by the neck as pirates until they are dead."[81]

The execution was scheduled for 21 January, but because the time between sentencing and execution was considered too brief for the pirates to make peace with their God, it was postponed to 18 February.[82] In prison, the convicts were visited by John Cheverus, the Roman Catholic Bishop of Bos-

---

[78]Sleeper, *Jack in the Forecastle*, 442; and *The National Register* (Washington), 9 January 1819.

[79]Hopkins, "*Plattsburg* Mutiny," 140.

[80]Hamblin, *United States Criminal History*, 393 and 394-396. When working on the slave mutiny on *Amistad*, John Quincy Adams requested the correspondence concerning *Plattsburg* in his search for precedents. Hopkins, "*Plattsburg* Mutiny," 140.

[81]*The National Register* (Washington), 9 January 1819.

[82]*Ibid.*; and Sleeper, *Jack in the Forecastle*, 427.

ton, as well as by other Catholic clergymen. The criminals reportedly regretted their actions, and the Scandinavians Raag and Peterson even converted to Catholicism. While the public consensus appears to have been that the sentence was just, many pitied Fogelgreen because of his youth.[83]

On the day of the execution, the convicts were placed in a wagon, and a procession moved through the city to Boston Neck, the narrow isthmus which connects Boston to Roxbury.[84] This location, on the shores of the aptly named Gallows Bay, was the city's main execution site. A crowd of 20,000 people reportedly turned out. When the men were thrown from the gallows, Peterson's halter broke; he fell to the ground but was immediately led back up to the platform. After all were dead, two Boston surgeons received the bodies for dissection and study.[85]

The Norwegian Inquiries

Although the mutiny in *Plattsburg* did not concern the Norwegian authorities, the extensive smuggling of coffee was impossible to ignore. An investigative commission was appointed in October 1816, and a new commission was appointed the next year, to investigate and rule on the case. The investigation turned out to be complicated, with seventy-six witnesses being questioned. Among other issues, there was uncertainty about whether the buyers of the coffee should have suspected that it had been smuggled. In the end, twenty-five persons from Mandal and its hinterland were charged. The evidence suggests that there were close relations between the mutineers and the local population of Kleven.[86]

For example, this was the case with the shoemaker Jørgen Ørbeck Gundersen. While *Plattsburg* was in the harbour, there was hectic activity in Gundersen's house. His father-in-law, the elderly pilot Jon Olsen, lived in the same house and served as a sheriff in the parish. Olsen had brought *Plattsburg* into Kleven and received fifty *piastres* from Frank Frederick, who also left his belongings in Gundersen's house. The shoemaker's apprentice, Hans Olsen Bøeg, told the investigators that he had assisted in carrying nine bags of money from *Plattsburg* to his master's house. When Frederick returned to fetch his possessions after his short voyage to Scotland, he complained that some of the

---

[83]Hamblin, *United States Criminal History*, 400; and Sleeper, *Jack in the Forecastle*, 428.

[84]Sleeper, *Jack in the Forecastle*, 427-428.

[85]Hamblin, *United States Criminal History*, 400; Hopkins, "*Plattsburg* Mutiny," 140; and Sleeper, *Jack in the Forecastle*, 428.

[86]Bugge, *En Sørlandsby*, 97-98; and Hundstad, *Klevefolk*, 73.

bags were missing. According to local gossip, Gundersen had stolen some of the money and invested in farmland in the surrounding area. The prosecutor argued that Gundersen should be jailed for two years for the theft of 250 *piastres*, although in the end he was only convicted of smuggling. His father-in-law was also accused of cooperating with the mutineers. It was claimed that despite his "rather immoral desire for money," he should have realized that there was something suspicious going on. The commission, however, declined to convict him.[87]

Witnesses confirmed that the mutineers had spent their money in an unusual fashion. Gundersen had sold a watch and an umbrella to the sailors for the pretty sum of 55.5 *piastres*.[88] The prosecutor claimed that by overlooking the behaviour of the so-called master and crew, the citizens who dealt with them must have realized that illegal activities had occurred. The commission accepted this argument and found that most of the suspects had violated the law by buying goods from persons they ought to have known did not have the right to sell them. Of course, there was also the smuggling.[89]

In the Supreme Court

The convicted persons in 1820 appealed to the Supreme Court of Norway, which reversed all the convictions except for smuggling. The fines for smuggling were high; those convicted had to pay double the assessed value of the coffee. The captain, Michael Rolfsen, had smuggled eleven and a half bags of coffee; his fine was 766 *specidalers*.[90] In addition to fines, each person had to pay the high legal costs involved. While the defender was paid fifty Norwegian *specidalers* per person, the Attorney General, Bredo Morgenstierne, demanded 100 *specidalers*. It seems that the eccentric Morgenstierne did not prosecute this case very well, appearing in court unprepared and "without the necessary shortness and clarity." As a result, he was fined thirty *specidalers* himself.[91]

One of Rolfsen's neighbours, Govert Olsen, was a manual labourer who, like many in Kleven, also ran a small inn, and one or more members of the crew spent the night there. Olsen also kept some coins for Gundersen. During the trial, when asked if he knew where the money had come from, Olsen replied that they came from piracy. This admission suggests that the

---

[87]Hundstad, *Klevefolk*, 77-78 and 303-304.

[88]*Ibid.*, 304.

[89]*Ibid.*, 74; and Bugge, *En Sørlandsby*, 98.

[90]Hundstad, *Klevefolk*, 75 and 329.

[91]Hundstad, *Klevefolk*, 74 and 78; and Bugge, *En Sørlandsby*, 98.

locals were told about the conspiracy. According to the local vicar, however, Olsen had limited mental capacities, so it was concluded that he did not know the difference between piracy and privateering. Olsen was sentenced to pay the court costs, but when his estate was settled in 1821, he was still 113 *specidalers* in arrears despite selling most of his furniture before his death.[92]

Why did the Supreme Court reject the accusations that the buyers of the coffee knew its origin? The answer appears to be that the Court found that the "authorities" should have intervened if they found the circumstances suspicious; since they had not done so, the buyers of the coffee had no reason to suspect anything illegal.[93] For the citizens of Mandal, however, the highest local "authority," although unofficial, was Consul Giertsen, who was deeply involved in the case himself.

"One Who Ought Not to be Continued in Office..."

When *Plattsburg* arrived in Kleven, Giertsen was in a serious financial crisis. Like many established commerce dynasties, his family was struggling to survive the postwar economic conditions.[94] When the arrival of *Plattsburg* seemed to promise a chance to make easy money, the Consul must have seized the opportunity eagerly. During the trial of the mutineers in Boston, testimony stated that Giertsen (here called "Gascar") had agreed to take all of the coffee. According to the mutineers, 356 bags of coffee were smuggled ashore. Then the American consul arrived, and the mutineers tried to escape.[95]

The Norwegian authorities never uncovered evidence that Giertsen intended to smuggle all the coffee. Still, he had committed a serious crime. The prosecutor of the investigative commission found Giertsen's involvement in the affair especially disturbing. Giertsen was the foremost citizen of Mandal but still lied to the commission. His relation to Stürmer was so close that the commission concluded that the consul knew about the mutiny. Stürmer had bragged that he could do whatever he wanted because he had Giertsen in the palm of his hand. The investigators believed that this meant that he had shared his dreadful secret with Giertsen.[96]

In the Supreme Court, Giertsen was only convicted of smuggling, but this was enough to ruin his reputation and business. To the Norwegian authori-

---

[92]*Ibid.*, 75-77 and 248-249.

[93]*Ibid.*, 74.

[94]Eliassen, *Mandal bys historie*, II, 38-44.

[95]Hamblin, *United States Criminal History*, 398.

[96]Hundstad, *Klevefolk*, 74.

ties, Giertsen was forever more connected to a bloody mutiny. An 1821 note from the Swedish foreign minister, Lars von Engeström, to Lord of the Treasury, William Vesey-FitzGerald, argued that Giertsen should "not...be continued in office, having been implicated in the mutiny of an American vessel, where the captain was killed and other outrages were committed." Vesey-FitzGerald made personal contact with Engeström on the matter and also spoke with the Foreign Secretary, Viscount Castlereagh. Giertsen was subsequently relieved of his duties as the British Vice-Consul.[97] His death in 1825 marked the end of the family firm and of an economic era in the city of Mandal. The *Plattsburg* case shows that all levels in the local community engaged in smuggling. Moreover, this clearly was not an isolated case.

Smuggling and the Outport Economy

When the Danish official Christen Pram made a voyage along the southern coast of Norway in 1805, he was observed owling and smuggling being undertaken openly, especially in those outports which did not have trade privileges. Sailors, pilots and even innkeepers were involved in these transactions.[98]

Some parts of this business were probably not so disturbing. As in all harbours, the local population in the outports was involved to a certain degree in "innocent" exchanges with visiting sailors. By selling smuggled goods in small quantities to the peasants in the hinterland, outport people could obtain wood and agricultural products which were not produced locally.[99] It was also accepted by the authorities that the sale of commodities to visiting crews had to be tolerated. Trade privileges or not, the visitors required articles such as ropes, tobacco, salt and fresh water.[100]

The case of *Plattsburg* showed, however, that the illegal transactions could be much more extensive. In some ways, this case was a novelty. Captains and seamen from time to time stole from the cargo to earn extra income. But to sell an entire cargo was an oddity. The desire of local people to undertake illegal transactions indicates that this was not the first time that smuggling was conducted in Kleven. The cases mentioned in the archives were probably only the tip of the iceberg. In the outports of southern Norway, there are

[97]Bugge, *En Sørlandsby*, 99-100. The documents concerning this matter were discovered by the Norwegian historian Jacob S. Worm-Müller in the archives of the Foreign Office in London. They are printed *in extenso* in Bugge's book.

[98]National Archives of Norway, Department of Special Collections, Ms. No. 14a II.

[99]Hundstad, "Uthavnssamfunnene på sørlandskysten," 72.

[100]*Ibid.*, 52-53.

strong oral traditions about smuggling. Indeed, residents can still point to places where the goods were hidden. Colonial goods, such as coffee and sugar, as well as spirits and wine, were particularly easy to trade.[101]

Pilots were often involved in smuggling, which seems to have been broadly accepted.[102] In the *Plattsburg* case, the head pilot, Nils Pedersen, was found guilty of smuggling. Pedersen had also with "great desire" begged *Plattsburg*'s "master" for a handkerchief with powdered sugar, one bag of ship's biscuits and a bottle of vinegar. Despite getting a heavy fine, his position as head of the pilots does not seem to have been disputed.[103]

The Supreme Court seemed to feel that it was more important to set an example of smuggling than to claim that the suspects ought to have known anything about the preceding incidents. The authorities took illegal trade and smuggling very seriously because such activity could damage the state's most valuable income – customs duties.[104]

To prevent smuggling, small customs houses were established in some outports. In the decades after the *Plattsburg* incident, the number of such stations was increased until most of the outports had customs officers. To help with their inspections, they built small "lookout cabins" on hills overlooking the harbour, although there is no evidence that they prevented smuggling and owling. There are several stories about customs officers turning a blind eye to smuggling, at least when it was on a relatively small scale, because they had to live in outports where smuggling was important.[105] Indeed, some of the suspects in the *Plattsburg* case claimed that they did not understand that their transactions were illegal because the customs officers were present. In the trial, two customs officers and two of their subordinates were accused of unprofessional conduct. In the Supreme Court, however, all of them were acquitted by claiming that Stürmer had poisoned their wine with sleeping medication.[106]

---

[101]*Ibid.*, 56-57.

[102]*Ibid.*, 57.

[103]Hundstad, *Klevefolk*, 75 and 333-334.

[104]Carl Lund, *Det Norske Tollvesens historie* (2 vols., Oslo, 1969-1977), II, 154-155 and 308-323.

[105]Hundstad, "Uthavnssamfunnene på sørlandskysten," 58-59.

[106]Bugge, *En Sørlandsby*, 97-98; Hundstad, *Klevefolk*, 75; and Hamblin, *United States Criminal History*, 398. Witnesses in the American court case, however, claimed that the customs officers were merely drunk.

Both oral and written sources indicate that corruption flourished among the customs officers. When Claus Urbye in the port of Eikvåg passed away in 1818, his relative, Bishop Claus Pavels of Bergen, wrote that he had wines at Urbye's house that he had never known before. This was because Urbye was a customs officer, and "in this respect humble and compliant. Ships of all nations regularly visited the harbour, and he received wonderful gifts from them."[107]

In the economic system of the outports, smuggling and owling were clearly beneficial. The importance of such transactions is impossible to calculate, but they undoubtedly influenced the local economy. It was probably not a coincidence that the crew of *Plattsburg* regarded a harbour in southern Norway as a safe destination; Stürmer even proclaimed that he had conducted "business" in this region before.[108]

Conclusion

The narrative of "The Silver Schooner" should not be regarded as a mere novelty. The contextualization of the ship and its owners provides an example of the early nineteenth-century global shipping networks. The incident also sheds light on the maritime world of a small coastal community in southern Norway where micro-economics were constantly influenced by macro-economics, and the local population was directly involved in worldwide networks of shipping and commerce. In the process, they contributed to the integration of Norway into the international world, economically, socially and culturally.

Sometimes these external links could be dangerous, as during wars or epidemics, but they could also be dramatic, as in the case of *Plattsburg*. For the historian, such incidents give us a rare opportunity to look behind the façade of a local community in a way that most other sources do not.

Even though the mutiny on *Plattsburg* occurred during a time of peace, it is a narrative in which *war* is a keyword. The ship was built in the style of a privateer, and most of the crew had recent experience in privateering or in the navy. The line between a pirate and a privateer could be indistinct, and traumatic experiences during conflicts may have influenced the cold-blooded actions of some of the crew members. The economic depression following the War of 1812 led Isaac McKim to devise new business strategies in which *Plattsburg* played an important role. The same economic instability also likely affected Consul Giertsen's involvement in smuggling. The postwar in-

---

[107]"The Diaries of Bishop Claus Pavels," 18. November 1818, 454, http://www.dokpro.uio.no/litteratur/pavels/frames.htm.

[108]Hamblin, *United States Criminal History*, 392.

ternational political climate may also have made the diplomatic negotiations over the mutineers more difficult.

In outports like Kleven, only a limited oral tradition has survived, perhaps due to the constantly changing environment in the harbour. Reminiscences of "The Silver Schooner" are still exchanged, even if the name *Plattsburg* has been long forgotten. Thorbjørn Egner's textbooks have been vital in preserving the story for subsequent generations, but in the process written and oral versions have become jumbled. Yet one detail of the narrative seems particularly durable: that the barrels of silver coins were buried on the nearby island of Gismerøya. The written sources are of limited assistance in confirming this, and perhaps only our imagination can guide us further. In the confusion following the visit of *Plattsburg*, it might have been possible for someone to have hidden some of the valuable cargo. Frank Frederick, who returned to Kleven, reportedly complained about missing valuables and allegedly claimed that he had "disposed of certain portions of his plunder." But we are unlikely to ever learn the truth, since when most of Gismerøya was levelled for industrial development in the 1980s, the last remaining hope of finding any silver dollars from "The Silver Schooner" vanished.

In A Peculiar Position: Merchant Seamen in Norwegian Health Policy, 1890-1940

Elisabeth Solvang Koren

An analysis of the health policies directed at seamen can deepen our understanding of their position in society and how they were perceived. Policies concerning seamen's health have been shaped by forces emanating from both the maritime world and agencies ashore. Broader developments in public health laid the groundwork for the provision of health services to seamen, but seamen were seen as marginal figures by many health professionals. Their mobility, long absences and age and gender profiles made them elusive targets for public health measures. This situation was depicted in 1951 by Karl Evang, the director of the Norwegian Directorate of Health and co-founder of the World Health Organization:

> From almost every point of view - social, economic and medical - the seafarer occupies a peculiar position...Public health experts will know that it is not sufficient to apply the same rules and provide the same facilities for seafarers as for the population on shore.[1]

Policies to improve the health of seamen have been largely ignored by scholars, but an intriguing essay by the British historian Sally Sheard did analyze health policies in the port of Liverpool between 1875 and 1939.[2] Sheard noted that the measures adopted for seamen were influenced mainly by a desire to protect the population ashore from contagion. The Port Sanitary Authority (PSA) saw seamen as a risk to the city's inhabitants. From 1874, the PSA concentrated on detecting the presence of infectious diseases, especially cholera, plague and yellow fever, among seamen landing in Liverpool. In the first two decades of the twentieth century, Liverpool's policies shifted to focus on venereal diseases (syphilis and gonorrhoea), and seamen were provided with free,

---

[1]Karl Evang, "Health and Welfare of Seafarers: An International Problem," *International Labour Review*, LXIII, No. 1 (1951), 1-2.

[2]Sally Sheard, "Mixed Motives: Improving the Health of Seamen in Liverpool, 1875-1939," in Laurinda Abreu (ed.), *European Health and Social Welfare Policies* (Santiago de Compostela, 2004), 321-336.

easily accessible treatment. Sheard stressed that while other diseases caused problems for seamen, they were ignored by the PSA.

Sheard depicted the well-being of seamen as a field where the interests of public health were often more important than the status of those who served at sea. Inspired by her study, I decided to examine Norwegian health policies toward seamen to see whether attitudes were similar. To what extent did seamen occupy a "peculiar position?" Were the health measures adopted really aimed at protecting the shore-based population? Using Norwegian sources, this essay addresses these questions.

We would expect to find great differences between the health policies in Liverpool and Norway. Liverpool was one of the world's largest ports, in 1920 handling more than 17,000 ships of 16.5 million net registered tons (nrt) from every continent.[3] By comparison, in the same year about 8000 vessels of 4.4 million nrt passed through all Norwegian ports combined. The largest port, Christiania, handled approximately 2000 ships of 2.7 million nrt, most from northern Europe or the United States.[4] Thus, the risk of contagion from abroad was much less in Norway, and hence it would be reasonable to expect that its policies would be less motivated by a desire to protect the populace from imported diseases. Unfortunately, it is impossible to compare Norway and Liverpool systematically using the existing literature; at any rate, it is questionable whether comparing a city with a country is sensible. Nonetheless, I will refer to the Liverpool experience to provide some context for Norwegian policy.

This study concentrates on the period 1890-1940. In the 1890s, new health measures for seamen were introduced after public debates about conditions in the Norwegian fleet. The study concludes in 1940, when health policies for seamen were fundamentally altered after Norway was occupied by German forces, and Norwegian seamen were separated from their homeland, sailing out of foreign ports in the Allied cause. The health services provided during World War II have been studied by the historian Guri Hjeltnes and the medical doctor Anders Gogstad.[5] But apart from their research, and that of the historian Johan Nicolay Tønnessen on the health measures introduced in the 1890s, there is little on the topic in Norwegian historiography.

---

[3]Francis E. Hyde, *Liverpool and the Mersey: An Economic History of a Port, 1700-1970* (Newton Abbot, 1971), 168; and Graeme J. Milne, "Maritime Liverpool," in John Belchem (ed.), *Liverpool 800: Culture, Character and* (Liverpool, 2006), chap. 4.

[4]Norway, Statistisk Sentralbyrå, *Norges Skipsfart 1920* (Christiania, 1921) tables 2 and 3.

[5]Guri Hjeltnes, *Sjømann – lang vakt* (Oslo, 1995); and Anders Chr. Gogstad, *Slange og sverd: Hjemmefront og utefront Leger og helsetjenester, 1940-1945* (Bergen, 1995).

This article is based on research in the archives of the Ministries of Social Affairs and Commerce, as well as the records of the Medical Director, supplemented where appropriate by published sources.[6] Between 1890 and 1939, the health of seamen was the responsibility of both ministries. In addition, various Christian and charitable associations attempted to improve seamen's health and welfare. The Norwegian Seamen's Mission is the most well-known, but in the area of health, the Scandinavian Association for Seamen's Homes Abroad (Foreningen for Skandinaviske Sjømandshjem i Fremmede Havne) and the Norwegian Red Cross Society (Norges Røde Kors) were more important both in facilitating access for seamen to medical services and in preventing illness among seafarers.

The Seamen's Committee

Seamen's health became part of the public agenda in the 1890s. In 1891, the government appointed the so-called "Seamen's Committee" to propose ways to improve health conditions for seamen serving in the Norwegian merchant marine. The situation in Norwegian shipping and the state of the Norwegian social reform movement form the backdrop for this development.

During the 1890s, Norwegian shipping suffered large losses of both ships and crew. In the worst year, 1894, ten percent of the fleet was lost in shipwrecks and other marine disasters. The fleet was old by international standards and contained a high proportion of sailing vessels, many bought second-hand from abroad. Contemporaries tended to blame the losses on overloading and participation in low-cost, and often dangerous, trades.[7] Safety at sea was debated in newspapers and the *Stortinget* (Parliament), in part due to the British Merchant Shipping Act of 1875 which introduced the Plimsoll line for British vessels.[8] This idea was controversial in Norway, and debates over the issue

---

[6]All archival sources used in this article are located in the Norwegian National Archive (*Riksarkivet*, RA). These include the records of Norges Røde Kors (Norwegian Red Cross); Socialdepartementet, Medisinalkontor (Ministry for Social Affairs, Office for Medicine); Handelsdepartementet, sjøfartsavdelingen, sjømannskontor (Ministry for Trade and Shipping, Office for Seamen); Handelsdepartementet, sjøfartskontoret (Ministry for Trade and Shipping, Office for Shipping); Medisinaldirektøren, kontoret for lege- og sunnhetsvesen (Medical Director, Office for Physicians and Public Health); and Medisinaldirektøren, overlegen for tuberkulosen, kontoret for lege- og sunnhetsvesen, tuberkulosesaker (Medical Director, Director for Tuberculosis, Office for Physicians and Public Health, Tuberculosis).

[7]Espen Søbye, "1894 - *annus horribilis*," *Fra forrige årtusen*, No. 10 (Oslo, 2000).

[8]Samuel Plimsoll, *Our Seamen: An Appeal* (London, 1873; reprint, Havant, 1979). For an introduction to other actors promoting seamen's welfare from the 1860s,

continued until a similar regulation was finally introduced in 1909. These debates formed part of the context for the discussions about seamen's health.

As in other industrialized countries, the question of working conditions became part of the agenda in Norway during the second half of the nineteenth century as deplorable conditions in many workplaces attracted increased attention. Social reformers demanded protection for the workers, and when the social-liberal party *Venstre* formed the government in 1884, it decided to address the "social question."[9] Working hours and conditions were regulated by law beginning in 1892 when the Factory Inspection Act introduced inspections to eliminate dangerous conditions and to prevent workplace accidents. The aim of the bill was to reduce health and safety risks, to protect workers from dangerous chemicals and to promote a healthier environment.[10]

The idea that the workplace environment could be harmful and that the state should mandate precautions to protect workers was transferred easily to the maritime workforce. The two processes were connected, as the *Venstre* politician Gunnar Knudsen chaired both the commission which prepared the Factory Inspection Act and the Seamen's Committee. Yet even though the state took steps to regulate working conditions, the liberal orientation meant that no radical measures were adopted. This was true especially when it came to shipping, where policymakers were especially careful not to harm the Norwegian position in an international industry.[11]

The Seamen's Committee was appointed to suggest ways to improve health conditions and safety for Norwegian seamen. Its first step was to collect information about the actual situation in the Norwegian merchant fleet. The Committee conducted a significant investigation. Its secretary, the social reformer and former priest in the Norwegian Seamen's Mission, Eugène

---

see David M. Williams "Mid-Victorian Attitudes to Seamen and Maritime Reform: The Society for Improving the Condition of Merchant Seamen, 1867," *International Journal of Maritime History*, III, No. 1 (1991), 101-126, reprinted in Lars U. Scholl (comp.), *Merchants and Mariners: Selected Maritime Writings of David M. Williams* (St. John's, 2000), 229-252. For a French perspective, see Christian Borde, "Safety at Sea and the Conduct of Shipping: Three International Conferences, 1889-1929" (Unpublished paper presented at the Eleventh Annual Conference of the European Business History Association, Geneva, Switzerland, September 2007 (http://www.unige.ch/ses/istec/EBHA2007/papers/Borde.pdf).

[9]Rune Slagstad, *De nasjonale strateger* (Oslo, 1998), 134-135 and 151-153.

[10]Øyvind Bjørnson, "Perspektiver på arbeidsmiljøets historie," *Arbeiderhistorie* (1997), 5-32.

[11]Slagstad, *De nasjonale strateger*, 152; and Camilla Brautaset and Stig Tenold, "Globalisation and Norwegian Shipping Policy, 1850-2000," *Business History*, L, No. 5 (2008), 565-582.

Hanssen,[12] travelled along the Norwegian coast to interview masters and seamen about their experiences and to solicit their views on subjects such as safety measures, diet and medical equipment on domestic vessels.[13] Hanssen also prepared a statistical analysis of Norwegian seamen to provide an overview of the age, marital status and mortality of the crews.[14]

After completing its study, the Committee in 1894 presented three proposals to the government relating to safety and diet to improve working conditions for seamen and to prevent illness at sea. Only one, however, was adopted immediately: from 1895 it was made compulsory for all Norwegian vessels over 100 nrt engaged in foreign trade to be equipped with a medical chest and to carry a medical manual authorized by the Ministry of Social Affairs. In addition, all vessels trading overseas had to adhere to detailed dietary regulations.[15]

In the short term, the Committee did not have much influence on maritime hygiene. In fact, there already was a clause in Norwegian maritime law dating from 1860 which required all masters to provide their crews with sufficient foodstuffs and medicine. But the prescriptions introduced in 1895 were different than those in the 1860 law, which basically required only that all vessels provide sufficient food and medicine in accordance with "existing practice."[16] In other words, it merely supported established standards. The Seamen's Committee was more ambitious in its recommendations because it wanted to raise those standards. Moreover, its proposals were not based solely on experience but also on the medical and social knowledge of its members. This represented a shift in the approach to seamen's health in that the state was now to define the standards to be met.

---

[12]Edv. Bull and Einar Jansen, "Hansen, Eugène," *Norsk Biografisk Leksikon* (19 vols., Oslo, 1921-1983), V, 409-411.

[13]Eugéne Hanssen, "Beretning fra de for Sømandskomitee, til Erhvervelse af oplysninger om forskjellige Spørgsmål, Komiteens Arbeide betræffende afholdte Møder med Skibsredere, Skibsførere og underordnede Sømænd: Bilag til Sømandskomiteens indstilling, Bilag til Ot. prp. 25," *Stortingsforhandlinger* (Christiania, 1902).

[14]Eugéne Hanssen, *Statistiske Oplysningerom norske Sjømænd: Deres fartstid, invaliditet, ulykkesrisiko etc.: Bilag til Sømandskommiteens indstilling* (Christiania, 1900).

[15]"Forskrifter om Medicinforsyning og Kosthold paa norske Skibe," *Norsk Medicinallovgiving*, 21 July 1894.

[16]*Lov om Søfarten, Givet den 24de Marts 1860*, §15. For an overview of the practice, see Knut Weibust, *Deep Sea Sailors: A Study in Maritime Ethnology* (Stockholm, 1969), 98-104.

The primary importance of the Committee was that it collected information, identified problems and suggested possible strategies to improve the health conditions for seamen. Moreover, its way of perceiving the problem influenced debate on the topic for three decades.

Measures in the Wake of the Committee

Preventing the spread of communicable illnesses ashore was a key goal of the health policies adopted in Liverpool. While this does not seem to have been a motive in creating the Norwegian Seamen's Committee, the measures it suggested built on the belief that seamen occupied a "peculiar position," that is, the health hazards they faced were different than those ashore.

The Seamen's Committee built on an understanding that the environment on board vessels, including inadequate diet, lack of access to medical facilities, damp, cramped cabins and stuffy air, led to medical problems. The Committee suggested measures to improve all of these. The first step was to improve hygiene, and from 1895, the medical chest and medical manual were made compulsory. The manual not only helped the captain when crew members needed medical assistance but also gave advice on how to prevent illness in the first place. The manual depicted the ship as an unhealthy environment, reflecting the belief that the ship itself could cause poor health.[17] Further, poor hygienic standards facilitated the spread of contagious diseases among the crew. By law, the master was obliged to know the contents of the manual and to follow its advice on cleanliness and disinfection to protect the crew.

Improvement of the cabins was another strategy recommended by the Committee to promote health at sea. Merchant vessels had all the characteristics that contemporary physicians associated with illness: they were dark, stuffy and humid.[18] The Committee proposed minimum sizes for cabins; these were implemented in the 1903 Safety at Sea Act, which mandated that every man in the forecastle should have a minimum of 1.6 square metres of floor space and 3.4 cubic metres of air.[19]

---

[17]"Ot. prp. Nr. 25 (1901-1902): Angaande spørsmaalet om indførelse af statskontroll med skibes sjødyktighed m.v." *Stortingsforhandlinger* (Christiania, 1902); and Vilhelm Uchermann, *Lægebog for Sjømænd: Veiledning for Skibsførere og Styrmænd i Sundheds- og Sygepleie ombord i Handelsskibe* (Christiania, 1895), 6-7. For a discussion of the same features on an emigrant ship, see Robin Haines, *Doctors at Sea: Emigrant Voyages to Colonial Australia* (New York, 2005), 61.

[18]Kari Tove Elvbakken, *Hygiene som vitenskap: fra politikk til teknikk* (Bergen, 1995), discusses the development of Norwegian hygiene.

[19]"Forslag til forskrifter;" and *Lov om statskontrol med skibes sjødyktighed m.v.*, § 43.

While these new rules might seem meagre, the 1903 Act was controversial because politicians were hesitant to require costly measures that could make Norwegian shipping less competitive. The controversies mainly surrounded the idea of introducing a compulsory freeboard-mark on Norwegian ships. The political elite in Norway spent years debating this issue. Conservatives argued that introducing safety standards for the fleet would place an intolerable burden on shipping. Indeed, the issue of safety at sea was one of the most contentious of its time; intertwined with such discussions, the subject of seamen's health and their work environment also became controversial.[20]

Only a few years later, however, complaints were made that the rules were inadequate to prevent tuberculosis. After pressure from the National Association for Tuberculosis, medical experts and members of parliament, new and more ambitious rules were introduced in 1916.[21] Indeed, the First World War paved the way for regulating the shipping industry to protect maritime labour.[22] As the ideology of social hygiene became accepted, improved housing and living standards for the poor ashore had been introduced.[23] Improvement of the conditions of cabins at sea was an extension of this.

The rules introduced in 1916 represented a great improvement, even though they applied only to newly built ships. They were also appreciated by the seamen themselves.[24] Steamships of more than 1000 tons were required to provide two-man cabins for the crew, while on large sailing vessels, four-man cabins were made standard. On smaller ships, less rigorous rules applied, but the universal requirement of a galley and a separate room for washing nonetheless led to better conditions.[25]

---

[20]Johan N. Tønnessen, "Fra klipperen til motorskipet," in Worm-Müller (ed.), *Den norske sjøfarts historie*, II, book 3, 135-148; and Dag Bakka, Jr., *Hundre år for sikkerhet til sjøs: Sjøfartsdirektoratet, 1903-2003* (Oslo, 2003), 31-33.

[21]"Ot. prp. 33 (1915): Om forandringer i lov om statskontrol med skibes sjødyktighet av 9de juni 1903 med tillægslov av 18de september 1909," *Stortingsforhandlingene* (Christiania, 1915).

[22]Atle Thowsen, *Vekst og strukturendringer i krisetider, 1914-1939* (Bergen, 1983), 129-130; and Finn Olstad, *Vår skjebne i vår hand: Norsk sjømannsforbunds historie, Vol. I* (Oslo, 2006), 79-81.

[23]Aina Schiøtz and Maren Skaret, *Folkets helse – landets styrke: Det offentlige helsevesenets historie i Norge, 1603-2000* (2 vols., Oslo, 2003), II, 226; and Ida Blom, *Feberens ville rose* (Bergen, 1998), 58-60.

[24]Olstad, *Vår skjebne i vår hand*, 79.

[25]"Kgl. res. Forskrifter for lugarer m.v. paa registeringspliktige fartøier (fiskefartøier undtat)," *Norsk lovtidende, 2. Avdeling*, 1 September 1916.

Maritime hygiene included the issue of diet. The difficulty of preserving and storing food at sea, combined with the parsimonious attitudes of many shipowners, led to a number of health problems. As a result, the Committee recommended improvements in seamen's diets.[26] Ironically, its prescriptions exacerbated the situation by prescribing larger quantities of preserved food which contained insufficient amounts of vitamin B1; this led to an increase in the incidence of beriberi from the mid-1890s.[27] In its defence, the role of vitamins in preventing beriberi was not yet clear, and the aetiology of the disease was a mystery still debated by specialists.[28] The illness was frightening and difficult to prevent with traditional hygienic measures. It also seemed that the illness exacted a greater toll among Norwegian seamen than among those serving on the ships of other nations.

The situation was taken seriously by the authorities, and beriberi received much attention. Unlike many other aspects of seamen's health policies, diet at sea was heatedly debated by the public. The authorities appointed a new committee to investigate the causes of the illness and to suggest measures to prevent its spread. This committee supported the hypothesis that beriberi was caused by inadequate nutrition. The authorities designed their preventive strategies based on this conclusion, and new dietary regulations were introduced in 1905. Thereafter, fewer incidents of beriberi were reported. The regulations were revised again in 1913, building on new knowledge about essential components in food that were necessary for good health.[29] In the interwar period, beriberi was rare in the Norwegian merchant fleet, although it still occurred on whalers.[30]

We now know that beriberi is caused by an insufficient intake of vitamin B1. We can conjecture that the illness was more prevalent on Norwegian

---

[26]"Forskrifter om Medicinforsyninge og Kosthold paa Norske Skibe," *Norsk Medicinallovgiving*, 21 July 1894.

[27]Harald Engelsen, *Skibshygienens saga* (Oslo, 1932); and Axel Holst, "Om den norske skibs-beriberi og om skjørbuk," *Norsk Sjøfartsmuseums skrifter*, No. 5 (Oslo, 1929).

[28]Kenneth J. Carpenter, *Beriberi, White Rice, and Vitamin B: A Disease, a Cause, and a Cure* (Berkeley, 2000); Norway, Beri-beri-komiteen, *Indstilling fra Beri-Beri-Komiteen* (Christiania, 1903); and Axel Holst, "Om beri-beri: Foredrag i Kristiania sjømandsforening 11te mai 1910," *Tidsskrift for Den norske Lægeforening*, XXX (1910), 623-630 and 678-689.

[29]Elisabeth Koren, "Beriberi: Sickly Airs, Lazy Sailors or Diet?" in Astri Andresen, Tore Grønlie and Teemu Ryymin (eds.) *Science, Culture and Politics: European Perspectives on Medicine, Sickness and Health* (Bergen, 2006).

[30]Holst, "Om den norske skibs-beriberi."

vessels due to a combination of long voyages in sailing ships and the extensive use of preserved food.[31] It is also possible that Norwegian seamen were more susceptible than others even before going to sea due to poor diets at home.

In the Norwegian debates about beriberi, the risk of its spread to the population ashore was seldom mentioned. Nor were the measures to improve the physical environment on board motivated by a wish to protect the Norwegian populace from disease. On the contrary, the rules were designed to improve the situation for the seamen themselves. In this respect, it seems that the Norwegian authorities had different motives for preventing illness among seamen than those found by Sheard in Liverpool.

Screening and Isolation

The Norwegian Safety at Sea Act (1903) made it mandatory to have a cabin for the isolation of sick crew members, and the law introduced obligatory medical examinations in the fleet.[32] The aim was to avoid the spread of diseases among the men on board. Particular interest was taken in tuberculosis; most seamen were in the twenty to twenty-nine year age group where the illness took its greatest toll.[33] In the years following 1903, the rules concerning health checks were adjusted several times, but the essence of the system remained: seamen were obliged to provide a certificate proving they were free of dangerous or communicable illness, included tuberculosis, before signing on a ship. They further had to prove that they had sufficient hearing, sight and colour vision.[34]

Medical examinations for seamen were unique in Norway for a long period. While people with transmittable tuberculosis were forbidden to work with food, they were not required to have medical exams before being hired.[35] From 1920, military recruits were examined for tuberculosis, and during the 1930s screening was introduced for school children and miners.[36] Until then, seamen were the only group for whom a medical examination was demanded.

---

[31] *Ibid.*

[32] *Lov om statskontrol med skibes sjødyktighed m.v.* (1903), §§ 84 and 85.

[33] Blom, *Feberens ville rose*, 11-13.

[34] *Om statskontrol med skibes sjødyktighed m.v.*, §§ 84 and 85; and "Veiledning for læger," *Norsk medisinallovgiving*, 22 May 1906.

[35] Ida Blom, "Opplysningskampanjer i kampen mot tuberkulose fram til ca. 1940," *Tidsskrift for den norske Lægeforening*, CXXII (2002), 73.

[36] Aksel Ongre and Jan Sommerfelt-Pettersen, "Tuberkulose blant sjøfolk – fra yrkesrisiko til fravær, men fortsatt navalmedisinsk utfordring," *Marinesanitetens Skriftserie*, No. 6 (2010), 8; S.W. Brockmann, "De militære lungeundersøkelser," *Tidsskrift*

Why were seamen subject to such examinations when other workers were not? The Seamen's Committee had considered introducing exams but concluded that this was not feasible.[37] The new committee did not divulge any particular inspiration for the idea, but it might have borne in mind the examination of emigrants; pre-embarkation medical checks were required on Norwegian emigrant vessels from 1863.[38]

The risk of contagion on board vessels was well understood by medical experts. Demanding a health certificate from crew members arguably was a strategy to avoid epidemics without placing financial burdens on shipowners. But risk alone cannot explain the introduction of the health examinations because they were not required for fishermen or seamen on domestic routes, even though the risk of transmittable diseases admittedly was just as high, or perhaps even higher, in these trades.[39] To understand the screening of seamen in international shipping we need to consider how they were treated if they became ill. Illness among seamen in the foreign trades placed a financial burden on the state.

The master had long been responsible for his crew, and if men became sick in a foreign port, the ship had to provide medical care and cover their expenses for homeward transport. From 1893, though, the ship's liability was restricted to covering the journey home and paying for care for four to six weeks.[40] The seaman retained his right to care, but the state bore part of the cost, thus relieving shipowners of some of the expense. This meant that seafarers who were ill prior to beginning a trans-oceanic voyage could be very expensive for the state. Even though financial considerations were not mentioned in the drafting of the law that introduced screening, this must have been one of the motivations for introducing the examinations. Venereal disease, on the other hand, was considered to be the seaman's fault, and the ship was responsible neither for his care nor for the journey home.

---

for den norske Lægeforening, LVII (1937), 980; [Sentralkontoret for skjermbildefotografering], "Skjermbildefotograferingens forhistorie i Norge," *Den norske nasjonalforeningen mot tuberkulose*, Nos. 5 and 6 (1943); and Schiøtz and Skaret, *Folkets helse*, I, 210 and 248-253.

[37]"Forslag til forskrifter," 26-27.

[38]Bakka, *Hundre år for sikkerhet til sjøs*, 17.

[39]S.W. Brockmann, "Tuberkuløse fiskere og fiskabaater," *Tidsskrift for Den norske Lægeforening*, XLII (1922), 565-567.

[40]"Oth. Prp. nr. 27 (1892) Ang. Udfærdigelse af en Sjølov og en Strandingslov," *Stortingsforhandlingene* (Christiania, 1892), 104; and *Sjøfartsloven* (1893), § 98.

A discussion at the International Conference on Health in the Merchant Marine, convened by the Norwegian Red Cross Society in 1926, put the Norwegian system in international perspective. Two British delegates, Mrs. Neville-Rolfe and Mr. Bowden from the British Social Hygiene Council, strongly opposed the idea of examinations.[41] This reflected national differences in attitudes toward preventive strategies.

Indeed, while Great Britain did not require mandatory medical examinations for seamen, many shipowners demanded that they have such tests before being hired.[42] This may suggest a difference in the political willingness of the state to intervene. Indeed, the Canadian sociologist Peter Baldwin has shown that the British were more hesitant than Scandinavians to use statutory intervention in preventative medicine.[43] But the difference may also have been caused by the varying degrees of liability; the Norwegian authorities bore a heavier financial burden when seamen were sick abroad than did the British. On the other hand, British shipowners had a greater financial incentive to demand medical examinations than did their Norwegian counterparts.[44]

Sailortown as a Health Hazard

In the early 1920s, the understanding of the health risks faced by Norwegian seamen was altered in two respects. First, public health experts and social reformers turned their attention to conditions ashore. Second, new actors took an interest in seamen's health and welfare. These were intertwined, and the 1920 Genoa Conference marked the starting point for new approaches to the subject.

The Genoa Conference was formally the Second League of Nations International Labour Conference. These conferences were international meetings where representatives of workers, employers and governments discussed working conditions and welfare.[45] At the 1920 conference, maritime labour was the focus. Four themes were on the agenda: working hours, unemploy-

---

[41] *Report of the Oslo Conference Convened by the Norwegian Red Cross Society and the League of Red Cross Societies on the Health of the Merchant Seaman, June 28th-July 5th* (Paris, 1926), 96-97.

[42] *Ibid.*, 171.

[43] Peter Baldwin, *Contagion and the State in Europe, 1830-1930* (Cambridge, 1999).

[44] As far as I know, no one in either Britain or Norway has conducted any systematic analysis on the different policies of shipowners on these issues.

[45] Hector Bartolomei de la Cruz, Geraldo von Potobsky and Lee Swepston, *The International Labour Organization: The International Standards System and Basic Human Rights* (Boulder, CO, 1996), 5-10.

ment, child labour and an international seamen's code. In addition, seamen's health was discussed, and on the initiative of the British National Council for Combating Venereal Disease, a resolution about seamen and venereal disease was passed which claimed that venereal disease was more widespread among seamen than among other groups and that the International Labour Office (ILO) should take steps to combat the disease. Free treatment, information programs and wholesome entertainment were proposed.[46] Conditions for seamen in port were discussed in following conferences, culminating in 1936, when it was agreed to recommend that participating countries improve conditions in their ports by restricting the sale of alcohol and drugs, introducing street lighting, providing wholesome entertainment, and promoting "by every possible means...the family life of seamen."[47] The prevention of venereal disease was to have a high priority.

The term "venereal disease" was used to refer to syphilis and gonorrhoea, two illnesses that if untreated could cause sterility, mental disorders, rheumatism and cardiovascular problems. Venereal disease could also lead to blindness, injuries and stillbirth in babies born to sick mothers. These children, considered "innocents," increasingly attracted attention after the First World War and defined many of the public health measures introduced to prevent venereal disease.[48]

The British historian Paul Weindling has explained the attention to venereal disease by reference to its spread in Europe and the US after the First World War. In addition, a more permissive approach to sexual morality made it possible to discuss the venereal disease more openly than before, with the result that a wider spectrum of preventive measures was applied. The year 1910 represented a milestone in the treatment of syphilis. Salvarsan, or arsphenamine, was perhaps not the "magic bullet" its creators proclaimed, but the new drug meant much shorter, more effective and less harmful treatment and made it possible to cure patients fully. The initiative to get the ill to undergo treatment increased correspondently.[49]

---

[46]*League of Nations International Labour Conferencem Second Session, Genoa, 1920* (Geneva, 1920), xiii, 447 and 595.

[47]*League of Nations International Labour Conference, Twenty-first Session, Geneva, 1936* (Geneva, 1936), 315.

[48]Elisabeth Koren, "Från Moral til Hälsa?" in Anna Jahnsdotter and Yvonne Svänstrøm (eds.) *Sedligt, renligt, laglig: Prostitution i Norden, 1880-1940* (Stockholm, 2007), 186-189.

[49]Paul Weindling, "Social Medicine at the League of Nations Health Organisation and the International Labour Office Compared," in Weindling (ed.), *International Health Organisations and Movements, 1918-1939* (Cambridge, 1995), 134-153.

The Genoa Conference and the subsequent labour conferences influenced the way the problems were perceived in Norway and laid the foundation for measures to improve the situation. As the Seamen's Committee had shaped the understanding of the seamen's situation for at least two decades after 1891, the ILO played much of the same role in the interwar years. Indeed, Norwegian doctors and social reformers made frequent reference to the ILO's 1920 conference.

The new approach to the seamen's situation ashore also made its way into the mass media and was disseminated to the wider public. In 1928, the Norwegian newspaper *Aftenposten* published reports from European ports which claimed that "sailortowns" destroyed the morals and health of seamen. These reports resembled those of the ILO in both tone and content. Seamen, they suggested, were tricked and taken advantage of by crimps, shipping masters and loose women. Alcohol made them less alert and more easily fooled. Venereal disease was widespread in international port cities.[50] Journalists, admittedly with a taste for the colourful aspects of the activities in the port areas, even claimed that seamen were at a greater risk ashore than at sea.[51]

New Actors, Health Promotion and Medical Care

The increased attention to the subject of seamen's health in the wake of the Genoa Conference attracted the interest of new actors. The Norwegian Red Cross Society became interested in the subject, and on the initiative of the medical doctor Harald Engelsen tried to put seamen higher on the agenda of the International League of Red Cross Societies.[52] After the First World War, Red Cross Societies in many nations expanded their activities to include problems not caused by war. The Norwegian Red Cross Society concentrated on promoting public health, in particular children's health. In addition, the Society prioritized seamen's health from 1923.[53] In this, Engelsen's personal interest and promotion of the subject played an important role.

As well, the Scandinavian Association for Seamen's Homes Abroad took a greater interest in seamen's health. This philanthropic association was founded in 1901 by shipowners and naval officers to provide seamen's homes

[50]The reports were published in *Aftenposten* in the autumn of 1928 and compiled in Carl Huitfeldt, *Gullfisk og haier* (Oslo, 1929).

[51]Huitfeldt, *Gullfisk og haier* (Oslo, 1929), preface.

[52]Harald Engelsen, "Report of the Norwegian Red Cross: The Rôle of the Red Cross of the Improvement of Health in Merchant Marine," *League of Red Cross Societies, Third Session of the General Council, Paris, April 28-May 2, 1924* (Paris, 1924).

[53]Martin Sæter, *Over alle grenser. Norges Røde Kors 100 år* (Oslo, 1965).

in foreign ports, to promote seamen's welfare and to prevent seamen from deserting from the merchant fleet. In the years following the 1920 shipping crisis, it was the most important organization working in the interests of Norwegian seamen. The Norwegian Seamen's Mission also began to expand into welfare work for destitute seamen abroad, although it tended to concentrate on religious welfare, the focus since its founding in 1864.[54]

These associations emphasized other aspects of seamen's health than did medical officials, and their involvement put the focus more clearly on conditions ashore. The Scandinavian Association for Seamen's Homes Abroad and the Norwegian Red Cross Society distributed leaflets on venereal diseases to seamen well before the medical authorities did.[55] The charity associations also provided health services to seamen; after 1923, for example, the Scandinavian Association for Seamen's Homes Abroad provided seamen with free medical treatment when needed.[56] The Red Cross Society also operated dispensaries in Norwegian port towns in the mid-1920s.[57]

In the same period, Norwegian authorities provided medical care for seamen with venereal disease to a greater extent than before. The 1923 Seamen's Act for the first time regulated all aspects of maritime labour in the same law. The right to medical treatment when ill was retained, but the clauses regulating it were amended slightly. The greatest change was that seamen gained the right to free treatment for contagious venereal diseases in order to prevent their spread, although non-contagious venereal diseases and other illnesses and injuries considered to be the seaman's fault were excluded.[58] In 1935, Norway subscribed to the Brussels Agreement, which granted seamen of all participating nations free treatment for venereal disease. By signing this pact, Norway agreed to provide free treatment for seamen with this affliction in Norwegian and foreign ports.[59]

---

[54]Bjørn Johanson, *Kirke i verdens hverdag: Den norske Sjømannsmisjon, 1864-1989* (Bergen, 1989), 40-41.

[55]Aug. Maurice Augustson, *Det farende folk: Arbeidet for de nordiske sjøfolk gjennom tyve aar – En oversikt* (Christiania, 1922), 15.

[56]Art. H. Mathisen, *Foreningen for skandinaviske sjømannshjem i fremmede havner, dens arbeid for sjømenn* (Oslo, 1946), 9.

[57]*Report of the Oslo Conference*, 103-107.

[58]*Sjømannsloven* (1923), § 28; Cf. "Om sjømenn som lider av tuberkulose og kjønnssykdom: Rundskriv fra Socialdepartementet," *Norsk Medicinallovgiving*, 17 March 1934.

[59]*Stortingsforhandlinger* (1934), 7b, 2193; and Paul Weindling, "The Politics of International Co-ordination to Combat Sexually Transmitted Diseases, 1900-1980s,"

Since the concern about venereal disease among seamen in the 1920s called for new preventive strategies, in addition to the provision of free treatment, Norwegian authorities and charity associations began to issue information pamphlets and to distribute packets containing chemical prophylaxis, ointments that could protect men from syphilis and gonorrhea if used immediately after exposure. While the use of such remedies was debated because they were associated with extra-marital sexual activity, from 1927 all Norwegian ships in the foreign trade had to provide them to the crew. This was at least five years before they were available to the rest of the population.[60]

In his vast comparative analysis of European health policies, Peter Baldwin examined the debates about chemical prophylaxis. Most belligerents had distributed the ointments to their troops during the First World War. After the war, there were debates about whether they should also be available to civilians. Baldwin has shown that although this treatment was controversial, the ointments became available in most European countries by the end of the 1920s.[61] Although the government was reluctant, the Red Cross Society and the general public strongly supported their distribution to Norwegian seamen.[62] Information about venereal disease was given to seamen to an extent that likely would have been considered indecent if provided to any other group except perhaps soldiers.[63] Still, some of the terms used in the leaflets led to protests from maritime organizations.[64]

Why did venereal disease among Norwegian seamen generate such a diversity of measures? One motivation was its high incidence. Another oft-mentioned reason was concern for the population back home. Venereal disease remained contagious for years after it was contracted, and a desire to protect

---

in Virginia Berridge and Philip Strong (eds.), *AIDS and Contemporary History* (Cambridge, 1993), 96.

[60]Karl Evang (ed.), *Populært tidsskrift for seksualell opplysning* (Oslo, 1933), 262-264. I have not succeeded in identifying exactly when the packets were first available in Norwegian pharmacies.

[61]Baldwin, *Contagion and the State*, 461-468.

[62]"Forslag til lov om foranstaltninger mot kjønnssykdommer med motiver m.v. 1923, bilag til Ot. prp. nr. 5" (1947), *Stortingsforhandlinger* (Oslo, 1947).

[63]See Ida Blom, "Fighting Venereal Diseases: Scandinavian Legislation, c. 1800 to c. 1950" *Medical History*, L, No. 2 (2006); and Blom, "Contagious Women and Male Clients: Public Policies to Prevent Venereal Diseases in Norway, 1880-1960," *Scandinavian Journal of History*, XXIX, No. 2 (2004), 97-117, for overviews on Norwegian attempts to prevent venereal diseases.

[64]RA, Socialdepartementet 3, Medisinalkontor No. 277, correspondence.

the seamen's (future) families was often mentioned by the authorities and many of the charitable organizations. Children whose mothers had contracted venereal disease had an increased risk of being blind, disabled or even stillborn. According to the Norwegian Red Cross Society, venereal disease "has the greatest prevalence and intervenes deepest into the homely happiness."[65]

The information materials also demonstrated a concern for the health of women and children. Seamen were encouraged to think about "the woman back home" before approaching other women.[66] The authors implored the men not to harm their future innocent children, warning of the tragedies they could cause: "A small child, without guilt of its own, blind, blind for life, because its mother or father has given in to temptation and violated the unwritten law of purity surrounding the relation between man and woman."[67] The fight against venereal disease among seamen was clearly conducted with the health of the Norwegian population in mind.

Conclusion

This analysis has demonstrated that Norwegian health policy for seamen was shaped primarily by four forces: overall developments in Norwegian public health; a wish to protect Norwegian citizens from imported contagions; financial considerations; and attitudes about the statutory regulation of shipping.

The concentration on venereal disease from about 1920 mirrored Sheard's findings in Liverpool. The motive in combating this disease was the health not only of seamen but also of the population as a whole. Norwegian seamen were to a great degree associated with these contagions, especially after the First World War, and a wide variety of measures were employed to fight them. The argument given for doing so was the risk that seamen could infect Norwegian women with the disease. Venereal disease could cause sterility, mental disorders and rheumatism among adults, and blindness and even death to babies and young children. A seaman infected abroad could be contagious for many years and represented a considerable risk to his Norwegian girlfriend or wife long after he first contracted the disease.

---

[65]"...har den største utbredelse og som griper dypest inn i den hjemlige lykke." *Ibid.*, "Plan for Norges Røde Kors' arbeide for bedring av Hygienen i Handelsmarinen," December 1923.

[66]Arne Forstrøm, *Helseråd for* Sjøfolk (Oslo, 1938); and Niels Steen, *Bevar ditt legeme: Aapent brev til vore unge sjøfolk* (Christiania, 1922).

[67]"Et lite barn, uten egen skyld, blindt, blindt for livet, fordi mor eller far har gitt etter for fristelsen og krenket den renhetens uskrevne lov som omgir kjønnsforholdet;" Kr. Andersen, *Hvad unge sjømenn bør vite* (Oslo, 1930), 5-6.

Some steps taken by Norwegian authorities to prevent illness among seamen, however, had motives other than the protection of the shore-based population. The screening introduced in 1903 and the measures to improve hygiene and diet were designed to protect the health of the seamen themselves. Thus, the Norwegian policy seems more complex than what Sheard found in Liverpool. The differences between Britain and Norway in this respect had many causes, rooted both in the maritime sphere and in national public health ideologies. Baldwin has identified a greater willingness in Scandinavia than in Britain to resort to statutory intervention for the sake of health. Further, the different types of shipping of the two countries presented discrete challenges to public health. Many fewer seamen landed in Norway, and they came mostly from Western Europe, representing only a slight risk of contagion.

In addition, financial motivations may have been more important to the Norwegian health authorities. In Norway, because the state bore part of the costs for ill seamen, it had an obvious incentive to prevent illness. The screening of men before enlistment must be understood in this context. Moreover, the drive to prevent venereal disease was intensified in the 1920s at the same time the state began to pay for seamen suffering from this ail

ment. It is possible, however, that the relationship is best understood in reverse. It might have been that the Norwegian authorities covered part of the expenses for illness among seamen because the health of this group was prioritized.

Still, on balance it is clear that concerns about health were not very important in the formulation of maritime policies in this period. Beriberi was an exception because it aroused public interest and generated heated debates. To some extent, the same can be said about the prevention of venereal disease among seamen, a problem which was intertwined with a broader debate about seamen's morals and lifestyles. As a result, many aspects of seamen's health were left to doctors with a special interest in the subject.

During the period studied here, public health services in Norway were greatly expanded. Concern was often expressed that seamen did not have the same access to health and welfare services as did other groups. Absence from home, unsafe working environments and less than wholesome leisure activities made it both difficult and expensive for the Norwegian state to cater to seafarers. In short, seamen were indeed in a "peculiar position." Public health experts and social reformers nonetheless agreed on steps to improve the situation. In turn, these measures laid the foundation for the establishment of health and welfare services to Norwegian seamen during the Second World War, when seamen's health was given a higher priority.[68] They also formed the basis for new health services for seamen introduced later in the century.

---

[68]Hjeltnes, *Sjømann – lang vakt*; and Gogstad, *Slange og sverd*.

The Norwegian-American Line: State Incentives and Mediations with Dominant Market Players

Per Kristian Sebak

Introduction

On 7 June 1913, the eighth anniversary of Norwegian independence, the Norwegian-American Line's *Kristianiafjord* set sail from Bergen on its maiden voyage to New York. Among the numerous dignitaries on the first leg, which had started from Christiania (Oslo) three days earlier, were King Haakon VII, the Norwegian cabinet and most members of parliament.[1] The inauguration of the Norwegian-American line had both national and international significance. From a national perspective, it marked the end of a decade-long process to gain entry for Norway in the transatlantic passenger business. At the same time, it brought Norwegian shipping for the first time into the most capital-intensive form of shipping: large passenger liners operating on the transatlantic passenger run. Moreover, Norway now had a sustainable passenger service connecting the country directly with the large Norwegian communities in the United States. The line was sustainable in that it was supported by state subventions and agreements with the dominant players in the transatlantic passenger trade. In an international context, the establishment of the Norwegian-American Line was significant because it was one of only a handful of new, independent transatlantic passenger companies established during a period (1900-1914) marked by collusion in the form of conferences, high barriers to entry and record numbers of passengers.

This essay will investigate how the Norwegian-American Line, despite national and international barriers, came into being from four key perspectives: how the initiatives were shaped, mediations with the Norwegian state, state incentives in the form of subsidies and negotiations with the dominant market players. In a broader international context, this will provide rare insights into the prerequisites, constraints and complex process of inaugurating capital-intensive shipping lines in general and transatlantic passenger lines in particular in the early part of the twentieth century. The investigation will be

[1]Erik Vea, Johan Schreiner and Johan Seland, *Den norske Amerikalinje, 1910-1960* (Oslo, 1960), 123-124.

based primarily on Norwegian parliamentary reports (*Stortingsforhandlinger*), records of the Norwegian Ministry of Foreign Affairs and documents from the Atlantic Conference. It will comprise six parts. The first and second sections set the events in a wider context and provide an opportunity to reflect on the key contemporary structures of the transatlantic passenger business in general and for Norwegian overseas liner traffic in particular. The third and fourth parts will address two opposing initiatives, one national and one Scandinavian, for a transatlantic line that took shape in 1908 and laid the foundation for the ultimate Norwegian-American Line. The fifth section will explore the ensuing state incentives for subsidizing the line, while the final part looks at mediations with the dominant market players.

International Context

In the early 1900s, the transatlantic passenger business was marked by two key features. First, despite record passenger numbers, it had an oligopolistic market structure dominated by British and German companies, and American capital. By 1903, following a fifteen-year period when at least ten large transatlantic passenger lines were absorbed or discontinued, there were only five notable groupings of transatlantic passenger companies in Northern Europe: the Hamburg-America Line (HAPAG), North German Lloyd, the International Mercantile Marine Company (IMMC, including the White Star Line), the French Line and the British Cunard Line. A new company, such as the Norwegian-American Line, that intended to enter the transatlantic passenger business from Northern Europe had to deal with one or several of these actors. Moreover, due to the volatility of the business, not least because of the sharp fluctuations in the number of third-class passengers (migrants), both annually and seasonally, only firms with some sort of state backing proved sustainable in the long term.[2]

The second key feature of the early 1900s was that the dominant firms in the market collaborated in various conference agreements. To use Robert G. Greenhill's definition, shipping conferences are best understood as "essentially cartels or oligopolistic arrangements whereby sellers, independent but associated shipping companies, combined to set prices and services to their custom-

[2]Drew Keeling, "Transport Capacity Management and Transatlantic Migration, 1900-1914," *Research in Economic History*, XXV (2008), 227-231; Keeling, "Costs, Risks and Migration Networks between Europe and the United States, 1900-1914," in Torsten Feys, *et al.* (eds.), *Maritime Transport and Migration: The Connections between Maritime and Migration Networks* (St. John's, 2007), 150; and Vivian Vale, *The American Peril: Challenge to Britain on the North Atlantic, 1901-1904* (Manchester, 1984), 32-143.

ers."[3] In the transatlantic passenger business, this meant fixing ticket prices, allocating markets and regulating most other aspects of the business. Most notably for this discussion, in February 1908 the Atlantic Conference was established between the Liverpool-based North Atlantic Passenger Conference ("British lines") and the continental Nordatlantischer Dampfer Linien Verband (NDLV).[4] The arrangement included a joint secretary based in Jena, Germany. A separate Mediterranean Conference was also established. Combined, the entire European migrant (third-class) market was divided into three submarkets; British-Scandinavian (including Finland), Continental (ports from St. Petersburg to Bordeaux), and Mediterranean. They were controlled by two inter-linked, transnational conferences: the Atlantic Conference and the Mediterranean Conference.[5]

National Context

Although by 1900 Norway possessed the world's third largest merchant fleet after Britain and Germany, and was among the most important sources of immigrants to the United States, it was only around the turn of the century that the country's shipping industry underwent a structural change characterized by large-scale shipping companies capable of entering the capital-intensive overseas liner trades, including the transatlantic passenger business. This shift came about through the amalgamation of a number of smaller Norwegian companies, along with the introduction of joint-ownership structures and new forms of management.[6] As in Denmark, which had been involved in overseas liner traffic since the 1880s, Norwegian firms interested in the liner business were all joint-stock enterprises, with a spatial concentration in the region of the

---

[3]Robert G. Greenhill, "Competition or Co-operation in the Global Shipping Industry: The Origins and Impact of the Conference System for British Shipowners before 1914," in David J. Starkey and Gelina Harlaftis (eds.), *Global Markets: The Internationalization of the Sea Transport Industries since 1850* (St. John's, 1998), 55.

[4]Erich Murken, *Die grossen transatlantischen Linienreederei-Verbände, Pools und Interessengemeinschaften bis zum Ausbruch des Weltkrieges: Ihre Entstehung, Organisation und Wirksamkeit* (Jena, 1922).

[5]Torsten Feys, "A Business Approach to Transatlantic Migration: The Introduction of Steam-shipping on the North Atlantic and its Impact on the European Exodus, 1840-1914" (Unpublished PhD thesis, European University Institute, 2008), 170-171 and 476.

[6]Helge W. Nordvik, "The Shipping Industries of the Scandinavian Countries, 1850-1914," in Lewis R. Fischer and Gerald E. Panting (eds.), *Change and Adaptation in Maritime History: The North Atlantic Fleets in the Nineteenth Century* (St. John's, 1985), 134-148.

capital, Christiania.[7] There was also a significant political dimension stemming from Norway's independence from Sweden in 1905. This was important because sustainable overseas liner traffic usually required state funding in the form of subventions. State involvement in shipping was thus a method both of confirming political independence and building a nation through shipping and trade. The efficacy of this approach had already been demonstrated in the wake of Belgian independence in the 1830s and was also a significant component of German and Italian state policies following their unifications.[8]

The first subsidized Norwegian line to operate beyond the North Sea was Otto Thoresen's freight line to Spain and Italy in 1894.[9] Fourteen years later, the first subsidized Norwegian transatlantic line, Gottfred M. Bryde's freight-based Norwegian Mexico Gulf Line, was opened. By 1915, Norwegians operated seven overseas lines connecting Scandinavia with Australia, India, Africa and the Americas. In his study of shipping conferences, Arvid Frihagen explained that Bryde's company immediately ran into "trouble" with the Cuba-Mexico Conference and was only "permitted" to carry freight to and from Scandinavia following negotiations with HAPAG.[10] Circulars from the Atlantic Conference also reveal that Bryde's line was monitored closely, especially when one of its agents announced that the line was willing to take passengers from Norway and Rotterdam to America. In September 1912, the Atlantic Conference was reassured that Bryde had "no intention to enter the passenger traffic."[11] In practice, this meant it would stick to transporting freight, with only a small supplement of passengers, and would not interfere with the Conference's interests. This example demonstrates the leverage that dominant market players had over latecomers in transatlantic liner services. Norwegians were also hampered by a lack of experience in dealing with oligopolistic market structures in general and conferences in particular. Indeed, the first conference in which Norwegian shipowners played an important role was the Baltic

---

[7]Johan N. Tønnesen, "Fra klipperen til motorskipet: Jern- og stålseilskuter. Siste treseilskutetid," in Jacob S. Worm-Müller (ed.), *Den norske sjøfarts historie* (6 vols., Oslo, 1923-1951), II, part 3, 357-358.

[8]Torsten Feys, "The Battle for the Migrants: The Evolution from Port to Company Competition, 1840-1914," in Feys, *et al.* (eds.), *Maritime Transport and Migration*, 27-47; and S.G. Sturmey, *British Shipping and World Competition* (London, 1962; reprint, St. John's, 2010), 18-19 and 31.

[9]Tønnesen, "Fra klipperen til motorskipet," 380.

[10]Arvid Frihagen, *Linjekonferanser og kartell-lovgivning* (Oslo, 1963), 46.

[11]Municipal Archives of Rotterdam (MAR), Holland America Line (HAL), 318.04/208, 12 January and 17 December 1910 and 2 September 1912.

and White Sea Conference for tramp shipping that was organized in 1905.[12] Their experience and competence were enhanced during the next ten years when Norwegian companies became part of conferences controlling shipping to and from North and South America as well as several other trades.

A Norwegian Line to America: National versus Scandinavian Unity

To understand the process that led to the creation of the Norwegian-American Line, we must examine two opposing alternatives that took shape in 1908. In addition to the political aspects, both were driven by two additional factors. First, the market situation was promising. Norwegian exports to North America were increasing, and the demand for passages between Norway and the United States was relatively strong. Second, the prospects for a Norwegian line to America were stimulated by the parliamentary decision in 1894 to construct a railway line between Bergen and Christiania that was to open in 1909. With this rail connection, the fastest route for passengers between eastern Norway, the country's most populous region, and North America was via the port of Bergen. In addition, Bergen had good steamship connections with ports along the Norwegian coast from Christiansand in the south to the Russian border in the north. Moreover, there was the possibility of linking Bergen with the Swedish railway network, making a Norwegian line to America important to Swedish interests as well.

The two competing initiatives involved a Norwegian alternative, based on a desire to increase national unity, and a Scandinavian alternative (also known as the "*Birma* Plan") based on cooperation between Norway, Sweden and Denmark. The proceedings around these two alternatives were complex, controversial and somewhat confusing. They have been the subject of several publications, especially concerning the involvement of key politicians, most notably the Norwegian prime ministers Gunnar Knudsen and Johan Ludwig Mowinckel, and to a lesser extent Christian Michelsen. The controversy over the two plans persisted well into the 1930s, particularly relating to which scheme was supported by whom, who said what, and who demonstrated the most national loyalty.[13] For Norwegians, the events of 1908 were thus a major topic. But from the perspective of the dominant market players, they were not nearly as important. The primary goal of the established lines was to contain

[12]J.F. Myhre, *Twenty Years with the Baltic and White Sea Conference: Memoirs* (Liverpool, 1927); and Frihagen, *Linjekonferanser*, 55.

[13]Endre Johannesen Svanøe, *Hvorledes vi vandt Den Norske Amerikalinje: En historisk oversigt* (Oslo, 1926); Endre S. Stephensen and Endre Johannesen Svanøe, *Et 30-aars tilbakeblik: Kampen om Den Norske Amerikalinje og Linjens konstituering* (Oslo, 1933); and Stephensen and Svanøe, *Den norske Amerikalinjens Oprettelse* (Oslo, 1938).

Norwegian and Swedish participation in the North Atlantic, which because of the conference agreements was an especially important market for the British lines.

The initiative behind the Norwegian alternative had its roots in 1902 when Captain Stephen Stephensen, who had long experience in Østlandske Lloyd's service between Christiania and Newcastle which also carried emigrants for British transatlantic lines, joined forces with the Norwegian-born naval engineer Johannes Bull in Scotland and the engineer Endre O. Svanøe, who already shared similar ideas from his work for the Norwegian State Railway in the building of the railway between Bergen and Christiania. Bull was approached especially to deal with the British transatlantic lines.[14] The stakes were raised in 1907 when Magnus Andersen, the first head of the Norwegian Mercantile Marine Division (*Sjøfartskontoret*), the government agency responsible for ship inspections, was appointed to head the working committee. In addition to preparing an application for a government subvention, Andersen's prime mission was to bring together all those who had shown interest in the scheme so that their names could appear on the invitation for share subscriptions. By early 1908, the list comprised 178 men from every corner of Norway, including all the stock exchange committees, most of the county governors and many leading shipowners and exporters.[15] It had truly become a national undertaking.

One of the companies most threatened by the Norwegian initiative was the Danish United Steamship Company (DFDS). Founded in 1866 and operating a wide range of steamship services in Europe and to North and South America, it had been involved in the transatlantic passenger business since 1898 when it acquired the Thingvalla Line, which operated a service between Copenhagen, Christiania, Christiansand and New York. Even though it did not join any of the transatlantic passenger conferences before 1909, DFDS had an agreement with the British and German lines which effectively restricted its market to Scandinavian and Finnish passengers. Norwegians were the company's most important customers.

Captain Cold, DFDS' new managing director from April 1908, believed that if there was to be a Norwegian line, the best option for DFDS would be to reorganize its own American service into a syndicate involving DFDS, a Norwegian and possibly a Swedish division, and the Danish East Asiatic Company, which at the time operated the Russian-American Line from the port of Libau. The minutes of DFDS board meetings disclose that a proposal for a "Scandinavian-Russian New York Line" was made on 7 July

---

[14]Svanøe, *Hvorledes vi vandt Den norske Amerikalinje*, 14.

[15]Magnus Andersen, *70 års tilbakeblikk på mitt virke på sjø og i land* (Oslo, 1932), 257.

1908.[16] The same minutes also reveal that the prime objective was to "stop the Norwegians." Although the company believed that the Norwegian working committee would "come to their senses" and scrap its proposal once it realized that it would have to "combat the English [transatlantic companies]," the Danes had several strong incentives to take immediate action.[17]

First of all, 1908 was a poor year for all transatlantic passenger lines, severely affecting revenues. Second, more pressure was put on DFDS when the company learned on 21 April that a separate Swedish American line was being planned involving cooperation between Swedish interests and the American banker J.P. Morgan and the IMMC. Although DFDS immediately soon learned through its connections in "Hamburg and England" that there was "no truth to the matter,"[18] this was not completely true. Wilhelm Lundgren had presented a plan for a Swedish America line earlier that month, but these did not proceed further at this stage.[19] Moreover, there was the role of Isak Glückstadt, the head of *Den Danske Landmandsbank*, a director of both DFDS and the East Asiatic Company and the main creditor for the Copenhagen Free Port. Since its opening in 1894, the Free Port had not succeeded in transforming Copenhagen into a major European transit port.[20] Nevertheless, considerable freight between North America and western Norway went through the Free Port, and much of this freight could be lost if a direct line was opened between Bergen and New York.[21] In sum, a subsidized Norwegian-American Line would badly affect all of the Danish parties, particularly *Den Danske Landmandsbank*.

In the summer of 1908, the Danes had one major possibility to thwart the Norwegian project. While Magnus Andersen's *Birma* Plan for a Norwegian line had attracted the interest and support, at least on paper, of a wide range of Norwegian shipowners, businessmen and dignitaries, he still had not approached the two most decisive institutions, the banks and the government of Prime Minister Gunnar Knudsen, who was known to support some kind of

---

[16]DFDS Archive, Copenhagen, Bestyrelses forhandlingsprotokol, V, 262.

[17]*Ibid.*, V, 267.

[18]*Ibid.*, V, 251.

[19]Algot Mattsson, *Vägen mot Väster: En bok om emigrationen och Svenska Amerika Linien* (Stockholm, 1982), 99-100.

[20]Anders Monrad Møller, Henrik Dethlefsen and Hans Chr. Johansen, *Sejl og damp: Dansk søfarts historie, Vol. 5* (Copenhagen, 1998), 141-142.

[21]Andersen, *70 års tilbakeblikk*, 265.

Norwegian participation in overseas liner traffic.[22] In addition, none of the few Norwegian experts on large-scale shipping had been consulted. To win the support of Norwegian and Swedish creditors for a Scandinavian alternative to stop the Norwegians, Glückstadt suggested approaching two of Norway and Sweden's most influential bankers, Nicolai Kielland-Thorkildsen, head of the Norwegian *Centralbanken*, and Knut Wallenberg, head of *Stockholms Enskilda Bank*, Sweden's most powerful private bank which was involved in numerous Swedish entrepreneurial initiatives.[23]

Towards the end of July, just as the Norwegian committee was more or less ready to make its plan public, the East Asiatic Company's *Birma* (hence the name "*Birma* plan"), usually sailing for the Russian-American Line, departed from Copenhagen on a special mission to the Christianiafjord, Bergen and Stockholm to win political and financial support for a Scandinavian alternative. The delegates onboard included Glückstadt, Cold and Admiral Richelieu of DFDS and Hans N. Andersen, the managing director of the East Asiatic Company. A letter of intent was signed in Bergen on 24 July implying that a Norwegian syndicate would operate a service between Scandinavia, Russia and New York together with DFDS and the East Asiatic Company. The signatures included Otto Thoresen and Halfdan Wilhelmsen, Norway's most prominent shipowners, and Nicolai Kielland-Thorkildsen. Christian Michelsen, the former Norwegian prime minister, had expressed his support in principle, albeit without promising any further involvement, and the scheme was embraced by Prime Minister Knudsen.[24] The extent of Swedish involvement was unclear at first, but it was stated that "a Swedish route" would be established, and *Birma* also stopped on the outskirts of Stockholm to meet Knut Wallenberg.[25]

The delegation recognized fully that a vital precondition was to reach an agreement with the Atlantic Conference. According to board minutes, DFDS resolved on 4 August to approach "Ballin [HAPAG's managing director] and the British lines" about the scheme.[26] HAPAG and North German

---

[22]Lauritz Pettersen, *Bergen og sjøfarten III: Fra kjøpmannsrederi til selvstendig næring, 1860-1914* (Bergen, 1981), 287-288.

[23]Francis Sejersted, "Nationalism in the Epoch of Organised Capitalism – Norway and Sweden Choosing Different Paths," in Alice Teichova and Herbert Matis (eds.), *Nation, State, and the Economy in History* (Cambridge, 2003), 96-112.

[24]Norway, Riksarkivet (National Archives, RA), Ministry of Foreign Affairs (NMFA), 1167/I, 24 and 25 July 1908.

[25]Søren Thorsøe, *et al.*, *Skandinavien-Amerika Linien – DFDS' passager- og fragtfart på Amerika* (Copenhagen, 2001), 135.

[26]DFDS, Bestyrelses forhandlingsprotokol, V, 263.

Lloyd, the leading continental companies, initially opposed the project, especially because of the East Asiatic Company's involvement. But a step toward overcoming this occurred when the East Asiatic Company reached a preliminary agreement with the Atlantic Conference on 26 August for its Russian-American Line, with the result that it withdrew from the Scandinavian alliance. DFDS was encouraged to join the Atlantic Conference on the understanding that the British lines would protect it in the event of competition from Norwegian or Swedish national lines. Nonetheless, DFDS remained committed to the Scandinavian scheme.

A meeting was scheduled in Liverpool on 9 September between DFDS and the British lines. According to Kielland-Thorkildsen, before the meeting DFDS asked its Norwegian colleagues to solicit the view of the Norwegian government on the matter, believing that a promise of state involvement would influence the British lines.[27] To this end, a meeting was convened in late August between Prime Minister Knudsen, Foreign Minister Wilhelm Christopher Christophersen, Kielland-Thorkildsen, Wilhelmsen and Johannes Irgens, the Norwegian ambassador to London who happened to be in Christiania on holiday. After the meeting, Christophersen telegraphed Norwegian Consul General Ottesen in London instructing him to present the following text at the Liverpool meeting:

> Actually strong efforts are made in the Norwegian press and among the public in order to form an independent Norwegian America Line, and appeals are made to national sentiments. In my opinion the national interests will be satisfied with the proposal which, it is understood, will be laid before the directors of the White Star, Cunard and Allan lines at Liverpool on Monday. The Norwegian foreign minister would therefore appreciate a decision by which these proposals were accepted, as he believes that national dissatisfaction and intended competition from Norway thus would be avoided.[28]

The solid backing of the Norwegian government for the Scandinavian alternative soon became the subject of controversy, but two months later Foreign Minister Christophersen dismissed the critics by claiming that advocates of the Norwegian alternative did not see the necessity of joining the conference. Furthermore, it was "among the Norwegian foreign service's primary duties to assist Norwegian businesses during the establishment of foreign con-

---

[27]RA, NMFA, 1167/I, 18 November 1908.

[28]*Ibid.*, 4 September 1908.

nections."[29] Although the Norwegian government had not promised any kind of subvention or other financial assistance, the reference in Christophersen's telegram to "national interests" being "satisfied" suggests that the government had rejected the need for an independent Norwegian line. It can be assumed that DFDS and those Norwegians who backed the Scandinavian scheme knew that state intervention in practice would disadvantage the competing Norwegian scheme, especially since both alternatives were being launched at the same time.

Despite the presence of the Norwegian consul general at the Liverpool meeting, the British lines still "firmly declined to consider any Norwegian participation in the transatlantic passenger business."[30] Notwithstanding this position, Irgens had already been mandated to approach the British transatlantic companies, Oswald Sanderson of the Wilson Line and British authorities on his return to London to win their support for Norwegian participation in the DFDS scheme. Sanderson was an especially powerful figure when it came to any Norwegian participation in the transatlantic passenger business because his company carried the vast majority of emigrants from Scandinavia to Britain for the British transatlantic lines and would therefore be affected by a direct Norwegian service. Indeed, Norwegian interests, and particularly the government, had on at least two occasions experienced the wrath of the Wilson Line. Most recently, the government had been forced to keep a subsidized line to Britain in the 1890s and early 1900s well clear of Wilson's hub in Hull.[31] In addition to his company's position in North Sea traffic, Oswald Sanderson was also the brother of Harold Sanderson, a director of the White Star Line and thus part of the IMMC, the most powerful alliance in transatlantic passenger traffic.[32]

In the end, the Norwegian delegates did not meet Oswald Sanderson. Because he was unavailable, Irgens instead met in London on 22 September with Arthur Wilson, chairman of the board and son of the Wilson Line's founder, where he expressed his hope "that the Wilson Line would find it reasonable that Norway in this manner [with DFDS] joined the America business, and that Wilson would use his influence on the 'pool' lines to get the company going." Wilson told Irgens that while he was sympathetic, he wanted the ser-

[29]*Ibid.*, 23 December 1908.

[30]DFDS, Bestyrelses forhandlingsprotokol, V, 265; and RA, NMFA, 1167/I, 11 September 1908.

[31]Wilhelm Keilhau, *Norges Eldste Linjerederi: Jubileumsskrift til Det Bergenske Dampskibsseskabs 100-års dag* (Bergen, 1951), 212 and 238-243.

[32]Brian Dyson, "The End of the Line: Oswald Sanderson, Sir John Ellerman and the Wilsons of Hull," in David J. Starkey and Alan G. Jamieson (eds.), *Exploiting the Sea: Aspects of Britain's Maritime Economy since 1870* (Exeter, 1998), 59-78.

vice to be confined to the routes west of Christiansand because he believed that the waters between there and Christiania were already crowded. At the same time, in "keeping with tradition," Wilson made it clear that his company would "fight" anyone who threatened its service at Gothenburg, where the Wilson Line had particularly strong ties.[33] Indeed, as far back as 1844, John West Wilson, Arthur Wilson's late brother, had taken up residence in Gothenburg where he built a strong brokerage business for the Wilson Line's activities in addition to serving on the city council and other bodies.[34] The position of the Wilson Line clearly complicated Swedish participation in the Scandinavian scheme.

While Norwegian diplomacy was mobilized to broker a deal with the British companies, the Danish foreign services did nothing, much to Irgens' surprise. This suggests that the Norwegian authorities, inexperienced as they were in dealing with shipping conferences, had miscalculated the nature of the relationship between states and conferences. There is no evidence that the Danish authorities were approached about the Scandinavian alternative, and such contact would have been unlikely because DFDS most often left such mediation to others. Irgens also received similar feedback from British authorities. He approached Sir Walter Howell, head of the Board of Trade, and Sir Charles Hardinge, under-Secretary at the Foreign Office, in search of their support. Howell said that he would find it "completely incomprehensible" if the British lines found that "Danish steamers were transferred to Norwegian flag [for a Scandinavian alternative]," but added that it was "difficult" for the Board of Trade to meddle in this matter. Similarly, Hardinge stressed that neither the Foreign Office nor the government would take any action against the conferences.[35]

Irgens, Kielland-Thorkildsen and Wilhelmsen finally met with Harold Sanderson on 26 September in Liverpool. Irgens got the impression that DFDS had not given Sanderson the full details of the proposed Scandinavian scheme, notably that calls would be made at Bergen. While Sanderson sympathized with the idea of Norwegian participation in the transatlantic passenger business, particularly considering the vast sums expended on the rail line between Bergen and Christiania, he was concerned that a national Norwegian line would lead to a similar Swedish line. This was a concern of the British transatlantic lines in general because they had focussed their Scandinavian activities on Sweden, which they regarded as the most important market. Knowledge of this situation was also why Sweden had been largely left out during the pre-

---

[33]RA, NMFA, 1167/I, 22 September 1908.

[34]Oscar Wieselgren (ed.), *Svenska män och kvinnor, Vol. 8* (Stockholm, 1955), 389.

[35]RA, NMFA, 1167/I, 26 September 1908.

liminary negotiations for the Scandinavian plan. In the end, Sanderson suggested that the Norwegian and Danish delegates propose at the next meeting of the Atlantic Conference, where both British and continental lines would be present, that two DFDS steamers would be transferred to the Norwegian flag and that calls would be made at Bergen.[36]

The Atlantic Conference meeting that voted on the Scandinavian scheme took place in Paris on 21 October. Although there are no extant minutes of this meeting, Kielland-Thorkildsen submitted a detailed report to the Norwegian foreign minister on 18 November which suggests that the Scandinavian delegation included Wilhelmsen, Glückstadt, Cold and himself; there were no Swedish delegates. The Danes were still willing to exclude Sweden from the scheme. The Norwegians disagreed, however, arguing that leaving out Sweden would enable "damaging" future competition in the form of a subsidized Swedish line. Wilhelmsen, the most powerful Norwegian shipowner, contended that it would be better to confront Swedish competition now rather than later.[37] The British lines agreed, and this led to the signing of a contract on 23 October which stipulated that a line could be established comprising two Danish, two Norwegian and one Swedish steamer. The service was allocated 3.35 percent of the combined westbound continental and British-Scandinavian third-class market, and four percent of the eastbound traffic.[38] The contract's introduction, which was due to come into effect on 1 January 1909, stated that:

> In view of the agitation in Norway and Sweden for National Flag Lines to North America, the Scandinavian American Line undertakes to support an arrangement whereby its own United States service will be reduced to two steamers, and a new Norwegian line with two steamers, will be established, and the Scandinavian-American Line will oppose any further extension as regards Denmark, Norway, or Sweden, and further bind themselves not to increase their own service.

It is telling that the contract was between the Atlantic Conference and DFDS; in other words, the Danish company was legally responsible. This likely reflected the fact that conference members already had well-established connections with DFDS. As far as Swedish participation was concerned, the contract stipulated that in addition to deploying only one Swedish steamer, calls at Gothenburg could be made no more than fifteen times per year, in ad-

---

[36]Norwegian National Archives, Ministry of Foreign Affairs, 1167/I, 26 September 1908.

[37]*Ibid.*, 18 November 1908.

[38]DFDS, Bestyrelses forhandlingsprotokol, V, 271.

dition to calls at Helsingborg. As for Norway, the line was permitted to maintain DFDS' America service via Christiania and Christiansand, in addition to making twenty calls annually at Bergen. Moreover, it could carry only "Scandinavian and/or Finnish passengers."[39] On 7 November, the agreement was ratified by DFDS, with Wilhelmsen and Kielland-Thorkildsen signing on behalf of the Norwegian division and Knut Wallenberg on behalf of the Swedish division.[40]

Opposition from Norway and Sweden

The contract signed in October and ratified in November 1908 did not mean that everything was settled for the new Scandinavian-American passenger service. On 11 September, while Irgens was lobbying the British lines and authorities on behalf of the Scandinavian alternative, Magnus Andersen of the working committee for an independent Norwegian national line requested Johannes Bull, his advocate in Britain, to commence negotiations with the British members of the Atlantic Conference.[41] Bull communicated with Harold Sanderson of the White Star Line, Henry Allan of the Allan Line, and Lord Pirrie, whom he already knew because both were in the shipbuilding industry. Pirrie had considerable influence in the British shipping industry through his post as vice-president of the IMMC; as well, his shipyard, Harland and Wolff, was a likely candidate to build the new company's steamers.

Andersen was under the impression that the rules of the Atlantic Conference gave preference to a national over a commercial line for admission. National lines, he believed, were those which enjoyed subventions, such as mail contracts and admiralty funding, while commercial lines were basically outsiders. Unfortunately for Andersen and the proponents of an independent Norwegian alternative, there was no such clause in the Conference's by-laws. In practice, however, the Conference had entered into agreements with companies backed by subventions, notably Canadian Pacific and the Russian Volunteer Fleet.[42] It is possible that Andersen had interpreted this as a rule which would apply automatically to a Norwegian national line.

At this stage, efforts to promote an independent line became ever more bewildering, not least because of the lack of negotiating experience among the Norwegians. The problem began when Henry Allan showed Bull a copy of the telegram confirming Foreign Minister Christophersen's support for

[39]MAR, HAL, 318.01/62, agreement CC.

[40]RA, NMFA, 1167/I, 7 November 1908.

[41]Andersen, *70 års tilbakeblikk*, 270.

[42]Feys, "Business Approach to Transatlantic Migration," 284, 286 and 477.

the Scandinavian alternative. This was soon picked up by the Norwegian press and led to confusion and controversy; indeed, it even triggered calls for the minister's resignation. Irgens was accused of "intervening and disturbing the negotiations between the Norwegian-American Line and the English conference lines." Moreover, Bull alleged that the British lines, believing that Norwegian participation in the Scandinavian scheme in effect concerned a national line, had signed an agreement under false pretences. Irgens dismissed these allegations, claiming that he knew nothing of any ongoing negotiations between Andersen's projected line and the conference and was only acting in accordance with his mandate.[43]

The seriousness - or absurdity - of the situation became even more apparent when Bull alleged that the matter "opens out matters of real State importance" and requested audiences with King Haakon VII of Norway (who was in Britain at the time) and his father-in-law, King Edward VII of Britain. The British king's "gracious intervention" was needed because "his tact and powers of diplomacy could undoubtedly immediately see a solution" and because "the Norwegian diplomacy, young and untried as it is, [had] failed very badly, and deliberately brought about a state of matters which necessarily must have wide-reaching and unfortunate consequences, unless they are handled with the utmost delicacy."[44] Irgens was not convinced and dismissed the request, writing that King Haakon was "very busy" and that there was "of course no opportunity" to involve King Edward in this matter.[45]

The circulars of the Atlantic Conference reveal that Bull's interventions in Britain were followed up on 25 November 1908 with a formal application from Andersen on behalf of a Norwegian national line. It requested that "our Company, when fully constituted, may be admitted as a member of the North Atlantic Conference Lines [*sic*], it being our sincere wish to respect and to work in agreement with all established interests." He underscored that the proposed company was the "expression of a strong and legitimate wish among Norwegian representative men and Corporations" and that it was to "receive from the Norwegian state both mail subsidies and Admiralty contributions," despite the fact that at the time the latter had not been confirmed by the Norwegian parliament.[46] Understanding that the Atlantic Conference had already entered into an agreement with DFDS for the Scandinavian alternative, he strongly lamented the "division from DFDS," alleging that the company "ut-

---

[43]Andersen, *70 års tilbakeblikk*, 272-274; and RA, NMFA, 1167/I, 27 October 1908.

[44]RA, NMFA, 1167/I, 17 and 28 November 1908.

[45]*Ibid.*, 1 December 1908.

[46]MAR, HAL, 318.04/208, 8 December 1908.

terly [lacked] the qualifications to become a National line, or a line qualified to receive mail subventions and Admiralty contributions." Further, he averred that the committee "must under these circumstances on behalf of the subscribers to its Prospects protest against the description of the competing Line as a National Line for Norway in any meaning of the word." In other words, Andersen was under the impression that DFDS had portrayed the Scandinavian alternative as a Norwegian national line.

There is no reference to responses from any of the conference members to Andersen's application. One explanation for this silence may have been that it only added to the confusion. The signed agreement with DFDS included a pool which effectively limited the extent of Scandinavian involvement in the passenger business. In addition, the Norwegian government had expressed its support. Why, then, should the Atlantic Conference take any notice of Andersen's application? At the next Atlantic Conference meeting in Paris on 3 February 1909, the only mention of Scandinavia was to an "Agreement with Scandinavian American Line [DFDS]."[47] Because the transatlantic lines were dealing with several major economic challenges at the time, there were limits as to how much effort could be channelled into the local bickering in Scandinavia.

Yet while everything was pointing to the success of the Scandinavian alternative, the strongest opposition to the scheme came from Sweden, where the press reported in mid-November 1908 that the "Danes had arranged a so-called Danish-Norwegian-Swedish line with only one boat to Sweden." This was in fact the beginning of the end to Scandinavian collaboration. Swedes particularly resented that their country had such a limited role in the scheme given that their country had the highest volume of exports and the largest number of passengers bound for America. Resentment also smouldered in Norway, particularly in relation to the government's alleged preference for the Scandinavian alternative. On 23 January 1909, Kielland-Thorkildsen confirmed that the scheme had been abandoned.[48] In effect, national pride, as well as tensions among the three Scandinavian countries, had undermined Norwegian participation in a direct passenger service between western Norway and North America. These problems also blocked any immediate prospects for a more straightforward connection from large parts of Scandinavia to the US.

Founding of the Norwegian-American Line and Incentives for Subvention

With the collapse of the Scandinavian alternative, the working committee for an independent Norwegian line proceeded with renewed vigour. On 1 February 1909, as the government continued to reply to criticisms over its support

[47] *Ibid.*, 3 February [1909].

[48] Andersen, *70 års tilbakeblikk*, 291.

for the Scandinavian alternative, the working committee submitted an application to parliament for a subvention. It now became an issue for the entire parliament rather than just a government that had openly supported the futile Scandinavian alternative. The application was first considered by the Road Committee (*veikomite*), which normally was the first to consider proposals for infrastructure projects requiring state funding. The committee decided in April 1909 to hand the matter over to the Ministry of Public Labour (*Departementet for offentlige arbeider*), thus excluding the Ministry of Foreign Affairs which had been heavily involved in the Scandinavian alternative. With parliamentary approval, the Ministry of Public Labour appointed a special ministerial committee to consider the application. This committee, which commenced work in March 1910, comprised six experts representing all of the major commercial centres in Norway. Five months later, on 27 August 1910, the joint-stock company *Den norske Amerikalinje A/S* was formally constituted. The ministerial committee submitted its recommendations on 9 June 1911, on the basis of which the Ministry of Public Labour recommended a subvention of one million *kroner* for the two years ending on 30 June 1915. This was state funding of an "extraordinary nature," as the proposition stipulated. By comparison, in the budget year 1911-1912, parliament had committed a total of only 650,000 *kroner* to Norwegian and international shipping lines. On 8 June 1912, the proposition was approved by a clear majority in the *Storting*.[49]

There was a significant difference between the main reasons given for a subvention in the initial application of February 1909 and the final proposition on which parliament voted. In the initial application, the rationale for a subvention was based primarily on the ability of the steamers to be used as auxiliary cruisers, with reference to the British Admiralty's arrangement with Cunard in 1903, as well as for mail contracts. The ministerial committee concluded that there were insufficient grounds to grant a subvention for either of these rationales. It argued that the current mail service via Britain or using DFDS was "fully satisfactory," and could find no grounds for granting funds on the grounds of the vessels' suitability as "auxiliary cruisers," in part because this would have a negative impact on an already strained defence budget.[50]

Although some advantages for trade and tourism were acknowledged, it was emigration that the committee regarded as a "factor of utmost impor-

---

[49]Norway, Stortingsforhandlinger, Ot. prp. og med., 1912, 2b, "Betænkning ang. Spørsmaalet om statsbidrag til A/S 'Den norske Amerikalinje,'" 10; and Stortingsforhandlinger, Ot. prp. No. 86 (1912).

[50]Stortingsforhandlinger, Ot. prp. og med., 1912, 2b, "Betænkning ang. Spørsmaalet om statsbidrag til A/S 'Den norske Amerikalinje,'" 23 & 25; and Stortingsforhandlinger, Ot. prp. No. 86 (1912), 1.

tance for the question of state funding for a Norwegian America line."[51] Outmigration by this time was increasingly resented in Norway, especially after the founding of the Society for the Limitation of Emigration (*Selskapet til Emigrationens Indskrænkning*) in 1908.[52] Indeed, the Ministry of Social Affairs appointed a committee in 1912 to consider new legislation aimed at restricting and better regulating emigration.[53] Yet the committee considering the subvention for the Norwegian-American Line argued that a direct Norwegian line would not lead to an increase in migration, believing that "the coming generation" would still find it natural to seek a livelihood outside Norway "on about the same scale as now." Moreover, it pointed to the many existing travel options.

At the same time, the committee found it regrettable that more had not been done to make it easier for the emigrant to return home or "at least as far as possible keep him as an associate in the native land's intellectual life and if possible also in its economic life." On this basis, the committee argued that the government should "promote re-migration" and ensure that emigrants not only became "useful citizens in the new country" but also pioneers in Norwegian trade, industry and intellectual life. A direct Norwegian line, connecting emigrants more firmly with their native land, would be an important remedy. Finally, the committee contended that an America line would be an important tool to maintain better control over the migrant traffic, stressing that this fit particularly well with the new emigration legislation under consideration.[54]

In the context of a newly independent state which wanted to restrict emigration and promote re-migration, parliament had a real incentive to approve a subvention of an "extraordinary nature" for the new line.[55] Still, it is not clear how the Norwegian government could claim that a direct national line could play a significant role in promoting re-migration. After all, German and British companies operated almost daily direct and fast passenger services from America to Britain and Germany, respectively, but the return rate among British (including Irish) and German immigrants was relatively low.[56] This sug-

---

[51]Stortingsforhandlinger, Ot. prp. No. 86 (1912), 3.

[52]Hans Norman and Harald Runblom, *Transatlantic Connections: Nordic Migration to the New World after 1800* (Oslo, 1987), 125.

[53]Norges offisielle statistikk, *Utvandringsstatistikk* (Oslo, 1921).

[54]Stortingsforhandlinger, Ot. prp. No. 86 (1912), 3.

[55]*Ibid.*, 4.

[56]Mark Wyman, *Round-Trip to America: The Immigrants Return to Europe, 1880-1930* (Ithaca, NY, 1993), 11.

gests that national sentiments and contemporary concerns about emigration may have been used deliberately as a mask to convince parliament of the need for a subvention, but that the real incentive was to consolidate trade routes. This also reflects Svein Ivar Angell's observation in his comparison of Swedish and Norwegian modernization strategies that shipowners sought political power to ensure that their trade could operate under the best possible conditions.[57] After all, the connection between the Norwegian-American Line and the political elite was particularly strong given that Gunnar Knudsen served as head of the board of representatives of the Line between 1911 and 1914 at the same time he was serving a second term as prime minister from January 1913 (he was also prime minister from 1908 until February 1910).[58] Moreover, the Line's management and board of directors included representatives from the petty bourgeoisie throughout Norway. It is clear that in addition to enhancing national terms for Norwegian shipping, the Norwegian-American Line could benefit Norwegian shipping as a whole by facilitating direct access to the most exclusive elite in world shipping.

The Norwegian-American Line and the North Atlantic Passenger Conference

When the working committee submitted its application for a subvention in February 1909, it stressed in a separate post the importance of "reaching an understanding" with "The North Atlantic Conference Lines" [i.e., the Atlantic and the North Atlantic Passenger conferences]," in addition to "seek[ing] cooperation with other lines."[59] The committee believed that the conferences would support an undertaking if it were widely supported in Norway. This pledge was also repeated when a revised application was submitted in March 1911, stating that "as soon as the time is right it will seek the acceptance of the transatlantic passenger lines" and "seek conditions that [are] acceptable for the Norwegian line."[60] Yet the ministerial committee and subsequent government proposals did not emphasize the relationship with other companies. The committee only alluded to the fact that the subvention would be important in "a

---

[57]Svein Ivar Angell, *Den svenske modellen og det norske systemet* (Oslo, 2002), 228.

[58]Vea, Schreiner and Seland, *Den norske Amerikalinje*, 429.

[59]*Angaaende Statsbidrag til en regelmæssig Dampskibsrute under norsk Flag for Post, Passager- og Fragtfart mellom Norge og Amerikas Forenede Stater*, 24.

[60]Stortingsforhandlinger, Ot. prp. og med., 1912, 2b, "Betænkning ang. Spørsmaalet om statsbidrag til A/S 'Den norske Amerikalinje'" and "Betænkning ang. Spørsmaalet om statsbidrag til A/S 'Den norske Amerikalinje.'"

possible competitive battle."[61] Moreover, apart from the DFDS board minutes which mentioned the progress of the Norwegian-American Line mostly from press reports, the new line does not appear to have received much attention from any of the existing lines.[62]

There was an obvious explanation for why the conferences were barely mentioned in the proposal. A confidential note from the ministerial committee to the Ministry of Public Labour in June 1911 disclosed that "because of the matter's sensitive nature it is difficult to address this issue in a report that is open to the public."[63] In other words, an in-depth explanation of the significance of conferences was deliberately omitted in order to strengthen the likelihood of public support. The committee informed the ministry that the Atlantic Conference possessed considerable means to "crush" any new competitor, though it believed that as a state-subsidized enterprise the Norwegian-American Line would not encounter any difficulties provided that it sought to collaborate with the conferences. The committee also informed the ministry that the US government had recently filed a petition against the Atlantic Conference for violating the Sherman Anti-Trust Act, which had been passed to bring action against cartels.[64]

Though there is reason to believe that some members of the Norwegian parliament were familiar with shipping conferences, there is equally good reason to suggest that it was mislead when it voted on the proposition for an "extraordinary" subvention. Indeed, parliamentarians might well have voted differently had they known that the conferences had the ability to "crush" a Norwegian line. After all, shipping conferences were still unfamiliar to Norwegian politicians and even to most Norwegian shipowners.

In the circulars put out by the Atlantic Conference, the first significant reference to the new Norwegian-American Line appeared in February 1913, only four months before it was due to begin operations. A Liverpool representative of the Line approached the secretary of the North Atlantic Passenger Conference on 5 February 1913 to explain that it wanted "to work in harmony with the Conference Lines, observing all rules regarding the control of agents, payment of commission, and their willingness to agree on rates." This interaction had come about because Benham and Boyesen, the Norwegian-America Line's general agent in New York, had received a number of applications from migrant agents in the US, many of them Norwegians, who wanted to sell tick-

[61]Stortingsforhandlinger, Ot. prp. No. 86 (1912), 5.

[62]See, for example, MAR, HAL, 318.04/208-211.

[63]RA, Ambassaden i Washington D.C., 211, 9 June 1911.

[64]Alfred D. Chandler, Jr., *Scale and Scope: The Dynamics of Industrial Capitalism* (Cambridge, MA, 1990; reprint, Cambridge, MA, 2004), 72-73.

ets for the company on the assumption that the line would join the conference. The conference agreements, however, prevented them from doing this if the Norwegian company was not a member of the Atlantic Conference. The Norwegian-American Line did not want to join the conference because of the on-going American investigation of the transatlantic companies for violations of the Sherman Anti-Trust Act, "into which [the Norwegian-American Line] naturally [did] not wish to be dragged at the start." Furthermore, because the Norwegian line was state-funded, joining the Atlantic Conference also depended on the pending emigration law.[65] The Norwegian-American Line therefore sought an intermediate agreement with the Atlantic Conference so that migrant agents in the US could work for the company even though it was not a member of the conference.

The secretary forwarded the request to all members of the Atlantic Conference, and the Red Star Line, North German Lloyd and Holland America all agreed that the matter should be sorted out by the British lines with the proviso that the Norwegian-American Line not be able to book any "continental" passengers.[66] DFDS, which by then was also a member of the Atlantic Conference, recommended that "some Agreement" ought to be made with the company, especially because of the "efforts" by the line "to open friendly negotiations." In other words, its attitude towards an independent Norwegian line was considerably more favourable than it had been in 1908, reflecting the fact that it was now protected by the Atlantic Conference. DFDS' only major concern was about freight traffic. DFDS dominated separate freight lines between Scandinavia and North America in cooperation with the Wilson Line, North German Lloyd and HAPAG. For this reason, DFDS recommended that an agreement on freight be concluded before negotiating about the passenger business. Cunard, the most important British player, was likewise in favour of an agreement with the Norwegian-American Line, especially because the line had the full support of the Norwegian government. Yet the most important incentive appears to have been the pending Norwegian emigration legislation. As the Cunard Line stressed, "it is quite possible that [the law] may introduce reprisals against Foreign Steamship Companies, should any aggressive steps be taken against the Norwegian Company."[67] In other words, Cunard believed that complying with the Norwegian request could provide protection against any further unwelcome state intervention in the transatlantic passenger business, though it stressed that the concessions should not be more than absolutely necessary. This also fits well with what Torsten Feys discovered about the attitude of the continental lines towards the Austro-Americana line and Cana-

[65]MAR, HAL, 318.04/211, 5 February 1913.

[66]*Ibid.*, 17 February 1913.

[67]*Ibid.*, 27 February 1913.

dian Pacific in the early 1900s: "[r]ather than risking both the implementation of new barriers on their trade and a costly rate war, the Continental lines preferred to cede a small slice of the cake to entrants [that received government support]."[68]

As a result, a freight agreement was signed in Copenhagen on 14 March 1913 between the Norwegian-American Line and DFDS, HAPAG, North German Lloyd and the Wilson Line to "work in harmony and thus avoid the breakdown of the freight rates." This meant fixing all rates between Norway and New York. The Norwegian-American Line was confined to picking up freight at Norwegian ports and could not "interfere" with other business conducted by the conference lines. Moreover, the final clause stated that "[t]his Agreement is subject to an arrangement being arrived at in regard to the Passenger business."[69] On 11 April 1913, a separate agreement was made in Liverpool between the Norwegian-American Line and the members of the North Atlantic Passenger Conference and DFDS. As with the freight agreement, it imposed several restrictions on the Norwegian-American Line, including fixed ticket rates; prohibitions against calls at Norwegian ports other than Christiania, Christiansand, Stavanger and Bergen; and a ban against carrying passengers who were not Norwegian, Danish and Swedish nationals (ethnic Norwegians with American citizenship were permitted, however). The line was to have freedom to advertise in any Swedish newspaper, but it was to keep an agent only in Stockholm, and it was committed to following the "Agent Rules and Regulations."[70]

This agreement clearly underlines the negotiating power of the dominant market players and shows that mediation on their strict terms was the preferred route. Foreign shipping lines had again demonstrated an ability to dictate Norwegian state policies, as the Wilson Line had done in the 1890s. For example, Trondheim could not be included in the service, despite the fact that several Norwegian politicians had argued that once the line was fully operational, this restriction should be lifted. Indeed, the contract between the government and the line even stated that "[C]all at Trondheim is included as soon as the company's material and consideration of the route's profitability allows it."[71] Finally, there is no indication that the agreements of March and April

[68]Feys, "Business Approach to Transatlantic Migration," 477.

[69]DFDS, 278b/1912-37 sager vedr. søfartskonferencer, 14 March 1913.

[70]MAR, HAL, 318.01/62, "Agreement on Scandinavian Third Class Passenger Business."

[71]Stortingsforhandlinger, Ot. prp. og med., 1912, 2b, "Betænkning ang. Spørsmaalet om statsbidrag til A/S 'Den norske Amerikalinje,'" 27; and Stortingsforhandlinger, Ot. prp. No. 86 (1912), 14.

1913 were picked up by the Norwegian press or presented to the Norwegian parliament, again demonstrating a limited understanding of the structure of shipping conferences by Norwegians.

Conclusion

The early twentieth century was marked by oligopolistic market structures and high barriers of entry for newcomers in the transatlantic passenger business which resulted in relatively few players dominating the business. These conditions also limited the number of new companies despite a record number of transatlantic passengers. By addressing how the Norwegian-American Line was created, this essay has not only uncovered additional barriers to new services but also how the dominant market players compromised to allow the entry of new companies when it served their interests.

The creation of a Norwegian shipping line to America was subject to various incentives, positions, strategies and interests of state and private actors in Norway as well as in Denmark and Sweden. There was a division between those who supported a Norwegian national line and those who advocated a service involving collaboration among the three Scandinavian countries. Indeed, the issue of a Norwegian line even led to disagreements among various Norwegian actors, a point clearly illustrated by the existence of two competing alternatives. Part of the debate over which scheme would best serve national interests was due to the limited experience Norwegians had with capital-intensive companies and oligopolistic market structures.

At the same time, the analysis has illustrated how the establishment of a transatlantic passenger line was subject to inter-state relations and contemporary national policies. Indeed, incentives and strategies for a Norwegian transatlantic line were shaped in part by the ill feelings between Norway and Sweden after the recent dissolution of their union. The debate was also embedded in state policies about nation-building, the best way to combat Norwegian outmigration and how to promote re-migration from America.

As for the dominant market players, the discussion has shown how their market position and leverage were not absolute in relation to newcomers in the transatlantic passenger business, especially if a national government was involved. Indeed, in 1908 the Atlantic Conference entered into an agreement with the futile Scandinavian alternative in part because it had the support of the Norwegian government and in part because DFDS, with which it had already collaborated, was involved. Five years later, it again made concessions to the Norwegian-American Line. Cunard, which had a particular interest in the Scandinavian emigrant market, admitted that this was done because it was better to make some concessions than to risk possible retaliation in the pending Norwegian emigration legislation. Still, the dominant market players in both instances clearly showed their negotiating power by placing strict limitations on the Norwegian-American Line, a move which also affected Norwegian state policies, especially when it came to the question of which Norwegian ports the new company could use.

After the Boom: The Political Economy of Shipping in Norway in the Interwar Period

Eivind Merok

The outbreak of hostilities in August 1914 marked the beginning of a spectacular boom-and-bust period for international shipping. Extraordinary levels of demand, coupled with shortages of shipping tonnage, caused freight rates to increase eleven-fold. Moreover, vessel prices rose markedly as investors sought to reap the benefits of the boom.[1] Controlling the world's fifth largest fleet, Norwegian shipowners earned windfall profits. The downturn, however, was equally sharp. By June 1920, freight rates had halved from their wartime peak, and vessel prices had fallen dramatically. Having rushed to replace lost vessels at high prices during the postwar boom, shipowners found that their fortunes had altered dramatically. By June 1921, around 500 Norwegian vessels, representing around 1,314,000 deadweight tons (dwt), were laid up, and these high rates of unemployment became a consistent feature of the interwar period.[2]

The boom and bust in the shipping sector posed extreme challenges for Norwegian policymakers who, in attempting to control the investors in shipping shares, introduced wide-ranging legislation and increased the tax rate for shipping companies considerably. These efforts, however, were insufficient, as expanding shipping earnings drove a speculative frenzy among speculators and the general public. Cleaning up after this boom, so to speak, proved to be a challenge. Losses in shipping permeated the financial sector, and traditional shipping banks found that the value of collateral, such as shipping shares and vessels, had been decimated. As a result, almost all the leading shipping banks were either forced to cease operations or suspend lending.[3] The

[1]The figures underlying this analysis are from Gelina Harlaftis, *A History of Greek-Owned Shipping: The Making of an International Tramp Fleet, 1830 to the Present Day* (London, 1996), appendix table 6.3.

[2]Stig Tenold, "Crisis? What Crisis? The Expansion of Norwegian Shipping in the Interwar Period," in Lars U. Scholl and David M. Williams (eds.), *Crisis and Transition: Responses to Economic Turmoil in the North Sea Region, 1790-1940* (Bremerhaven, 2008), 117-134.

[3]Sverre Knutsen, "Staten og kapitalen i det 20. århundre: regulering, kriser og endring i det norske finanssystemet, 1900-2005" (Unpublished PhD thesis,

shortfall in export earnings from shipping and other sectors also aggravated the current account deficit and diminished the value of the Norwegian currency. Attempting to bring the *krone* back to its prewar parity, the Norwegian Central Bank [Norges Bank] introduced deflationary policies from the mid-1920s that greatly aggravated the economic difficulties, resulting in low aggregate growth throughout the decade.[4]

It is surprising, to say the least, that the boom during World War I, and the subsequent financial crisis in the 1920s, would set the stage for a large-scale expansion and technological modernization of the Norwegian merchant fleet. From 1923 to 1938, the Norwegian fleet experienced the most rapid growth (4.5 percent per annum) among the world's leading shipping nations. As a result, the Norwegian share of world tonnage doubled. The most dramatic change, however, was the shift toward a more capital-intensive investment strategy, as Norwegian shipowners invested more heavily in modern, motor-driven vessels from the late 1920s than did any other shipping nation.[5]

To account for this trend, scholars have focused on Norwegian entry into the tanker business because this segment was central to the broader technological change.[6] The most prevalent explanation in the literature focuses on the alliance between Oslo-based shipowning companies and Swedish shipyards. Since Swedish yards had excess capacity and ample financial resources, they could offer financing to shipowners who lacked access to more traditional sources of finance.[7] While the generous financial arrangements offered by foreign shipyards do help to explain the lure of entering the tanker industry, it

---

University of Oslo, 2007); Knutsen, "From Expansion to Panic and Crash: The Norwegian Banking System and Its Customers, 1913-1924," *Scandinavian Economic History Review*, XXXIX, No. 3 (1991), 41-71; and Helge W. Nordvik, "Bankkrise, bankstruktur og bankpolitikk i Norge i mellom-krigstiden," *Historisk tidsskrift* (Norway), LXXI, No. 2 (1992), 170-192.

[4]Fritz Hodne and Ola Honningdal Grytten, *Norsk økonomi i det tyvende århundre* (Bergen, 2002).

[5]Tenold, "Crisis? What Crisis?"

[6]Jørgen Gunnerud, "Tankskipseventyret i Oslo, 1925-1939," *Sjøfartshistorisk årbok 1991* (Bergen, 1992), 35-170; Knut Utstein Kloster, *Perler på en snor: Eventyret om norsk tankfart* (Oslo, 1953); and Leif Nørgård, *Tankfartens etablerings- og introduksjonsperiode i norsk skipsfart, 1912-1913 og 1927-1930* (Bergen, 1961).

[7]Håkon With Andersen, "Laggards as Leaders: Some Reflections on Technological Diffusion in Norwegian Shipping, 1870-1940," in Kristine Bruland (ed.), *Technology Transfer and Scandinavian Industrialisation* (Oxford, 1991); and Stig Tenold, "Norway's Interwar Tanker Expansion - A Reappraisal," *Scandinavian Economic History Review*, LV, No. 3 (2007), 244-261.

ignores the more overarching shift in demand for technology among Norwegian shipowners. Accounting for the demand for these new technological solutions cannot rely solely on generous business arrangements because it is reasonable to expect that similar offers were made, but not taken up, to shipowners in other countries. Moreover, it is cogent to ask how shipowners in Norway managed to sustain a high level of investment throughout the interwar period despite experiencing a draconian domestic financial crisis.

To begin addressing these challenges, this essay investigates the consequences of World War I on the business environment for Norwegian shipping companies. While most authors recognize that the First World War was a watershed for Norwegian shipping, few have attempted to gauge the impact of shifts in both the political and economic environment on the period that followed.[8] Indeed, the only account of government policies towards the shipping industry during the war is generally dismissed as being strongly biased.[9] Other studies that have dealt with the impact of government policies aimed specifically at shipping have generally concluded that their impact was limited.[10] But I will argue that the choices made by Norwegian policymakers during World War I and its immediate aftermath had a decisive impact on developments in the interwar period. Between 1916 and 1920, the Norwegian government introduced a complete reform of the legal bases for the shipping industry, and this new regime remained virtually unaltered during the interwar years.

This essay examines the emergence of a new policy regime for shipping in Norway during and after WWI, and seeks to clarify the consequences of this policy regime. The article is organized as follows. In the first part, I will identify significant changes in the regulatory framework affecting the industry that were introduced during World War I. Lawmakers enacted both a new law on incorporation and a new tax code within a brief period, but these laws were significantly altered by little-known processes after the conflict. A

---

[8]The classic studies are still Wilhelm Keilhau, *Norge og verdenskrigen* (Oslo, 1927); and Johan Schreiner, *Norsk Skipsfart under krig og høykonjunktur, 1914-1920* (Oslo, 1963). The most up-to-date study of the shipping industry during World War I is found in Morten Hammerborg, *Skipsfartsbyen: Haugesunds skipsfartshistorie, 1850-2000* (Bergen, 2003).

[9]John O. Egeland, *Kongeveien: Norsk skipsfart fra århundreskiftet til den annen verdenskrig* (Oslo, 1973). For modern assessments of Egeland's book, see Helge W. Nordvik, "Norwegian Maritime Historical Research during the Past Twenty Years: A Critical Survey," *Sjøfartshistorisk årbok 1990* (Bergen, 1991), 241-278; and Arild Marøy Hansen and Atle Thowsen, *Sjøfartshistorie Som Etterkrigshistorisk Forskningsfelt, Vol. 3: Etterkrigshistorisk Register* (Bergen, 1991).

[10]See, in particular, Atle Thowsen, *Krise og krisetiltak i norsk tankskipsfart, 1929-1936* (Bergen, 1979); and Thowsen, *Vekst og strukturendringer i krisetider, 1914-1939* (Bergen, 1983).

key component of these changes was the introduction of a temporary law exempting capital income from taxation. In the second part, I will discuss the impact of these laws for both the financial and shipping industries. The essay concludes with a discussion of the implications of the new economic and political regime for investment strategies by Norwegian shipping companies in the interwar period.

I

Few if any neutral states were as affected by the wartime boom as Norway.[11] Strong demand for Norwegian exports and shipping services created a veritable bonanza in the domestic economy, fuelling speculation among all classes of the population. The shipping sector played a pivotal role in this. Gross freight income expanded seven-fold compared to the prewar years and increased its share of total export earnings to around fifty percent.[12] The promise of windfall profits in shipping also fuelled the speculative boom in the stock market. According to the business journal *Farmand*, "the rather undeserved gold flow that has washed ashore in our country has brought a feverish, breathless haste to become rich."[13] Speculators in shipping stocks were able to earn fortunes literally overnight due to the spiralling share prices, and shipping companies raised 1.4 billion *kroner* to fund new investments during the war.[14]

The wartime boom therefore brought both the necessity and the opportunity for legal reform. The 1915 elections returned a more radical parliament, with increased representation for the Labour Party and a clear majority for the ruling Venstre (Liberal) Party. While Venstre had formidable shipowners in its ranks, the party also catered to a wide constituency with left-leaning representatives comprising a key faction. After the election, Venstre could afford to ignore protests from special interests as it dealt with wartime issues.[15]

---

[11]Monica Værholm and Lars Fredrik Øksendal, "Letting the Anchor Go: Monetary Policy in Neutral Norway during World War I," *Norges Bank Working Paper 2010/28* (Oslo, 2010).

[12]Calculations on the basis of Statistisk Sentralbyrå (SSB), *Økonomisk Utsyn, 1900-1950* (Oslo, 1955).

[13]*Farmand* (Oslo), 18 November 1916, quoted in Værholm and Øksendal, "Letting the Anchor Go," 9.

[14]While share values were obviously affected by inflation, it serves as some comparison to note that the sum of all share issues in the interwar period (1919-1939) was 621 million *kroner*. SSB, *Historisk Statistikk 1968* (Oslo, 1968), table 264.

[15]Leiv Mjeldheim, *Den gylne mellomvegen: Tema frå Venstres historie, 1905-1940* (Bergen, 2006).

A more worrying change from shipowners' perspective was a shift in the public perception of the industry. Soaring freight rates and rising import prices caused widespread concern over the nation's supplies. When shipping companies reported spectacular profits, they quickly became the leading scapegoat for the country's woes. In the opening session of the *Storting* in 1915, the Labour Party's Magnus Nilsen voiced a radical critique, arguing that "shipowners are increasing freights to heights never before witnessed... [and] using the crisis to lay burdens on the working people. Their actions are poised to bring the entire economy down."[16] While such remarks might be expected from Labour, similar comments came from Jens Bratlie of the Conservative [Høire] Party, who blamed government for not controlling the situation: "with a merchant fleet many times larger than what is needed to supply our nation, such problems could easily have been avoided."[17]

The response was not long in coming. The government formed by Venstre used its parliamentary majority to pass wide-ranging wartime regulations in its first months in office, increasing general corporation taxes as well as special wartime rates. Headed by prominent shipowner Gunnar Knudsen, the government introduced a war-profits tax on 18 August 1915, increasing the general tax level for companies significantly. Despite significant opposition from individual shipowners, parliament passed the tonnage tax with limited debate and nearly universal support across party lines, not only because the extraordinary demands on the state during the war necessitated new methods of raising revenue but also due to the popular belief that increasing freight rates were responsible for the general price increases. In the end, the new law led to significant increases in the tax bills for shipowners, who argued that they were being treated unfairly while other industries were left untouched.[18]

The speculative boom in shipping stocks, as well as public reports of misconduct, provided ample reasons for parliament to provide a new legal regime for incorporated shipowning companies. Presenting the case to the *Storting,* the Minister of Justice, Lars K. Abrahamsen, himself a former sailor and shipowner, argued that the present situation demanded immediate action because "elevated freight rates had led to a strong, and in the Justice Department's opinion, unhealthy speculation in shipping shares."[19] Even the Ship-

---

[16]Magnus Nilsen, "Arbeiderpartiet," in *Stortingstidende, forhandlingene* (Oslo, 1915), 42. This translation, and all others unless noted, are mine.

[17]Jens Bratlie, "Høire," in *ibid.*, 45.

[18]The introduction of extraordinary wartime taxes on shipping is covered extensively in Egeland, *Kongeveien;* Keilhau, *Norge og verdenskrigen*; and Schreiner, *Norsk skipsfart under krig og høykonjunktur*.

[19]*Stortingstidende* 1916, Ot. prp. nr. 5, 20.

owners' Association found reason to support the move. The Association's Kristiania branch expressed its concern over "the speculative boom" in the industry in a letter to parliament in 1916, arguing that a new law was needed to put in place minimum requirements for investors.[20]

While proper safeguards for outside investors were clearly needed, Knudsen went further. In these and several other comments, he argued that parliament had an obligation to regulate the industry to prevent it from making unsound speculative investments. The only viable long-term strategy for shipping companies, in Knudsen's mind, was to invest when vessel prices were low, operate with limited leveraging and deliver steady profits to owners through the strict control of costs.[21] This view of proper shipping strategy was in stark contrast to the asset speculation that had been occurring since 1914. By August 1916, the stock indices for shipping companies had quadrupled over prewar levels, and the volume of share issues had increased to 400 million *kroner* compared to thirty million *kroner* in 1914.[22]

The passage of a new incorporation act, coupled with a revision to the general tax code, clearly reflected the dual ambitions of curbing speculation and closing existing loopholes in the tax regime. The legislative process raised issues that had previously received little attention in the public debate. In hammering out the final details of the tax laws, lawmakers found it extremely difficult to regulate "speculative" companies while also safeguarding sound business ventures. This problem was particularly acute when it came to regulating the way companies would calculate the depreciation of real capital.

Although the existing tax code did contain some rules to regulate this, these led to confusion among local tax officials by singling out speculative companies or transactions as targets for taxation. According to the 1911 law, companies founded to acquire vessels "to later be sold at an advance" were obligated to pay taxes on their gains. The law did not, however, offer any clarification about how to separate companies established "primarily for speculative purposes" from those that enjoyed profits due to increases in asset prices.[23] Moreover, to ensure that single-ship companies did not apply exces-

---

[20]*Ibid.*, 23.

[21]For a general impression of Knudsen's views, see Gunnar Knudsen, *Erindringer, 1905-1925* (Porsgrunn, 1998).

[22]The figures for share issues are in current *kroner* and are taken from SSB, *Historisk Statistikk 1968*, table 264. Similarly, the share index is not deflated and is taken from Keilhau, *Norge og verdenskrigen*, tabeller til kapittel XIII, table 2.

[23]The interpretation here is based on the evidence given by four tax lawyers to the Shipowners' Association, reprinted in *Norges Rederforbunds Cirkulære, 1916-1917*,

sive rates of depreciation, the law explicitly stated that the companies would be taxed if the sale value or insurance premium on a vessel exceeded its book value. Again, the intent of the law was clearly to hinder aggressive amortizations, and leading lawyers consulted by the Shipowners' Association concluded that only income derived from an "unwarranted" amortization would be taxable.[24] The boom in vessel prices increased the importance of these considerations, and the *Storting* sought to clarify the matter. The revised tax stated explicitly that "any profit derived from sales of vessels would be taxable under the established tax law," removing any reference to speculative companies. It then reaffirmed this by clarifying that the gains from the sale of vessels, building contracts, shares or parts in a *partsrederi* should be taxed as income.[25]

Within a year, then, parliament had managed to end much of the confusion surrounding the registration and taxation of shipowning companies. Responding to public outcries, the *Storting* seems to have successfully addressed most of the concerns about speculative practices in the shipping industry, as well as closing existing loopholes in the tax law. Requiring that shipping companies be responsible for the entire tax bill, under a more stringent national code, in effect removed many of the opportunities for tax evasion.

These legislative achievements came under pressure in the later stages of the war. The primary cause was a shift in the role of shipping in the foreign economy. Up until 1917, freight income had shored up the Norwegian external balance, and the shipping industry had contributed greatly to increasing the government's tax revenues. After massive losses of vessels, however, the impact of the shipping sector on the domestic economy shifted, as the contribution from freight earnings fell and the industry started to draw upon its currency holdings. The underlying investment cycle driving this pattern is clearly present in the tonnage statistics. Figure 1 represents the aggregate growth in the fleet expressed as percentage of the total fleet caused by reductions (sales abroad and losses) and additions (newbuildings in Norway and acquisitions from abroad). As is evident from the figure, wartime losses, combined with a decline in new additions, resulted in a steep aggregate decline in tonnage in 1917 and 1918. The rebound thereafter is equally apparent, as new additions in 1919 and 1920 of around 230,000 and 499,000 gross tons represented about eleven and twenty percent of the total fleet in the respective years.

---

cirkulære 4, "Fra Vælferdsutvalget til Rederforbundets Medlemmer (Kristiania, 22/06-1916)."

[24]*Ibid.*

[25]The law was passed in March 1916 and is presented in Ot. Prp. Nr. 10 (1916).

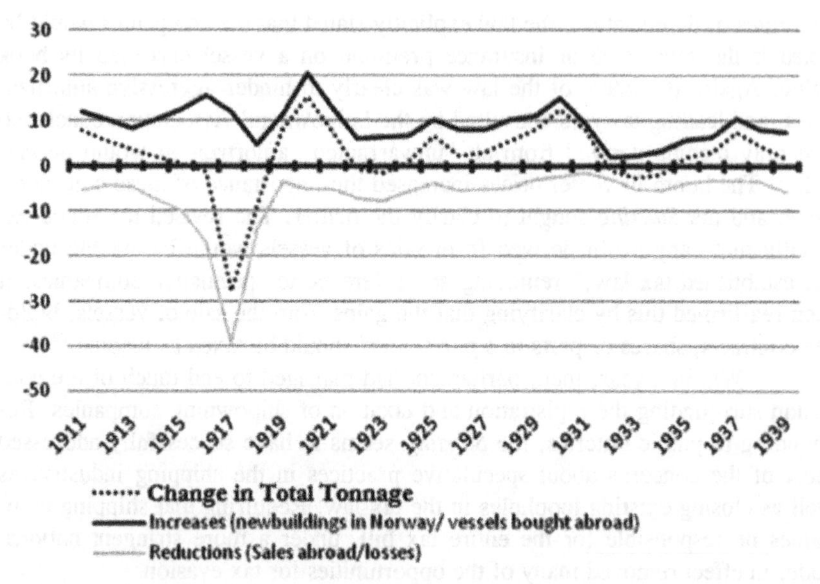

Figure 1: Gross Tonnage: Growth, Increases and Reductions, 1911-1939 (percent of total tonnage)

Sources: Statistisk Sentralbyrå (SSB), *Statistisk Årbok 1925* (Oslo, 1926), table 81; SSB, *Statistisk Årbok 1929* (Oslo, 1930), table 79; SSB, *Statistisk Årbok 1931* (Oslo, 1932), table 83; and SSB, *Statistisk Årbok 1940* (Oslo, 1940), table 116.

In order to fund new investments, shipping companies drew on balances in Norwegian and foreign banks. The shipping sector's drain on financial resources posed extreme challenges for the Norwegian financial sector and the stability of the exchange rate. When seeking to address this challenge, the government found that it had few opportunities for doing so as shipping companies had placed a sizable share of their currency earnings abroad. When attempting to identify the cause of this situation, a currency committee charged with investigating the crisis made some startling observations about the Norwegian currency market. As the committee collected information from various sources, it was revealed that most of the foreign exchange earnings acquired by Norwegians were controlled by fewer than forty companies, with shipping companies predominating. Another worrisome finding was that a small fraction of these earnings was being placed in the Norwegian market. According to evidence gathered by the committee, only thirty percent of Norwegian currency holdings were placed in Norwegian banks (including the Central Bank), an extremely low proportion compared to the corresponding figure of seventy-five percent for Swedish banks.[26]

While the reliance on foreign banks had probably been a long-standing feature in the shipping sector, this had been accentuated as a result of currency risks introduced during the war. With the suspension of gold convertibility in August 1914, the Central Bank had introduced a *de facto* floating currency regime; after a brief depreciation, the *krone* gained value throughout 1915 against all major currencies. In 1916, shipowners were complaining about the currency situation to the Shipowners' Association, detailing the difficulties of entering into chartering contracts when "the profitability of these contracts will change in the next day as a result of the whims of the currency markets."[27]

The build-up of foreign reserves was also a response to the increased tax rates. As we have seen, the tax rates were increased considerably during 1916. Since no mechanism existed to ensure that foreign assets would be taxable, there were considerable tax incentives to keep funds abroad. The committee's first advice to the government therefore was to amend the law to force shipowners to declare such holdings on their tax returns. Another route attempted to attract these holdings was to place restrictions on the currency market by introducing a centralized currency exchange controlled by leading Norwegian banks. When debating the introduction of such measures, Thomas Fearnley, Jr., himself a large shipowner, stated bluntly "that there are no powers that could prevent me from presenting a sterling freight check to my British banker in London rather than presenting it to a bank in Norway, and the idea of regulating our foreign exchange in such matters is not only futile, it is counterproductive."[28]

Debating the measures to reverse the situation, the members of the currency committee became aware of a rule that allowed shipowners to avoid taxation of capital income earned during the war if the profits were reinvested in a new vessel within a year.[29] This rule had been introduced after lobbying

---

[26]RA, S-4063-D-L0165-003, mappe, Valuta-Valutarådet-Avgjort av Kongen, "Innstilling fra Valutarådets Arbeidsutvalg," 4 June 1920. Although the report was published in June 1920, it was presented to the Currency Committee for its meeting on 12-13 March 1920.

[27]*Norges Rederforbunds Beretning, 1916-1917*, "Sak 740: Valutakursenes svingninger." See also *Norges Rederforbund Cirkulærer 1917*," cirkulære 72: Valutasituasjonen," August 1917.

[28]RA, S-4063-D-L0166-0002, mappe, Valuta-Valutarådet, Møtereferater og korrespondanse med Wilhelm Keilhau, 1920-1921, "Referat fra møte," n.d. (probably May-June 1920).

[29]*Ibid.*, S-31600-EL0042-0003, mappe, Valutarådet I, 1920-1924, "Stenografisk referat fra valutarådets møte," 12 March 1920.

from the Shipowners' Association as an extraordinary measure to alleviate the challenges posed by the growing vessel losses in the spring of 1917.[30] Viewed as temporary, the law initially established stringent criteria for the exemption. It applied solely to insurance profits and stipulated that a rebate could only be claimed by writing down what was considered to be the excessive price paid for a newly acquired vessel. The Shipowners' Association later lobbied successfully for the extension of this rule to all classes of capital income. To complement the law, changes were made in the tax code to allow shipowners to make extraordinary write-downs of vessel values when market conditions dictated.[31]

The implications of the new law were obvious in the postwar period. Reports received by the currency committee from Bergen Kreditbank - a leading shipping bank - claimed that shipowners were rushing to acquire new vessels in order to exempt wartime profits from taxation.[32] Debating the issue in a meeting in March 1920, representatives from banks and industry expressed great surprise upon learning the full extent of the tax rebate given to shipowners. The industrialist Johan Throne Holst pointed to the unfairness of such rules applying only to shipping and stated that it was astounding that the industry was given the right to conduct extraordinary write-downs on assets, especially since the general tax laws prohibited such actions.[33] Representatives from banks further urged the committee to remove the rebate. Citing several examples of high-profile shipowners, the bankers argued that they were contracting new vessels primarily to avoid taxes on wartime profits.[34]

The majority of the committee pressed strongly for recommending that the tax rebate be removed immediately. Summing up the argument, the legal expert Arnold Ræstad argued that the evidence presented to the committee overwhelmingly suggested that the rebate had only led to the excessive contracting of vessels and was therefore endangering the stability of the entire financial system. As such, there could be no grounds for retaining the law.[35]

---

[30]Norges Rederforbund to Ministry of Trade, 10 May 1918, reprinted in *Norges Rederforbund Beretninger, 1917-1918*, 26-28 (author's translation).

[31]*Norges Rederforbunds Beretning, 1918-1919*, "Sak nr. 1104 Skattefritagelse på Assurancegevinst."

[32]RA, S-4064-D-L0166-001, mappe, Valutarådet Fds. Finanskontor, 1920, Bergen Kreditbank to Chairman of the Currency Committee, 24 January 1920.

[33]*Ibid.*, "Stenografisk referat fra valutarådets møte."

[34]*Ibid.*, 20.

[35]*Ibid.*, 24.

The Ministry of Finance, however, did not agree. After consulting with the Ministry, the committee discovered that such a suggestion would not be accepted. Following a joint meeting among Prime Minister Knudsen, the currency committee and the Shipowners' Association, it became clear that any recommendation to remove the tax rebate was off the table.[36] Instead, the currency committee proposed that the government amend the law to make all capital income exempt from taxation if the assets were placed in the Norwegian credit market and not used for ordering vessels before 1924.[37] By delaying the acquisition boom, the committee hoped that the infusion of financial assets held by the shipowning community could stabilize the currency.[38]

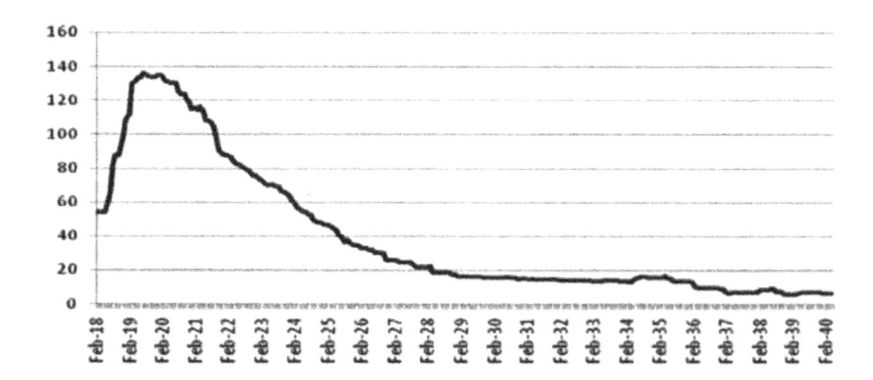

Figure 2: Tax Deposits from Norwegian Shipowners in Norwegian Banks, 1918-1940 (million *kroner*)

Notes: The figures are based on the reports made by shipowning companies to the Ministry of Finance in order to qualify for a tax exemption. Tax deposits refer to the sums placed in certified accounts in Norwegian banks to cover the taxes that would be owed if the company failed to meet the criteria established under the law.

Source: Norway, Riksarkivet (RA), S-S-2393-E-L0055-0001, "Beskatning ved tap av skip og ved salg til utlandet 1917-"

---

[36]*Ibid.*, RA-S-4063-D-L0166-0002, Valuta, Valutarådet/Mappe, Møtereferater og korrespondanse med Wilhelm Keilhau, 1920-1921, brev til K.G. Bomhoff, n.d. (probably March 1920).

[37]*Norges Rederforbund Cirkulære 1921*, cirkulære 8, "Forandringer i Depositionsloven," 2 August 1921.

[38]RA, S-3160-EL0042-0003, mappe, Valutarådet II, 1920 "Utskrift av protokoll ført i valutarådets møter den 12. og 13. mars 1920."

Any hope that these measures would counteract the drawing down of assets in Norwegian banks proved futile. Under the original act, shipping companies were obliged to make a deposit that would cover any tax liability that would be incurred if it failed to invest in a new vessel. The sums involved, typically forty to fifty percent of the insurance profits, were overwhelmingly placed in Norwegian banks, even prior to the passage of the law mandating this practice in June 1920. Accounts of these deposits kept by the Ministry of Finance reveal that the deposits made by shipowners climbed rapidly between February 1918 and May 1919, but then began to decline. As figure 2 shows, the deposits reached their apex of 133 million *kroner* in May 1919, but then fell continually until late 1929, when they had stabilized at around eighteen million *kroner*.

The consequences of the failure to stem the import of new vessels soon became apparent. The continued slide in the external value of the *krone* during the summer of 1920 meant that the situation was becoming critical for shipowners with contracts in Britain. A report by the Shipowners' Association suggested that among its members, eighty-five companies had entered into contracts for which the outstanding obligation amounted to £21.8 million. Out of this, the companies reckoned that they could cover about £7.6 million from their currency holdings in Britain, while about £14.8 million had to be met either by assets held in Norway or future earnings. The sterling liabilities for 1920 alone were estimated in excess of five million pounds, and £4.7 million more was due in 1921.[39] The falling value of the *krone* further induced shipowners to hoard foreign exchange. In January 1920, Bergen Kreditbank reported that shipowners had grown uneasy about the weakening of the currency and were massively buying sterling to cover future liabilities on vessels. It urged the Central Bank to intervene to stabilize the situation.[40]

Commenting on the matter, *Farmand* reported that government action was now imperative because the debt situation threatened to bring down the industry.[41] Facing an increasingly desperate situation, the government finally intervened. After negotiations between the Shipowners' Association, the leading commercial banks and the Ministry of Finance, it was agreed that the government would act as the borrower for a currency loan placed by a bank consortium abroad. Under the arrangement, the government would distribute the foreign exchange raised by the loan to Norwegian commercial banks which would offer it exclusively to shipowning companies. In return, the banks and

---

[39]*Ibid.*, S-4063-L0166-0001-Valuta, Valutarådet Fds. finanskontor, 1920, Rederforbundet to Finansdepartementet om behovet for valuta, 17 July 1920.

[40]*Ibid.*, Bergen Bank to Norges Bank, 24 January 1920.

[41]*Farmand* (Oslo), 9 October 1920.

their shipping company clients agreed to place significant sums in a public loan to be issued in the Norwegian market.[42]

The final terms were controversial and became known as the most expensive loan ever raised by the Norwegian government, primarily due to the fact that it was payable in dollars and carried a high nominal interest of eight percent.[43] This interpretation is misleading, however, because the cost of the loan was paid by the commercial banks and their clients. The shipping companies were already exposed to currency risks through their contracts with the shipyards, and the alternative to the loan was expensive cancellations. As for the tax rebate on capital income in the shipping sector - believed to be the key factor driving the crisis - no action was taken. Instead, the legislation was extended through a series of temporary laws throughout the interwar period.

A final revision, brought about through the initiative of Gunnar Knudsen after he had resigned from government, changed the law so that there were no limitations on the extent of asset depreciations that could be written off and extended the tax rebate to the acquisition of second-hand tonnage in Norway. Reviewing the final outcome, the Shipowners' Association urged all members to report their claims to the Ministry of Finance because companies which had claimed tax rebates under previous schemes were eligible for the new and improved rebate. According to its legal advisor, Eivind Eckbo, capital gains would now be completely exempt from taxation if used for the acquisition of new vessels rather than being limited to write-downs on "excessively priced" ships. Eckbo also reported that he had received confirmation that there would be "no limitations that prevented shipowners from writing down the value of the vessel to, for instance, 1 *Krone*."[44]

The final outcome of the process was thus a complete reversal of the principles that had guided the policy changes incorporated in the law passed in 1916. The principle of that law - and indeed one of its chief goals - was to reign in speculative asset play in the industry. From 1917, however, virtually all gains from such practices were exempted from taxation if the proceeds were re-invested in vessels. While passed as a temporary taxation law, the rules were extended through new temporary bills throughout the interwar period. The only remaining demand on shipowners seeking to utilize the rebate was a commitment to re-invest in shipping. Furthermore, the ability to make

---

[42]RA, S-4063-D7-L0172-003, mappe, Valuta, Bankkonsortiets Valutalån I, 1922-1926, v-2-6, Gjenpart av Finansdepartements skrivelse to Andresen Bank A/S, 4 September 1920.

[43]See, for instance the discussion in Hermod Skånland, *Det norske kredittmarked siden 1900* (Oslo, 1967).

[44]*Norges Rederforbunds Cirkulære 1921*, cirkulære 8, "Forandringer i Depositionsloven," 2 August 1921.

extraordinary write-downs on capital became a permanent feature from 1921, and the limitations on such depreciations were removed.[45]

The shipping crisis that ensued made the full implications of these decisions difficult to identify, both for contemporary observers and later historians. By prioritizing the need to replenish the merchant fleet, the government led by Gunnar Knudsen set the course for the events that would unfold during the 1920s.

II

In its annual report for 1921-1922, the Shipowners' Association noted that the industry was facing the most dramatic depression yet experienced.[46] As freight rates plunged, it became clear that the re-investment boom of 1919 and 1920 could not have been timed less fortuitously. By the time the new vessels entered the market, freight rates had collapsed. The much-quoted standard freight rate for coal from Wales to Alexandria fell from around forty-nine shillings in 1919 and 1920 to about sixteen shillings in 1921.[47] The downward movement of freight rates led to a collapse in vessel prices: the average price for a 7500-ton cargo vessel fell from £180,000 during the war to about £60,000 in 1921.[48]

The financial implications of the fall in vessel prices for shipowning companies, investors and banks were staggering. While it is not possible at present to gauge the full impact of these write-downs, the information from publicly listed companies gives some indication of the magnitude of the losses. Shipping stocks were reduced to roughly one-fifth of their peak levels between May 1918 and April 1921.[49] Another indication was the write-downs of capital made by listed shipping companies. Between 1919 and 1930, listed shipping

[45]The details of these laws, and the implications for the shipping industry, were spelled out by the legal advisor to the Shipping Association in *Norges Rederforbund Beretninger, 1921-1922*, Vælferdsavdeling, "Depositionslovene av 1921."

[46]*Ibid.*, 6-7.

[47]The Wales-Alexandria freight rate was a much used reference point by shipowners communicating with the Shipowners' Association. The freight rate data was collected by Bergen Børs and later republished in SSB, *Statistisk Årbok 1928* (Oslo, 1929), table 85.

[48]Harlaftis, *History of Greek-Owned Shipping*, appendix 6.3. The figures in the text refer to averages for the years 1921-1925 and 1929-1933.

[49]Estimation based on the stock indices published in Jan Tore Klovland, "Historical Stock Price Indices in Norway," in Eitrheim, Klovland and Qvigstad (eds.), *Historical Monetary Statistics for Norway*. The peak value of the shipping index occurred in May 1918 (491), and the index had a value of 109.4 in April 1921.

companies wrote down their capital by about 250 million *kroner*, a figure representing about twenty-five percent of the paid-in capital in 1919.[50]

The losses in the stock market naturally reduced the availability of external capital for the industry. While shipping companies had raised enough capital to fund their entire investments during the war, the stock market became significantly less important from 1921.[51] As is evident from figure 3, the amount raised in real terms fell significantly from 1920 and remained at far lower levels for the entire interwar period. In nominal terms, the write-downs conducted by existing shipping companies listed on Norwegian stock exchanges far exceeded the value of new capital raised throughout the 1920s. As a result, the contribution from the stock market was negative in terms of the capital invested in shipping from 1921 to 1929.[52]

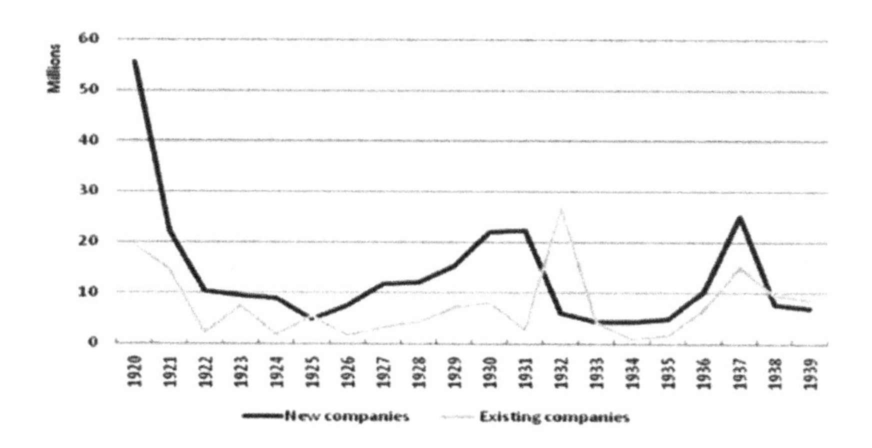

Figure 3: Capital Raised by Shipping Companies through New Issues, 1920-1939 (constant 1938 prices)

Note: The deflator used is taken from SSB, *Statistisk-økonomisk oversikt over året 1939* (Oslo, 1939) in order to preserve comparability with the official statistics published for the period

Source: SSB, *Statistisk årbok* (Oslo, various years).

---

[50]SSB, *Statistisk Årbok* (Oslo, various years), tabeller over Norske aktieselskap anmeldt til Handelsregistrene.

[51]Skånland, *Det norske kredittmarked*.

[52]SSB, *Statistisk årbok* (Oslo, various years), tabeller over Norske aktieselskap anmeldt til Handelsregistrene.

Because commercial banks had offered loans on the basis of shares as collateral, the fall in share prices directly affected the banking industry as well. The banking crisis of the 1920s has been widely discussed in the literature, often in connection with the policies to return the *krone* to gold parity.[53] While bank failures were frequent, the implications for the liquidity of the financial system were mitigated somewhat by support from the Central Bank and the government. In total, however, the banking sector reduced its loans to the public from 5575 million to 3524 million *kroner* from the end of 1920 to 1926. The single most important reason for this reduction in lending was write-downs on bad loans. These losses – a staggering 1235 million Norwegian *kroner* – were covered mainly by the banks' own funds through write-downs on stock capital and earnings.[54]

The total reduction in capital in the commercial banking sector naturally affected the availability of funds for the shipping industry. While there are no reliable figures on lending to the shipping sector prior to the mid-1920s, estimates for the period thereafter indicate a significant shift in the sources of loan capital for the industry. Samples published by Hermod Skånland (see figure 4) indicate that the domestic commercial banks reduced their lending significantly from 1927. In real terms, the reduction meant that the total funds available were halved, while this was offset somewhat by increased borrowing abroad. The implication was clear: during the 1930s, the net contribution to the shipping industry from the commercial banking sector was negative.

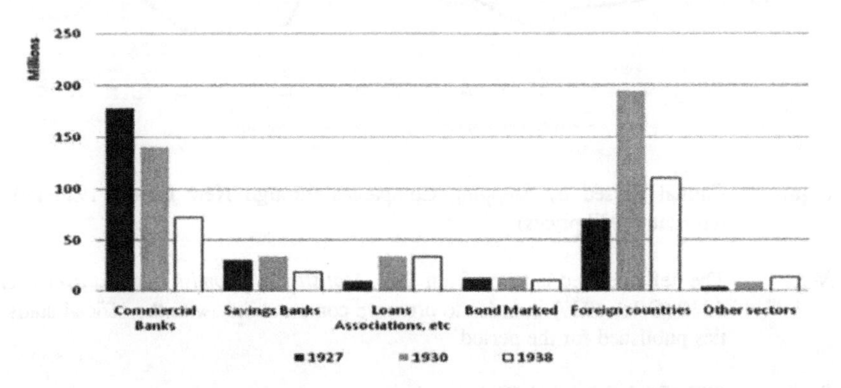

Figure 4: Loans to the Shipping Industry, 1927-1938 (constant 1938 prices)

Note: See figure 3.

Source: Hermod Skånland, *Det norske kredittmarked siden 1900* (Oslo, 1967), 89.

---

[53]For a review of the literature, see Knutsen, "Staten og kapitalen."

[54]Skånland, *Det Norske Kredittmarked*, 156.

Largely as a result of the postwar crisis, both the stock market and the banking sector ceased to be important sources of external finance for the shipping industry. Nonetheless, the shipping industry managed to sustain remarkably high levels of investment throughout the interwar period, as estimates of real investment in five-year periods from 1920 documents indicate (see figure 5). Not only did the shipping community manage to fund considerable levels of investment during the worst of the crisis from 1920 to 1925, but the investment rates rose sharply thereafter.

One critical explanation for the high investment levels maintained involved the tax rebates offered to shipping companies on capital income earned during the war. Official statistics recorded that 889 vessels were lost during the war, representing close to 1.3 million gross tons.[55] While the total size of the gains from these assets are impossible to ascertain because shipowners kept a large part of the proceeds in foreign banks to avoid taxes, we can identify the sums involved for companies that chose to register their capital income under the tax regime. This includes 335 vessels of close to one million dwt (see table 1). These vessels alone represented a book value of around 167 million *kroner*, while the total wartime insurance profits reported under the arrangement amounted to around 350 million *kroner*.

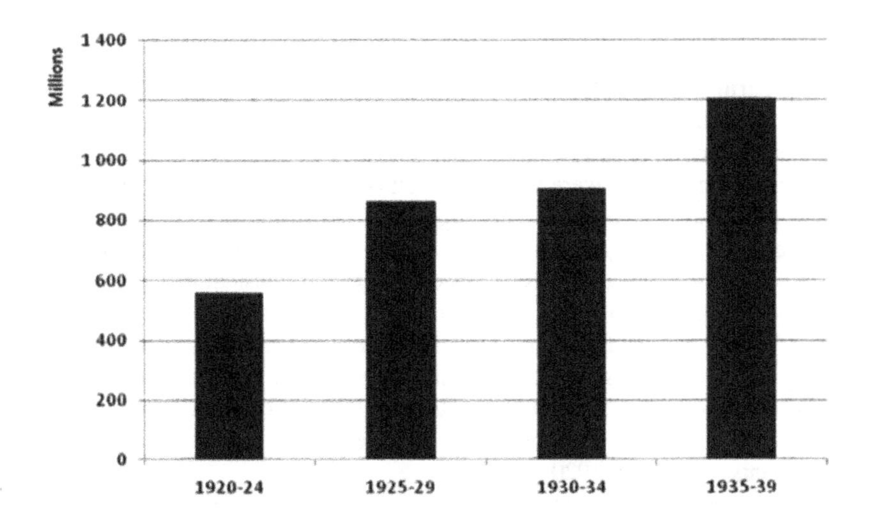

Figure 5: Investments in Vessels, 1920-1939 (constant 1938 prices)

Note: See figure 3.

Source: SSB, *Økonomisk utsyn, 1900-1950* (Oslo,1955), table 37.

[55]SSB, *Historisk Statistikk 1948* (Oslo, 1949), table 131.

Table 1
Insurance and Sales Profits, 1915-1918

	1915	1916	1917	1918
Insurance Profits	1,086,568	28,733,286	215,546,009	104,980,145
Insurance Payments	2,030,000	42,651,827	331,295,563	141,679,990
Sum of Book Value	943,431	13,877,048	115,692,748	36,710,588
Tonnage (Dwt)	18,400	93,975	625,908	254,730
Number of Vessels	3	35	207	90

Source: RA, S-S-2393-E-L0055-0001, mappe, Finans og tolldepartementet, 1. skattekontor, L, "Register over skipssaker, Beskatning ved tap av skip og ved salg til utlandet 1917-."

A sizable proportion of these investments must be considered a direct subsidy. Under the wartime tax regime, most shipowners faced an effective tax rate of forty to fifty percent, and as a result were obligated to offer guarantees of up to half of the insurance profits. Based on the deposits offered by Norwegian shipowners under the scheme, it is therefore possible to ascertain precisely what tax savings were involved. Looking at losses during the war exclusively, Norwegian shipowning companies placed 160 million *kroner* as deposits for taxes payable. This tax rebate therefore represented twenty-six percent of the total ordinary income and wealth taxes collected by Norwegian municipalities during the war.[56]

The importance of these sums for investments during the 1920s became highly controversial, with the Shipowners' Association alleging that most of the insurance profits were lost as a result of unwise investments made at the height of the postwar boom.[57] This suggestion, however, is highly misleading. As is evident from figure 6, wartime profits were reinvested throughout the 1920s, most of them after vessel prices had fallen considerably. Only about twenty-seven percent of the wartime profits reported under the law were reinvested by the end of 1920, and a sizable share of the net investments made during the decade was financed by insurance profits from the war. In real terms, wartime profits accounted for close to 158 million *kroner* of investment capital, and reinvested wartime profits represented around a third of the total investments made from 1920 to 1925.

When recovering from the crisis, the shipping community was able to utilize financial resources accrued as a result of wartime losses. Understanding why shipowners were able to weather the storm in the first half of the 1920s

---

[56]SSB, *Historisk Statistikk 1948*, table 219.

[57]See, for instance, the introduction to the annual statement from the Shipowners' Association in 1923 in *Norges Rederforbunds Beretning, 1923-1924*. This interpretation is also presented in Egeland, *Kongeveien*.

does not, however, fully account for the shift in investment strategies. From the early 1920s, an increasing share of shipping investments went towards newly constructed vessels, leaving Norwegian shipowners with a fleet that was significantly newer than the world average by 1938. Moreover, by 1938 over sixty percent of the tonnage in the Norwegian fleet consisted of motor-propelled vessels, compared to around twenty-six percent in the world fleet.[58] Similarly, the proportion of the fleet consisting of smaller vessels fell dramatically. In 1912, 65.7 percent of Norwegian tonnage consisted of vessels smaller than 2000 tons, but by 1938, this had fallen to 19.5 percent.[59]

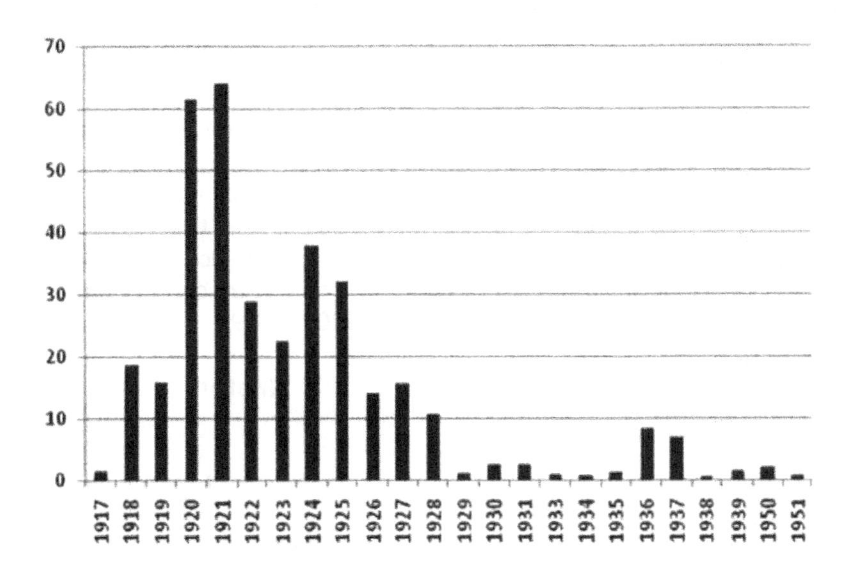

Figure 6: Re-investment of Wartime Insurance Profits, 1917-1951 (million *kroner*)

Notes: The estimates are based on the profits that shipowning companies reported to the Ministry of Finance in order to qualify for a tax exemption. Profit here indicates any insurance payments exceeding the book value of the vessel. The year of reinvestment is found by the release date of the funds deposited to cover any tax liability if the shipowning company failed to meet its obligation under the law.

Source: See figure 2.

---

[58]Tenold, "Norway's Interwar Tanker Expansion;" and Tenold, "Crisis? What Crisis?"

[59]This estimate is based on SSB, *Historisk Statistikk 1948*, table 132. It includes all sail, steam and motor vessels above 100 net tons.

One should be wary, however, when dating the timing of this transition based on published statistics because these data naturally reflected a lag compared with actual investments. As well, a sizable portion of the registered fleet consisted of vessels that rarely entered the international cross trades. Most available measures indicate, though, that the investment pattern was changing by the early 1920s. Looking at additions to the registered fleet in isolation, for instance, shows that net additions of motor vessels exceeded those of steam from 1925. This feature is even more pronounced when viewing the leading shipping towns in isolation. Omitting investments in sailing vessels, the four leading shipping towns – Haugesund, Bergen, Tønsberg and Oslo – represented on average seventy-three percent of the total fleet for the entire period (see figure 7). While the investment pattern in Oslo clearly diverged from the rest due to extremely high investments in motor-propelled vessels from 1925 onward, by 1932 the shift towards motor vessels was evident in all the leading shipping centres. In all four, the disinvestment in steam vessels started around 1923 and amounted to a total reduction of gross steam tonnage on register of nearly 300,000 (representing around twenty percent of steam tonnage registered in those cities in 1920). This reduction was not mimicked in other areas, as the total steam tonnage on registry outside these four centres increased by about eight percent from 1920 to 1939.

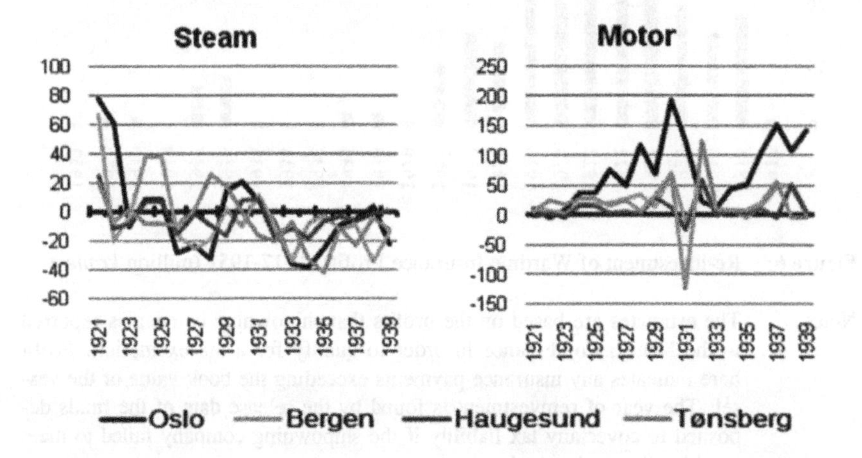

Figure 7: Net additions of Steam and Motor Tonnage in Oslo, Bergen, Tønsberg and Haugesund, 1921-1939 ('000 gross tons)

Source: SSB, *Statistisk årbok* (Oslo, various years).

In attempting to account for this, scholars have surprisingly overlooked one of the most direct signals received by shipowners when deciding how to invest. The shipping crisis of the early 1920s made the unemployment of vessels a serious concern to the shipping community. By the summer of 1921, approximately forty percent of the Norwegian fleet was laid up. Attempting to identify the causes of this problem, the Shipowners' Association discovered that costs had shifted dramatically as a result of the war. While official statistics offer little guidance about the true nature of these changes, the statistical material gathered by the Shipowners' Association suggested that total operating costs had tripled between 1914 and 1921 in nominal terms.[60] Studies of wage costs (excluding board and lodging) have largely confirmed this impression. In the decade following 1910, Ole Grytten found that wages in the merchant fleet increased by 500 percent in nominal terms, before halving in the next decade.[61]

A committee of the Ministry of Trade charged with investigating lay-up rates in the Norwegian industry revealed that there were some warning signs. In its final report, the committee suggested that the Norwegian industry had been disproportionately affected by a downturn in activity in the late 1920s. By January 1928, 8.7 percent of gross tonnage in the Norwegian fleet was laid up, while the corresponding figures for other European fleets varied between 0.6 percent in Holland and 5.8 percent in Sweden. When seeking to explain this, however, the committee was confronted with a scarcity of data on comparative costs in major merchant fleets. Attempting to verify its initial hypothesis that Norway suffered from relatively higher manning costs proved unsuccessful. A comparison of the actual wage costs accrued by a sample of forty Norwegian vessels with those that would have been borne had the same vessels been registered under other flags showed that Norwegian wage costs were remarkably similar to those elsewhere. A similar analysis of the manning scales in various countries produced the same result. In short, the Norwegian manning scale was similar to most other leading merchant shipping nations, although the committee found that insurance payments accrued by Norwegian vessels were somewhat higher than the standard rate abroad.[62]

The scarcity of data faced by the committee should preclude any overconfident interpretation. Its findings did not support the hypothesis that relatively higher operating costs in Norway led to a more rapid adoption of capital-intensive investment strategies. A more solid form of evidence assembled

---

[60] *Norges Rederforbunds Cirkulære 1922*, "Skibsreder Fr. Odfjells's og Advokat Kaare Schønings inledningsforedrag paa vegne av Norges Rederforbund for voldgiftsretten den 1. august 1922."

[61] Ola H. Grytten, "Nominal Wages, 1726-2006, Classified by Industry," in Øyvind Eitrheim, Jan T. Klovland, and Jan F. Qvigstad (eds.), *Historical Monetary Statistics for Norway, Part II* (Oslo, 2007), table 6.A.2.

[62] Norway, Handelsdepartementet, *Innstilling fra Skibsopleggskomiteen* (Oslo, 1928).

by the committee does, however, provide an important insight into the incentives for this technological shift. When breaking down lay-up rates by tonnage class, the committee discovered that they were significantly skewed. While as little as 3.3 percent of the fleet consisting between 3000 and 4000 gross tons was laid up, a staggering twenty-nine percent of vessels smaller than 1000 gross tons was unemployed. A major reason for the high lay-up rates, the committee concluded, was that the Norwegian fleet still comprised a higher proportion of smaller vessels.[63] While this does not provide positive evidence of the existence of significant economies of scale in the period, it does suggest at the very least that shipowners had a very clear signal from the freight market during the 1920s. Smaller vessels, and in particular smaller tramp ships, found it very difficult to find profitable employment, with direct financial consequences for the owners.

On one point, however, the committee did find empirical support for a claim about Norwegian exceptionalism. When comparing the taxes paid by shipping companies in Norway with the rates in other countries, the committee found that Norwegian shipowners were paying considerably more. Comparing the accounts of three companies, the committee found that Norwegians paid considerably higher taxes than did shipowners in all other countries except Germany. For instance, the committee reported that Norwegian shipping companies had a tax burden between two and a half and seven and a half times greater than in Sweden. In the examples used by the committee, the major difference was taxes on companies' assets, since Germany was the only other country to levy such a tax. In addition, the Norwegian companies paid a slightly higher tax on income than did Swedish and Danish shipowners.[64]

While the results of these comparisons were highly dependent upon the examples chosen, they do illuminate some particular features of the Norwegian tax regime. When viewed from the perspective of a company attempting to minimize its tax burden, two points stand out. First of all, aggressive leveraging of investments would minimize what was perceived as punitive taxation on assets held by a company. Second, paying out dividends to investors offered significant tax savings, as the rate of taxation on dividends was lower than on assets held within the company. A final point, albeit not noted by the committee, was that in Norway all income accrued from asset sales was exempt from income tax. As we have seen, this part of the tax code was an inheritance from the early 1920s, originally aimed at channeling wartime profits into re-investment in vessels. Shipowning companies continued to enjoy

[63]*Ibid*. The complete estimate of lay-up rates as a share of different tonnage classes was: vessels between 500 and 1000 gross tons, 28.8 percent; 1000-2000 gross tons, 16.9 percent; 2000-3000 gross tons, 12.6 percent; and 3000-4000 gross tons, 3.3 percent.

[64]*Ibid*., 18-29.

this privilege in the interwar period. Figure 8, which records all registered asset gains exempted from taxation, shows that throughout the interwar period, Norwegian shipping companies registered capital gains of about sixty million *kroner* that was exempt from taxation.

While the total sums exempted under this tax arrangement during the interwar period paled in comparison to the profits accrued during World War I, the effects of the incentives for individual companies could be quite considerable. Consider the career of the young entrepreneur Leif Høegh. After establishing his company in 1927, Høegh expanded his fleet during the 1930s. In a surprising move, he ordered a series of new tankers from Swedish shipyards in the midst of the tanker depression, directly contradicting the efforts of the international tanker cartel to limit the construction of new ships.[65] The tax accounts in the Ministry of Finance give some hint of the potential advantages of such a strategy. Two of the vessels, bought in 1937 and 1938 at a total cost of 5.6 million *kroner*, were sold after a year, bringing in revenues of 8.4 million *kroner*. The 2.8 million *kroner* profit was exempt from taxation and was reinvested in new vessels in 1940.[66]

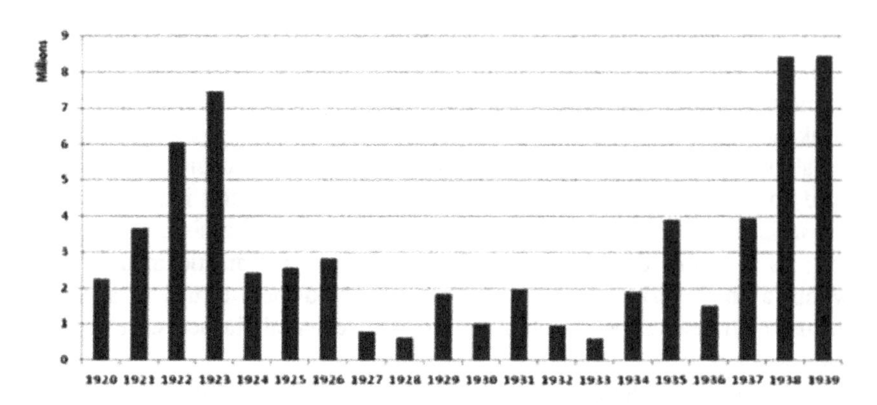

Figure 8: Capital Income from Vessels Lost or Sold, 1920-1939

Note: Capital income refers to sales prices or insurance payments exceeding the book value of the vessel.

Source: See figure 2.

[65]Atle Thowsen, "Leif Høegh - utdypning" in *Norsk Bibliografisk Leksikon* (Oslo, 2010).

[66]RA, S-S-2393-E-L0055-0001, "Beskatning ved tap av skip og ved salg til utlandet 1917- ."

By exempting all capital gains from taxation if they were reinvested in new vessels, and by allowing shipowners to make extraordinary depreciations of assets when market conditions favoured such a strategy, lawmakers had established a policy regime that was highly beneficial for those shipping entrepreneurs who made capital-intensive investments. The strategies of the "biggest gamblers" relied heavily on leveraging, and the fortunes of individual companies were highly dependent on the movement of vessel prices.[67] The bigger the "bet," the more advantageous these tax rules became. When investing after 1921, shipping companies benefitted if vessel prices rose, as any realization of this appreciation in capital was not taxable. If vessel prices fell, shipping companies could make extraordinary write-downs of their assets, thus limiting the tax on current earnings. If vessel prices later improved, any proceeds from sales would again be exempt from taxation.

Conclusion

An overview of the development of the Norwegian shipping industry during the interwar period leads to two seemingly contradictory observations. First, the industry began the 1920s in what might be judged as a negative macroeconomic environment as the floating currency regime underscored the risk of operating from a small country and the banking crisis of the 1920s significantly weakened the industry's traditional sources of finance. Surprisingly, though, the shipping industry recovered quickly from the postwar depression and managed to sustain strong rates of investment throughout the interwar period. These investments increasingly were concentrated in expensive, modern vessels; as a result, the Norwegian fleet underwent a dramatic modernization within a short period. In brief, Norwegian shipowners turned to a capital-intensive strategy as its traditional sources of external finance were dramatically weakened.

Previous attempts at resolving this dilemma have focused on the entrepreneurs who entered the tanker sector. As scholars have studied these companies, they have identified the resources mobilized by individual companies, either in the form of the long-term charters negotiated with oil companies or through financing deals with foreign shipyards. While not disputing these findings, I have asked a slightly different question: What had changed in the industry's economic and political environment, and how can these changes help us to understand the developments that followed?

Directing attention towards the economic and political framework surrounding Norwegian shipping has the additional benefit of placing the industry

[67]The term is taken from Vidar Hole, *The Biggest Gamblers: Structure and Strategy in Norwegian Oil Tanker Shipping During the Era of Growth, 1925-1973* (Bergen, 1993).

in a more relevant context. As the leading contributor to export earnings in Norway, shipping played a pivotal role in the economic cycles both during and after World War I, and considerations about its future earning potential were given great weight in policy deliberations. As a result, monetary and fiscal policy issues were central to reforming the shipping industry. This was particularly true during the war, and the wartime experiences form a crucial backdrop for understanding the shipping policies implemented in the interwar period. The outbreak of war and the boom that followed were periods of much legal reform. Responding to the speculative bubble, policymakers established a new tax code, closing existing loopholes and significantly raising the tax rate. Establishing these laws, however, necessitated several clarifications in the tax code, but these were later revised significantly under very different economic circumstances. Wartime losses coupled with extraordinary earnings created a pent-up demand for vessels, and when this demand was unleashed it had detrimental consequences for the already precarious Norwegian balance of payments. Shipping policy thus became ingrained in monetary policy, and concerns for the stability of the financial system trumpeted the policy ambitions and attitudes in parliament.

It is ironic that the final outcome of this process would be the creation of a policy regime that rewarded precisely the type of behaviour that the original laws were attempting to curb. In exempting capital income from taxation, policymakers were attempting to aid the industry in rebuilding the fleet after massive wartime losses. By stimulating demand for vessels during the postwar boom, this law significantly worsened the prospects for the interwar period, and extraordinary financial demands from the industry set the stage for a prolonged financial crisis.

The shipping crisis of the early 1920s revealed that dramatic changes had occurred in the economic and political environment of the shipping industry. First of all, the losses accrued by investors and shipping companies seriously weakened the financial sector, eroding traditional sources of financial capital. In the 1920s, the shipowning community could ameliorate the worst consequences of the financial crisis by mobilizing capital income accumulated during the war. In the 1930s, however, the industry was increasingly forced to rely on financing from abroad. Second, shipowners in the postwar period confronted significantly altered cost considerations. While the true nature of these changes is still elusive, statistics on lay ups provide indisputable evidence that by investing in smaller tramp vessels - the predominant form of investment before 1914 - shipowners were at risk of not being able to find employment for their fleets. Finally, the shipping industry operated in a tax regime that rewarded capital-intensive strategies by exempting capital income from an otherwise prudent tax code.

In short, the political economy of shipping in the interwar period was highly beneficial for entrepreneurs willing to make bold investments in larger, more expensive vessels, leveraging their investments heavily and betting on future asset prices to generate extraordinary profits. It is perhaps not surprising that these were precisely the kinds of entrepreneurs who would dominate the Norwegian shipping industry's transition from "laggards to leaders" during the interwar years.[68]

[68]This term is used by With Andersen, "Laggards to Leaders," to describe the technological transition.

International Maritime Trade Politics and the Case of Norway, 1948-1990[1]

Andreas Nybø

Introduction

The politics of international shipping changed fundamentally between the 1960s and the 1980s. From World War II until the early 1960s, the field was dominated by actors from a few countries in Western Europe and North America. The level of government involvement in deep-sea maritime transport was fairly limited. A few decades later, this activity was much more politicized. Further, international shipping policy decisions were developed in complex international processes involving a broad spectrum of international organizations, transnational industries and inter-governmental networks.

The aim of this article is twofold. First, it will discuss developments in international shipping politics from the immediate post-World War II decades until the late 1980s. It will focus especially on the formation of international organizations and networks and will examine how they influenced the politics of shipping. The key objective is to understand the dynamic development of an international - or perhaps transnational - policy field. What were the roles of the different organizations and networks in the policy field, and how did they develop over time? How did the various entities - organizations, networks and governments - affect each other? Second, it will discuss the role of Norwegian actors in the field of maritime trade politics. It seeks to understand the dynamics of the field and to analyze their actions and reactions to developments in international shipping politics. Who were the actors which created the Norwegian policies? What were their strategies? How did they work? And did they have any influence on policies at the international level? This part will both provide a broader understanding of Norwegian international maritime trade politics and serve as an example of how actors adapted to changes in the field in general.

---

[1]The author would like to thank the Organisation for Economic Co-operation and Development (OECD), the Norwegian Shipowners' Association and the Norwegian Ministry of Foreign Affairs for granting access to archival materials, and the participants at a workshop on Norwegian shipping history in Oslo in February 2011 for comments and suggestions.

Some clarifications should be made at the onset. First, the primary focus of this study is *politics* rather than *policies*, that is, the aim is to analyze the circumstances and context of policy decisions rather than the policies themselves. Second, it discusses international, rather than national, shipping politics. To some degree, the national and international dimensions cannot be separated, but it is the international dimension that is my main concern. Third, the article focuses on maritime trade politics as opposed to technical regulations, manning policies and the like.

The history of shipping politics since World War II has been the subject of a number of studies. The most comprehensive investigation arguably is Alan Cafruny's 1987 book which shows that international shipping became more regulated and politicized during the 1970s and 1980s.[2] While my conclusions do not diverge very far from his, I will add to the work of Cafruny and others by focusing on international organizations and the connections among them. The main argument is that between the 1960s and the 1980s, not only did government involvement in shipping increase but it also came to involve an increasing number of actors and arenas for negotiations. The importance of international organizations and networks grew considerably from the 1960s, both in shipping politics and in other areas.[3] In this essay, I will go beyond the development of individual organizations to discuss how, together with state and non-state actors, they comprised a complex decision-making network within the field of international maritime politics. In recent years, the increased number and importance of international organizations has made them important objects for study in international relations research. Some international relations scholars have labelled the transformation of international politics since the 1960s as a shift from international politics to global governance. James Rosenau has defined this development as a "multiplication of spheres of authority."[4] Several scholars have claimed that this has led to a weakening of the

[2]Alan W. Cafruny, *Ruling the Waves: The Political Economy of International Shipping* (Berkeley, 1987).

[3]The development within many of the organizations relevant to shipping has been discussed by previous scholars, most extensively by Bruce Farthing, who in his excellent overview of international shipping even included the addresses and telephone numbers of the various organizations; see Bruce Farthing and Mark Brownrigg, *Farthing on International Shipping* (Colchester, 1987; 3rd ed., London, 1997). There are also several studies with narrower scopes, including Anna Bredima-Savopoulou and John Tzoannos, *The Common Shipping Policy of the EC* (Amsterdam, 1989); and Okechukwu C. Iheduru, *The Political Economy of International Shipping in Developing Countries* (Wilmington, DE, 1996).

[4]Klaus Dingwerth and Philipp Pattberg, "Actors, Arenas and Issues in Global Governance," in Jim Whitman (ed.), *Palgrave Advances in Global Governance* (New York, 2009), 42.

role of states in international politics, while others have suggested that rather than reducing the influence of states, it has instead changed their strategic approaches.[5]

The second part of the paper will focus on the approach of Norwegians to international shipping politics, and particularly to international organizations and cooperation. Despite the importance of shipping to Norway's economy, the role of the industry in Norwegian external politics has not been given much attention by historians.[6] Political decisions regarding shipping were often made by civil servants or the shipping industry itself rather than by political leaders; consequently, shipping was only occasionally at the centre of Norwegian foreign policy debates. It is thus not surprising that international shipping politics does not occupy a prominent position in the historiography on Norwegian foreign relations. Still, it is crucial to investigate these kinds of "low-level" strategies, not only to understand specific developments in shipping politics but also to gain a better understanding of the role of Norwegians in international trade politics.

In addition, a study of the approach taken by Norwegians to changes in international shipping politics enables us to examine how they operated in the international political system. But this essay will not provide a comprehensive discussion of how the "globalization" of shipping politics affected Norwegian interests. To do so would require a much more extensive analysis, especially into Norwegian *national* shipping policies.[7] Instead, my aim here is to provide a framework for understanding how Norwegian actors related to changes in the international arena and how this contributed to shifts in Norwegian policies and strategies. This will also be useful for understanding how these actors approached the shifting realities of international politics.

---

[5]See, for example, Iver B. Neumann and Ole Jacob Sending, *Governing the Global Polity: Practices, Mentality, Rationality* (Ann Arbor, 2010).

[6]In the two volumes of the multi-volume series on Norwegian foreign policy, *Norsk utenrikspolitikks historie*, which cover this period, shipping politics is not accorded much attention. See Knut Einar Eriksen and Helge Øystein Pharo, *Kald krig og internasjonalisering, 1949-1965* (Oslo, 1997); and Rolf Tamnes, *Oljealder, 1965-1995* (Oslo, 1997).

[7]There are some studies on the relationship between "globalization" and national shipping policies. See, for example, Evangelia Selkou and Michael Roe, *Globalisation, Policy and Shipping - Fordism, Post-Fordism and the European Union Maritime Sector* (Cheltenham, 2004), which covers primarily the post-1990 period; and Camilla Brautaset and Stig Tenold "Globalisation and Norwegian Shipping Policy, 1850-2000," *Business History*, L, No. 5 (2008), 565-582, which studies the link between economic globalization and Norwegian domestic shipping policies.

Atlantic Unity and Conflict, 1948-1970

A study by the Maritime Transport Committee (MTC) of the Organisation for Economic Co-operation and Development (OECD) in 1986 summarized the development of international shipping politics since the 1950s:

> During the fifties and sixties, the main problems which had concerned [OECD] Member countries had been themselves. However, in the seventies and more recently, the ever-growing influence by governments, primarily of developing and state trading countries, upon ocean shipping has led to significant departures from the free circulation of shipping and fair competition in this area, with the resulting need for OECD Member countries to defend the principles of liberalisation and, where possible, to extend its scope in the maritime sector.[8]

While this description reflects the self-image of many OECD countries as the defenders of liberal shipping policies, it seeks to justify more government intervention in the name of liberalization as well. Moreover, it summarizes to some extent developments in international shipping politics from the 1950s to the late 1980s.

International shipping politics in the decades after World War II were dominated by North Atlantic countries. This was understandable, since Western European and American shipowners controlled a majority of the world's merchant fleet. This commercial dominance was reflected on the political side of international shipping. The "Atlantic Regime," as Cafruny called it, kept shipping politics fairly liberal, although there were important political differences among the Atlantic partners. The US government and shipping industry was more inclined to advocate the use of protectionist measures to maintain the *status quo*. Western Europeans, on the other hand, preferred a *laissez-faire* regime, with relatively little government involvement. It should be noted, however, that many European countries used domestic regulations – on manning, tax policies and currency issues – to protect their national interests. Nevertheless, disagreement over the level of government involvement was the main fault line in international shipping politics during the first two postwar decades.

Among the most important forums for shipping debates was the Maritime Transport Committee of the Organisation for European Economic Co-

---

[8] Archives of the Organisation for Economic Co-operation and Development (OECD), Paris – MT(87)I, Part V, Maritime Transport Committee, Annual Report 1986.

operation (OEEC). The OEEC was established in 1948 as part of the arrangement to distribute Marshall Plan aid. One of the other main tasks of the MTC, which was created at the same time, was to monitor maritime trade to ensure it complied with a clause in the agreement between the US and the European aid recipients which required that at least fifty percent of the goods transported under the Plan be carried in American vessels.[9] Both the OEEC and MTC were continued after the Marshal Plan ended in 1952. The focus, however, shifted from securing American cargo reservations to debating the role of governments in international shipping. Subsidies, flag discrimination and flags of convenience were among the most debated topics. The OEEC also passed a "Code of Liberalisation" which was binding on maritime transport. Throughout the 1950s, the MTC remained a forum for Europe's traditional maritime nations in the struggle to achieve liberal international shipping regulations.

In 1961, the OEEC was transformed into the OECD, with the addition of the United States and Canada, both of which became members of the MTC as well. In the negotiations leading to this reorganization, there was an intense debate over the role of the MTC. The Europeans wanted it to remain a tool to increase cooperation and liberalization in international maritime transport, while the US preferred it to become a forum for consultation, without a defined objective of liberalizing international shipping. In the end, the Code of Liberalisation was continued, but with a provision for the US to opt out.[10]

The next year, ten European traditional maritime nations established an informal trans-governmental network called the Consultative Shipping Group (CSG).[11] It met regularly, often on a monthly basis. Consultations at the ministerial level were held when it was deemed "necessary to concert policy on major shipping issues."[12] The CSG's original objective was to enhance cooperation in the battle against US protectionism. The CSG was a useful supplement to the re-organized MTC because it provided a venue for informal

---

[9]John O. Egeland, *Vi skal videre* (Oslo, 1971), 304, as cited in André Garborg Rustand, "Allierte på kollisjonskurs? Norge og den amerikanske skipsfartspolitikken, 1948-1960" (Unpublished MA thesis, University of Oslo 2009), 43.

[10]Farthing and Brownrigg, *Farthing on International Shipping*, 103.

[11]The original members were Belgium, Denmark, France, Greece, Italy, Netherlands, Norway, the UK, Sweden and West Germany. They were later joined by Finland and Japan. Great Britain, National Archives (TNA/PRO), Foreign and Commonwealth Office (FCO), 76/13, memo by Shipping Policy Division, 7 October 1970. Finland and Japan also joined the OECD, and consequently the Maritime Transport Committee (MTC) in 1969 and 1964, respectively. TNA/PRO, Ministry of Transport (MT), 59/3256, brief for the President's visit to Japan, August 1965.

[12]TNA/PRO, FCO 76/780, P.F. Newman to Mr. Hitch and Mr. Taylor, 23 September 1973.

discussions and served as a pressure group *vis-à-vis* the Americans. In Washington, official representatives of CSG countries formed the so-called "Cotton Club" as a forum for discussions with US officials. From the late 1960s, the CSG served as a platform for strategy coordination on maritime transport issues other than US policies.

Shipowners' organizations also played an important role in setting maritime policy on both the national and international levels. Industry representatives in many countries had close ties to governments, participating formally and informally in decision making on policies and strategies.[13] Representatives from these associations were part of some national delegations to the MTC and prepared official briefs and strategy documents for national delegates.[14] The CSG cooperated closely with international shipowners' organisations, particularly the Council of European National Shipowners' Associations (CENSA), which was established in 1963.[15] In addition, other organizations served as arenas for policy debates among shipowners and as pressure groups *vis-à-vis* governments and international organizations.[16] Although it is difficult to measure the impact of shipowners' associations on international maritime transport policies, they undoubtedly had some influence, at least in Europe. Indeed, there is little evidence in the sources of conflict between European shipowners and the governments of CSG countries. One reason for this obviously was the close business-government dialogue which created a common understanding of goals and strategies among industry representatives and government officials.

During the post-WWII era, international maritime transport became an issue within the United Nations (UN). The Inter-Governmental Maritime Consultative Organization (IMCO) was established by the UN in 1948 and came into existence ten years later. The purpose of the organization was to increase the technical regulation of maritime transport. Several European traditional maritime nations, especially the Scandinavian countries, were sceptical

---

[13]Evidence of discussions among industry and government officials appear frequently in both Norwegian and British archival sources.

[14]OECD, DAF/MTC/75.17, note by Secretariat, 27 March 1975.

[15]TNA/PRO, MT 59/3218, United Nations Conference on Trade and Development (UNCTAD), review of studies and activities in the field of shipping and ports, 12 January 1967.

[16]The number of such organizations was vast, but among the most important were the International Chamber of Shipping (ICS), established in 1921; the Comité des Associations d'Armateurs des Communautés Européennes (CAACE), comprising national shipowners' associations in EEC countries, established in 1965 (known as the European Community Shipowners' Associations since 1990); and the International Tank Owners' Association (Intertanko), established in 1934.

of this supra-national body which they feared would develop beyond their control.[17] Nevertheless, they all had joined the IMCO by 1959.[18] The IMCO had a successful start, especially in the passage in 1965 of an updated version on the Convention for the Safety of Life at Sea, originally adopted in 1914. After the *Torrey Canyon* disaster in 1967, pollution became an important issue within the IMCO. Still, the role of the IMCO was frequently debated. Several US administrations in the 1960s argued that it should become more involved in trade issues, in addition to technical and environmental topics.[19] Although the Europeans considered this, it was decided to leave the IMCO with its original mandate.[20]

The United Nations Conference on Trade and Development (UNCTAD) was founded in the early 1960s to boost economic growth in the developing countries. UNCTAD's first meeting was held in 1964, and it soon became an important forum for the so-called "North-South" debates. In 1965, UNCTAD established a Committee of Shipping to promote "understanding and co-operation in the field of shipping and to study and report on economic aspects of shipping."[21] The Committee comprised forty-five members from both developing and developed nations which had some interest in maritime transport policies. The establishment of this Committee was a first step away from the Atlantic-dominated regime of the post-World War II era. It was obvious from the start that the Committee would increase pressure on the European traditional maritime nations, but as a British government report put it, "most countries would rather use the U.N.C.T.A.D. to educate the l.d.c.s. [least developed countries], however thankless the job may be."[22] This proved not only thankless but also futile because developing nations were not interested in being "educated" and soon proposed radical changes to international shipping policies.

The Europeans' prospect of maintaining their dominant position in international shipping politics seemed remote. As one UK official stated, "[w]e

---

[17]Farthing and Brownrigg, *Farthing on International Shipping*, 70-71.

[18]See International Maritime Organization (IMO), http://www.imo.org/About/Membership/Pages/MemberStates.aspx.

[19]TNA/PRO, FCO 76/474, W. Lak to Consultative Shipping Group (CSG) members, 27 August 1968.

[20]*Ibid.*, FCO 76/231, letter from H.A. Dudgeon, 19 October 1971; and FCO 76/474, R.F. Cornish to CSG members, 13 September 1968.

[21]*Ibid.*, 76/10, information paper by the UNCTAD Secretariat, 25 September 1969; and draft report of the Committee of Shipping, 30 April 1970.

[22]*Ibid.*, MT 59/3501, note by J.R. Steele, 2 July 1965.

face a period of change in shipping...Our objective should be to tailor the changes so that they do as little harm as possible to world trade"[23] But the European traditional maritime nations were sailing in difficult waters. Negotiations within UNCTAD were complicated, in part due to the group system within the organization. Among the three most important groupings was the Group of 77, comprising the developing nations; the East Bloc, also known as Group D; and group B, which included the Western countries. The developing countries, many of them newly liberated after a century or more of colonialism, wanted radical change and pushed hard for measures to strengthen their commercial fleets as a part of the New International Economic Order, a concept that dominated the North-South dialogue for decades.[24] The East Bloc for obvious reasons stood with the Group of 77 on questions relating to increased government regulation of maritime transport, and frequently objected to the capitalist principles put forward by Group B countries. Disputes within Group B over both issues and strategies made the task of blocking proposals for more government intervention in shipping increasingly difficult, and one of the main aims among many Western European traditional maritime nations was to prevent a Group B split. While the Group B nations managed to weather the storm fairly well until the late 1960s, the worst was yet to come.

The New International Maritime Order, 1970-1990

It was obvious by the late 1960s that the liberal order of the preceding decades was under considerable pressure. The challenge from the developing countries and from UNCTAD was about to transform shipping politics and lead to the emergence of new actors. While transatlantic issues remained important, they were no longer paramount. One of the main characteristics of shipping politics of the 1970s and 1980s was that decisions were made within a number of symbiotic international networks and organizations. Westerners were under threat commercially; although the majority of the world fleet was still registered in OECD countries, this was about to change with the shipping crisis of the mid-1970s.

Until the late 1960s, debates between the traditional maritime nations and the developing nations had been centred primarily on principles and the structure of the intergovernmental "consultation machinery" of UNCTAD and other organizations.[25] Progress was slow, and some developing countries, es-

---

[23]*Ibid.*, internal UK briefing note, May 1965.

[24]See, for example, Robert L. Rothstein, *Global Bargaining: UNCTAD and the Quest for a New International Economic Order* (Princeton, 1979).

[25]TNA/PRO, MT59/3501, summary of conclusions adopted by the Trade Committee (OECD), 27 October 1965.

pecially in Latin America, began to pass legislation aimed at increasing their fleets. Brazil was the leader in this development. In 1969, the country

> introduced sweeping measures of cargo reservation with the expressed object of achieving a 50/50 sharing of cargoes, as well as a tax credit on manufactured exports carried in national vessels...The Government of Brazil...also intervened in conference agreements to secure a radical alternation in pooling agreements in the interest of its national line.[26]

What worsened the situation for many European countries was the American attitude towards Latin American cargo-reservation schemes. After Richard Nixon took office in 1969, the US undertook a review of the country's shipping policies and in the following years entered into several arrangements with the Brazilian government and others.[27] These agreements were criticized by the Europeans, and the Norwegian representative to the OECD characterized them as "the most serious examples of flag discrimination to date."[28]

The most controversial proposition put forward by the developing countries, however, was the regulation of liner shipping. The liner trades were to a large degree controlled by international cartels, the so-called "conferences," which determined freight rates and allocated quotas and sailing routes. Since the end of the war, these conferences had largely been allowed to continue as before, despite the adoption of stricter anti-trust legislation in Europe. Government regulation of conferences was among the issues debated between the Europeans and the US in the early 1960s, but it was with the establishment of UNCTAD that it became a substantive issue in maritime politics.[29]

The developing countries claimed that high freight rates obstructed exports and the economic development of poor nations.[30] They suggested that governments should monitor conference rates and intervene when necessary.[31]

---

[26]OECD, MT(70)5, MTC Annual Report 1969, 22 May 1970.

[27]*Ibid.*; and TNA/PRO, MT 59/3258, note by B.E. Bellamy, 18 September 1969.

[28]OECD, MT(70)7, MTC, shipping policy matters, 3 July 1970.

[29]See, for example, TNA/PRO, MT 59/3501, G.R.W. Brigstocke, note of conclusions of the meeting of the MTC, 22 October 1965.

[30]*Ibid.*, FCO 76/10, UNCTAD Committee of Shipping, summary records of meeting, 29 April 1970.

[31]TNA/PRO, FCO 76/10, draft report of meeting of UNCTAD Committee of Shipping, 29 April 1970.

The US government in the early 1960s had already given the Federal Maritime Commission authority to regulate freight rates that were seen as "so unreasonably high or low as to be detrimental to the commerce of the United States."[32] The European countries, however, regarded conferences as private business agreements and did not want to interfere with their operations; they therefore suggested that governments should encourage the customers of shipping companies to form shippers' councils that could negotiate with conferences.[33] The general idea was that these councils could balance the power between the shipping companies and their customers. A British Shippers' Council had been established in 1955, and in the following years similar bodies were founded throughout Europe. The new national shippers' councils soon formed international organisations, most prominently the European Shippers Council. The international shippers' council held annual meetings with CENSA and soon developed into a political pressure group rather than a negotiating body. In 1963, the Shippers' Council and CENSA agreed upon a "Note of Understanding" regarding principles and procedures for the determination of freight rates and the settling of disputes between shippers and conferences.[34] Despite their questionable impact, cooperation between shippers and shipowners became the prime example for the traditional maritime nations of the utility of self-regulation in maritime transport. In 1971, the European Shippers Council and the CENSA, encouraged by the CSG governments, agreed upon a "code of practise for conferences."[35] The obvious reason for this code was to prevent discussion of an UNCTAD code on conferences.

Self-regulation by the conferences was not sufficient for the developing countries. First of all, the power of the shippers' councils was limited and was not regulated by any laws.[36] Further, the question of freight rates was only one of several issues the developing countries had with liner conferences. More important, at least in a nation-building perspective, was the role of national lines and their ability to enter established conferences. In UNCTAD meetings, developing countries emphasized that their national lines were often

---

[32]OECD, MT(70)5, MTC Annual Report 1969, 22 May 1970.

[33]TNA/PRO, FCO 76/10, draft report of meeting of UNCTAD Committee of Shipping, 29 April 1970.

[34]*Ibid.*, OECD Secretariat to MTC members, 19 August 1965.

[35]OECD, MT(72)5, MTC Annual Report 1971, 4 May 1972.

[36]TNA/PRO, FCO 76/10, UNCTAD Committee of Shipping, summary records of meeting, 22 April 1970.

denied access to conferences or accepted only after long delays, and even then only allocated very limited shares.[37]

At an UNCTAD meeting in 1972, the Group of 77 proposed the development of a world code on liner conferences that would be acceptable to all parties, and the Group B countries agreed in principle. What such a code should include, however, was a matter of dispute. The developing countries wanted the code to include cargo reservations and the right for governments to regulate freight rates; not surprisingly, this was rejected by Group B. A special group was then established to continue work on a code.[38] Although it met in January and June 1973, there were still disagreements on a number of issues. In November 1973, a so-called "Conference of Plenipotentiaries" met in Geneva under the auspices of UNCTAD to discuss the code. While considerable progress was made, a final code was not agreed upon until the Conference of Plenipotentiaries reassembled in the spring of 1974. On 8 April 1974, the Conference adopted a "Code of Conduct for Liner Conferences" (hereafter the UNCTAD Code), with seventy-two countries voting in favour, seven against and five abstaining.

The most controversial measure in the Code was a cargo-reservation scheme which gave the exporting and importing nations equal rights to reserve cargoes for their national lines, while "third-country shipping lines, if any, shall have the right to acquire a significant part, such as twenty percent."[39] In practice, this meant a 40-40-20 sharing of trade, something which obviously would be detrimental for cross-traders. The UNCTAD Code was only legally binding on those countries that ratified it, and would come into force only after being approved by at least twenty-four countries with at least twenty-five percent of world tonnage.

Seven of the OECD member countries voted for the UNCTAD Code, the same number voted against it, and a further five countries abstained. Among the supporters were the Federal Republic of Germany, France and Belgium, all founding members of the Consultative Shipping Group. Only a few years earlier, the CSG nations had appeared to be united against increased government intervention in shipping and in promoting self-regulation of the liner trades.[40] On the other hand, once it was clear that some degree of regulation was all but inevitable, political pressure from the developing countries, as

---

[37]*Ibid.*, draft report of meeting of UNCTAD Committee of Shipping, 29 April 1970.

[38]OECD, MT(73)3, MTC Annual Report 1972, 8 May 1973.

[39]*Ibid.*, MT(74)5, MTC Annual Report 1973.

[40]TNA/PRO, FCO 76/393, internal briefing note by the UK Department of Trade and Industry, 11 April 1972.

well as public opinion in the West, required the developed nations to at least appear constructive in discussions about reform and economic development. During 1972, a split emerged within the CSG, primarily between France and West Germany on one side and Britain and the Scandinavian countries on the other.[41] In the midst of this difficult political situation, international shipping markets collapsed. In the wake of the 1973 oil crisis, demand for international maritime transport fell and freight rates plummeted. It soon became obvious that the crisis was structural rather than cyclical, and the difficult market situation continued to trouble the shipping industry for more than a decade. In its wake, there was a seismic shift in the ownership of merchant tonnage. While in 1970, 64.5 percent of the world fleet was registered in OECD countries, by 1987, the OECD's share had declined to thirty-four percent.[42]

After the adoption of the UNCTAD Code in 1974, both the OECD and the European Community began to examine the compatibility of the UNCTAD Code with their own regulations. The OECD Council was divided on the issue, but asked its members to reaffirm their commitment to the OECD Code of Liberalisation.[43] There is little doubt that the UNCTAD Code, despite not being totally incompatible with OECD regulations, represented a clear break with the liberal practices that had dominated the Maritime Transport Committee and particularly the CSG since the early 1950s. Still, sceptics could not use the OECD to force the others not to ratify the UNCTAD Code, and the MTC remained an arena for consultation rather than action.

The European Community, on the other hand, had both the will and the legal power to pressure member states which were inclined to approve the Code. Although international shipping was excluded from the Treaty of Rome, the European Court in 1974 ruled that its general provisions regarding competition and non-discrimination were also applicable to ocean shipping. Under heavy pressure from the European Commission, Belgium, France and West Germany decided to abstain from ratifying the UNCTAD Code until it was decided whether it was compatible with EC regulations.[44] In September 1974, the Commission concluded that certain measures in the Code conflicted with European regulations and suggested a process to adjust the terms in order to

---

[41]*Ibid.*, FCO 76/394, Inter-departmental Group on UNCTAD, report of UK delegation, 4 August 1972.

[42]Stig Tenold, *Changes in the Distribution of the World Fleet, 1970-1987* (Bergen, 2000), 5.

[43]OECD, MT(75)5, MTC Annual Report 1974, 14 May 1975; and DAF/MTC/75.47, follow-up on the UNCTAD Code, 19 December 1975.

[44]Norway, Ministry of Foreign Affairs (NMFA), 44.36/15B, vol. 5, Ketil Børde to NMFA, 31 July 1974.

secure ratification by all Community members. The Commission's proposal was accepted, to the surprise of many participants.[45] This started a long process of negotiation within the European Community on a common approach to the Code, which finally ended in 1979 with a compromise which established a common basis on which member countries could ratify the Code.[46] The most important part of the European compromise was that the cargo-sharing scheme should not apply to trade between member states. In the wake of this compromise, several other OECD countries ratified the UNCTAD Code with similar reservations, leaving the US as the most prominent outsider. The Code came into force in 1983, and by the mid-1980s most European traditional maritime nations had ratified it. Since ratification by countries with at least twenty-five percent of the world fleet was required for the Code to come into force, the EC compromise clearly was instrumental in its implementation.

The development on the UNCTAD Code in the 1970s marked the definitive end to the post-World War II shipping policy regime. Some degree of government regulation of international shipping was unavoidable, but given that trade between most developed countries was continued on a commercial basis without government interference, the Code was acceptable even to the most liberal actors in the field. Still, the Code was only one of several developments in shipping politics between the late 1960s and the 1980s. Parallel to the discussions on the Code, a series of bilateral trade agreements which included maritime transport were agreed. Increased national subsidies to shipping and shipbuilding in the wake of the shipping crisis also worried those who favoured liberal shipping policies. Another threat to the traditional maritime nations was the emergence of new actors in international shipping. Of particular concern to many OECD countries were the increased fleets of the East Bloc countries. These so-called "state trading countries" did not have to take the same commercial considerations as did Western shipowners and consequently were able to continue their operations without fear during the shipping crisis. Indeed, these countries used the crisis to expand heavily in the liner trades.

The European compromise began a process of unification of shipping policies among OECD countries. Most prominently, it was the first step towards common European legislation on ocean shipping. The first package of such shipping legislation was passed in 1986. This contributed to establishing the Community more permanently as an important maritime trade policy arena and moved the focus of some Europeans away from the MTC, CSG and CENSA to the European Community and its shipowners' association, CAACE. Nevertheless, the common approach to shipping contributed to reconciling the

---

[45] *Ibid.*, W.G. Solberg to NMFA, 2 October 1974.

[46] OECD, DAF/MTC/80.16, MTC Draft Annual Report 1979, 17 April 1974.

differences among European nations that threatened to tear the alliance apart during the 1970s.[47]

After the situation in Europe was stabilized in the late 1970s, the process of unifying the policies of the OECD members started. The UNCTAD Code, which the US and Japan never signed, was only one of several bones of contention. The MTC initiated a programme to harmonize member countries' shipping policies. After a thorough investigation, an inventory of conflicting policies was published in 1983. The document formed basis for prolonged and difficult negotiations. In 1984, the United States passed a new shipping act which brought the US regulatory system more into line with the practices of other OECD countries.[48] Finally, in 1987 the OECD Council agreed on a resolution based on the common principles of shipping policy. The OECD resolution marked a milestone in maritime trade politics, as this was the first time that all developed countries had agreed on a detailed document covering a large number of shipping policies.[49] The common approach was a result not only of the work done within the OECD but also in the European Community, the CSG-US dialogues, bilateral and regional networks, shipowners' and shippers' associations and UNCTAD. Despite the fragile nature of the OECD consensus, Western nations seemed better suited for productive cooperation on maritime trade policies than they had been for a long time.

By the late 1980s, international shipping markets were recovering. From the perspective of the Western nations, it appeared that some developing countries, especially in Latin America, were liberalizing their shipping policies.[50] Nevertheless, several other developing nations, especially in Africa, continued their regulatory regimes, and OECD countries had disputes over subsidies and protectionism.[51] More concerning for many traditional maritime nations was that their share of the world fleet was reduced tremendously between the onset of the shipping crisis and the late 1980s. The growth of the Southeast Asian fleets was one reason for this, but just as important was the flagging-out of fleets by Western shipowners. Nationality gradually became less important to shipping companies which preferred to register their ships in tax havens or countries with fewer regulations about manning and other re-

[47]Norwegian Shipowners' Association (NSA), 1-4, Nordisk skipsfartssamarbeid, V, internal note by Alf Bergesen, 22 January 1974.

[48]OECD, MT(85)1, part I, MTC Annual Report 1984, 24 April 1985.

[49]*Ibid.*, MT(87)1, part I, MTC Annual Report 1986, 12 March 1987.

[50]*Ibid.*, MT(85)1, part I, MTC Annual Report 1984, 24 April 1985.

[51]OECD - MT(90)1, Part I - MTC Annual Report 1989, 12 February 1990.

quirements. This obviously changed the nature of world shipping politics, as national and commercial issues became less important.

In short, international maritime trade politics changed substantially from the late 1940s to the late 1980s. The first couple of decades were dominated by Western European and North American nations. The debate usually centred on subsidies and flag discrimination. Although many Western European countries were critical of American shipping policy, the field remained quite stable and friendly until the 1960s, and international shipping was hardly regulated at all. The most important arena for shipping policy debates in this period was the Maritime Transport Committee of the OECD. From the early 1960s the level of conflict between the European maritime nations and the US increased. The Europeans established the Consultative Shipping Group to coordinate their strategies towards the US. At the same time, several developing nations entered the policy field, demanding more regulation of international shipping in order to strengthen their ability to develop their own shipping industries. UNCTAD became the battleground for the conflict between actors seeking more regulation and those who favoured more liberal policies. Soon this debate moved to other arenas, and the debate on the UNCTAD Code became the dominant issue in the CSG and the OECD. The Code also became the first maritime trade issue discussed within the European Community. It is obvious that international shipping became more politicized and that the number and importance of international organizations increased from the mid-1960s to the 1980s. In addition, the field grew more complex during these decades. Organizations such as UNCTAD and OECD were interdependent, and decisions taken in one arena affected those in others. These developments also changed the strategies of actors in the field, as we shall see when we study the Norwegians in the next section.

Norway in International Shipping Politics

During a visit to Norway in 1965, British Minister of State Roy Mason stated that "Norway was the foremost and strongest supporter of...liberal international shipping policies. He referred to Anglo-British co-operation on this issue in many international organisations."[52] These few words from the Minister's speech pretty much sum up the main lines in Norwegian international maritime trade politics. Norway was one of the most eager *laissez-faire* countries, which is understandable given that more than two-thirds of the Norwegian fleet was involved in the international cross-trades.

---

[52]TNA/PRO, MT 59/3256, note by K.J. Jordan, 21 May 1965; and *Verdens Gang* (Oslo), 21 April 1965. Mason was Minister of State with responsibility for shipping in the Board of Trade; see Elisabeth Sleeman (ed.) *The International Who's Who, 2004* (London, 2003), 1105.

This part of the essay examines the approach of Norwegians to international shipping politics. First, I will identify the main actors to gain an idea of how decisions were made. Second, I will discuss their strategies toward shipping politics. Alan Cafruny claims that small countries like Norway lacked influence in international politics.[53] He might be correct, since Norway probably had only a limited influence on overall developments. The country's lack of political and economic power obviously required Norwegians to cooperate with people from other countries. But with whom did the Norwegians cooperate? Where and how did they cooperate? How did Norwegian actors adapt to developments in international shipping politics? And what influence, if any, did Norwegians have?

Norway was among the strongest defenders of liberal international maritime trade policies during the entire period. Compared with most other countries, even the traditional maritime nations, shipping remained among the nation's most important export industries. From the mid-nineteenth century to the 1970s, shipping was actually *the* most export important industry in terms of revenues. Throughout this period, the industry was largely oriented towards international markets; only a small part of the goods carried by Norwegian vessels was of Norwegian origin.

The importance of the industry gave shipowners a special standing in Norwegian society. As one British report stated in 1970, "[i]n a country which abolished its aristocracy in the last century and prides itself on its egalitarianism, the title 'shipowner' (it is used as a title) is one to conjure with." Before World War II, several shipowners held high offices in the Norwegian government, including the office of prime minister. After the war, this changed as the Labour Party came to dominate politics. Nonetheless, despite some disagreements over currency restrictions after war, the shipping industry and the Norwegian government cooperated fairly closely.[54] As in most other traditional maritime nations, the industry was to a large degree left free from government regulations during the postwar decades. The government seems to have acknowledged the shipping industry's contribution to the economy and realized that its international exposure made it particularly vulnerable. Stricter regulation would decrease the competitiveness of the Norwegian fleet. Further, access to international markets was crucial for Norwegian shipping, so the Norwegian government had to lead by example and impose as few restrictions as possible.

The relationship between the Norwegian government and industry representatives was very close. The intimate relationship between the Minis-

---

[53]Cafruny, *Ruling the Waves*, 203.

[54]TNA/PRO, FCO 33/1267, T.F. Brenchley to Sir Arthur Douglas-Home, 8 October 1970.

tries of Trade and Foreign Affairs and the Norwegian Shipowners' Association (NSA) was the result of a strong consensus between civil servants and industry representatives about the main objectives of Norwegian international maritime trade policy. It was not uncommon for them to use phrases such as "our approach" in discussions between the NSA and the ministries.[55] The NSA was an integral part of Norwegian international shipping politics. The Shipowners' Association had daily contact with government officials and received copies of most relevant correspondence, telegrams and reports. In addition, the NSA participated in official Norwegian delegations to international forums such as the MTC, CSG, Nordic consultation meetings and European Community discussions. It was also common for NSA employees to research and write the official briefs for the Norwegian delegation. The leaders of the Seafarers Union, on the other hand, usually were excluded from debates about international shipping politics, even when the Labour Party was in government.[56] Finally, there were several cases of key actors shifting between jobs in the ministries and the NSA, something which doubtless solidified the ties even more.[57]

As a recipient of aid through the Marshall Plan, Norway joined the OEEC in 1948 and was a member of the MTC from the beginning. In the following decades, the MTC became the preferred arena in the Norwegian battle against subsidies, flag preferences and other restrictive shipping politics.[58] The structure of the MTC and members' attitudes towards shipping policies suited the Norwegians well. Government officials, politicians and the NSA were far more sceptical about the IMCO where the traditional maritime nations would not have the same dominant position as in the MTC. Norwegians feared that the US and other countries would use the IMCO to impose regulations on maritime trade. After a prolonged debate in the 1950s, however, the Norwe-

---

[55]NMFA, 44.36/6.84, file 2, Asbjørn Larsen to Kjell Rasmussen, 30 July 1971.

[56]This resulted in a furious debate in the mid-1980s, when the leader of the Norwegian Seafarers Union discovered that the shipowners had participated in official Nordic consultation meetings, while the labour organizations were excluded. NSA, 2-220.2, Henrik Aasarød to Asbjørn Haugstvedt, 11 March 1986.

[57]Eivinn Berg was perhaps the most prominent of these. During his career, he held a number of key positions in the Ministry of Foreign Affairs, both abroad and at home, and he was the director of the NSA in the 1970s. He also served as Secretary of State for Foreign Affairs in Kåre Willoch's Conservative government during the 1980s. Other persons with careers in both the ministries and the NSA include Karoline Lennartson Bøhler, Sigurd Endresen and Thor Chr. Hildan.

[58]Rustand, "Allierte på kollisjonskurs?" 46.

gian government decided to join the IMCO in order to influence the organization from within.[59]

During the 1960s, Norway took an active role in the MTC and in the establishment of the CSG.[60] Together with the other traditional maritime nations, Norwegians were particularly concerned about US legislation in the first half of the 1960s. As the developing countries entered the field of shipping from the mid-1960s, Norwegians were among the most critical voices against greater government regulation. Norwegian delegates used the MTC and CSG to draw attention to government involvement in the shipping industry of member and non-member countries.[61] Still, it was evident that Norwegians had to increase their efforts if they were to prevent a substantial increase of regulation in international shipping. It was also clear that they had to adapt their strategies to the new directions in international maritime politics.

Cooperation with other European maritime nations was the primary strategy pursued by Norwegians to defend the liberal shipping political order. This strategy worked fairly well for a time, but from the mid-1960s, some actors in Norway began to voice concerns over the willingness of some Western European nations to sacrifice liberal principles.[62] Given the development in connection with the UNCTAD Code, these concerns soon proved to be real. The first step in the Norwegian approach to adapt to the emerging situation was to increase cooperation with its closest allies, the United Kingdom and the other Scandinavian countries.

The relationship among Norway, Sweden and Denmark has historical roots, and in shipping politics the three countries had close ties. Contacts with Finland increased after the country became a member of the OECD in 1969. The international turbulence presented challenges to all of the Nordic countries. Although there were substantial differences among each of their shipping industries, they all shared a common interest in maintaining liberal international shipping policies. To try to ensure this, government representatives from Norway, Denmark, Sweden and Finland met regularly for so-called "coordination meetings." Around 1970, these increased in frequency and were held as often as four times a year, depending on the need to prepare and coordinate strategies for international meetings. The meetings were typically attended by four or five people from each country, usually senior officials from ministries

---

[59]*Ibid.*, 53-61.

[60]TNA/PRO, FCO 33/1267, Brenchley to Douglas-Home, 8 October 1970.

[61]See, for example, OECD, MT(70)1, MTC policy matters, 5 February 1970; and MT(71)5, MTC consultation on members countries' shipping policies, 25 May 1971.

[62]TNA/PRO, MT 59/3256, note by K.J. Jordan, 21 May 1965.

of trade and foreign affairs and representatives from each of the countries' shipowners' associations. These conclaves contributed on many occasions to common Nordic strategies for international negotiations.[63]

Norway also maintained close contacts with British representatives, both through bilateral discussions and meetings among the Nordic countries and UK representatives.[64] When the split among CSG countries emerged in the early 1970s, the Anglo-Nordic group was the strongest proponent of *laissez-faire* principles, but that did not mean that they necessarily shared the same views on how best to maintain a liberal shipping policy. After the adoption of the UNCTAD Code in 1974, it became evident to the Norwegians that it would be difficult to deny concessions to the developing maritime countries. The strategies might have been affected in part by the general Norwegian attitude to North-South debates, where Norway was usually portrayed as among the more progressive developed countries.[65] Probably more, the Norwegian political actors wanted to broker a compromise in Europe to prevent further fragmentation among the Western countries. A common understanding with the other CSG and OECD countries could be used as a basis for negotiations with the East Bloc and the less-developed nations. The general idea was that it was essential to first influence the countries close to you and then to cooperate with those in the second and third second tiers. This is an example of how Norwegian actors adapted to the changed situation in international shipping politics during the 1970s.

In 1974, Danish and British representatives clung firmly to the position that they should refuse any kind of government regulation of liner conferences. Norwegian, Swedish and Finnish actors, on the other hand, were disposed to accept cargo reservation for developing countries, but not for developed nations.[66] Norway actually took the most radical position among the Anglo-Nordic countries, something that must have been seen as quite surprising given that only a few years earlier, Norwegians had portrayed developing

[63]NSA, 1-4, Nordisk skipsfartssamarbeid, V, Sigurd Endresen, internal memo, 12 June 1975; and Reginald Norby, memo, 18 April 1972.

[64]*Ibid.*, Nordisk skipsfartssamarbeid, VI, minutes of meeting with NMFA, 7 February 1974; and TNA/PRO, FCO 76/393, internal UK brief, 11 April 1972.

[65]NSA, 1-4, Nordisk skipsfartssamarbeid, V, minutes of meeting with MTC and NMFA, 6 July 1972. According to some people, the Norwegians were only "progressive" when their interests were not at stake. See, for example, Helge Hveem, "Norway: The Hesitant Reformer," in Cranford Pratt (ed.), *Internationalism Under Strain: The North-South Policies of Canada, the Netherlands, Norway and Sweden* (Toronto, 1989), 104-154.

[66]NSA, 1-4, Nordisk skipsfartssamarbeid, V, Norby, memo, 1 February 1974.

countries as third-parties trying to meddle in the business of the traditional maritime nations.[67] Nevertheless, this must be seen as an indication of how important a compromise among the Western countries was for Norwegians.

The situation involving the UNCTAD Code was further complicated by the Norwegian refusal to become a member of the EC after a referendum in 1972. Shipowners had eagerly promoted Norwegian membership in the Community and by the late 1960s regarded the EC as an important actor in international shipping politics. The Norwegian shipping community watched with great disappointment as their primary allies and close trading partners, Denmark and the UK, joined the European Community in 1973 while Norway remained outside.[68] In subsequent negotiations for a trade agreement between Norway and the Community, shipping services was given little attention by the Norwegian delegation, which instead focused on exports, especially frozen fish fillets.[69] The shipowners again were left in the lurch.[70]

In addition to the role of the European Community in the UNCTAD Code debates, many in the Norwegian shipping community feared that the Europeans would form an exclusive trading block. Close relations with the Community were important, and the links with the UK and especially Denmark were valuable in giving Norwegians insight into the on-going process of deciding shipping policy within the Community. On numerous occasions, the Norwegian government and the Norwegian Shipowners' Association received information on progress within the Community from Danish officials and the Danish Shipowners' Association. Negotiating common positions with the Danes and the British could also give Norway some influence on the development of European policy in this field. Norway's role in the process that ended with the European compromise on the UNCTAD Code in 1979 is difficult to determine, but it is worth mentioning that the final position was in line with the Norwegian proposition in 1974.

In addition to trying to influence the EC through Denmark and the UK, Norwegians sought other channels. The CSG and MTC, for instance, could be useful in moderating French and German views regarding shipping

---

[67]NMFA, 44.36/6.84, H.J. Darre Hirsch to Per Borten, 22 December 1970. The term used by Darre Hirsch to describe the developing countries was "*utenforstående land*."

[68]NSA, 1-7B4-XIII, NSA press release, 26 September 1972.

[69]See, for example, TNA/PRO, Board of Trade (BT) 241/2554, J.O. Wright, internal memo, 9 April 1973.

[70]NSA, 1-7B4-XIV, David Vikøren to Jens Evensen, 2 February 1973.

policies.[71] During the 1970s, the NSA urged the Norwegian government to establish closer contacts with European bodies, but because the politicians had to balance the interest of the export industries and strong domestic opinion against European integration, they approached Brussels only reluctantly.[72] In 1977, however, Norway and the European Commission established formal consultation on shipping issues.[73] The NSA tried to keep a closer watch on EC activities. As the Community grew more important as an arena for shipping policy debates during the 1970s and 1980s, the NSA tried to get closer cooperation with the EC shipowners' organisation, CAACE. In the early 1970s, the NSA even tried to become a member, but it was refused because Norway was not an EC member.[74] It might be added, though, that the NSA actually became a member some twenty years later. During the 1970s and early 1980s, however, the NSA had to use other forums, such as CENSA or Anglo-Nordic shipowners' networks, to promote their ideas. The NSA tried as well to influence EC bodies directly. From the late 1970s, it frequently sent representatives to Brussels to discuss shipping matters with officials and politicians. On several occasions, the NSA suggested sending an official Norwegian shipping representative to Brussels, but this position was not established until 1985.[75]

After the EC reached a compromise on the UNCTAD Code, Norway, as did most other European OECD members, decided to ratify the convention. When Denmark, Sweden and Norway ratified the UNCTAD Code on 28 June 1985, the chapter of the Convention entitled "Declarations and Reservations" stated the Danish reservations, while the paragraphs on Sweden and Norway simply read "[s]ame declaration and reservation, identical in essence as those made by Denmark."[76] In the years following the European compromise, Norwegians took an active role in establishing a shipping policy consensus among

---

[71]*Ibid.*, 1-4, Nordisk skipsfartssamarbeid, V, Bergesen, internal note, 22 January 1974.

[72]For more on Norwegian relations with the EC in the 1970s, see, for example, Toivo Miljan, *The Reluctant Europeans: The Attitudes of the Nordic Countries towards European Integration* (London, 1977).

[73]NSA, 1-7B4, file "Adm. Direktør David Vikøren. Besøk i Brussel 24. og 25. oktober 1977;" and Evinn Berg, brief, 10 October 1977.

[74]*Ibid.*, Asbjørn Larsen, internal note, 24 October 1972.

[75]See note 73; and NSA, 1-7B4-XXIII, Rolf Sæther, internal memo, 15 August 1978.

[76]UNCTAD, *Convention on a Code of Conduct for Liner Conferences, Declarations and Reservations, XII, 6,* 3-6, http://r0.unctad.org/ttl/docs-legal/unc-cml/status/Convention%20on%20a%20Code%20of%20Conduct.pdf.

Western countries to try to increase the chances of keeping international shipping fairly liberal.

Norwegians feared that the European compromise would be "watered down."[77] It was thus crucial for Norway to reach a compromise within the MTC. This soon proved to be very difficult. Although the European compromise had united the European countries, it was impossible to persuade the US and Japan to ratify the Code. The differences between the parties seemed vast, and the development of a common OECD approach to shipping was hampered by the parallel negotiations over a common European shipping policy. The slow development greatly worried Norwegians in the early 1980s. An NSA report from 1984 stated that the negotiations were entering a critical phase and argued that it would become difficult to re-establish the dialogue if these failed. It was further added that a dialogue between the CSG and the US was the only way to reach a compromise.

> For Norwegian shipping a potential CSG-USA-agreement would be *the* great opportunity to avoid the shipping political situation we have feared for some time: where the OECD no longer functions satisfactorily, the EC turns in to a trading block, and USA and Japan are independent and strong enough to form their own politics, while Norway is left as the only large cross trader without connections or possibility to influence the development.[78]

The quote demonstrates first of all that the Norwegian position was very fragile, given that the country was both small and a European "outsider." Further, it shows how the actors navigated within the political system, where decisions in one arena were necessary for development in others.

The first point in the report was strengthened in 1986 when the European Community passed its first package of common legislation on maritime transport. Both the leaders of the NSA and the Director General of the Ministry of Trade and Shipping admitted that they were "worried" by the situation. Within the NSA, the European legislation was called "extremely disturbing."[79] Developments within the OECD were also greeted with pessimism by Norwe-

---

[77]NSA, 1-4, Nord. Skipsfartssamarbeid, Sæther, internal memo, 13 September 1979.

[78]NSA, 2-221.1, Council of European National Shipowners' Associations (CENSA), internal NSA report, 24 October 1984 [my translation].

[79]*Ibid.*, 2-229.10-7, minutes of meeting between the NSA and the Ministry of Trade and Shipping, 17 January 1987; and Kjetil Djønne and Arild Wegener, internal memo, 8 January 1987.

gians. Although a "common approach" among the OECD countries was very much in the interest of Norwegians, the OECD was seen as too weak in the battle against protectionism.[80] For most traditional maritime nations, a common approach within the OECD was acceptable, but for the Norwegians who feared becoming outsiders, a weak OECD was much more worrisome.

Like the rest of the traditional maritime nations, Norway was severely impacted by the shipping crisis. From the early 1970s, the shipping industry's importance to the country's export revenues declined from around forty percent to about fifteen or twenty percent in the 1980s.[81] In addition to the international shipping crisis, the increased significance of the oil industry to Norwegian export revenues contributed to this. Nonetheless, the Norwegian shipping industry was deeply shaken by the shipping crisis, and from the early 1980s, shipowners started to register their vessels abroad. Between the late 1970s and the late 1980s, the Norwegian-registered merchant fleet was reduced by approximately seventy-five percent. Norway had the world's fourth largest national fleet in 1970, but by 1987 the country only had the eighteenth largest registered fleet.[82] The flagging-out of the Norwegian fleet caused many harsh reactions in Norway, but in the long run the reduced competiveness of Norwegian-registered vessels was unsustainable. The Norwegian solution was to establish an international ship register which partly re-established Norway as a major shipping power. Meanwhile, though, nationality had become less important in shipping, and both Norwegian shipowners and their government had to adapt to this new reality from the 1990s onwards.

Conclusions

This essay has discussed the development of international shipping politics from the end of World War II until the late 1980s, with a special emphasis on the role of international organizations and networks and the way Norwegian actors operated in the field. As Alan Cafruny noted, international shipping became more regulated and politicized in this period. This essay emphasizes as well the fact that the structure of international shipping policy negotiations changed as international organizations and networks became more important. The increased importance of new entities transformed the international maritime trade policy field from a stable and fairly simple system into a complex

---

[80] *Ibid.*, 2-222.1-1, Karoline Lennartson, internal memo, 15 November 1989.

[81] Stig Tenold, *Skipsfartskrisen og utviklingen i norsk skipsfart, 1970-1991* (Bergen, 2001), 32.

[82] Stig Tenold, "The Shipping Crisis of the 1970s: Causes, Effects and Implications for Norwegian Shipping" (Unpublished PhD thesis, Norwegian School of Economics and Business Administration, 2001), 156.

political web. The postwar Atlantic unity, which lasted until the mid-1960s, had few actors: Western European and North American governments and shipowners. Disagreements in this period centred primarily on national subsidies and flag discrimination. The system that evolved from the mid-1960s included many more actors. In addition, the self-regulation of the shipping sector came under pressure as many of the actors - both new and old - sought a higher degree of political regulation of international shipping. I have argued that the key to understanding how policy decisions were made in this new system is to analyze the *interdependence* between the various entities in the field - such as intergovernmental organizations, transnational networks, shipowners' associations and so forth.

Most of the organizations that became important in the maritime policy field in the 1970s and 1980s were established by the early 1960s. Their importance was nevertheless small until the late 1960s when the UNCTAD situation emerged. Developing countries wanted a regulation of international liner shipping in order to strengthen their own national fleets and thus suggested an international Code of Conduct for liner shipping in UNCTAD. The debates on the Code lasted for more than a decade, and when it was finally passed in the mid-1980s, it had been watered down significantly. Still, the debate on the regulation of liner shipping was a watershed in international shipping politics and a clear break with the earlier *laissez-faire* approach to international maritime trade policies. The adoption of the UNCTAD Code is also an excellent example of how the various international entities affected each other. The UNCTAD Code became the great issue in maritime trade policies during the 1970s and the early 1980s. The Code was debated not only in UNCTAD but also in the European Community, the OECD and in bilateral talks. Developments in all these different spheres were crucial for the final establishment of the UNCTAD Code. Similarly, when the OECD finally agreed on a common approach to shipping policy in 1987, this was a result of developments within UNCTAD, the European Community, CSG, CENSA and the OECD. In addition, progress was influenced by developments in the shipping industry and by national, bilateral and multilateral discussions on many fronts. These two cases are excellent examples of the interdependence among the various entities within the policy field. It should be stressed, though, that I do not claim that this is a complete analysis of international shipping policy decisions but rather that such decisions were a result of complex processes on many levels. In order to understand the development, it is thus necessary to take the complexity of the field into consideration.

The Norwegian case shows how one group of actors - Norwegian government officials and industry representatives - operated in the field. Government officials and industry representatives worked very closely throughout the period. The Norwegians in the first decades after World War II were reluctant to embrace international cooperation, preferring to use the MTC to limit the role of governments in shipping. From the late 1960s, though, they were forced to change their approach. The new strategy embraced discussions, mediations and pressures within a complex web of bilateral and multilateral consultations, networks and agreements. The main strategy of the Norwegian actors was to influence actors close to home first and then use this as a basis for negotiations with others. Although we need to be cautious not to exaggerate the changes either to the overall structure of shipping politics or to the actors in the system, the trend is nevertheless undeniable.

The Norwegian fear of being left as the only major cross-trading nation without great political and economic power or without being part of a larger community, such as the European Community, shows that even in the late 1980s Norwegians still perceived international maritime trade politics as important. It further demonstrates the difficulties that actors from small countries encounter when dealing with international politics. Still, the substantial efforts made to exert some influence shows that Norwegians believed that they could influence the direction of the international maritime policy.

Inheriting Strategies: Understanding Different Approaches to Shipping during the World War I Boom in Haugesund, Norway[1]

Morten Hammerborg

On 14 October 1915, John Knudsen Haaland married Aslaug Stolt-Nielsen in the Church of Our Saviour (Vår Frelsers kirke) in Haugesund, a small town on the west coast of Norway.[2] One week later, in the same church, his twin brother Christian Wegner Haaland wed Ida Karoline Knutsen. Not only did the brothers marry at roughly the same time, but each served as the other's best man. For residents of Haugesund, however, the most striking similarity between the two weddings undoubtedly concerned the brothers' choice of brides, for they married the daughters of two of the town's leading shipowners, Botholf Stolt-Nielsen and Knut Knutsen O.A.S. The twenty-year-old brothers, sons of a bank manager from a respectable though rather modest background, were about to embark on careers as shipowners just as World War I was beginning to affect maritime commerce (although Norway remained neutral). Despite the similarities, their careers had very different outcomes; one went bankrupt, while the other enjoyed immense prosperity and was one of the most important and respected men, both economically and politically, in Haugesund.

How did these results occur? Why did the twins end up at such different ends of the success spectrum? As happened so often in the volatile world of shipowning, the fates of these two men and their companies hinged on strategic

---

[1]I wish to thank the editors of this volume for their critical and constructive suggestions. I also wish to thank the participants at the workshop in Oslo where this essay was first presented, especially Stig Tenold and Camilla Brautaset. The article has also benefited greatly from the generous feedback from my colleagues Teemu Ryymin, Svein Atle Skålevåg and James Wood.
 Much of this article is based on Morten Hammerborg, *Skipsfartsbyen: Haugesunds skipsfartshistorie, 1850-2000* (Bergen, 2003). For the most part, I will exclude the archival references that can be found in that volume. In addition, I draw heavily on Øyvind Bjørnson, *Haugesund, 1914-1950: Dei trødde sjøen* (Bergen, 2004), and two biographies: Tor Inge Vormedal, *B. Stolt-Nielsen: Den glemte pioneren* (Haugesund, 2001); and Vormedal, *Knut Knutsen OAS: Høvdingen av Haugesund og Knutsen-imperiets vekst og fall* (Haugesund, 2001).

[2]Information on these marriages has been compiled from church books placed at my disposal by Mads Ramstad, director of Karmsund Folkemuseum in Haugesund.

decisions taken before or after a boom or bust.[3] It is often fairly straightforward to identify the decisions that led to riches or doom for various actors, but in this article I will concentrate on the strategies that underlay these decisions. From where did these differing strategies stem? How were they produced? How were they implemented?

Trying to understand why different actors made different strategic choices can be difficult. For example, it is possible to utilize the extensive literature on "economic man," differing concepts of (economic) rationality or the psychological processes involved in economic decision-making.[4] Instead, although somewhat overlapping with these approaches, I will view the shipowners' strategic choices as first and foremost social phenomena that were heavily influenced by the past. As Karl Marx famously declared, "[m]en make their own history, but they do not make it just as they please; they do not make it under circumstances chosen by themselves, but under circumstances directly encountered, given and transmitted from the past."[5]

In this article, I will examine the tension between the ways that the Haaland twins tried to "make their own history" under two different sets of circumstances having their roots in the past. To be more precise, through an analysis of their histories I want to explore how past practices can have a decisive impact on economic decision making. In both cases, the past was transmitted through a set of obligations and influences which can be traced to their respective fathers-in-law. First, we will see how personal background and experience came to shape two clearly distinguishable sets of inclinations and relatively stable economic strategies of the shipowners Stolt-Nielsen and Knutsen O.A.S. in the decades leading up to World War I. Next, we will explore how these differing practices in many ways were inherited by the young Haaland brothers. As I will show, the two different strategies remained the tools which shipowners used to navigate the choppy waters of the wartime boom.

The resilience of these strategies and the habitual manner in which they were executed led to patterns of behaviour that are best thought of as "*modi operandi*." A *modus operandi* is a consistent way of operating. It is

---

[3]For an excellent study that illustrates this point, see Stig Tenold, *Tankers in Trouble: Norwegian Shipping and the Crisis of the 1970s and 1980s* (St. John's, 2006).

[4]For a thorough discussion of the concepts of "economic man" and rationality regarding shipowners, see Berit Eide Johnsen, "Rederstrategi i endringstid: Sørlandsk skipsfart fra seil til damp og motor, fra tre til jern og stål, 1875-1925" (Unpublished PhD thesis, University of Bergen, 1998). For a classic study of economic decision-making, see Herbert A. Simon, "Theories of Decision-making in Economics and Behavioral Science," *American Economic Review*, XLIX, No. 3 (1959), 253-283.

[5]Karl Marx, *The 18th Brumaire of Louis Bonaparte* (London, 1852; reprint, London, 2001), 7.

shaped and regulated by past experiences and present circumstances. It takes the form of almost routinized patterns of action, in our cases in the form of business strategies.[6] These behaviours, however, are not immutable and can therefore change over time. Shipowners, like all social agents, are simultaneously structured and structuring beings, but radical breaks that lead to a decision to revise a *modus operandi* most often require a strong external shock.[7]

In the following, I will identify the *modi operandi* of the four shipowners based on their business strategies and analyze the relationship between the two generations of shipowners. To explain why the Haaland twins followed such different paths, we must look beyond the narrow time span of the boom and its aftermath. Instead, we must begin with their fathers-in-law. First, though, we need to examine the social and economic arena in which they acted.

Haugesund: City of Speculators

> The small town of Haugesund is located on the west coast of Norway. It looks rather insignificant, and in actual fact there is nothing unique about it, except that during the war it set a record for the number of millionaires. Norwegians at the time claimed that no other town in the world was as well endowed with large-scale capitalists.[8]

The quote above is from a leading Danish newspaper, *Berlingske Tidende*, described the town of Haugesund in the interwar period. In spite of being a rather small and provincial town, Haugesund was one of the leading shipping towns of Norway, renowned for the fervency with which its shipowners had speculated during the First World War boom, thus setting a "record in mil-

---

[6]"Strategies" in this article denote consistent patterns of behaviour displayed by actors through investment decisions, uses of credit, choices of business organization and dividend policies. The sources, except in the case of B. Stolt-Nielsen, do not permit us to generate insights into their thoughts and deliberations through journals, letters or similar records and hence must be inferred from their behaviours.

[7]My use of *modus operandi* bears a good deal of resemblance to Pierre Bourdieu's concept of *habitus*. I will, however, not pursue the similarities here. Readers seeking an insightful introduction to Bourdieu's analytical model may wish to consult the essays in Michael Grenfell (ed.), *Pierre Bourdieu: Key Concepts* (London, 2008).

[8]The quote is from *Berlingske Tidende* (Copenhagen); my translation. It is taken from Øyvind Bjørnson, "Knut Knutsen OAS," *Norsk Biografisk Leksikon*, V (Oslo, 2002), and also at http://www.snl.no/.nbl_biografi/Knut_Knutsen_O._A._S./utdypning.

lionaires." Due to its neutrality, Norway's large fleet remained commercially active during the war, carrying goods to the belligerents and generating enormous profits for Norwegian shipowners.[9] The speculation of these boom years brought unprecedented wealth to Haugesund, which was perhaps unrivalled in the intensity of its financial speculation.[10] Far more populous cities, such as Christiania (Oslo) and Bergen, were of course home to greater numbers of ships and shipowners, meaning that they derived larger profits than did Haugesund, but in relative terms, Haugesund's shipowners seem to have speculated more heavily than their competitors elsewhere.[11] For instance, as wartime losses reduced the nation's tonnage by 28.5 percent between 1914 and 1918, Haugesund's tonnage actually increased by sixty-five percent. This burgeoning fleet of modern ships meant that while in 1914, Haugesund grossed around 4.5 percent of national freight income, by 1920 it grossed 11.6 percent. Partly in response to this increased commerce, the town's population grew rapidly, almost doubling from 10,633 in 1910 to 20,236 in 1920, at which time the still-young town boasted one of the highest mean incomes in Norway.[12] The boom seemed to have blessed Haugesund; its future looked to be full of promise and glory.

Ten years later, however, hardly any of the shipping companies which had grown so rapidly between 1914 and 1920 still existed or else struggled on with a lone steamer. By 1930, Haugesund's share of Norwegian gross freight income was reduced to 6.5 percent, still higher than its pre-boom position but a sharp decline from its peak. All the banks that had been established by *nouveaux riche* speculators during the boom had been declared insolvent, and the few banks still in existence were reluctant to finance new ships. As well, unemployment raged, population stagnated and municipal revenues plunged, forcing ambitious infrastructure projects to come to a halt. The blessing had become a curse.

The reason for the disproportionate volume of speculation in Haugesund, as well as its rapid rise and subsequent stagnation, is to be found in the town's history and culture, particularly in its entrepreneurial roots. Haugesund was built on speculation in the herring trade: it was granted township rights in 1854 as a direct consequence of the extensive and rich herring fisheries just off

---

[9]For a classic introduction, see Johan Schreiner, *Norsk skipsfart under krig og høykonjunktur, 1914-20* (Oslo, 1963).

[10]For the impact on Haugesund, see Bjørnson, *Haugesund*, 21-101.

[11]Hammerborg, *Skipsfartsbyen*, 123.

[12]This information is taken from Norway, Census, 1900 and 1920, using the modern borders of Haugesund. See http://www.ssb.no/emner/02/01/folketellinger/kommunehefter/1990/index.html.

its shores, rights that entitled the town to export herring. As local entrepreneurs grasped this opportunity, economic life became cyclical and highly market dependent. A typical year began with merchants borrowing to buy herring, salt, and labour. Once the herring was caught, local vessels would transport the herring to European markets for sale. At the end of the year, debts were paid off, and profits hopefully were made. Speculation in fluctuating prices and markets was at the core of this business, which dominated Haugesund's economic life. When the herring exporters used their capital and expertise to expand into shipping in the late nineteenth and early twentieth centuries, the practice of speculation was reinforced. In 1900, a local newspaper hailed the town's speculators with the following homage:

> The steamship company has grown to a major industry in our town, and our young, capable and intelligent speculators, who at the right time demonstrated their courage and manliness [*mannshjerte*] to speculate, has made to some extent splendid businesses.[13]

Speculation permeated both economic life and civic ideals in Haugesund. When freight rates and ship prices spiralled upward after 1914, the "young, capable and intelligent speculators" of Haugesund were given an opportunity to prove their "courage and manliness." The result was unparalleled growth, followed by a devastating crash and decades of stagnation as these men waited for the return of favourable conditions.[14]

Treating the town as an object of investigation sheds light on what may have made Haugesund especially prone to the speculation frenzy of 1914-1920. What this analytical perspective misses, however, is that within this city built on speculation were a myriad of different approaches to shipping.

Formation of the *Modi Operandi* of the Fathers-in-Law

Even before their marriages into prosperous shipping families in the autumn of 1915, both John K. and his brother Christian Haaland had begun to establish themselves as shipowners. Still, there is no doubt that these fledgling enterprises were a direct result of their impending marriages, and the ships they purchased were bought with assistance and guarantees from their soon-to-be fathers-in-law. Such assistance to aspiring young men was a common feature in Haugesund, serving as perhaps the most frequent source of economic expan-

---

[13]Reidar Østensjø, *Haugesund, 1896-1913* (Haugesund, 1993), 102. See also Bjørnson, *Haugesund*, 52.

[14]The subtitle of Bjørnson, *Haugesund*, for the period 1914-1950 is aptly called "Dei trødde sjøen" ("They Tread Water").

sion in the years preceding World War I and leading to the creation of several "new" shipping firms (*rederier*).[15] The case of the Haalands is an excellent example of this economic expansion, for we can see how the ship-owners B. Stolt-Nielsen and Knut Knutsen O.A.S. not only gave over their daughters and dowries but also provided their sons-in-law with their preferred approach to commerce, ensuring that the commercial as well as the biological family would be perpetuated. In their shipping activities, the brothers would adopt the principles and codes of conduct of their respective patrons. While John K. and Christian were twin brothers and firm friends with a shared background, these similarities were soon obliterated under the influence of their new commercial obligations, which came to impose on the two young men very different *modi operandi* derived from the business practices of the families into which they married. As we will see, the backgrounds and approaches to shipping could hardly have been more different than between the two fathers-in-law.

B. Stolt-Nielsen was born in Haugesund in 1863. He was the son of Niels Nielsen, a lawyer who had moved from the capital, Christiania, after he had gone bankrupt in 1850. The Nielsen family was rather exceptional in the newly established town. Hardly any of the town's slightly less than one thousand inhabitants in 1855 possessed a higher education or extensive learning. Instead, the business community consisted mainly of autodidactic herring merchants and active or former skippers. This was to a large extent still true in 1886 when the twenty-three-year-old B. Stolt-Nielsen returned from commercial school in Christiania and military service to set up an insurance agency. Many of the older herring exporters and shipowners entrusted the educated, though inexperienced, Stolt-Nielsen with their business. In 1891, he was invited by a herring exporter and skipper to participate in the purchase of a small steamship. Although Stolt-Nielsen was a minority partner, he was asked to serve as the managing owner (*korresponderende reder*) of this venture.

The dominant form of ownership in Haugesund prior to 1914 was the single-ship *partsrederi* - usually translated as partnership, part-ownership or joint-ownership. This was a model also practised in other countries, such as Great Britain with its "sixty-fourths" system, but it had prevailed in Norway longer than elsewhere.[16] These partnerships required a manager to keep the books and to handle correspondence. The manager was not necessarily expected to provide the bulk of shipping expertise or financial resources, but he was sought as a partner for his knowledge of bookkeeping, letter writing and ability to communicate with prospective clients in the major European lan-

[15]For numerous examples, see Hammerborg, *Skipsfartsbyen*.

[16]See Stig Tenold, "Norwegian Shipping in the Twentieth Century," *Særtrykkserie*, No. 314 (2009), 57-77.

guages.[17] As communications improved, the *korresponderende reder* would take on a much more active role and emerge as the classic shipowner, or *reder*, who contracted for the building of ships, controlled numerous vessels and became the principal source of shipping expertise. Indeed, Stolt-Nielsen's career is a particularly good example of this process.

In the decades leading up to World War I, Stolt-Nielsen was invited to manage or establish a great number of single-ship partnerships.[18] By 1913, his management company (*rederi*) operated the second largest fleet in the town. Nevertheless, his actual ownership was far smaller than several other shipowners in Haugesund. Stolt-Nielsen stuck to the model to which he had been introduced early in his career, preferring to remain a minority owner of his "own" ships. In 1903, he owned less than thirteen percent of the shares in his fleet (with an estimated worth of about 135,000 *kroner*), a percentage that would remain more-or-less unaltered in the years to come.[19] His income, in addition to the dividends paid by his shareholdings and a small percentage of the turnover for managing the ships, stemmed mainly from his role as exclusive broker for the fleet. Stolt-Nielsen insisted on such exclusivity for all the partnerships he managed; unless he was awarded these terms, he refused to act as manager. A new partnership would in fact be created only after Stolt-Nielsen had contracted for a vessel. He then sold it to the partnership, profiting in the process. As exclusive broker, he negotiated all charters, brokered the ships' insurance and any future sales; for all this, he was paid a commission by the various partnerships. Since he lacked the resources to finance such a large fleet, he relied on an extensive network of passive investors to build up a fleet that he ran - and profited from - as *reder*.

This was a consistent pattern in Stolt-Nielsen's business strategy. Although his various actions and decisions in the coming years were also informed by market developments, technological change and his growing experience, it is easy to detect an overall *modus operandi* forged by his commercial background and, in particular, the way he entered shipping. It was a strategy that had proven its worth for two decades before the war broke out. No wonder, then, that he stuck to this recipe of minority ownership, reliance on other people's risk capital, and - most importantly although in the end ruinously - personally contracting ships in the years to come.

---

[17]See, for instance, the case of a school teacher in Haugesund who, with hardly any shares in the ships, was elected manager for several vessels in the 1870s; Hammerborg, *Skipsfartsbyen*, 57.

[18]*Ibid.*, 108-113.

[19]Haugesund Public Library, E.H. Kongshavn, "B. Stolt-Nielsen" (unpublished manuscript, 1986).

Knut Knutsen O.A.S. (1871-1946) entered shipping in a quite different fashion than did Stolt-Nielsen.[20] Knutsen was raised on an island just outside of Haugesund, the son of Ole Andreas Knudsen (1828-1908), which explains the abbreviation following his name (meaning "son of Ole Andreas"). Ole Andreas Knudsen was one of the numerous fishermen in the vicinity of Haugesund who became a skipper, herring exporter and shipowner during the second half of the nineteenth century. In close cooperation with his brother, John (1835-1908), he worked his way up from humble origins. Knut Knutsen O.A.S. was in effect to grow up as an only child, and therefore the sole heir, to the business (his two sisters died in infancy). The aging brothers Knudsen dissolved their business partnership in 1901, and from then until his death, Ole Andreas worked together with his son. Knut had already been active both in the herring business and as *reder* of a few ships, but through his father these activities were taken to a new level. Father and son took a major step away from the herring business when they contracted a 6000-deadweight ton (dwt) ship from a shipyard in Stockton on Tees. This ship, *O.A. Knudsen*, cost the staggering sum of 655,000 *kroner*, and was the biggest and most expensive ship in Haugesund when it arrived in 1907. In stark contrast to Stolt-Nielsen's rapid fleet expansion which relied on outside investors, the Knudsens paid almost the entire sum for their new vessel.

The desire to control their ships, not only as managers but also as owners, was not restricted to *O.A. Knudsen*. It was a principle that applied to all their ships, as well as their herring salteries and other assets. As Ole Andreas had owned everything together with his brother almost without external investors, so did he and his son. When Ole Andreas died in 1908, Knut Knutsen O.A.S. became the sole proprietor. Compared to Stolt-Nielsen's 1907 fleet of twelve ships, Knutsen's four ships do not seem very impressive, but in terms of personal capital, Knutsen was a far richer man than Stolt-Nielsen. As a general rule he held between eighty and ninety of the standard 100 parts in the various single-ship partnerships. The only outsiders normally allowed to purchase a small number of parts were the skippers of each ship, a practice that was customary in almost all the *partsrederier*.

In the years between his father's death and the outbreak of the war, Knutsen O.A.S. bought just two more ships. These were acquired in the same manner as before, and he kept between eighty and ninety parts for himself. The growth of his fleet again appeared slow compared to Stolt-Nielsen's. But if Knutsen O.A.S. may have seemed cautious and conservative, this was due to his principle of always keeping full control of his ships. His actions actually displayed a great ability and willingness to take risks through buying new and expensive tonnage without the aid of investors, but such a strategy also re-

[20]On Knutsen's family background, see Vormedal, *Knut Knutsen*. See also Hammerborg, *Skipsfartsbyen*, 136-139.

quired growth to be rather slow because he needed to build up his personal funds before new ships could be bought. This was the *modus operandi* that Knut Knutsen O.A.S. followed during his entire career, and it would in essence be the method by which he operated his business for the rest of his life.[21]

John K. Haaland: A Flying Starter

John K. Haaland was given the opportunity to become a shipowner through his marriage to Stolt-Nielsen's daughter Aslaug, but like so many young men in Haugesund from well-to-do families, he had set his eyes on a future in shipping from an early age. He went to Bergen to complete his schooling at a commercial high school before returning to Haugesund, where he went to work for one of the many herring exporting and ship-owning firms.[22] With the economic backing of Stolt-Nielsen, and by being admitted to his investor network, John K. Haaland started his career as *reder* by buying two medium-sized ships in 1915. The vessels, *Primo* (1500 dwt) and *Secundo* (2200 dwt), were bigger than the traditional steamers used to export herring, and John K. Haaland followed suit with a number of other young shipowners in the town who were attempting to enter international tramp shipping directly, instead of gaining experience first in the herring business.[23] Like his father-in-law, his partnerships also involved many different players - the 100 parts generally were split among about forty different investors. The biggest owner was Stolt-Nielsen with about twenty shares, while Haaland kept only about ten. His *rederi* got off to a flying start due to the war, and after less than a year as a *reder* he set out to make his great leap forward.

Like his father-in-law, he sought to achieve a rapid expansion by relying on external investors for funding. This was the basic similarity in strategy between Stolt-Nielsen and his son-in-law. However, John K. also employed what was then the rather new organizational form of a multi-ship company, which meant that his chosen means of expansion differed from Stolt-Nielsen's. Whereas Stolt-Nielsen continued to create single-ship partnerships (from 1915, single-ship, limited-liability companies that were run as partnerships) that paid in full for the ship he had contracted, John K. Haaland chose to organize his *rederi* as a multi-ship, limited-liability, joint-stock company. Limited-liability companies had already been in vogue in Christiania for some time. Legal

[21]For an overview of the career of Knut Knutsen O.A.S. and his firm, see Hammerborg, *Skipsfartsbyen*;, Bjørnson, *Haugesund*; and Vormedal, *Knut Knutsen*.

[22]His education and the composition of his first partnerships are described in an unpublished manuscript by E.H. Kongshavn about the Haaland family which was provided to me by Mads Ramstad of Karmsund Folkemuseum in Haugesund.

[23]For examples, see Hammerborg, *Skipsfartsbyen*, 127-129.

changes in the years after 1900 had made ships more acceptable to banks as collateral, and limited-liability companies could now purchase ships without its shareholders paying for them in full, relying instead on bank loans. The multi-ship company took these advantages to a new level and was hailed by many contemporaries as the most progressive way of organizing ship management.[24] By abandoning the single-ship organizational form, the company was no longer bound to only one vessel. This enabled a firm, at least in theory, to plan ahead, to continue operations even if a ship was lost or sold, to disperse risk between ships and to build up funds and attain credit more easily. In retrospect, the transition from single-ship partnerships to multi-ship, joint-stock companies was perhaps the most important prerequisite for success in the interwar period. As Stig Tenold has noted, this was how Norwegian shipping companies consolidated and developed into "proper enterprises built for longevity."[25]

John K. Haaland's decision to organize his business as a multi-ship company in October 1916 should therefore not be seen as an inherently foolhardy, misconceived or ill-advised strategy. The ability and willingness to invest in shipping were at an all-time high in Haugesund and elsewhere, and the 10,000 shares at 1000 *kroner* apiece quickly provided his company D/S A/S John K. Haalands rederi ten million *kroner* in capital. Following his father-in-law, John K. Haaland now was able to build up a fleet for which he was the manager (as *reder*) but in which he would only hold a minority ownership.[26]

The first deal into which the newly established company entered was to buy Haaland's single-ship companies *Primo* and *Secundo*. In March 1917, after one of the vessels had been sunk by a German U-Boat, the company bought a one-year-old vessel of more than 5000 dwt for about five million *kroner*, with fifty percent of this sum coming from third-party loans. At the same time, the company also bought four building contracts for new ships from B. Stolt-Nielsen. Stolt-Nielsen had taken his old business of ordering ships personally and then selling them to another level during the boom, and he involved his son-in-law and his son-in-law's company in this practice. We will return later to this business of selling and buying building contracts, as this would be the reason for Stolt-Nielsen's, and in part also for John K. Haaland's, downfall.

It was one thing to secure contracts for new vessels during the boom years, but quite another to get these ships delivered safely and on time. The shipyards had great problems securing building materials, and even if this

---

[24]About the debate on this in Norway, see Atle Thowsen, *Vekst og strukturendringer i krisetider, 1914-1939* (Bergen, 1983), 33-35.

[25]Tenold, "Norwegian Shipping," 70.

[26]The following sections are based on Hammerborg, *Skipsfartsbyen*, 140-145.

problem were resolved, delays often slowed production. There were many reasons for these difficulties, though for the most part the delays were the result of sharp rises in the price of labour and raw materials, costs which had to be paid for out of a fixed contract that provided for payments at the earlier market prices and rates of exchange. As a result of these price rises during the building period, shipyards not only saw their profits vanish, but could actually lose money by delivering a ship according to the terms of the contract.[27] Shipowners, eagerly awaiting the arrival of vessels in order to take advantage of the astronomical freight rates, had to compensate the shipyards to speed up delivery. This was true for all four contracts that John K. Haaland's rederi bought from Stolt-Nielsen.

While the first three were delivered by a shipyard in Bergen in 1918 and early 1919 without serious complications because the *rederi* met all the yard's demands for increased prices, the final contract proved far more difficult for the company. This contract was with a Dutch shipyard, but delivery was postponed several times. In the spring of 1919, the board decided to agree to an increase in the building price if the yard would start construction immediately. In August, two representatives from the *rederi* travelled to the Netherlands and negotiated a fifty-percent increase on the contract (255,000 *guilders*); in return, the shipyard promised to deliver the vessel within ten months. By then John K. Haaland had sold on the contract, but when the Dutch did not deliver the ship on time, the deal fell through. The *rederi* was now being held to ransom by the shipyard and had little room for manoeuvre. Desperate to obtain the ship, Haaland persuaded the board to award the shipyard another 100,000 *guilders* as a sign of good will, a gesture that finally led to the delivery of the vessel in late August 1920, just as the boom was coming to an end.

With the Dutch project still undecided, in December 1919 the board of representatives met to discuss the situation. Since freight rates were still at an all-time high, the company needed more ships to continue its growth, so they decided to order two more ships, this time in the United Kingdom. These vessels (7000 dwt and 5000 dwt) were much bigger than the delayed Dutch ship (2062 dwt). The first ship from a British yard was delivered in March 1920, financed primarily by the sale of an older vessel. John K. Haaland was reluctant to sell the ship, but finally bowed to pressure from the company's bankers who were beginning to get concerned about ratio of loans to collateral. The second and larger vessel, *Aslaug Haaland*, was delivered in April 1921, about six months after the markets had crashed. By this time, the Dutch ship

---

[27]Many shipyards would soon introduce a new, more flexible form of contract (*glideskalakontrakter*) where the price of the vessel was dependent on the development of costs. For a discussion of this in Bergen, see Thowsen, *Vekst og strukturendringer*, 241.

had been delivered, payments were due on *Aslaug Haaland*, and the company was experiencing acute cash flow issues.

By following the principles of his father-in-law - rapid expansion relying on external investors - Haaland, as a minority owner, had in effect been at the mercy of his investors during the boom. The investors demanded a high rate of return due to the record freight rates and the ever-increasing price of the shares. In order to satisfy them, and to keep the company's share prices attractive, Haaland had paid out huge dividends rather than building the capital. Indeed, he drastically reduced the paid-up capital, which by August 1919 had been reduced by fifty percent. The professed advantages of a multi-ship company depended on a constant build-up of funds; without the financial strength to endure a drop in rates while at the same time taking delivery of ships on order, the company was doomed regardless of its organization.

When Haaland was unable to make his payments, Haugesund Privatbank was forced to reimburse the shipyards. At the same time, Norwegian inflation had made the British pound considerably more expensive; in January 1920, the exchange rate was 18.16 *kroner* to the pound, but by September it was 26.60 *kroner*. *Aslaug Haaland* cost the company an astounding 6.1 million *kroner* and proved to be its downfall. When it was delivered in April 1921, the bank demanded the five other ships of the firm on which it held mortgages and took full control. It ordered the company to go public and to issue new stock, but the board of representatives found this totally unrealistic; investment capital, which only a year earlier had been abundant, was now non-existent. As a result, the bank started selling off ships, even as prices plummeted. The fire sale of assets combined with an inability to raise new capital would have spelled disaster for any business. *Aslaug Haaland*, planned to be the crown jewel of Haaland's empire, was sold to investors in Melbourne, Australia, for 1.5 million *kroner*, a loss of 4.6 million *kroner* in just over a year on that vessel alone.

All the banks in Haugesund, including several that had been established during the boom, went bankrupt following the devastating losses inflicted on them by the shipping firms. The losses, however, were not restricted to the firms; the main problem likely was the direct funding of many of the speculators.[28] The banks had fuelled this speculation and enabled many of the shipbuilding contracts by guaranteeing investments and extending huge overdrafts backed only by stocks in shipping companies or shipbuilding contracts. When the value of stocks and the ships themselves plummeted almost overnight, and when shipbuilding contracts went from sure things to future losses,

---

[28]The oldest bank, Haugesund Privatbank, survived only because it was taken over by Bergen Privatbank in 1922 after a deal was struck in which all depositors with more than 50,000 *kroner* agreed that ten percent of their holdings be awarded equity in the Bergen institution. See Hammerborg, *Skipsfartsbyen*, 145; and Bjørnson, *Haugesund*, 107-119.

the banks' collateral became almost worthless. The activity that brought perhaps the biggest losses, and which also destroyed John K. Haaland's personal fortune and brought down his father-in-law, was the practice of ordering new ships, not with the intent to operate them but to sell them and cash in on the rapidly rising prices for new tonnage.

In the autumn of 1922, John K. Haaland began negotiations with his creditors. His company was under the control of the bank which was trying to sell off the ships. But even more seriously, by participating in his father-in-law's asset play in shipbuilding contracts, he was also deeply in debt personally. In 1920, Haaland's assets had been valued at about three million *kroner*, but by 1922, as the value of his assets declined, his personal debts totalled 2.4 million *kroner*. Because the banks saw few opportunities for recovering their losses, they let him strike a deal in which he was to pay only ten percent of his debts (bringing yet another loss to the banks of more than 2.1 million *kroner*). By borrowing 170,000 *kroner* from his twin brother Christian, using his future inheritance from their mother as collateral, he was able to meet the banks' demands. In the end, he was left with only one ship that had been registered in a single-ship company outside of the main company, and he operated this in a modest way until his death in 1934 at the age of forty-two. When his estate was settled, his brother, Christian, still had an outstanding claim of 150,000 *kroner*.

The Demise of B. Stolt-Nielsen

Stolt-Nielsen had always insisted that his single-ship, joint-stock companies - the organizational form he adopted in 1915 - should perform as the partnerships had been obliged to do, paying in full for each vessel when it was delivered.[29] The ships were therefore free of debt, and investors would have to finance, either from their own funds or by borrowing, to become partners. This "archaic" approach in which his companies did not finance ships through bank loans, left the fifteen or so companies in which Stolt-Nielsen was involved debt free, possessing a fleet of fully owned new ships. This meant that his businesses were in excellent condition to weather the falling markets after the crash in the second half of 1920.[30] This rather conservative, low-risk approach to

[29]This practice was not unique to Stolt-Nielsen. See, for example, Helge W. Nordvik, "Entrepreneurship and Risk-Taking in the Norwegian Shipping Industry in the Early Part of the Twentieth Century: The Case of Lauritz Kloster, Stavanger," in Lewis R. Fischer (ed.), *From Wheel House to Counting House: Essays in Maritime Business History in Honour of Professor Peter Neville Davies* (St. John's, 1992), 323-348.

[30]Some of the companies paid handsome dividends well into the 1920s. On Stolt-Nielsen's economic status in the early 1920s, see Bjørnson, *Haugesund*, 154-161.

running his single-ship companies stood in stark contrast to the high risks he took when placing shipbuilding contracts.

As we have seen, Stolt-Nielsen had a long tradition of ordering ships and then selling them to the partnerships he was to manage. The four contracts he sold to his son-in-law's *rederi* in 1917 were just the tip of the iceberg. During the boom, Stolt-Nielsen dramatically expanded his business of ordering and selling shipbuilding contracts not only to his own single-ship companies but also to others. As prices for both existing and future tonnage soared, Stolt-Nielsen made great profits by securing and later reselling building contracts to investors eager to garner profits from the record freights (and therefore willing to pay just about any price for anything that would float). The lyrics to a song at a Christmas party of the Haugesund Shipowner's Association in 1933 recalled those halcyon days: "Even a ship without hull, came in at 50,000 pounds."[31]

Stolt-Nielsen speculated heavily in this business, ordering forty-three ships totalling 259,400 dwt during the war.[32] The vast majority of these contracts were negotiated with the intent to sell the vessel before delivery. He also bought fourteen second-hand ships. In comparison, his actual fleet at the end of the war comprised only twelve ships totalling 65,500 dwt. As long as ship prices continued to increase, the sale of contracts was a highly profitable business. In 1916, for example, he sold off nine contracts, earning him 1.3 million *kroner* in net profits. He later wrote of these years that "Gold flowed over everything."[33] If he had left it to the limited-liability companies to order the ships themselves, he would have missed out on these profits. On the other hand, by ordering ships outside these partnerships, he left himself vulnerable to the crash.

Stolt-Nielsen's business in trading in shipbuilding contracts was mainly organized by a consortium including himself, his son-in-law, his nephew, his office manager and two Bergen investors. Stolt-Nielsen owned about sixty percent. The participants pledged their personal capital for the liabilities and debts of the consortium. In 1919, one of the Bergen banks estimated that Stolt-Nielsen's debts and liabilities to it alone were more than twenty-one million *kroner*.[34] When the crash obliterated the market for selling

---

[31]"Selv en båt foruten bunn, kom i femti tusen pund" (my translation). This is taken from Vormedal, *B. Stolt-Nielsen*, 41.

[32]Hammerborg, *Skipsfartsbyen*, 133-134.

[33]"Det randt guld av alt" (my translation). Vormedal, *B. Stolt-Nielsen*. 32, letter dated 7 November 1925.

[34]This also included some businesses in Haugesund that Stolt-Nielsen had guaranteed. Particularly devastating was a guarantee for a friend starting a lumber busi-

the contracts, the participants in the consortium soon were unable to pay their debts. Cancelling contracts was costly, and the consortium could not pay off all the shipyards. It was once again left to the banks that had issued the guarantees to suffer the losses.

Early in the 1920s, Stolt-Nielsen was the manager of a large, debt-free and highly modern fleet that was still profitable, but he had incurred heavy personal debts to his banks, which were now desperate to convert their claims into cash wherever and however they could. As a result, they refused to negotiate a settlement with Stolt-Nielsen that would allow him to operate the ships and, hopefully, repay portions of his debts. In addition to concerns over the stability of the markets, the banks also had reason to be concerned about Stolt-Nielsen's private life after he was elected to parliament in 1919, an event that led him to move to Christiania where he adopted an extravagant and costly lifestyle. Faced with these conditions, the banks understandably were reluctant to grant Stolt-Nielsen a deal that would have permitted him to retain control of the companies. Instead, the banks wanted to sell off his ships and receive whatever payment they could get. Because Stolt-Nielsen was a minority owner in these companies, he was dependent on other shareholders to support him against the banks. The problem for Stolt-Nielsen was that almost all the investors in his companies had had to turn over their stocks to the banks because they were mortgaged as security for loans they could no longer repay. He had also surrendered most of his stock to one of the banks as a guarantee for the business of the consortium.

The banks therefore effectively controlled the companies and used their position to force Stolt-Nielsen out as manager. They then instructed the new manager to sell the ships and dissolve the companies.[35] Stolt-Nielsen therefore shared the fate of his son-in-law and many other Haugesund shipowners in the interwar period, managing just a single, small and aging steamer in increasingly marginal freight markets. The bulk of the approximately forty *rederier* in Haugesund in the decades to come would operate just one or two small steam vessels, sorry remains of the grand designs and enterprises from the time when Haugesund set "a record for millionaires."

---

ness, which cost him two million *kroner*. For a detailed description, see Bjørnson, *Haugesund*, 155.

[35]The process that led the banks to stop dealing with Stolt-Nielsen is complex. For a detailed account, see *ibid.*, 154-161; and Hammerborg, *Skipsfartsbyen*, 148-152. For a contrasting view, see Vormedal, *B. Stolt-Nielsen*.

Christian Haaland: Seemingly Failing

Christian Haaland seemingly entered shipping in much the same fashion as his twin brother.[36] He also had been sent to Bergen for schooling and went for one more year of commercial school in Christiania before going to London to learn the shipping business. With the help of his father-in-law, he also bought two ships in 1915, the year of his marriage. But there the similarities with his twin brother came to a halt. His first vessel, the twenty-five-year-old herring steamer *Annaho* (900 dwt), was a modest investment at 110,000 *kroner*. This purchase was probably guaranteed by Knut Knutsen O.A.S.; of the twenty shares, Knutsen bought nine through an investment company called A/S Commercial. Christian owned nine as well, and the captain took the two remaining shares. This single-ship, joint-stock company functioned as had the old partnerships by financing the ship in full. The notable difference *vis-à-vis* Stolt-Nielsen and John K. Haaland was that the *reder*, together with his immediate family, retained total ownership control, as Christian Haaland adopted his father-in-law's *modus operandi*. This was also true for the second ship, *Idaho*, a much larger but still rather old 5100-dwt vessel which cost 950,000 *kroner*. Haaland and A/S Commercial each held forty-five shares, while the remaining ten were divided between Haaland's mother and the captain of the ship.

Knutsen helped Christian Haaland to get started, and the two would cooperate closely in the coming decades, but he was unwilling, or perhaps unable, to finance all his son-in-law's enterprises. In 1917, a year after his twin brother had started his large multi-ship company, Christian Haaland created a joint-stock, multi-ship company open to non-family investors (*folkeaksjeselskap*). Knutsen and his son-in-law deviated in part from the principle of "no outsiders" and no mortgages on the ships, although they still retained control by taking about sixty-five percent of the 5000 stocks in A/S Asker, as they named the company. Instead of obtaining funding and then looking for ships, as for the most part John K. Haaland did, Christian chose to buy an entire shipping company from Christiania with a fleet of four ships. The fleet was comprised of three new ships of about 8000 dwt, one of which was the first tanker owned in Haugesund, and a 5500-dwt vessel that was more than twenty years old. Most important, the three most costly ships were on long-term charters of between four and six years when Haaland bought them. This deal reflected a desire to take on less risk than his twin brother. He chose to buy a fleet with a guaranteed income, and most important, he bought completed ships instead of contracting for the construction of vessels in the highly volatile shipbuilding markets during the First World War. To consolidate his economic position, he sold off his first vessel, *Annaho*, which had increased in

[36]The following is based on Hammerborg, *Skipsfartsbyen*, 199-203.

value by almost nine-fold in just over two years; the deal brought Haaland and Knutsen almost half a million *kroner* each.

In the first few years, however, it must have seemed that Christian had made an unfortunate choice in buying three ships on long-term charters. Although expenditures for insurance, coal, surveys and repairs continued to rise during the boom, three of Haaland's vessels sailed for fixed rates contracted early in the war when freight rates were lower; the ships were therefore hardly able to cover their expenses. The company also had to make payments on the loan of more than two million *kroner* it had taken out to buy the fleet. Risk aversion, if timed badly, could bring down companies during these years. Yet as luck would have it, even though the fourth ship in the fleet was by far the smallest, oldest and least expensive vessel in the fleet, because it was unchartered it was able to take advantage of the soaring freight rates and sustain the rest of the fleet. It was chartered in 1918 at a very good rate and over the next four years earned a net profit of 3.2 million *kroner*, effectively supporting the operations of the struggling multi-ship company. When one of the chartered ships was lost in a hurricane in 1918, bringing an insurance payment of two million *kroner*, the company's standing was further strengthened. Because he and his father-in-law controlled the company, investors could not force it to increase dividends, which enabled Haaland to build up company funds. Christian Haaland also refrained from buying or contracting ships in the postwar boom, concentrating instead on consolidating the company's position with its three remaining ships.

Christian Haaland also made some other investments before the crash, most notably in contracting for the building of another tanker in Canada which was delivered to a single-ship company in 1918. But none of these transactions rendered him vulnerable when the crash came. He had proved his ability to operate in the heated market of the boom by starting a multi-ship company that was partly dependent on external investors and bank loans, but he did so cautiously. Even if the company struggled for a period due to the long-term charters, and in essence was saved by the one unchartered ship and the insurance on the one that disappeared, Christian Haaland was never in trouble. He had other sources of income, including the older ships he had not included in the new enterprise, and most important, he did not leave himself vulnerable by taking part in consortiums specializing in asset plays. Despite massive earnings, he continued to be cautious in the postwar boom. This was most evident in the single-ship company D/S A/S *Idaho*. His second ship, *Idaho*, had generated large earnings for A/S Commercial - in 1916 alone the vessel made a profit of one million *kroner* - before it was torpedoed in the fall of 1918. The indemnity agreement gave the company almost three million *kroner*. This money could be exempted from taxation if it was spent on buying ships - a tax regime that further fuelled the disastrous shipbuilding contracts that many shipowners entered into towards the end of the boom - but could only partly finance a new ship of the same size in the bloated market prior to 1921. Haaland successfully applied to the authorities to have the deadline extended well into the 1920s. When prices plummeted, this company, without ships but with millions in capital, would be the vehicle he used to follow his father-in-law into motorized tanker and liner shipping in the interwar period. This strategy, again, was a near carbon-copy of Knutsen's actions.

Knut Knutsen OAS: Rise to Greatness

The business philosophy of Knut Knutsen O.A.S. remained virtually unaffected by the boom. This does not imply that he did not participate, gamble or take risks in the dramatic years during and after the war, but he did so in the manner in which he had always conducted his business. Following his actions through this period is for the most part like reading a reinforced narrative of Christian Haaland's actions, albeit with some notable exceptions because he was already an established and wealthy shipowner prior to the war. Knutsen was not dependent on external investors, and did not found a multi-ship company as did his son-in-law. He could have chosen to do so, of course, and gained access to risk capital from speculators that would have enabled him multiply his fleet, but this would have been a radical break with his *modus operandi* and was probably never considered. Knutsen would stay the course on which he had embarked decades before; he would never depend on investors and would always keep between eighty and ninety percent of the ownership in all his vessels. He wanted absolute control of both ownership and revenue. When Stolt-Nielsen contracted for more than forty ships inside and outside of his single-ship companies, making contemporaries predict that he was destined to become the nation's largest shipowner, Knutsen proceeded at a far slower pace.[37]

Although he was not a minority owner, his investments were still rather brisk and by no means without risk. In 1915, he bought three ships, which of two were new, but the prices this early in the war were still comparatively modest, with the most expensive costing 775,000 *kroner*. As prices soared, Knutsen decided to contract for the building of several ships in the United States, with deliveries spread out through 1917. Turning his attention overseas was not unique to Knutsen; increasing problems in obtaining building materials at home and the unavailability of shipyards in the belligerent countries had led a number of neutral shipowners to place orders at American

[37]As *Land og Folk* commented about Stolt-Nielsen in April 1918, "[i]t is on a sound basis for a journalist to risk prophesying that the biggest shipowning firm in Norwegian shipping before long will belong in Western Norway's most dynamic city: Haugesund" (my translation).

yards.[38] Indeed, Christian Haaland also contracted for one ship overseas, thereby again echoing his father-in-law's business decisions. The 8800-dwt sister ships *Golden Gate* and *Key West*, at a cost of US $790,000 apiece, were delivered in the summer of 1917. The last ship he ordered, *Jeanette Skinner*, also of 8800 dwt but with steam turbine propulsion and costing US $1.2 million, would never find its way to Haugesund, however, because it was requisitioned by the US Shipping Board in August 1917 as a consequence of American entry into the war earlier that year.

At the time, Knutsen must have perceived this as a devastating blow, for the ship would undoubtedly have generated great profits for its owner over the next few years. But the requisition proved to be a blessing in disguise. After the war, the Norwegian Shipowners' Association and US authorities negotiated a deal to compensate Norwegian shipowners whose vessels had been requisitioned. As a result, Knutsen O.A.S. was awarded US $2.1 million dollars and nearly 650,000 *kroner* as settlement. According to a fellow Haugesund shipowner, Knutsen left the US dollar settlement in American banks for the next couple of years before bringing it back to Norway. During that period, as the Norwegian *kroner* devalued against the US dollar, the compensation became even more advantageous to Knutsen. In 1919, the average exchange rate was 4.11 *kroner* to the dollar, but in 1921 it was 6.81 *kroner*, so Knutsen may in fact have earned as much as fifteen million *kroner* as a result of the requisition of *Jeanette Skinner*. Moreover, these funds were available to him in the mid-1920s when ship prices were far lower than during the boom. Therefore, even without external investors (of which there were none, at least in capital-poor Haugesund of the 1920s), he could launch an ambitious new building program. Throughout the interwar period, Knutsen O.A.S. purchased a large number of new motorized liners and tankers. He also developed, together with his son-in-law and in time also his own son, Ole Andreas Knutsen (1899-1993), a revised market strategy in which the ships in his newly established lines would comprise a low-risk part of the company, supplying stable, continuous income. The tankers, on the other hand, were operated without charters in the spot market where they were exposed to the volatility of the market. Christian Haaland also followed this recipe, chartering his liners to Knutsen Lines and independently running his own tankers unchartered. The strategy proved highly successful, making Haaland a shipping company of substance on the national level. It also made Knutsen O.A.S. one of the three leading shipping companies of Norway and Knut himself perhaps the richest man in the country.

It is important to recognize that during the boom years Knutsen possessed no special knowledge or insight that was unavailable to other shipown-

---

[38]See Schreiner, *Norsk skipsfart*; Vormedal, *Knut Knutsen*; and Nordvik, "Entrepreneurship."

ers, nor did he have a "King Midas" touch that made everything he touched turn into gold. When the United States entered the war, obtaining new ships from American shipyards became impossible because the country's shipbuilding capacity was needed for the war effort. Knutsen therefore turned his attention to a shipyard with which he had good relations in Bergen. He placed orders for five ships of between 3000 and 4500 dwt. But due to a lack of materials, the large number of contracts and a much extended building and delivery cycle, these were never delivered before the crash in the autumn of 1920. When the markets collapsed, Knutsen wanted to cancel the contracts. This was expensive, and Knutsen was told that the cost for two of the ships would be 1.5 million *kroner*. In an attempt to avoid this expenditure, Knutsen tried to buy the shipyard with the intent of closing it and hence being free of the contracts. The yard's board of directors declined his offer, however, due to the many workers who would then face unemployment.[39] Knutsen ended up paying the cancellation charges for the two ships, and took delivery of one ship in each of the years 1922, 1923 and 1924. They were all paid for by the settlement from the American authorities, and all three were transferred to the wealthy, but until then ship-less company, D/S A/S Jeanette Skinner.

Although Knutsen's track record during the boom was not flawless, and while the glorious result was partly due to the blessing of the requisition in 1917, it is still clear that his established strategy was largely responsible for his success. Until *Jeanette Skinner*, all his companies were old-style partnerships, in effect ships largely owned and controlled by a single man. As a result, he raked in record freight incomes from all his ships. Most important, this strategy enabled him and his son-in-law to stay away from the disastrous asset plays conducted by consortiums which relied heavily on borrowings from banks and personal guarantees from their members. Even if according to the ship registries he was only the fourth biggest shipowner in Haugesund after the war, and seemingly was hopelessly overshadowed by Stolt-Nielsen, he and his son-in-law had already laid the foundation for the brilliant successes their companies were to experience in the decades to come.

Conclusion

When Christian Haaland died in 1952, he left behind a thriving shipping company that continued until the 1990s, when a generational change induced the family to sell out. Christian left behind a legacy as one of Haugesund's great entrepreneurs, businessmen and politicians, serving three times as mayor, as president of the Norwegian Shipowners' Association and as a deputy member

[39]Henrik Myran and Kåre Fasting, *Herfra går skibe: Aksjeselskapet Bergens Mekaniske Verksteder, 1855-1955* (Bergen, 1955), 165; and Vormedal, *Knut Knutsen*, 40.

in the Norwegian Parliament. His bankrupt twin brother, dead by that time for almost twenty years, was mostly forgotten.

This article has explored how, despite similar starting points, the twin brothers' different strategic choices during the boom years led them to end up in such different circumstances. It is clear that the choices they made were heavily influenced by their respective fathers-in-law. By marrying into shipping families with different business philosophies, their own *modi operandi* were shaped. John K. Haaland was taught by B. Stolt-Nielsen that shipping was best conducted by managing a large fleet that relied on external investors for capital and by contracting for ships personally. Christian Haaland, however, followed the Knutsen tradition of not only managing but also holding the majority ownership of the ships he operated. These varying choices had an import effect on their companies' rates of growth: John K. aimed for volume to make a profit, while Christian concentrated on running fewer ships. Both strategies involved risks, and the development of markets in the end determined success. The entry of the Haaland brothers into shipping coincided with one of the most intense booms ever experienced in international shipping and a tremendous crash a few years later. Their strategies, which in a period of more stable markets could easily have produced very different results, made for two distinctly divergent fates. The element of luck clearly cannot be dismissed from such an analysis.[40]

It is useful to note how two very different business strategies could yield positive results in one period but, when circumstances changed, could increase the likelihood of achieving success by following one while the other led to bankruptcy. The cases of B. Stolt-Nielsen and John K. Haaland should perhaps serve as reminders that the demise of companies or entrepreneurs in the aftermath of a boom often require more complex, multifaceted and historically detailed explanations than merely referring to "speculation fever," "speculative frenzy" or similar quasi-psychological metaphors.[41] The foundation for the successes of Knut Knutsen O.A.S. and Christian Haaland cannot meaningfully be understood by reducing them to presumed personal qualities that prevented them from being caught up in such "euphoria." Explanation must take into consideration developments prior to the boom and how past strategies continued to influence decisions, some of which led to success and others to ruin.

The fates of the various actors aside, what is striking in this study is the important influence of the past on decision making. I argue that the strate-

---

[40]For a case study concentrating on the role of chance, see Peter N. Davies, "Business Success and the Role of Chance: The Extraordinary Philipps Brothers," *Business History*, XXIII, No. 2 (1981), 208-232.

[41]For an historical analysis rife with such metaphors, see John Kenneth Galbraith, *A Short History of Financial Euphoria* (New York, 1993).

gies employed by the shipowning families (and the factors we must consider in explaining their formation) should not be seen merely in the narrow context of a wartime boom and its aftermath. Indeed, the commercial strategies pursued in Haugesund during this period cannot be reduced to mere opportunistic responses to market fluctuations. On the contrary, the differing wartime behaviours of the shipowners studied here were consistent with their established business strategies, often forged and developed over decades and passed on from one generation to the next. These different strategies proved both durable and resilient in confronting the heated conditions of the boom. This is not to say that an actor's choices were predetermined, but rather that established patterns in his or his family's commercial life provided crucial information in mapping out future moves, and that this information was often quite independent from the wider economic trends that prevailed during the boom years.

The twin brothers Haaland of course made choices which brought them either riches and glory or ruin and doom. But they did not choose with absolute freedom; their choices were not only a result of the present but also of the past. In short, their choices had a history, and without an understanding of this it is impossible to understand them. The strategies chosen by the twin brothers during the boom, decisions that set them up for different fates due to extraordinary developments in the market, were in this sense very much inherited.

Why Did They Fail? Business Exits among Norwegian Shipping Companies since 1970

Trygve Gulbrandsen

Introduction

Between 1970 and 1987, the population of Norwegian shipping companies was considerably diminished. About two-thirds of the companies with ships registered in Norway that existed in 1970 were no longer operating in 1987. The reduction in the number of shipping firms was particularly strong during the years before 1980 and the three years prior to 1987. According to Stig Tenold, the majority of the firms that exited withdrew from shipping because of weak markets and poor incomes. Moreover, most of them were small.[1]

The high turnover among shipping firms, however, has not been a unique Norwegian phenomenon. Ioannis Theotakis and Gelina Harlaftis demonstrate that in Greek shipping as well a large number of shipping firms and shipowners have exited the industry. As in Norway, the businesses that left were mainly small. At the same time, the Greek-owned fleet has been characterized by a steady entry of new shipowners and companies, creating a dynamism which has spurred both technological and organizational innovations.[2]

The large number of departures from Norwegian shipping was a result of the general crisis in shipping which spanned much of the 1970s and 1980s. The causes of this crisis and how it affected the population of Norwegian shipping firms have been well analyzed elsewhere.[3] In this article, I want to go behind the general picture and study in more detail why and how some specific shipping firms failed to continue. Was the general shipping crisis the main

---

[1]Stig Tenold, *Skipsfartskrisen og utviklingen i norsk skipsfart, 1970-1991* (Bergen, 2001).

[2]Ioannis Theotakis and Gelina Harlaftis, *Leadership in World Shipping: Greek Family Firms in International Business* (London, 2009). On the issue of new entrants and innovation, see Helen Thanopoulou, Ioannis Theotokas and Anastasia Constantelou, "Leading by Following: Innovation and the Postwar Strategies of Greek Shipowners," *International Journal of Maritime History*, XXII, No. 1 (2010), 199-225.

[3]Tenold, *Skipsfartskrisen*.

reason for their failure? Or were the exits the outcome of inadequate strategic responses to the challenges and problems it caused? To what extent did the failures result from firm- or owner-specific factors, possibly interacting with the difficult economic conditions in the shipping markets? These are some of the central questions posed in this study. In order to answer them, I have chosen to examine four medium-sized shipping companies that exited from shipping during the 1980s and the 1990s. All were well-known firms that had been founded in the first half of the twentieth century. They operated in different markets, though, and thus represent the breadth of Norwegian shipping. Business failures are seldom studied by either business or maritime historians. This article may thus contribute new knowledge to both disciplines.

Previous Research

Business failures or exits may refer to several different situations, and it is necessary to distinguish among them. For example, the discontinuance of the ownership of a business and the discontinuance or closure of the business itself can be two different things. A large number of what appear to be business exits are in reality transfers to new ownership. Further, the discontinuance of ownership may be involuntary or voluntary. Involuntary transfers of ownership may be the result of hostile takeovers or may have occurred because business partners wanted the owner to be replaced. In the case of voluntary changes of ownership, the original owner may have sold the business in order to focus upon other commercial activities, or he may have planned to start a new business.[4] Some owners sell their firms because of old age or illness, or because they want to enjoy a more sedate life.[5] Other owners exit due to a failure to generate sufficient income to finance their private life.[6] As David Stokes and Robert Blackburn have noted, many firms that closed were fairly well managed but failed to generate adequate incomes.[7] Richard Carter and Howard Van Auken claim that half of all closed firms were relatively successful at the

---

[4]David Stokes and Robert Blackburn, "Learning the Hard Way: The Lessons of Owner-Managers Who Have Closed Their Businesses," *Journal of Small Business and Enterprise Development*, IX, No. 1 (2002), 17-27.

[5]Nobuyuki Harada, "Which Firms Exit and Why? An Analysis of Small Firms Exits in Japan," *Small Business Economics*, XXIX, No. 4 (2007), 401-414.

[6]Richard Carter and Howard E. Van Auken, "Small Firm Bankruptcy," *Journal of Small Business Management*, XLIV, No. 4 (2006), 493-513.

[7]Stokes and Blackburn, "Learning the Hard Way," 17-27.

time they ceased operations.[8] The discontinuance of the business may take the form of bankruptcy where creditors suffer substantial losses, or a business may be liquidated before bankruptcy in order to prevent further losses.

Previous research has identified several factors or circumstances behind business failures. Much of this research, however, has focussed on small firms, often with short histories. In contrast, here I examine some medium-sized shipping firms which existed for several decades before they exited the industry. Nonetheless, the findings in the research on small business failures may be useful in understanding these shipping companies. The factors behind business failures discussed in the literature may be grouped into four categories: the general economic climate or economic conditions; factors relating to the owner, such as his or her education and experience; problems inherent in the firm and its strategy; and factors connected with family ownership, a characteristic of most Norwegian shipping firms.

Kent Millington found that long-term interest rates, unemployment and inflation were the economic variables with the greatest impact on business failures.[9] Similarly, when bankruptcy was associated with the failure, Jim Everett and John Watson discovered that higher interest rates significantly contributed.[10] On the other hand, it appeared that the likelihood of failure increased with the lagged rise in unemployment. This led to conclude that many marginal businessmen may have decided to move out of business and into paid employment when opportunities to do so improved. Mirjam van Praag found that the higher the general rate of business failures, the more likely an individual would be to leave the business to avoid the increased risks.[11] According to LuAnn Gaskill, Howard van Auken and Ronald Manning, many failures were due to the owners' poor skill sets.[12] Van Praag found that previous experience in the same industry increased the chances of survival.[13] The reasons for prob-

---

[8]Carter and Van Auken, "Small Firm Bankruptcy," 493-513.

[9]Kent J. Millington, "The Impact of Selected Economic Variables on New Business Formation and Business Failures," *Journal of Small Business Finance*, III, No. 2 (1994), 177-179.

[10]Jim Everett and John Watson, "Small Business Failure and External Risk Factors," *Small Business Economics*, XI, No. 4 (1998), 371-390.

[11]C. Mirjam van Praag, "Business Survival and Success of Young Small Business Owners," *Small Business Economics*, XXI, No. 1 (2003), 1-17.

[12]LuAnn R. Gaskill, Howard E. Van Auken and Ronald A. Manning, "A Factor Analytic Study of the Perceived Causes of Small Business Failures," *Journal of Small Business Management*, XXXI, No. 4 (1993), 18-31.

[13]Van Praag, "Business Survival," 1-17.

lems that led to an exit might be in the firm and its chosen business strategy. Not surprisingly, Janet Bercovitz and Will Mitchell have demonstrated that failed businesses were usually less profitable than those that survived. They also found that the scale or size, measured as the amount of sales, of a firm contributed to its long-term survival, and that a broader scope in the form of number of multiple product lines also had a positive effect on the chances of survival. On the other side, their study showed that increased activity in unrelated sectors had a negative impact on the probability of survival; in other words, diversification is beneficial when the activities involved are closely related.[14] Stephen Perry concluded that failing businesses were characterized by less formal planning than in those that survived.[15] Carter and Van Auken discovered that failed businesses experienced liquidity shortages, while Van Praag also highlighted the availability of capital as a prerequisite for survival.[16]

In the extensive literature on family businesses, several authors have related business failures to characteristics of the owner-family.[17] For instance, it has been claimed that a disorderly generational succession of ownership and management may sap the energy and divert the attention of owners away from making important decisions. Other scholars have pointed to the hazards of incompetent or unmotivated inheritors and lax control over the efforts of family managers. It has also been debated whether risk-aversion and a strong emphasis on family control might prevent the owner-family from making necessary investments in new products, technologies and markets. Another problem is the proliferation of owners in those family businesses which reach the third generation. A large number of family-owners may make it more difficult to agree on important strategic issues. All of these potential problems or challenges in family-owned businesses may weaken their chances of survival.

All the studies referred to above are statistical studies based upon quantitative data, most of them utilizing cross-sectional analysis. Relatively few scholars, however, have paid attention to failures as outcomes of long-

---

[14]Janet Bercovitz and Will Mitchell, "When Is More Better? The Impact of Business Scale and Scope on Long-term Business Survival, while Controlling for Profitability," *Strategic Management Journal*, XXVIII, No. 1 (2007), 61-79.

[15]Stephen C. Perry, "The Relationship between Written Business Plans and the Failure of Small Businesses in the US," *Journal of Small Business Management*, XXXIX, No. 3 (2001), 201-208.

[16]Carter and Van Auken, "Small Firm Bankruptcy," 493-513; and Van Praag, "Business Survival," 1-17.

[17]For a short review of the literature, see Trygve Gulbrandsen and Even Lange, "The Survival of Family Dynasties in Shipping," *International Journal of Maritime History*, XXI, No. 1 (2009), 175-200.

term processes where the businesses pass through various stages on their way to a final exit. A notable exception is a study by Donald Hambrick and Richard D'Aventi, who describe business failures among large corporations as "downward spirals."[18] They found that failing companies showed signs of weakness well before the culmination of the process. For instance, the failures had lower equity-to-debt ratios than survivors as early as ten years prior to bankruptcy. Their operating performance as measured by returns on assets also significantly lagged behind the survivors for every year examined. The owners and managing directors in the failing companies were victims of perceptual errors which the authors term "false encouragement." As long as the economic environment was favourable and the firms had sufficient cash to cover short-term obligations, the decision-makers carried on as usual. At the same time, though, profitability was suffering and their room for manoeuvre was diminishing. When the economic environment worsened, the owners and managing directors of the failing firms resorted to "strategic excesses." Faced with more grave problems, they chose either passivity or hyperactivity. Many of them vacillated between extreme strategies. The firm's death was a protracted process which accelerated during abrupt environmental downturns.

In this essay, I want to follow up on the process perspective on failures. I will describe the histories of the respective companies, but in so doing I will focus particularly upon the last fifteen or twenty years of their existence. I will examine to what extent the circumstance and factors discussed in previous research may explain why the four shipping companies failed and examine how different circumstances combined to cause their exit from the industry.

The Four Cases and Sources of Information

I have chosen to examine the fates of four shipping companies: Ivaran, Herlofson Shipping Co. A/S, HAV/Helmer Staubo and Co. and Laboremus/Einar Bakkevig's Rederi. Ivaran sold its last remaining ships in 1999 to Kristian Siem. The company continued for a couple of years by chartering vessels, but this activity soon came to an end as well. Ivaran continued as a legal entity into the first years of the twenty-first century, but in fact it was an empty shell and no longer engaged in shipping. The last owner of Herlofson Shipping Co., Sigurd Herlofson, declared bankruptcy in 1990. Tore Staubo, the last owner of HAV, sold his shares to the Havtor group in 1993, and in 1994 HAV was merged into Havtor. In 1989, Laboremus was merged into I.M. Skaugen. Four years earlier, Svein Bakkevig and his shipping firm had been replaced as the managers of Laboremus.

---

[18]Donald C. Hambrick and Richard A. D'Aventi, "Large Corporate Failures as Downward Spirals," *Administrative Science Quarterly*, XXXIII, No. 1 (1988), 1-23.

These four companies have been chosen for three reasons. First, I wanted to study well-established shipping firms which at a certain time in their existence were either relatively large or medium-sized enterprises. Their age, reputation and size make it particularly interesting to discuss why they exited the shipping industry. Second, I have chosen companies which operated in different markets in order to see how the conditions in the particular markets influenced the fate of the firms. Third, in order to find sufficient information about these failing shipping firms, I selected companies that had left the industry relatively recently. This gave me the opportunity to interview persons who were owners or managers, or who followed the companies closely during the final stages of their existence. I have interviewed Eirik Holter-Sørensen, the last owner of Ivaran; Tore Staubo, the last owner-manager of HAV; and Svein Bakkevig, the last owner-manager of Laboremus. In addition, I interviewed Ivar Saunes, Emil Gamborg and Finn Messel, all of whom were directors of Herlofson Shipping. The first was a director until 1977, while Gamborg was senior director until 1983, and Messel was managing director from 1986 to 1990, the year the company declared bankruptcy. During the 1980s, Saunes was a director in the shipping department of the largest Norwegian bank at that time, Den Norske Creditbank (DnC), a position which gave him an excellent vantage point from which to view the shipping industry as a whole; I have benefitted greatly from his insights. In addition, I have used the published histories of the companies or biographies on individual shipowners. I discovered early on that when a business closes, many significant documents and archives generated by the firms tend to disappear. Company histories and biographies, together with the interviews, gave me valuable information when other written material on the firms was scarce. I have also used articles in the newspapers *Aftenposten* and *Dagens Næringsliv* as sources.

The Histories of the Four Shipping Companies

Ivaran[19]

In 1902, Ivar Anton Christensen, based in Haugesund, a town on the southwest coast of Norway, solicited investors in order to acquire a steamship. This can be seen as the origin of Ivaran. Ten years later, Christensen had eleven steamers and had become the biggest shipowner in Haugesund.[20] In 1913, he

---

[19]The material in this section comes from an interview with Eirik Holter-Sørensen; and Bård Kolltveit, *Bridge Across the Seas: Ivaran's Rederi A/S, 1902-1907* (Oslo, 2007).

[20]For a broader study of the development of the shipowning community in Haugesund, see Morten Hammerborg, *Skipsfartsbyen: Haugesunds skipsfartshistorie, 1850-2000* (Bergen, 2003).

moved his business to Oslo, the capital. In 1920, Christensen merged three of his companies into one joint-stock company called A/S Ivarans Rederi, an event usually seen as the formal beginning of the firm. Christensen operated tramp ships, but he saw a greater potential in the overseas liner trades. At the time, however, it was regarded as too hazardous financially for a Norwegian shipowner to operate a steamship line in the cross trades. To overcome this, Ivaran realized that the only viable way to enter the liner trades was through a partnership with an already established operator. In 1927, Ivaran therefore entered into an agreement with the US-based shipping firm Garcia and Diaz to establish a new limited-liability company, A/S Linea Sud-Americana, which entered the liner trade between the east coast of the US and Argentina, Brazil and Uruguay. The depression that followed the 1929 Wall Street collapse hit Linea Sud-Americana as well. In 1932, Christensen decided to end his cooperation with Garcia and Diaz. Ivaran took over full ownership of the company, and the same year Ivaran entered into an agreement with another American partner, Moore and McCormack Co. Inc. Formally, the new partner became the American agent for Ivaran, but in reality, the Ivaran vessels sailed under Moore and McCormack's colours.

Christensen also wanted to enter the oil transport business.[21] In 1924, he ordered a tanker and managed to secure a ten-year charter with a US company. This ship proved to be a well of solid and stable income until it was sold in 1936. The earnings from this ship enabled Christensen to compensate for deficits in the company's liner trade. Nonetheless, Ivaran could not escape the negative effects of the depression, and share capital was written down in 1929, 1931 and 1932. Moreover, shareholders received no dividends between 1925 and 1934. Christensen died in 1934, and his brother-in-law, Sverre Holter-Sørensen, took over as general manager.

In 1936, the US Congress passed a new Merchant Marine Act, the purpose of which was to provide state support to develop liner services under the American flag. As a result, Ivaran's cooperation with Moore and McCormack came to an end, and Ivaran had to operate under its own flag. Ivaran found a new general agent in the US and managed to go out on its own. In cooperation with a company based on the Philippines, De La Rama, Ivaran also entered the liner trade between the US and East Asia with good financial results. By 1940, the fleet managed by Sverre Holter-Sørensen on behalf of

---

[21]In this Christensen was not alone. Norwegian shipowners expanded substantially in the tanker trade during the post war years. The classic study is S.G. Sturmey, *British Shipping and World Competition* (London, 1962; New ed., St. John's, 2010). For a more up-to-date analysis, see Stig Tenold, "Norway's Interwar Tanker Expansion - A Reappraisal," *Scandinavian Economic History Review*, LV, No. 3 (2007), 244-261. See also Eivind Merok, "After the Party: The Political Economy of Shipping in Norway in the Interwar Period," *this volume*.

A/S Ivarans Rederi and various affiliated companies comprised nine dry-cargo ships and two oil tankers.

As did other Norwegian shipping companies, Ivaran lost several ships during World War II. After the war, Ivaran reopened its liner trade with three modern C1-A ships acquired from the Americans. The first quinquennium after the war was characterized by a shortage of tonnage in both the East Asian and South American trades; Ivaran benefitted from this shortage and enjoyed favourable profits. While the cargo liner trades might not be the most profitable branch of shipping during periods of great prosperity, it is also less vulnerable during times of depression. For this reason, Ivaran was reluctant to re-enter the fluctuating tanker trade after the war. At the end of 1949, Ivaran disposed of three ships in the US-South-America trade, five ships in the US-East Asia service and two ships in general tramp trade.

Ivaran now faced progressively stronger competition in its markets. Fluctuating freight volumes and a growing discrimination in trade policy against third-flag carriers led to increasing difficulties for Ivaran. Fierce competition in the East Asian trade motivated Ivaran to terminate Ivaran Lines Far East after more than twenty years of operation. In contrast to the changing conditions in the Asian trade, the South American service generated reliable profits during the 1950s. But even this trade soon became more challenging as growing flag discrimination in Brazil and Argentina and new shipping lines attempting to enter the US-South American trade forced several lines to abandon their service. In 1967, Ivaran and six other third-flag liner operators were forced to accept a pool agreement under which eighty percent of the Brazilian trade was to be shared equally between US and South American lines. The remainder was left to the few third-flag carriers remaining.

At the beginning of the 1970s, Ivaran's cargo liners began to show their age. But Ivaran hesitated to take the financial risk of investing in expensive new vessels. During the decade, Ivaran decided instead to sell five of its ships and charter them back for specified periods. Various other vessels were also acquired on time charters. In 1976, Ivaran finally decided to take the plunge and order new cargo liners. Two new container ships were delivered in 1978, which comprised the entirety of its wholly owned cargo liner fleet. In 1980, Ivaran turned its service into a full-fledged container line. But larger vessels were required to handle container traffic efficiently, so in 1983 Ivaran joined the German shipowner Claus-Peter Offen in a limited partnership which took over the contracts for two new and larger container ships which Offen had ordered from a German yard. When these vessels were delivered in 1984, they were chartered by Ivaran for four years but were operated under the German flag and were managed by Offen.

From 1984 onwards, the protectionist measures in Argentina and Brazil against third-flag carriers began to ease. For instance, in 1985 Brazil declared that cargo lines serving the country no longer had to be members of conferences or cargo pools. By that time, Ivaran was the only non-national carrier of any significance still active in the US-South American trade. Two other Norwegian shipping companies had ceased operating liners between North and South America. While the changed situation opened new opportunities for Ivaran, free trade also meant more competition. To face this challenge, Ivaran established its own agency network organized as a wholly owned Ivaran subsidiary with offices in the US, Canada, Mexico, Venezuela and the Caribbean. Two more container ships were bought by another limited partnership initiated by Offen in 1985; these were again German flagged and managed by Offen.

Despite the company's priority on the liner trades, during the 1970s and 1980s Ivaran also entered the offshore industry. In 1974, Ivaran initiated a partnership, named K/S Ivaran Drilling A/S Co., which ordered a drilling platform from a Norwegian shipyard.[22] Ivaran subscribed forty percent of the investment capital. But K/S Ivaran Drilling ran into difficulties from the very start. At the time it ordered the rig, it was not fully financed. Moreover, there was no charter attached to the contract. When the market quickly deteriorated, the prospects of profitable employment for the rig looked remote. The building contract was cancelled with the loss of the entire invested capital. Fortunately, Ivaran had more luck with supply services. In 1974, it took possession of a new supply vessel and shortly thereafter ordered a second. Both vessels were operated through a pool, named Stad Seaforth, led by two other shipping companies. The cooperation through the pool led to satisfactory charters. At the end of 1984, Ivaran had three wholly owned supply ships and had shares in three others. Favourable tax rules motivated a large number of investors to join limited partnerships which invested in supply vessels. The result was a considerable tonnage surplus which led to lay-ups and operating losses in many of the partnerships. K/S Stad Seaforth suffered the same fate. The partnership had poor results in 1986. Heavily in debt, the partnership had to renegotiate its financial commitments. The capital was entirely written off, and the ships were sold. In 1990, Ivaran had an ownership stake in only a single supply ship.

The company even turned to the more sophisticated area of gas transport, a highly specialized sector dominated by a handful of operators.[23] More-

---

[22]Drilling and other offshore-related activities became a favoured investment for many Norwegian shipping companies during the 1970s and 1980s. Some details are provided in Stig Tenold, "The Shipping Crisis of the 1970s: Causes, Effects and Implications for Norwegian Shipping" (Unpublished PhD thesis, Norwegian School of Economics and Business Administration, 2001), 353-363. See also Jan Karl Karlsen, *The Mobile Rig Industry* (Bergen, 1992).

[23]A short, general account of the growth of the gas shipping industry is provided by Martin Stopford, *Maritime Economics* (London, 1988; 3rd ed., London,

over, the sector was characterized by high capital costs and an extremely volatile market. In short, it had great risk potential. In 1981, Ivaran sponsored the establishment of a limited partnership, K/S A/S Ivaran Gas Transport; A/S Ivarans was responsible for thirty percent of the shares. A gas carrier was ordered from a Norwegian yard and delivered in 1984. But by that time the gas market had weakened, and Ivaran's foray into gas transport ended with the ship being bought by I.M. Skaugen A/S.

In 1989 and 1990, Ivaran ordered four new containerships from a German yard. The first two were bought by Offen and hired out to Ivaran. The next two were bought by Ivarans Rederi and Ivaran Shipping, a wholly owned subsidiary established by Ivarans Rederi in 1990 as a result of a merger of several small firms within the Ivaran group. The purpose of this new ownership structure was to allow Ivarans Rederi to concentrate on liner operations, while Ivaran Shipping should take care of activities in tramp and bulk shipping, oil transport and the sale and purchase of ships. Other new container ships were delivered to Ivaran Shipping in 1993, 1994 and 1995. In 1994, Ivaran Shipping was forced to sell one of the new container ships to solve financial problems stemming from a huge loss caused by massive speculation in currency by the managing director of Ivaran Shipping, who had been appointed in 1991. Ivaran Shipping had a net loss of 170 million Norwegian *kroner* (NOK). It was also discovered that this director had kept commissions for himself and placed them in a Swiss bank account. He was later prosecuted for fraud and sentenced to five-and-one-half years in prison.

During the early 1990s, Ivaran attempted to extend its liner services. For instance, it started to call at ports in Venezuela, a large producer of gas and oil. More significantly, Ivaran opened Ivaran Lines Europe in 1992. Several ports in South America were included before vessels headed across the Atlantic to several cities in Europe. Ivaran also entered into various strategic alliances and slot agreements with shipping companies in Germany, the United States and South America.

In 1995, Ivaran owned four vessels and had twelve additional ships on charter. The firm's activities were relatively extensive. But increasing competition in the liner market between the US and South America led to falling rates, which caused substantial losses between 1994 and 1996. While rates increased somewhat in 1997, by now more than twenty lines were operating similar services. In particular, larger liner companies with more capital, such as Mærsk and Crowley, made their presence felt in the trade between the US and South America. Their strong capital base meant that they had a greater capacity than smaller companies to endure losses and wait for the competitors to withdraw from the trade. By the fall 1997, Ivaran's board decided to look for a buyer for

---

2009), 478-488. A study of the industry focusing on Norwegian participants is Ann-Elisabeth Svendsen, *Gass-skipsfart* (Bergen, 1992).

the liner services. The next year, the vessels engaged in these services, together with all the agencies in the US and Brazil and a large number of containers were sold to CP Ships Holding Inc. UK, a subsidiary of Canadian Pacific, based in Montréal. CP Ships went on to become one of the world's main liner operators. But by this time Ivaran faced a new problem - to find sufficient employment for its own ships and for the one it had on charter. When rates continued to fall, the company made another huge loss in 1998. Ivaran was now in default with all its creditors. The end of the story was that to comply with the requirements of its creditors and shareholders, Ivaran sold its remaining vessels to Kristian Siem.

During the last ten years of Ivaran's existence, the main owner, Eirik Holter-Sørensen, had to cope with conflicts within the owning family and with several attempts at hostile takeovers. At the end of the 1980s, he and his cousin, Westye Holter-Sørensen, were the main owners of Ivaran. The two cousins also managed the company together. In 1989, Westye Holter-Sørensen and his family sold their shares to outside investors. So did Eirik Holter-Sørensen's brother, Jan Holter-Sørensen. The buyer was Foinco Shipping A/S, owned by an outside investor, Bernt Fossum. Soon, Foinco owned forty-two percent of Ivaran's shares. Eirik Holter-Sørensen kept control because the shipping company Awilco, owned by Anders Wilhelmsen, sold its eighteen percent ownership in Ivaran to Ivaran's German partner, Claus-Peter Offen. Anders Wihelmsen had previously worked as general manager at Ivaran, and the sale of his shares to Offen attested to his loyalty to his previous employer. But why did the cousin and the brother sell their shares to an outside investor and thus weaken the ownership position of Eirik Holter-Sørensen? The reason seems to be that Eirik had poor relations with his close relatives. According to Eirik's son, his father had not treated his brother well.

From this moment on, a lengthy struggle for control of Ivaran began. In 1990, Foinco's shares were taken over by Det Søndenfjeldske Norske Dampskibsselskap A/S, one of the oldest shipping companies in Norway. Three years later, Kristian Siem became the main owner of Søndenfjeldske, which for years had been a partner of Ivaran in its offshore activities. But now it showed its true colours. Soon after acquiring the Ivaran shares, Søndenfjeldske suggested that its shares be separated from Ivaran and put into a separate company. Holter-Sørensen rejected this suggestion. Søndenfjeldske also repeatedly demanded a seat on Ivaran's board, a demand that was not met. The reason for Holter-Sørensen's resistance was that he sensed that Søndenfjeldske's owners only had a financial interest in Ivaran, and he feared that they wanted to split up Ivaran and realize its value through sale. Conflicts and negotiations with Søndenfjeldske continued through most of the 1990s. In 1998, Ivaran gave in and invited Siem to become a member of the board. The next year Siem bought Ivaran's remaining ships.

It seems that these struggles, first with Erik Fossum and then later with Kristian Siem, demanded too much energy from Eirik Holter-Sørensen and probably diverted his attention from necessary strategic analyses and decisions. His son believes that his father and the administration of Ivaran could have dealt with the business challenges Ivaran faced during the 1990s had his father acquired the shares of his brother and cousin. Be that as it may, Holter-Sørensen never had the peace and quiet to contemplate the necessary decisions, and the result was the demise of the firm.

Herlofson Shipping Co.[24]

The first Sigurd Herlofson was born in 1879. Trained as a lawyer, he was also educated at the war college, lower level. In 1907, together with Bendix Jørgensen Grefstad, Herlofson established the shipping company Grefstad and Herlofson. This company soon became a substantial shipping firm, with nearly thirty sail and steam vessels. Herlofson withdrew from the firm in 1916, disenchanted by the excessive speculation that went on in the shipping market during World War I. Herlofson nonetheless retained a keen interest in shipping, which spurred him in 1926 to establish a new shipping company - Sigurd Herlofson Shipping Co A/S. Herlofson soon bought two tankers from the Anglo-Saxon Company and entered the tanker trade. After a few years, he sold the two ships and bought two motor tankers. In 1932, Gunnar Hvattum joined him as a partner, and in 1935 Herlofson's son, Peter Didrik, also became a partner. In 1933, Herlofson started a liner service transporting fresh fruit from the American west coast to Europe. When World War II erupted, Sigurd Herlofson Shipping disposed of four fruit ships, one cargo liner and three motor tankers. During the war, the firm lost four ships. In the autumn 1945, Herlofson bought two new fruit ships and two cargo liners. The next year, the firm ordered what at the time was the world's biggest tanker from Kockums Shipyard in Sweden. Sigurd Herlofson died in 1952 at the age of seventy-three. His son, Peter Didrik, took over as senior owner-manager. He continued to manage the firm together with Gunnar Hvattum until the latter died in 1963. Three years later, Peter Didrik's son, the second Sigurd Herlofson, became a partner.

After World War II, Herlofson started a new fruit line between America and Europe, named the Black Diamond Line. From 1945 to 1955, the shipping company had six ships in this trade. The competition in this market, however, increased to a point where their trade was no longer profitable for Herlofson Shipping. Ships were sold or leased to other shipping companies,

---

[24]The material in this section comes from interviews with Ivar Saunes, Emil Gamborg and Finn Messel; annual reports from the company, 1972-1982; and Einar Diesen, *Slekten Herlofson gjennom 400 år: En sørlandskrønike* (Oslo, 1975).

although Herlofson Shipping continued in a smaller scale in liners, as well as in bulk shipping and tankers. In 1970, Sigurd Herlofson merged eight companies which hitherto had been owned and managed by Herlofson Shipping Co. as subsidiaries. The new company disposed of thirteen ships. The merger also resulted in a decision to engage in business activities other than shipping. Herlofson Shipping had already started to invest in the oil business by ordering a semi-submersible oil rig, which was delivered in 1973. Through another company, Sigurd Herlofson also owned a substantial number of shares in the shipyard Fredrikstad Mekaniske Verksted. In the beginning of the 1970s, he bought nearly fifty percent of the shares in the construction firm Kaare Backer and also acquired part of the prestigious Grand Hotel in Oslo and a cold-storage plant in northern Norway. The motive for engaging in other business activities was to diversify his financial assets and hence his risk.

In 1972, the year before the oil crisis struck, Herlofson Shipping owned in whole or in part five tankers, had shares in four bulk ships, had recently ordered two new bulk carriers, possessed three-and-a-half small liner ships, owned twenty percent of a whaling factory ship and about half of the (ordered) advanced submersible oil drilling platform. Moreover, Herlofson Shipping owned seven percent of an oil company - Pelican and Co. - which had permission to drill for oil in the North Sea.

How did the oil crisis affect Herlofson Shipping? Reading its annual reports during the 1970s gives a good impression of how the problems in the shipping industry gradually affected the firm. In 1974, the year after the OPEC oil embargo, most of its ships were still operating, although two old motor tankers were laid up. Although the annual report described the difficult situation in international shipping, Herlofson had ordered two new ships from Fredrikstad Mekaniske Verksted, one large tanker and one oil/ore carrier, both for delivery in 1976. At its annual meeting in 1975, it was decided to pay ten-percent dividends on the shares.

The next year, most of the ships were still operating, but for some of them, rates now were too low to cover the running costs. As a result, one tanker and one bulk carrier, both of them older ships, were sold. Although the oil platform was managing fairly well, for the first time the company lost money and was unable to pay dividends. The problems continued in 1976. Most of the ships that were still employed were engaged in tramp trades at low rates. During the year, all four of the old liners and one tanker were sold. Even the oil platform operated at a deficit. The two new ships delivered from Fredrikstad Mekaniske Verksted had satisfactory long-term financing; due to a guarantee from the Norwegian Guarantee Institute for Ships and Oil Rigs (GI), the banks excused Herlofson Shipping from making repayments for three years.[25] Still, the company lost money for the second year in a row. In 1977, the shipping crisis hit Herlofson Shipping hard. Three of the tankers were laid up, including one of the large ones that had been delivered the previous year, and all the bulk ships were sold. The two remaining tankers were placed in tramp trades at rates which did not cover operating expenses. The factory ship lost money, and the revenues from the oil company Pelican only covered expenses. The only promising activity was the oil rig, which was hired by British Petroleum at a favourable rate. The problems continued during the next few years. As the firm continued to lose money and to accumulate debts, it was forced to sell more ships and to reduce the staff considerably. In addition, the administration moved to more modest offices.

The drastic measures were to a large extent initiated by a new director, Emil Gamborg, who was hired in 1977. In Herlofson Shipping, Sigurd Herlofson was still the managing director, with Gamborg acting as a deputy managing director. When he arrived at the firm, he soon discovered that the owner and the administration did not really understand the difficulties the company faced. They believed that the firm's economic situation, in spite of the shipping crisis, was fairly good, and that the ships were in good condition. In contrast, Gamborg saw that it was necessary to downsize the company by selling ships and reducing the number of employees. He discovered that there was no real leadership in the company and no clear strategy. In Gamborg's opinion, strategic decisions were influenced too much by the company's main shipbrokers. According to Gamborg, Sigurd Herlofson was at times a victim of advice from these shipbrokers that seemed to reflect the brokers' own economic interests. For instance, the shipbroker had a substantial share in Fredrikstad Mekaniske Verksted, from which Herlofson Shipping ordered the two ships that saddled the firm with substantial debts in the second half of 1970s and into the 1980s. Both Reidar Saunes and Finn Messel, previous directors, confirm the strong influence which the shipbrokers had on Sigurd Herlofson's decisions. The owner-manager himself was a likeable person, but he was not comfortable with being a responsible owner-manager. In addition, several years of economic problems seemed to have weakened his resolve. While he was good at calculating prices and costs, he did not like to make difficult decisions. He once told Saunes that he wished that he could retire before he reached the age of forty-nine. The firm also lacked an independent board which could oversee the decisions of the owner and his administration.

According to Gamborg, the lack of a concrete strategy manifested itself in an incoherent collection of ships which represented too much diversifi-

---

[25]The GI was established by the Norwegian government in 1975 "to try to alleviate the financial difficulties faced by the industry and to preserve tonnage in Norwegian hands;" see Stig Tenold, "Saving a Sector – But Which One? The Norwegian Guarantee Institute for Ships and Drilling Vessels Ltd.," *International Journal of Maritime History*, XIII, No. 1 (2001), 39.

cation. In addition, some of them were too old to be competitive. Gamborg also believed that the ships were too long, too narrow and too deep - in short, unsuited for the markets in which they operated. In spite of the outdated nature of several of the ships, the owner and the administration had been reluctant to dispose of them. Moreover, the company had a weak capital base and inadequate profitability. In this respect, Herlofson Shipping resembled those large, failing firms which, according to Hambrick and D'Aventi, showed early signs of basic weaknesses.[26] In addition, Herlofson Shipping concentrated too much on the tramp trades and had too few long-term charters. During his time as director, Gamborg sold off older ships and slashed the staff by about half. Gamborg left the company in 1983, and Finn Messel was engaged as the new managing director in 1986.

In 1981, Herlofson Shipping owned half of a large tanker which was operated through the shipping pool Sea Team OBOS, as well as seventy percent of a large motor tanker which operated on the spot market and 42.5 percent of an oil/ore ship which was also operated through Sea Team. The first of these three ships was laid up in 1981, and the next two were laid up the next year and later sold. In addition, Herlofson Shipping had small ownership shares in an oil/bulk carrier and a tanker. A tanker and the oil rig were sold in 1981. The income from the sales was used to reduce the company's debt. Herlofson also still held a small share (5.9 percent) in the oil company Pelican. At this time, while Pelican had drilled for oil for several years and had discovered some oil reservoirs, they were not commercially exploitable. At the end of 1981, Herlofson Shipping had 165 employees, 150 more at sea and another fifteen in the administration.

Herlofson Shipping and its affiliated companies also had a high debt load, most of which stemmed from the two new ships which were delivered in 1976. The company had arrangements with their main financial creditors and the GI, which eased the terms of repayment. These agreements were extended in 1981. Due to decreasing ship values, at the end of the 1970s the firm's creditors stepped in to protect their assets. According to the last managing director, Finn Messel, Herlofson Shipping at the beginning of the 1980s was in reality governed by the banks and the GI. The company had to sell assets to meet the demands from its creditors. Moreover, the company had to continue to reduce the number of employees.

In 1982, Herlofson Shipping altered its strategy by initiating several limited partnerships which acquired ships that were then managed by Herlofson. The partners were both international and Norwegian charterers and investors. To protect its control of the partnerships, Herlofson Shipping was careful to avoid allowing any of the partners to acquire large ownership stakes. The partnerships all had short time horizons, most of them only four years. The

---

[26]Hambrick and D'Aventi, "Large Corporate Failures," 1-23.

purpose of this strategy was to retain the company's capacity to manage ships and administer the transport of goods. At the same time, the owner and the senior managers hoped to generate enough profits from these activities to be able to build a new capital base for future investments. This strategy was reasonably successful, and the company again earned some profits. The various limited partnerships, however, were dissolved in 1986-1987.

At this point, the company embarked on yet another new strategy by chartering ships from other companies and operating them on contracts with various charterers. Herlofson employed a person who had previously worked for the Høegh Shipping Company and gave him the responsibility for this business. The plan was to carry grain to East Asia and to transport coal from Australia on the way back to Europe. The market for this trade was positive in 1987, and the prospects for this strategy seemed promising. At this time, Herlofson's debt burden was also manageable. In fact, the balance sheet looked satisfactory on paper. But it soon transpired that the timing of the company's charters and freight contracts was disastrous. The rates for chartered ships rose substantially, far beyond the rates at which Herlofson had contracted. The company nonetheless had to fulfil its commitments to the various charterers. These soon became a heavy burden. The result was that cash haemorrhaged from the company, and Herlofson Shipping suffered huge losses.

According to a well-placed observer, the ruinous consequences of the charter business were to a large extent the result of the actions of the person in charge of this business. He was described as a busybody who entered into a large number of charters and freight contracts that proved to be economically disastrous. The last managing director of the company, Finn Messel, confirmed this, but blamed himself for not having exercised greater control over this person's activities. But to be fair to Messel, the owner paid little attention to the activities of this employee either.

The capacity of the firm and the owner to deal with the problems was weakened at the end of the 1980s by two other events. Wanting to leave a lasting footprint on his hometown of Arendal, Sigurd Herlofson built a posh hotel there. Building the hotel tied up a good deal of the company's capital, and the property struggled to become profitable. In 1988, Sigurd Herlofson also entered into a conflict with his stepmother and his half-brother when both claimed that as minority owners they had received insufficient information about the company's state of affairs. As in similar cases, it is reasonable to assume that this conflict diverted still more of Sigurd Herlofson's attention from the task of running his firm.

In 1990, it was revealed that the managing director had transferred considerable sums from the employees' pension fund to other companies in the group. When the owner discovered this, he declared bankruptcy. The managing director was later convicted of fraud, although two previous directors believe that he did this to save the shipping company rather than to enrich himself.

A/S HAV: Helmer Staubo and Co.[27]

The limited-liability shipping company A/S HAV was founded in 1915 with Helmer Staubo and his father, Christian P. Staubo, as the main owners through their personal company, Helmer Staubo and Co. The father was already co-owner of the family-owned shipping firm John P. Pedersen and Søn. A/S HAV was the idea of Helmer Staubo, who not surprisingly became its acting owner manager. The company began with a single ship. Over the next few years, it bought new ships, financed by fresh issues of company stock. Father and son retained sixty percent of the shares, however, in order to protect the company from aggressive external investors. When the shipping market boomed during World War I, Helmer Staubo pursued a cautious strategy and was not tempted to chase easy profits. In 1918, Helmer Staubo also became a partner in the family firm John P. Pedersen and Søn.

During the 1920s, Helmer Staubo and Co. operated five modern steamships in European tramp trades and on short time charters. It was difficult, though, to earn acceptable profits due to low freight rates. The company therefore decided to sell its ships. During the 1930s, A/S HAV actively engaged in the profitable fruit trade between the West Indies and North America. At the end of the 1920s, Helmer Staubo also entered the tanker business by founding a new limited-liability shipping company A/S Havtank, which owned and managed a tanker during the 1930s. At the outset of World War II, Helmer Staubo had four ships, three of which were lost during the conflict. In 1942, Christian Staubo retired as a partner. And Helmer Staubo's eldest son, Knut Helmer Staubo, became a new partner in 1944. In 1950, Helmer's younger son, Jan, was elevated to partner as well.

After the war, Helmer Staubo and Co. acquired two second-hand and two newly built motor tankers. In 1947, A/S HAV and A/S Havtank established the so-called "Staubo Line," which operated two liners between North America and the eastern Mediterranean, although its participation in this trade ended in 1953 when the administration of HAV concluded that it would demand larger investments in order to become profitable. But in 1957, Helmer Staubo entered the liner trade again with two vessels sailing for the Black Diamond Steamship Corp., based in New York. Helmer Staubo continued in various liner trades up to 1966. With a new motor tanker delivered in 1949 and another one in 1951, Staubo also re-entered the tanker trade. Both ships

---

[27]The material in this section is based upon an interview with Tore Staubo; Tore Staubo, *Finanskriser - overlevelse mot alle odds* (Oslo, 2009); and Dag Bakka, Jr., *Hav I Storm og Stille* (Larvik, 1990).

were chartered by Anglo-Saxon Petroleum Co. for five years.[28] These time charters provided the company with a stable income, while the liner trade barely covered operating and capital costs. In 1955, HAV and Havtank ordered a new tanker and a dry-cargo ship, reflecting a conscious effort to diversify their risks; both ships turned out to be profitable. Inspired by the good results in the tanker trade, Helmer Staubo and Co. acquired new tankers in 1962 and 1968. In the latter year, together with the shipping companies John. P. Pedersen and Søn and I.M. Skaugen, Helmer Staubo and Co. chartered four tankers built for a Greek shipowner. These ships were operated in a pool by Staubo.

During the 1950s and 1960s, the company was managed in a careful and conscientious way, a management style that was influenced by Helmer Staubo's personal character. The father and both of his sons were also involved in various organizational activities outside the shipping company. Knut H. Staubo, for instance, served as president of the Norwegian Shipowners' Association in the 1960s, while his brother Jan was engaged in various sporting organizations and was later a Norwegian member on the International Olympic Committee.

Early in the sixties, A/S HAV and A/S Havtank looked for new business opportunities in South America. In collaboration with a Norwegian fish meal producer, the two shipping companies invested in a new fish meal factory in Peru. This investment opened up the prospect of transporting processed fish products from Peru to the US and Europe. Helmer Staubo soon became one of the biggest carriers in this profitable trade, although the production of fish meal generated only modest earnings. In 1973, Peru nationalized the fish meal industry, and in 1974 Helmer Staubo and Co. decided to end its activities in that country.

At the start of the 1970s, the founder of the firm, Helmer Staubo, retired from management at the age of seventy-nine. Thereafter, the business profile of the company shifted from being a cautious operation towards a more ambitious and risky strategy. In 1970, Helmer Staubo and Co. ordered five ships, three "handy-size" bulk carriers and two Very Large Crude Carriers (VLCCs). The bulk ships were financed mainly by the shipyards, backed by state guarantees, while the two VLCCs were financed through limited partnerships in which A/S HAV and A/S Havtank held thirty-five and thirty percent of the shares, respectively. The total financial participation of the two shipping

---

[28]Anglo-Saxon Petroleum Co. cooperated closely with Norwegian shipowners from the interwar years. Studies of this relationship include Atle Thowsen, "Fra krig tile krise vekst: Mellomkrigstiden - det store hamskiftet i sørlandets skipsfart," *Sjøfartshistorisk årbok* (1994), 7-134; and Gaute Chr. Molaug, "Det sørlandske Anglo-Saxon eventyr" (Unpublished MA thesis, University of Bergen, 2001). For a general study of the company, see Norman L. Middlemiss, *The Anglo-Saxon/Shell Tankers* (Newcastle upon Tyne, 1990).

companies was quite substantial. The two supertankers were delivered in 1973 and 1974, the first one before the war between Israel and the Arab nations triggered the subsequent oil embargo, the other one after the oil crisis was a fact. In the summer of 1973, Helmer Staubo and Co. also contracted with a Japanese yard for a relatively large motor tanker for delivery in 1977. At the same time, the affiliated family company, John Pedersen and Søn, ordered a sister ship. Neither of these two ships had charters when the shipping market collapsed in October 1973.

Helmer Staubo and Co. also wanted to participate in the emerging offshore industry. In 1973, A/S HAV and A/S Havtank joined I.M. Skaugen, which had just ordered a semi-submersible oil platform. The two companies subscribed to 8.5 percent of the vessel. Moreover, together with John P. Pedersen and Søn, Helmer Staubo ordered two supply ships from a German yard, both delivered in 1975. The two family firms joined the pool "Edda Supply Ships," which consisted of five member companies that together operated ten-to-twelve supply vessels. Helmer Staubo and Co. became the operator of the pool. In 1974, A/S HAV and A/S Havtank contracted for the building of two advanced drilling ships in the Netherlands. The first was due to be delivered in 1976 and the other in 1977. The intention of the owners was to gradually include more partners. The development in the offshore did not, however, motivate other investors to join the two firms. Accordingly, they were left with large financial obligations.

Owning and managing tankers, bulk ships, supply ships and oil rigs, and having huge financial obligations, Helmer Staubo and Co. was now facing a period of unprecedented crisis in the shipping industry. The new, ambitious, and incautious strategy presented the owners with huge challenges. As the shipping market deteriorated, the family firms now had obligations that were far beyond what the present market rates could cover. In 1974, Tore K.H. Staubo, Knut's son, joined Helmer Staubo and Co. At that time, he realized that despite the international crisis, his father and the administration believed that they had the situation well in hand. But to Tore Staubo, the budgets were too optimistic. It became clear to him that the company had too many tankers, too many orders for new ships and too much invested in offshore activities. These problems also became obvious to the owners and the administration, and over the next few years, they spent much time negotiating with frequently aggressive creditors and attempting to weed out the worst "cash drains" in their portfolio of ships and rigs. At the same time, it was important to them to keep sufficient tonnage to generate some profits and to provide a basis for the firm's continued existence once the markets improved. They also wanted to retain key personnel and competence. An important task was to handle the two drilling ships. Chase Manhattan Bank had made an advance on the building loan and feared that the security no longer covered their financial risk. In 1976,

Helmer Staubo managed to cancel the second of these two ships, albeit with substantial penalties, while the GI guaranteed the loan on the first vessel.

In 1977, Helmer Staubo disposed of a bulk ship which was still making profits, a drilling ship which also did reasonably well, a supertanker which barely covered expenses and another supertanker that was laid up. Both the supply ships operated at a loss, and the firm decided to sell them. It was only due to income from the chartered Greek ships that the shipping company managed to remain afloat. All available assets were now used to pay off the loans. In 1979, the owners managed to sell one of the two supertankers, but it was difficult to reach this agreement because the various owners in the limited partnership had different opinions on the necessity of such a sale. The amount which the sale generated enabled the company to pay off the rest of its loans. Simultaneously, the other supertanker, which had been laid up, was chartered for twelve months at a reasonable rate.

When the second drilling ship was delivered in 1976, it was chartered for four years to a French oil company. Because of the penalty fees on the cancelled sister ship, Helmer Staubo and Co. was left with a large debt. It managed, however, to find profitable charters for the drilling ship throughout the 1970s. In 1980, the firm opened negotiations with the GI for a settlement of their obligations and a refinancing of the loan from Chase Manhattan. In 1982, twenty percent of the drilling vessel was sold to a French company. Because of the worsening market for supply ships after 1976, the two supply vessels were forced to operate on the spot market. And even when they were chartered for twelve months in 1977, the rates were unsatisfactory, and both ships were sold in 1979. In 1979, A/S HAV and A/S Havtank were delisted on the Oslo Stock Exchange.

Towards the end of the 1970s, some burdensome shipping engagements were phased out, and in 1980, the remaining shipping activities provided satisfactory profits. But in 1982, the international shipping market again collapsed. As a result of a doubling of oil prices, international trade stagnated. In these conditions, the four-year contract for the drilling ship was valuable to Helmer Staubo and Co. In the following years, the operation of this vessel generated a steady cash flow that helped the company to discharge its loans. The remaining supertanker was sold in 1983. That same year, Tore Staubo took over as general manager, and in 1984, A/S HAV and A/S Havtank were merged into a single joint-stock company. In 1986, Helmer Staubo and Co. bought two new, smaller tankers at a Korean yard. Two limited partnerships were established to finance and formally own the tankers. Helmer Staubo and Co. took a majority ownership position (sixty-four percent) in the first limited partnership but subscribed to only 16.5 percent in the other. Both ships were operated by Helmer Staubo and Co. In 1987, the company operated four tankers, a bulk ship and the drilling vessel. That same year, the bulk ship was sold.

At the beginning of the 1980s, Helmer Staubo & Co. again became engaged in offshore projects. In 1980, the firm purchased forty percent of the shares in the limited partnership Stamar Supply A/S, which had just ordered a combined anchor handling and supply vessel. Helmer Staubo in 1984 became a partner in a limited-liability company which owned two other supply ships. Over the next few years, however, the market for supply ships became difficult. Due to excess tonnage it was difficult to obtain charters at acceptable rates, and the value of the ships decreased. The shipping company finally decided to leave the supply ship market, and the three ships were sold in 1986 and 1987.

The solid income earned by the drilling ship was noticed by investors in Oslo. The decade of the 1980s was characterized by a liberalization of the credit market and a rise in the stock market, so there was a large amount of available capital looking for lucrative investment opportunities. Tore Staubo attempted to exploit this situation by increasing the firm's capital through a general issue of shares in A/S HAV. By 1984, the company was again listed on the Oslo Stock Exchange. These strategic moves were risky for a family-owned and managed company in which the Staubo family traditionally controlled about sixty-five percent of the shares. When A/S HAV was reintroduced on the stock exchange, several members of the Staubo family chose to sell their shares to outside investors. At the start of 1985, Tore Staubo and his father controlled only about thirty-seven percent of the company.

During the winter, the share price rose rapidly. Two of the investors, a Swiss and Norwegian investment company (NIMBUS, headed by Per Grobstock), systematically bought shares in A/S HAV. By May 1985, they controlled forty-two percent of the shares. The new owners immediately began to demand a restructuring of the company. They proposed to merge A/S HAV with a British offshore company. To Tore Staubo, this proposition was only financially motivated because it was well known that A/S HAV had a great deal of cash on hand. Staubo felt that the two investors were only interested in maximizing the value of their shares and would then exit the company. He declined the proposition, supported by the board. The two financial investors continued to challenge the Staubo family. At the general meeting in 1986, they proposed that A/S HAV discontinue the management agreement with Helmer Staubo and Co. The two investors also strongly criticized some of Staubo's statements. According to Tore Staubo, the company's earnings suffered from the pressure from NIMBUS. In 1987, the shares of the two investors ended up in the hands of A/S Laboremus, another shipping company, controlled by I.M. Skaugen. A/S Laboremus also bought additional shares in A/S HAV. As a result of another general issue of shares, Tore Staubo by this time had less than a third of the shares in A/S HAV. In other words, he was facing a majority owner whose intention was, as with the previous two investors, to reorganize the company. To re-take control of the company, Tore Staubo raised a personal loan of NOK fifteen million to try to halt the plans of I.M. Skaugen. The stalemate between Staubo and Skaugen was finally solved by a split of A/S HAV, which was carried out in 1988. Nearly two-thirds of the company was transferred to a new company, which was taken over by A/S Laboremus. This part included the successful drilling ship and a large tanker. A/S HAV and Tore Staubo were left with a tanker, shares in three other ships and NOK forty-three million in cash.

After the split, Tore Staubo soon bought four second-hand bulk ships, all on behalf of limited partnerships in which A/S HAV held between nineteen and fifty-one percent of the shares. In other words, he continued to use this form of ownership to finance new vessels and to provide his shipping company with operational activities. Helmer Staubo and Co. continued to be active in 1989. The company focussed on the bulk trades, product tankers and the offshore. Three new ships and three oil rigs were bought, and Staubo established separate limited partnerships for each rig. When rig values rose considerably during the winter of 1989/1990, Tore Staubo exploited the opportunity and sold the rigs. In 1990 he also purchased two new semi-submersible oil rigs, again organized as limited partnerships and financed by loans from selected banks. He planned to finance his share of the project by raising new capital through share issues in A/S HAV. But in order to convince investors, he took fifty-five percent of the shares in the limited partnerships. To finance this, Tore Staubo raised a personal loan of NOK forty million, at that time a substantial amount. This loan was more than he was able to service, but he was reluctant to sell any shares in his company. The operation of the rigs was left to Wilrig A/S, which also took twenty percent of the shares in the two partnerships. One of the rigs was chartered by Petrobas, but the other had only sporadic charters and lost money. Banks started to push the partners to meet the financial obligations of the second partnership. Tore Staubo suggested to the partners that they merge the two partnerships so the income from the first rig could cover the deficit of the other. Wilrig, which was owned by the Wilhelm Wilhelmsen family, declined to support this solution. Staubo now also had serious difficulties servicing his personal loan, and he thus decided to sell both rigs to an American company. Tore Staubo later claimed that Wilrig, by obstructing the restructuring and the refinancing of the two oil rig partnerships, inflicted a mortal wound on A/S HAV. He felt that Wilrig and the Wilhelmsen family failed him at a crucial time. After the sale, A/S HAV had more than NOK 100 million in cash, but Staubo felt that this was too little to invest in new shipping or offshore projects. He therefore chose to sell A/S HAV.

A/S Laboremus - Einar Bakkevigs rederi[29]

The last case was a small shipping company, originally founded in 1910 as a whaling company but later turned into a publicly-held firm involved mainly in the tanker and gas trades. It was merged into a larger shipping company at the end of the 1980s.

Laboremus was founded by Tarald Dannevig and Lars Thorsen, with the shipping firm T. Dannevig and Co. as manager. In 1919, Dannevig became the sole owner, and Laboremus was involved in whaling on and off until 1937. Dannevig contracted his first tanker, a steam turbine ship, in 1922; a diesel tanker was added to the fleet five years later. Both ships operated on the spot market. Dannevig was quite reluctant to enter into long-term freight contracts with the large oil companies because he felt that such deals implied too much dependence on them.

With two small tankers in the 1930s, Dannevig's shipping company was a modest operator in the shipping market. Both ships were torpedoed during the war, and Dannevig duly received indemnities for them. To avoid taxation, Laboremus was expected to reinvest the money in new ships. Dannevig hesitated, however, to do so because the boom and collapse of the shipping market after World War I had evidently made him pessimistic about developments in the postwar market. In 1948, he bought a small steam tanker, which he again operated on the spot market, most of the time with cargo. Dannevig was criticized for not reinvesting more of the capital reserves, but he claimed that public restrictions, tax rules and the unions' wage and welfare claims made it too risky to invest in new tonnage.

In the 1950s, Laboremus could have been described as a financial firm as much as a shipping company. Substantial assets were invested in bonds and shares, in Norway and abroad. Dannevig seemed to prefer to keep assets in the form of securities and to receive a steady return on these investments. In 1954, he was seventy-five-years old, so it is possible that his risk-aversion was a function of his advanced age.

In 1950, the chief executive officer of T. Dannevig and Co., Oscar Bakkevig, was admitted as a partner. When Dannevig retired as an active owner-manager in 1954, Bakkevig's son, Einar, also became a partner in T. Dannevig and Co. Einar Bakkevig had extensive experience within shipping, having worked in shipbroking offices in several countries, passed the exam as average adjuster, headed the administration of another shipping firm and he started his own shipbroking company.

---

[29]The material in this section is based upon Svein Bakkevig, interview; Bård Kolltveit, *La oss arbeide: A/S Laboremus, 1910-1985* (Oslo, 1985); Laboremus, annual reports, 1981-1986; and material at www.skaugen.com.

In 1954, Laboremus finally contracted for a new ship, a medium-sized bulk carrier. Both of the Bakkevigs were eager to expand the company. Einar Bakkevig had many ideas to pump new vitality into the shipping firm. Tarald Dannevig, however, still held a majority of the shares, and Bakkevig soon discovered that he would use his position to veto any initiative that in his eyes was too risky. When Bakkevig suggested to the shareholders' committee in 1957 that Laboremus should contract for a new, relatively large dry-cargo ship, he was voted down by the Dannevig's representatives. In 1959, after successful negotiations with the Ford Corporation, Bakkevig recommended that Laboremus begin to transport cars from Europe to the US and Canada.[30] Once more, he was turned down by Dannevig and his representatives on the shareholders' committee.

In the elections to Laboremus' shareholders' committee in 1962 and 1963, Dannevig's supporters were replaced by people more sympathetic to Bakkevig's ambitions. At that time, he had begun to take an interest in gas transport. He was convinced that the demand for natural gas would increase and that gas transport had a promising future. At the beginning of the 1960s, he spent much time visiting producers and consumers of gas in order to establish a relationship and to build trust with potential charterers. And he attempted to learn as much as possible about the gas trade. He came to the conclusion that Laboremus ought to operate specialized gas tankers. The shareholders' committee endorsed his idea, and in 1965 the company bought its first gas tanker. In the next years, two more gas tankers were purchased for the carriage of ethylene. Since these ships were very expensive to build, the necessary capital was raised by a consortium with Laboremus as one of the participants.

During the 1970s, Laboremus continued to buy new gas tankers and chemical carriers. In 1977, the firm had ownership interests in eight such tankers, all managed by Einar Bakkevig's shipping company. Bakkevig had established a good international reputation within gas transport. But this trade was volatile, vulnerable to changing business cycles, and in 1976 Laboremus faced serious problems. A general economic recession and high costs in Norway combined with a substantial debt to strain the company's cash flow dramatically. As a result, Laboremus was unable to pay the instalments on its loans. The main banks allowed Laboremus to postpone its scheduled payment in 1977. But the situation did not improve, and in 1979 the company had a large accumulated deficit. It attempted to solve the problem in 1980 by selling one of the ships to a new limited joint-stock partnership in which Laboremus itself had a ten-percent share.

---

[30]Car transport was soon to become a major area of growth for Norwegian shipowners; see Espen Ekberg, "The Growth of the Deep-Sea Car-Carrying Industry, 1960-2008," *this volume*.

By 1980, Einar Bakkevig owned fewer than twenty-five percent of the shares in Laboremus. At this time, the other owners claimed a change in the company's governing structure. Fearnley and Eger, a large shipping firm, former business partner of Einar Bakkevig and one of the owners of Laboremus, demanded that the board be expanded with two new members. The motivation for this change likely was that the other owners wanted to protect their investments and hence wanted to have a firm hand on the wheel. Fearnley and Eger later joined I.M. Skaugen in forcing Svein Bakkevig out of Laboremus.

In 1981, Einar Bakkevig suddenly died, and his son Svein took over as manager of Laboremus and owner of the Einar Bakkevig shipping firm. He had joined his father as responsible partner in 1979, but he now faced the challenge of steering Laboremus into calmer waters. At the end of the 1970s and the beginning of the 1980s, competition in the gas market had grown. During this period, several Norwegian shipping companies looked to the gas trade for profitable business opportunities. We saw above how Ivaran, for instance, with no prior knowledge of gas transport, entered this trade. Moreover, favourable rules on depreciation motivated some Norwegian shipping companies to build new gas ships for which there was no demand.

In 1982, together with another Norwegian gas carrier, Svein Bakkevig initiated the creation of a gas pool, Norwegian Gas Carriers, to strengthen the participants' position in the international gas market. Four other Norwegian companies participated, among them Ivaran and Langfeldt/I.M. Skaugen. In 1982, Laboremus had three ships in this pool. The next two years, however, were difficult for Laboremus. Poor markets and weak earnings in 1982 and 1983 forced the company to expend much of its liquid reserves and to avail of a bank overdraft. Due to the increasing age of the ships, operating costs increased. Gas ships are technologically advanced and require more maintenance and upgrading than other vessels. With increasing age, these maintenance costs become more noticeable. In this situation, a new LPG/ethylene carrier was delivered. The debt incurred in buying this ship raised the company's total debt considerably. The year 1984 ended with a substantial deficit, but the value of the ships was still considerable, making the company interesting for outside investors. Rising share prices in 1982, 1983 and 1984 bear witness to the interest in Laboremus as an investment.

Norwegian shipping in the 1980s was characterized by the formation of larger business units through takeovers and mergers. Another initiator of Norwegian Gas carriers was the shipping company I.M. Skaugen, which was eager to attain a foothold in the gas market. I.M. Skaugen had been a car carrier, had engaged in oil drilling and had owned offshore supply vessels. The firm had experience in cruise shipping and the bulk trades, and now saw gas as an interesting field for expansion. The owners of I.M. Skaugen identified a need as well as an opportunity to restructure Norwegian Gas Carriers. Skaugen bought shares in another significant gas company and then purchased more than fifteen percent of the shares in Laboremus. Shortly after I.M. Skaugen had become a part-owner of Laboremus, Morits Skaugen, the heir of I.M. Skaugen, and Cato Holmsen, the company's managing director, persuaded the other owners to expand the company's capital stock, arguing that this would improve Laboremus' cash position and increase the ability to contract for new ships. In 1984, the share capital was raised twice, the second time with NOK ten million through a general issue. As a result of these operations, the number of shareholders increased from 200 to 700, and Laboremus received new capital which could be used for expansion. At the same time, however, Svein Bakkevig's ownership position in Laboremus was significantly diluted. The insurance company Storebrand held ten percent of the shares and offered Svein Bakkevig the opportunity to buy them. Had he bought these shares, he might have withstood I.M. Skaugen's hostile takeover. But Bakkevig did not have enough personal capital because the Bakkevig family had never been able to generate enough income from managing Laboremus to become a larger owner. Through the years, they had first and foremost been managers of Laboremus, not substantial owners. In 1985, the other owners agreed to relieve Bakkevig of his position as manager of Laboremus, and in 1989, Laboremus was merged into I.M. Skaugen, which at the same time became the dominant owner in Norwegian Gas Carriers.

Einar Bakkevig had become owner-manager when the founder of Laboremus, Tarald Dannevig, retired. Einar Bakkevig, the second generation in his own family, demonstrated that he had ideas to develop the shipping company further. With his strong position as a shareholder, Dannevig, even after his retirement, prevented Einar Bakkevig from realizing his plans. Laboremus thus illustrates that a fragmentation of ownership, in this case between business partners and not within an owner-family, can be devastating to the growth and effective management of a business enterprise. Laboremus and Einar Bakkevig might have fared much better had Bakkevig had more decision-making power and less interference from other owners. He could have created a profitable shipping business and built capital reserves at an earlier stage, but the lack of reserves made it difficult for Bakkevig to build a strong ownership position in Laboremus. Owning less than one-quarter of the shares in Laboremus made him vulnerable to opposition from the other owners and to takeover efforts from outside players. The economic difficulties of Laboremus spurred the other owners to take action and motivated external investors to restructure both Laboremus and the gas trade in Norway.

Why Did They Fail?

Previous research has shown that business exits can take place in various ways. The four cases discussed above illustrate this fact well. Only one of the four shipping companies, Herlofson, went out of business due to bankruptcy.

In contrast, Tore Staubo decided himself to sell A/S HAV, while Ivaran was compelled to sell its ships because of a crushing debt burden, and Einar Bakkevigs Rederi was forced out of its position as owner-manager of Laboremus after what can be described as a hostile takeover.

All four shipping companies discussed in this article were relatively old firms. Ivaran was founded in 1920, Herlofson Shipping Co. in 1926, A/S HAV/Helmer Staubo and Co. in 1915, and Laboremus in 1910. They were all medium-sized firms. In the mid-1970s, Ivaran owned two ships and chartered five others; Herlofson owned in whole or in part fourteen vessels and a drilling platform; Helmer Staubo and Co. owned shares in six ships; while Laboremus disposed of eight gas carriers. Their owners were well respected in the Norwegian shipping community. Why then did they fail?

The histories above demonstrate that the exit of each company was brought about through the interaction of several circumstances, decisions and events. In all cases, however, a principal reason for their difficulties was worsening conditions in their respective shipping markets, caused to a large extent by the international shipping crisis. But as I will discuss below, for these firms the deteriorating conditions became particularly challenging because of inadequate, or even ruinous, strategic decisions; inadequate governance; conflicts within the owner-family; a more favourable environment for takeovers in the 1980s and 1990s; and unforeseen and disastrous events.

Market Conditions and the Shipping Crisis

In the previous research on business failures, it has been demonstrated that the general economic climate affects the probability of survival. The histories of these four companies show that their fate was to a large extent determined by the shipping crisis during the 1970s and 1980s. Two of the companies - Herlofson and Helmer Staubo - were especially hard hit by this crisis. Both had a significant share of their tonnage in tankers and the bulk trades, the shipping markets that were hardest hit by the changing conditions. Both had also invested in offshore vessels. We saw above that soon after the crisis began, both firms encountered serious problems in finding profitable charters for their ships. At the same time, both had substantial loans. When freight rates fell and ships were idle more frequently, the loans became an obstacle to further operations. In the early years, both companies managed to ride out the storm by selling ships, dismantling unprofitable or high-cost shipping commitments and reducing debt. But despite these extensive adjustments, the two firms soon encountered new problems caused, at least to a certain extent, by new challenges in international shipping markets. The preceding histories demonstrate, however, that these challenges by themselves did not break the backs of the firms. Instead, it was their choice of strategic directions that caused their final failures. I will discuss this more below.

Ivaran's primary shipping activity was the liner trade, a sector that was not affected by the shipping crisis to the same extent as were tankers and the bulk trades. But nonetheless, Ivaran also experienced deteriorating conditions in their markets which made it difficult, if not impossible, to survive. Ivaran had for decades been a successful operator in the liner trade between the east coasts of North and South America. The company had weathered competition and discrimination against third-country carriers. In the beginning of the 1980s, Ivaran was in fact the "last man standing," the only non-national carrier of any significance in this trade. But at this moment the South American countries began to repeal their protectionist measures, and the subsequent liberalization of the trade attracted much stronger competitors with whom Ivaran was too small to compete. The company had insufficient capital and cash reserves to withstand the shrinking profits and simultaneously invest in new ships and an effective network of agents. Some of the new competitors that entered Ivaran's trades had "fled" in the face of excess capacity in the tanker and bulk markets. In that way, Ivaran, too, was affected by the international shipping crisis.

Compared with the other firms, Laboremus operated in a specialized but demanding segment of the shipping market. Gas transport requires both considerable capital and a high degree of competence on the part of both crew and administration. For these reasons, competition was not as intense as in the tanker market. Laboremus in fact managed quite well during the first phase of the shipping crisis. But as more shipping companies attempted to gain a foothold in the gas trade, the market became overcrowded and undermined the ability of Laboremus to generate sufficient income to service its debt. But it was not these market conditions that were the principal cause of Svein Bakkevig's departure and the demise of Laboremus but rather the hostile takeover orchestrated by I.M. Skaugen and Bakkevig's own lack of ownership power which led to the failure of Laboremus and Einar Bakkevig's Rederi.

Inadequate Strategy

All the companies encountered serious problems in the wake of the international shipping crisis. But in some cases, these problems were exacerbated by unwise strategies or even by the lack of a coherent strategy. A good example is Herlofson Shipping Co. According to Emil Garborg, who joined the company as a senior director in 1977, Herlofson had no clear strategy. The firm had a broad portfolio of shipping activities and investments. It was engaged in the tanker, bulk and liner trades, the offshore, and even owned a significant share of a factory ship. Moreover, the owner-manager had investments in several other industries. Gamborg also believes that the quality of the ships was questionable. Herlofson had probably diversified its investments too much. Its situation seems to confirm what Bercovitz and Mitchell found – that increased activity in unrelated sectors has a negative impact on the probability of survival.[31] After the firm managed to cope with the problems by downsizing its fleet and work force at the start of the 1980s, it shifted its strategy - and then revised it again a few years later. While the first strategic shift turned out reasonably well, the final change led directly to the company's failure. As shown above, the final strategy entailed chartering vessels and then operating them on contract for other charterers. The problem was the poor timing of these two different charter operations. On the one hand, the failure of this strategy was due to poor governance by both the owner and the managing director (see more about this below). On the other hand, the vacillation between different strategies is similar to the actions of the failing companies studied by Hambrick and D'Aventi which also were characterized by wavering between various courses of action.[32] In general, when market conditions change significantly, it is necessary to adjust the company's strategy. In the case of Herlofson, however, it seems that the changes of strategy were only partly based on a thorough analysis. Instead, there was an element of desperation in how the firm looked for new business opportunities. Herlofson also illustrates another main finding in Hambrick and D'Aventi's study. They found that the owners and managers of failing companies were often victims of "false encouragement," that is, they carried on as usual as long as they had enough cash to cover short-term obligations.[33] Similarly, when Gamborg joined Herlofson Shipping in 1977, he discovered that the owner and the administration, in the midst of the shipping crisis, believed that the situation was fairly good.

In Helmer Staubo and Co., the owner and administration were also the victims of "false encouragement." When Tore Staubo returned from the US in 1974 to join the family firm, he found that his father and uncle thought that they had the situation well in hand, despite the fact that the shipping markets were about to collapse. The main problem in Helmer Staubo, however, was that when the founder of the company - Helmer Staubo - retired at the beginning of the 1970s, his sons, Knut and Jan, launched an ambitious strategy based upon overly optimistic expectations about future trends in the shipping industry. While the founder had been prudent and cautious, his two sons in a short period threw the company into several new shipping projects, some of which, such as the purchase of two VLCCs, were large and costly. The many commitments incurred by the brothers took most of their time and energy in subsequent years. Through their unwise strategic actions, the owners landed the company in difficulties, the signs of which were a high debt load and fi-

---

[31]Bercovitz and Mitchell, "When Is More Better?" 61-79.

[32]Hambrick and D'Aventi, "Large Corporate Failures," 1-23.

[33]*Ibid.*

nancial losses. According to Hambrick and D'Aventi, such difficulties are often early warnings of later failures.

But it was not until the owners committed new strategic mistakes that their final fate was sealed. Knut's son, Tore Staubo, bore most of the burden of piloting Helmer Staubo into calmer waters. He seemed to have been more careful than his father. Nonetheless, the rationality of some of his strategic actions was questionable. For instance, after A/S HAV was split up by I.M. Skaugen in 1988, he hastily invested in seven new ships and three oil rigs. To persuade outside investors to participate in his new projects, he even took out a large personal loan. All the liabilities he contracted, combined with difficult markets for his shipping tonnage, proved to be devastating for the continued existence of his firm. In this respect, Staubo came to resemble his father and uncle who some years earlier had built up heavy debt burdens for the company. Equally unfortunate were his manoeuvres in the stock market, which resulted in a weakening of his ownership share and exposed him to unfriendly actions from external investors. I discuss these events at greater length in the next section.

I have shown how for decades Ivaran had been a successful liner operator in the trade between North and South America. But during the 1970s and 1980s, it made some questionable investments in other segments of the shipping industry. In the 1970s, Ivaran initiated a partnership which ordered a drilling platform. But as described above, the partnership ran into difficulties from the outset because the rig was neither fully financed nor chartered. The order soon had to be cancelled, with the loss of all the invested capital. Ivaran also had a short history in the supply ship market, and this venture also failed. Stranger still was that Ivaran attempted to enter the demanding gas trade without previous experience or knowledge. Moreover, the firm bought a gas tanker at a time when the market had already weakened; not surprisingly, this ship was soon sold. In light of the growing competition within Ivaran's main market, it is possible that this futile enterprise was an attempt to find alternative shipping activities for the company.

Weak or Eroding Owner Control

The four cases demonstrate that weak or eroding owner control can make it difficult for a family-owned shipping company to continue to exist. This factor has received some attention in the literature on family businesses, but the question of owner control has scarcely been addressed in previous research on business failures. The significance of this factor was most obvious in the case of Laboremus and Einar Rakkevig's Rederi. The owner-managers of Laboremus never had a sufficient ownership share to prevent others from taking over the company. Nor did the Bakkevig family have enough capital to increase their shareholdings at critical junctures, such as when the other owners increased the company's stock significantly through general issues which resulted in a further weakening of Svein Bakkevig's ownership position.

Insufficient owner control was also a problem in Ivaran and Helmer Staubo and Co. In Ivaran, Eirik Holter-Sørensen's brother and cousin undermined his control by selling their shares to outsiders. These sales seemed to have been motivated by intra-familial conflicts. The outside investors likely had purely financial motives for their investment, that is, they wanted to realize the value inherent in the company by splitting it up and selling the various parts. In A/S HAV/Helmer Staubo, the owner-manager found that family members sold their shares in the company when A/S HAV was re-listed on the Oslo Stock Exchange. As in the case of Ivaran, these shares ended up in the hands of outside owners who planned to break up A/S HAV in order to earn a quick profit. Tore Staubo may also have contributed to the undermining of his ownership control on several occasions. A couple of times during the 1980s he increased the company's share capital through new stock flotations in order to raise more capital to finance planned shipping ventures. Since developments in the industry involved the use of progressively larger ships, the company required an amount of capital which few firms could finance from their own reserves. As a result, raising new capital in the stock market became an important way of financing new ships. But for Tore Staubo, each new issue resulted in a dilution of his ownership share, exposing him to takeover attempts from outside players. He seemed to have been taken unaware by the new climate in the financial and stock markets during the 1980s and was surprised that several operators in these markets showed little consideration for traditional ideas about "gentlemanly" business practice. His ownership control was also weakened by his use of limited partnerships. Since in several cases he had only a minority position in these ventures, in difficult situations the partners found it difficult to reach unanimous decisions. In other words, these partnerships were often characterized by "collective action problems" which on several occasions prevented the company from reacting swiftly to acute economic problems.

Hostile Takeovers

In three of the companies, attempts at hostile takeovers added significantly to their problems. This is a topic which has not been given much attention in previous research on business exits. As described above, in Laboremus a hostile takeover was in fact the main reason why Einar Bakkevig's Rederi had to surrender both ownership and management to another shipping firm. In Ivaran and A/S HAV/Helmer Staubo and Co., various attempts at hostile takeovers drained much of the owners' energy and diverted their attention from important strategic and operational questions. While attempted takeovers were not the main reason why these companies failed, actions by outside investors aggravated an already strained situation and thus pushed the firms further along the path to exit.

Takeovers were the true children of the 1980s. The takeover mania began in the United States as an innovation in the financial and stock markets. So-called "asset players" discovered that they could reap considerable profits from buying low-priced companies and then restructuring and selling them. Another strategy was to split the firms up and sell the pieces at prices that were higher than the value of the company as a whole. As a result of the liberalization of the credit markets in Norway in the beginning of the 1980s, idle capital poured into the economy. As turnover in the stock market increased, so too did share prices. In the wake of this development, many owners of capital copied American investors and tried to generate profits from asset plays and takeovers. Many of these individuals were interested first and foremost in quick profits and had no intention of operating the businesses themselves. Others perceived that increasing globalization necessitated larger business units and used takeovers as an instrument to achieve mergers of small and medium-sized firms into larger and more powerful units. Whatever the motivation, in Norway these new strategies manifested themselves in a sharp increase in the number of takeovers and mergers until 1987, when the collapse in the stock market put a brake on the hectic trading of firms and corporate assets.[34] But as we have seen above, in the 1990s new players entered the arena and again attempted to reap profits from hostile takeovers. In shipping, some of these actions may have been necessary to restructure the industry. For instance, it is possible that the restructuring of the Norwegian gas trade accomplished by I.M. Skaugen was necessary.

Poor Governance

Some of the problems in both Herlofson and Ivaran can be traced to poor governance. I reported above that Herlofson's last managing director admitted that he had not adequately supervised the employee responsible for the extensive charter business that ultimately scuppered the company. Nor had the owner monitored this person's actions. Similarly, Ivaran's owners were shocked to discover that the managing director of the subsidiary Ivaran Shipping had run a huge loss through massive speculation in currency. Ivaran sued the company's auditor for not having discovered this in time, but the court decided that the board of the subsidiary and the owners were responsible for not having controlled the managing director.

Such incidents can be clarified using agency theory, part of which focuses on the risk of opportunistic behaviour by employed managers when their

---

[34]Trygve Gulbrandsen, *Eiere og kolleger: Medeierskap i norsk arbeidsliv* (Oslo, 1999).

interests are not aligned with those of the owners and their relationship with the owners is characterized by asymmetrical information.[35] The excessive chartering activities by Herlofson Shipping and the massive speculation in currency in Ivaran are both examples of opportunism on the part of responsible "agents" in the two companies. According to agency theory, the divergence of interests between principal and agent normally gives owners a strong economic incentive to oversee the actions of the agent. In the two cases discussed here, however, the owners did not seem to be sufficiently aware of the problems in their companies. Whatever incentives were inherent in their roles as owners, they did not induce them to exercise better control over their employees.

Exits as Protracted Processes?

In the section on previous research, I discussed the "process perspective" of Hambrich and D'Aventi.[36] According to these scholars, business exits are protracted processes where signs of a coming failure manifest themselves early in the process. Typical signs of future failures are low profitability and high debt. In line with this perspective, the histories of the four companies show that the road to failure was a protracted process. Each firm exhibited serious problems well before it left the industry. All had too much debt and performed poorly in many regards. But all of them managed to recover somewhat and to reconstruct themselves before new problems appeared. It seems reasonable to argue that had they chosen wiser strategies and made sounder decisions late in the process, they might have avoided their final demise. The problem was that they did not seem to learn from previous mistakes. Moreover, the owners of some of these companies were too eager to regain its previous position and as a result made decisions that finally sent them over the edge. A more careful and observant strategy late in the process might have saved both Herlofson and Helmer Staubo. In other words, for a shipping company an exit is not necessarily an inevitable result of a difficult situation, nor is it a path-dependent outcome. It may be possible to initiate a turnaround that helps a company survive. But as we have seen, in practice this seems to be very difficult to accomplish.

---

[35]Michael C. Jensen and William H. Meckling, "Theory of the Firm: Managerial Behavior, Agency Costs and Ownership Structure," *Journal of Financial Economics*, III, No. 4 (176), 305-360; and Kathleen M. Eisenhardt, "Agency Theory: An Assessment and Review," *Academy of Management Review*, XIV, No. 1 (1989), 57-74.

[36]Hambrick and D'Aventi, "Large Corporate Failures," 1-23.

Little Man, What Now?
Company Deaths in Norwegian Shipping, 1960-1980

Stig Tenold and Karl Ove Aarbu[1]

Introduction

The period from 1960 until the early 1970s is usually regarded as a prosperous period for shipping. Demand for seaborne transport increased rapidly, and massive investments led to growth and modernization in the world fleet. Larger vessels and new ship types invaded the markets traditionally served by general cargo vessels. Since the Norwegian shipping industry maintained its significant role in the international market through strategies based upon specialization and economies of scale, the period can be considered beneficial for it. Nevertheless, within the context of strong demand growth and new technological solutions, a substantial number of Norwegian shipping companies went out of business by failing to cope with the new opportunities. What factors can explain this apparent paradox?

The analysis in this paper is based on the 1960 population of Norwegian shipping companies.[2] Information about the size, geographical location and business strategies of the companies is linked to how the companies performed in the years from 1960 to 1980, with particular attention to whether they "survived" or "died" during this period. The results show that the fates of the companies in these two decades were closely related to their positions in

---

[1]The authors are grateful for financial support from Norges Forskningsråd and Norges Rederiforbunds Fond for NHH through the project "Nortraship" (Norwegian Transformations in Shipping). We are also thankful for comments from the editors and from participants at seminars in Oslo, Copenhagen and Uusikaupunki.

[2]The unit of analysis is the managing owner [*rederi*] - the company that arranged the operation and management of the ships - rather than the holding company that was the legal owner of the vessels. Although some managing owners controlled ships that were legally owned by more than one such holding company, the managing owners constituted the administrative level that was most relevant for the analysis; see Johan Seland, "Comment on Characteristics of Ownership," in Peter Lorange and Victor D. Norman (eds.), *Shipping Management* (Bergen, 1973), 30-35. The difficulty in determining the correct unit of analysis in Norwegian shipping is not new; see the discussion in Johan Einarsen, *Reinvestment Cycles and Their Manifestation in the Norwegian Shipping Industry* (Oslo, 1938), 120-122.

1960 and that the role of company size was of particular significance.[3] In the prosperous period from 1960 to 1973, more than half of the smallest companies disappeared. The casualties continued after the market collapsed, but by then even some of the larger companies began to fail as well.

The essay analyzes the basis for the reduction in the 1960 stock of Norwegian shipping companies, distinguishing between two periods characterized by radically different market conditions. The hypothesis is that the small companies which disappeared before 1973 became victims of the improved productivity of their competitors. By and large, the problems the small companies faced were a result of the booming market, which enabled financially stronger rivals to invest in superior tonnage to replace their own older, smaller and less-advanced vessels. The high cost of acquiring the new technology needed to remain competitive meant that smaller shipping companies were unable to renew their productive capital. During the 1960s, owners who refrained from investing in competitive capacity - for financial or other reasons - rapidly disappeared.

We also believe the combination of market conditions and investments is important to explain the disappearance of Norwegian shipping companies in the period from 1973 to 1980, though by then the trends had been reversed. As the deteriorating market conditions reduced revenues substantially, an investment strategy that was too aggressive could become just as problematic as a failure to modernize. Consequently, the victims were no longer only the small companies with limited abilities to invest in new tonnage but also larger firms that became overextended.

Our research was motivated by the data in figure 1, which show the proportion of companies that survived from 1960 to 1980, differentiated by the size of the enterprise in 1960. All the largest companies - here defined as those that owned ten or more ships in 1960 - survived into the 1980s. The number of the smallest companies - those owning only one or two ships - declined more or less continuously throughout the period. By 1980, three-quarters of the smallest shipping companies had chosen - or been forced - to ship the oars. Between these extremes, the number of companies with three to nine ships fell by about ten percent in the period up until 1973 but thereafter declined rapidly, with a particularly strong exodus from 1978 onwards.

[3]For a discussion of how "population studies" of companies may provide useful insights, see Leo J.G. van Wissen, "Demography of the Firm: A Useful Metaphor?" *European Journal of Population*, XVIII, No. 3 (2002), 263-279.

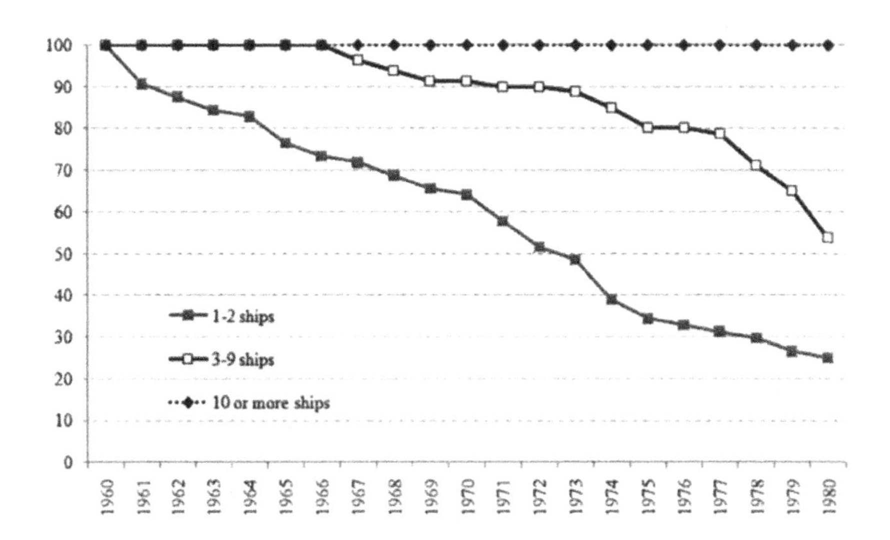

Figure 1: Proportion of Companies Still in Existence by Number of Ships in 1960 (percent, 1960-1980)

Note: Categories based on the number of ships above 5000 gross registered tons (grt) owned in 1960.

Source: Database of Norwegian shipping companies, compiled from *Det norske Veritas, Register over norske, svenske, danske, finske og islandske skip* (Oslo, various years).

After a general introduction to shipping cycles and technological change between 1960 and 1980, we examine the population of Norwegian shipping companies in 1960, sketching the differing fates of three categories of firms distinguished by the size of their fleets. In the next section, we analyze the pattern of company "deaths" and the resulting structural changes. Specifically, we show that the reduction in the number of companies was distributed unequally by both firm size and time. Finally, we introduce an econometric model that estimates the "life expectancy" of a company. This model confirms the findings of the previous analyses, but it adds to our knowledge by showing how much the various parameters (company size, average vessel size, age of the fleet, location and business strategies) influenced the fate of shipping companies. The results indicate that company size was by far the most important factor in determining their fates.

Shipping Cycles and Technological Changes

Although the shipping industry has always been characterized by strong cycles with sharp peaks and troughs in freight rates, it is possible to identify certain trends that shape its development in the medium term. The years analyzed in this essay can, in this respect, be seen as two separate paradigms. The first period (1960-1973) was marked by exceptionally strong growth in the oil tanker and major dry bulk markets, while the increase in demand for the transport of other goods was more modest. In the subsequent period (up to and including 1980), there was an absolute decline in the demand for tanker transport, while demand for the main dry bulk cargoes grew relatively slowly. Table 1 illustrates the transformation of the tanker and dry bulk markets from the first to the second period and shows the relative stability of the demand growth for other types of goods.

Table 1
Compound Annual Demand Growth in Three Market Segments, 1963-1973 and 1974-1980 (percent)

	Crude Oil and Oil Products	Main Dry Bulk (iron ore, coal and grain)	Other Cargoes (estimated)
1963-1973	14.5	13.3	6.4
1974-1980	-2.7	4.6	4.7

Source: Calculated on the basis of ton-mile data in Fearnley and Egers Chartering Co. Ltd., *Review* (various years), table 2.

The strong growth in shipping demand up to 1973 enabled the employment of a rapidly expanding fleet. While the increase in the number of vessels was relatively modest, growing by approximately fifty percent between 1960 and 1980, the carrying capacity of the merchant marine grew much faster due to the influx of large vessels that took advantage of economies of scale. Measured in grt, the world fleet grew more than three-fold over the two decades. Thus, the average ship in 1980 was more than twice as large as in 1960. In addition to this quest for economies of scale, the shipping industry was characterized by the introduction of new, more specialized tonnage. Such vessels - targeted at niches such as gas, car and chemical transport - became a cost-effective alternative to general cargo carriers.

The rapid technological development in shipping had important implications for companies that wanted to replace their existing fleets. The new, more competitive tonnage was sold at prices considerably higher than what the companies could raise by selling older ships. Figure 2 illustrates the replacement ratio, the value of an old vessel relative to the cost of a new ship, for the period 1965-1980. The term "replacement ratio" can be thought of as the maximum equity realized by disposing of a second-hand ship measured as the percentage of the price of a new vessel. For instance, by selling a 1956-built, 12,500-deadweight ton (dwt) closed shelterdecker (fifty-six CSD) in 1965, the owner would have been able to raise about forty-two percent of the funds needed to buy a new 18,000-dwt bulk carrier. By 1971, revenue from the sale of the same shelterdecker would have only contributed fifteen percent of the purchase price of a new 18,000-dwt bulk carrier.

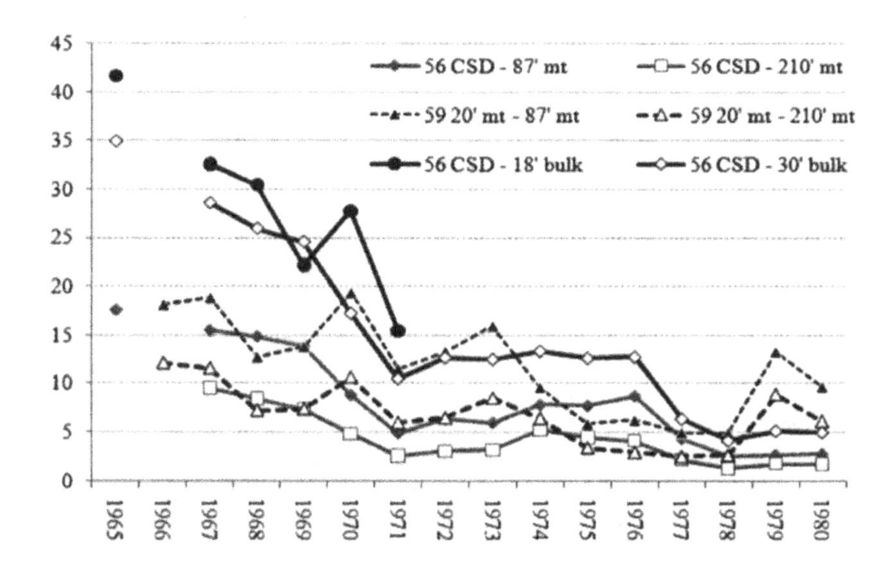

Figure 2: Replacement Ratios: Second-hand Values as a Percent of Newbuilding Prices, 1965-1980

Note: The terms 18', 20', 30', 87' and 210' refers to the size of the vessels in dwt, while "mt" refers to motor tankers. The source does not provide a second-hand price for 1956 CSDs in 1965. This value has been estimated on the basis of representative sales in the Norwegian market that year, as reported by Norwegian brokers.

Source: Authors' estimates on the basis of Fearnley and Eger's Chartering Co. Ltd., *Review*, various issues.

Tanker shipping is another segment in which Norwegian shipping companies were heavily involved. Here, the replacement problem was even more pronounced. In 1966, the owners of a seven-year-old, 20,000-dwt motor tanker would raise only eighteen percent of the funds needed to buy an 87,000-dwt tanker. Consequently, even if the older vessel was debt-free, the sale of the ship would be insufficient to raise the equity needed for new investments, which was usually twenty percent of the price of the new vessel.

Figure 2 indicates one of the reasons for the demise of Norwegian shipping companies in the period: the high cost of replacing older tonnage with new ships. It is likely that this process would affect smaller shipping companies adversely, but owners with larger fleets would be able to raise the resources need to acquire modern tonnage by substituting one new ship for several outdated ones. Thus, owners who had a "critical mass" of vessels would be able to follow the signals from the market and invest in competitive ships that utilized economies of scale.

Two factors amplified the disadvantage that small companies had in undertaking fleet modernization. The first is that larger companies almost certainly had better access to credit. Although a number of new financial institutions had been established, and access to credit from shipyards was improved during the 1960s, the demand for equity was still substantial. Typically, the owner's own input amounted to at least twenty percent of the price of the ship. The second disadvantage for smaller owners was the lack of specialized knowledge. According to one industry insider, there was a new need for "economic and financial competence. The traditional focus on operations and new cargoes was no longer sufficient to keep up with the new developments."[4] Large companies, with big organizations ashore, could acquire this competence by employing personnel with the requisite skills. For smaller shipping companies, with only a handful of employees, this was not an option.

The small companies in 1960 chose one of three strategies in the subsequent decades. First, some owners decided to leave shipping altogether. There were several reasons for this; limited financial resources, unfortunate investments, lack of successors, etc.[5] Second, some companies sold off their fleets but reinvested the revenues in parts of ships managed by other shipowners. In this manner, the ties to the shipping sector were retained, but at arm's length, although the companies disappeared as independent units. Finally, some small shipping companies adopted an offensive strategy, financing investments in larger tonnage through the use of retained earnings or external funds. As a result of the strong cycles in shipping, the income streams from otherwise identical investments might have varied immensely, depending on the timing of the purchase and sale of the ship and the revenue earned in the freight market. Although shipowners started out small, if they bought "cheaply," sold "dearly" and entered into long-term charters at the peak of the

---

[4]Tore Staubo, *Finanskriser – overlevelse mot alle odds* (Oslo, 2009), 159-160.

[5]Examples of the reasons behind the disappearance of companies can be found in Morten Hammerborg, *Skipsfartsbyen* (Bergen, 2003), 354-357; and Tore Nilsen, "Bergen og Sjøfarten V," *Sjøfartshistorisk Årbok 2001* (Bergen, 2002), 566-569. The tramp owners with old shelterdeck vessels were the most typical example of the reinvestment problem; see Dag Bakka, Jr., *Tramp – Norsk trampfart, 1945-1985* (Bergen, 2002).

market, it would have been possible to acquire the funds necessary for modernization.

Norwegian Shipping in 1960

The analysis of Norwegian shipping companies that disappeared takes the 1960 stock of companies as a point of departure and looks only at the fates of those that existed at that date.[6] Consequently, firms that were established after 1960 have not been included. While these omissions reduce the value of the analysis as a full-scale population or industry study, they also remove a lot of disturbing "noise" from the data. For instance, in the second half of the 1970s, several shipping companies were established on a temporary basis, sometimes at the behest of banks or other creditors, in order to oversee the sale of tonnage taken over from owners in financial distress. The inclusion of such companies in the data would lead to a double-counting of company deaths - first, when the original owners folded and again when the company established to carry out the liquidation had accomplished its task. The intentionally temporary nature of these companies would also mean that the death rates of the "newcomers" would appear to be much higher than was actually the case.

We have decided to end the analysis in 1980 - in the middle of the shipping crisis - due to the quality of the data. Before 1980, there was a relatively good correspondence between the Veritas registry, on which our data set is based, and the Norwegian fleet. After 1980, however, the authorities allowed shipowners to flag out their older, "technically obsolete" tonnage for up to two years in preparation for sale to foreigners.[7] The way this policy was implemented permitted a substantial degree of discretion, and from 1983 onwards there was relatively general access to registering ships abroad. This suggests that owners could disappear from our data set - and be counted as "deaths" - even though the company (and its activities) still existed.[8]

[6]Given that the focus is on companies engaged in international shipping, only those that owned ships greater than 5000 grt have been included. See Stig Tenold, *Tankers in Trouble: Norwegian Shipping and the Crisis of the 1970s and 1980s* (St. John's, 2006), for a more thorough discussion of the database.

[7]Norway, Parliament, *Stortingsmelding*, LII (1980-1981), "Om Skipsfartsnæringen."

[8]A related problem is the existence of companies that did not "die" before 1980 but were kept on "life support." Some owners were able to maintain their fleets as a result of government guarantees; see Stig Tenold, "Saving a Sector - But Which One? The Norwegian Guarantee Institute for Ships and Drilling Vessels Ltd.," *International Journal of Maritime History*, XIII, No. 1 (2001), 39-62. Given that this arrangement was open to all owners, regardless of size, it does not necessarily affect our results.

The data upon which this analysis is based nevertheless enable us to answer three important questions. First, how did those Norwegian shipping companies that existed in 1960 develop over the next two decades? Second, to what extent was there a relationship between the size of the companies in 1960 and their subsequent fates? Third, are there any other factors - for instance, the age of the fleet in 1960, strategic adaptation or the geographic origin of the company - that affected the probability of company survival?

In 1960, the population of shipping companies in Norway was characterized by a substantial degree of heterogeneity, and table 2 provides some descriptive statistics. The diversity is striking. Oslo was the largest port, with sixty-eight companies controlling a total of 401 ships above 5000 grt. At the other end of the scale, there were six ports with only one ship above 5000 grt.[9] Similarly, Wilh. Wilhelmsen - the largest company, owning sixty-one ships above 5000 grt - controlled a fleet that was two-thirds larger than the fleets of all the thirty-six single-ship companies combined.

Table 2
Description of the Database and Norwegian Shipping in 1960

		Average per Port/Company	Maximum	Minimum
Number of Companies	164	6.3 companies per port	68	1
Number of Home Ports	26			
Number of Ships	870	33.4 (port)/ 5.3 (company)	401/61	1/1
Ship Age		9.15	43	1
Fleet Age		9.14	27	1

Note: The difference between the average age of the ships and the average age of the fleets (which are comprised of the same ships) reflects the fact that the latter figure is an average of averages.

Source: See figure 1.

In addition to size, the shipping companies also varied with regard to their investment strategies. The majority followed a strategy of diversification, with investments in more than one business sector. Table 3 gives an overview of the dominant strategies of the 164 companies included in the data set. The

[9]These ports were Bodø, Kirkenes, Lillesand, Stokmarknes, Tromsø and Ålesund.

category "Main Segment" refers to the number of companies which had the majority of their investments in the given segment, while the term "No. of companies" refers to the number that had invested in the specific vessel type.

Table 3
Presentation of the Business Strategies in 1960

	Diversification	Tankers	General Cargo	Dry Bulk	Passenger	Smaller Vessels
Strategy	112	37	11	4		
Main Segment		114	35	15		
No. of Companies		132	88	41	2	64

Note: While the calculations and categories refer only to vessels larger than 5000 grt, the database includes information on whether the companies owned smaller ships as well. Those that owned such vessels, in addition to ships above 5000 grt, have been categorized as following a diversification strategy.

Source: See figure 1.

Table 3 reveals the strong position of tanker shipping in Norway – more than eighty percent of the companies in the data set had invested in tanker tonnage, and thirty-seven were "pure" tanker owners. More than two-thirds of the companies followed a diversified strategy, with investments in more than one market segment. For almost seventy percent of the diversified companies, the operation of tankers was their main activity.

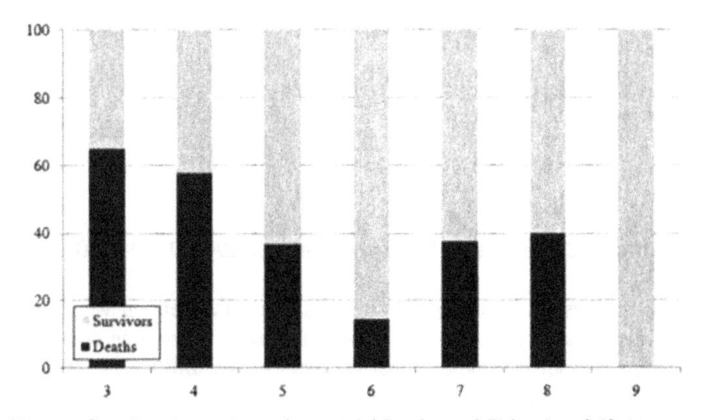

Figure 3: Deaths and survivors by Number of Ships in 1960 (percent)

Source: See figure 1.

Figure 1 showed that the pattern of survival differed greatly depending on the number of ships a company owned in 1960. The previous discussion of replacement suggests that a company's room to manoeuvre, and its potential strategic responses, was highly influenced by the size of its fleet. As with most types of categorizations, however, the distinctions between small, medium and large companies are a simplification that contains some arbitrariness at the margins. For instance, the challenges and opportunities of a shipping company with nine vessels were likely to be more similar to those of a ten-vessel company than to those of a three-vessel company. Figure 3 shows the relative share of "deaths" and "survivors" based on the number of ships the companies owned in 1960.

Figure 3 strengthens the point that the "outcomes" for three-ship companies were more similar to those of the smallest companies than to those of the nine-ship companies. This idea of a polarization of the companies owning from three to nine ships is further underscored when we consider *when* those companies disappeared. Until the late 1970s, all those that "died" had five ships or fewer in 1960 (see figure 4).

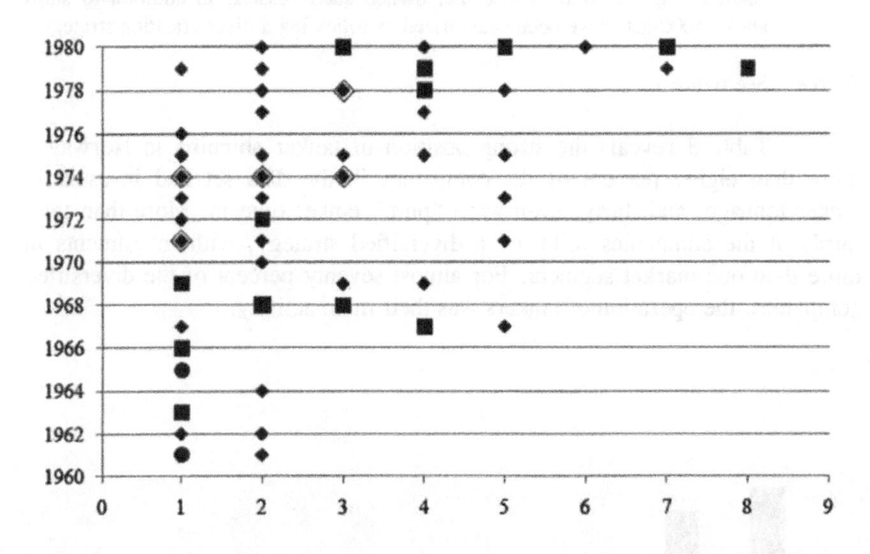

Figure 4: Disappearance of Companies by Number of Ships in 1960, 1960-1980

Note: The number of vessels is plotted on the x-axis and the year in which the companies disappeared on the y-axis. Diamonds indicate that one company disappeared, while squares indicate that two companies fulfilling the criteria disappeared. White-framed diamonds indicate that three companies disappeared, while circles indicate that more than three companies disappeared.

Source: See figure 1.

Based on figures 3 and 4, we have further split the companies into three categories. The first consists of the sixty-four firms, spread along the Norwegian coast, which operated with only one or two ships.[10] These are the "small shipowners," or "little men," in our analysis. Second, there were fifty-eight medium-sized companies that controlled fleets of three to five ships. Finally, there were forty-two companies that controlled six or more vessels in 1960. Table 4 provides an overview of the companies in the different categories and the striking differences in survival rates in the period 1960-1980. It suggests that the small companies began with evident handicaps; not only were their fleets relatively limited, but their vessels were on average both smaller and older than those of the companies in the other categories.

Table 4
Differences among Three Categories of Owners in 1960 and Their Survival Rates to 1980

	No. Ships	No. Companies	No. Ports	Mean Company Size	Mean Vessel Size	Mean Fleet Age (years)	Survival Rate to 1980
Small Companies	1-2	64	22	14,078	9793	10.1	25%
Medium-sized Companies	3-5	58	14	41,930	10,527	8.2	47%
Large Companies	6+	42	12	137,181	10,533	9.0	86%

Note: Six companies (one large, one small and four medium-sized) that disposed of their ships, but were registered as owners of drilling vessels, have been characterized as "surviving."

Source: See figure 1.

The Survival Model

Thus far we have focussed on the role of company size and have analyzed the situation using descriptive, univariate measures.[11] In this section we specify a

[10]The database reflects the "port of registry" reported in the Veritas registry. Thus, ships registered in ports other than the one in which the company was based have not been reassigned. This means, for instance, that Sig. Bergesen d.y. and Co. (medium-sized in 1960) and Wilh. Wilhelmsen (large) have been registered under Stavanger and Tønsberg, respectively.

[11]According to John Freeman, Glenn R. Carroll and Michael T. Hannan, "The Liability of Newness: Age Dependence in Organizational Death Rates," *American*

survival regression model where we simultaneously take into account a richer set of explanatory variables to study the survival pattern over a period of twenty years. It is important to note, however, that all the companies were established before 1960 and have therefore been at risk for death before that date. Because of scarce information about these companies before 1960, we are not in a position to model their full lifetimes. Rather, we model the risk of death from 1960 to 1980 given that the firms had survived until 1960.

We begin the analysis with a closer look at the survival pattern from 1960 to 1980 by depicting the Kaplan-Meier estimate for company survival. This shows the conditional probability for a company to survive until time $t+1$ or beyond, given that it already has survived to year t. Figure 5 shows that almost half of the companies survived beyond twenty years: since eighty-eight of the 164 companies survived until 1979, and seventy-nine survived until 1980, the median survival time was twenty years. The figure also indicates that the risk of death was quite low in the first ten years but that it increased slightly thereafter. Companies that were alive in 1980 are treated as censored.

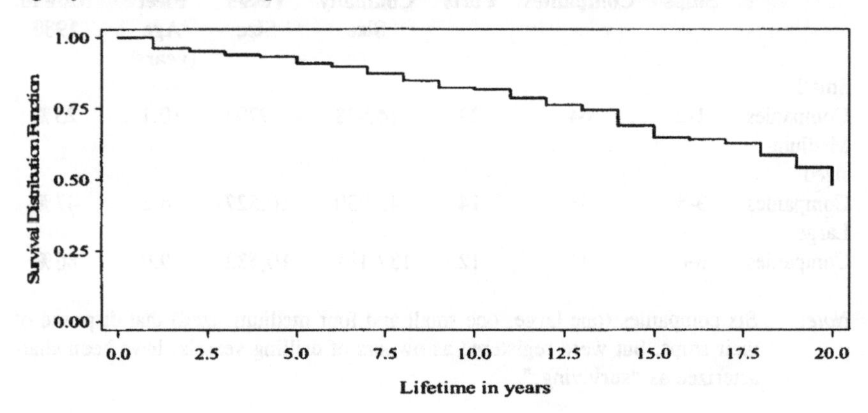

Figure 5: Kaplan-Meier Survival Function, All Companies, 1960-1980

Source: See figure 1.

As pointed out above, the survival pattern was clearly a function of company size. Moreover, we argued above that the companies naturally fit into three size categories: small companies with two ships or fewer; medium-sized

Sociological Review, XLVIII, No. 5 (1983), 693, "existing evidence in the relationship between organizational size and mortality is inconclusive." The authors refer to one empirical work from Norway that supports the idea that mortality rates among small organizations are high; see Frøystein Wedervang, *Development of a Population of Industrial Firms: The Structure of Manufacturing Industries in Norway, 1930-1948* (Oslo, 1965).

companies with three to five ships; and large companies with six or more ships. Figure 6 shows the differences in the survival patterns among these categories. Basically, this depicts the same pattern as shown in figure 1. But due to the differences in the size categories, there were company deaths in all groups. Thus, using this size division, we will be able to estimate the death hazard in all groups.[12]

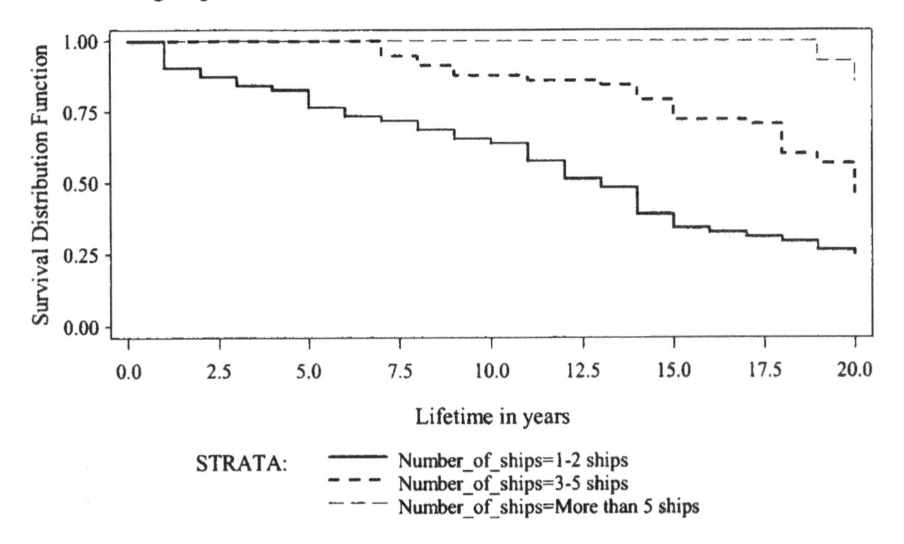

Figure 6: Kaplan-Meier Survival Functions for Different Company Sizes, 1960-1980

Source: See figure 1.

Figures 5 and 6 indicate that the death hazard increased in the second half of the 1970s. In order to verify this, we plot the logarithm of the survival function in figure 7. If this is a straight line, we can conclude that the death hazard was constant. If the curve is convex, however, this implies that the hazard increased over time. A concave curve indicates a decreasing hazard over time.[13]

---

[12]As previously noted, the survival functions may be affected by the existence of companies that survived through government guarantees. The Norwegian Guarantee Institute was only one of many arrangements to help shipowners with liquidity difficulties; similar support was given by banks and shipyards. We have therefore chosen not to introduce a "support from the Guarantee Institute" dummy variable into the model.

[13]See Paul D. Allison, *Survival Analysis Using SAS: A Practical Guide* (Cary, NC, 1995; 2nd ed., Cary, NC, 2010), 55-58.

The curves in figure 7 tend to bend upwards, which is a sign of convexity. Based on this observation, we set up a Weibull survival model, which accommodates this increasing hazard over time.[14] We included several covariates in the model. First, we constructed two indicator variables to capture the number of ships each company owned. The indicator variable "small" was equal to one if the company owned one or two ships in 1960, while the indicator variable "medium" was equal to one for companies with three to five ships in that year. Companies with more than five ships in 1960 served as a reference group in the regression. We also included the main port to which the company was assigned. As the number of observations was limited, we included the two most important ports - Oslo and Bergen - in the regression.[15] Finally, we included a dummy variable for the "GC" (general cargo) strategy. The GC variable captures the effect of this strategy relative to the others that were pursued in the 1960s.

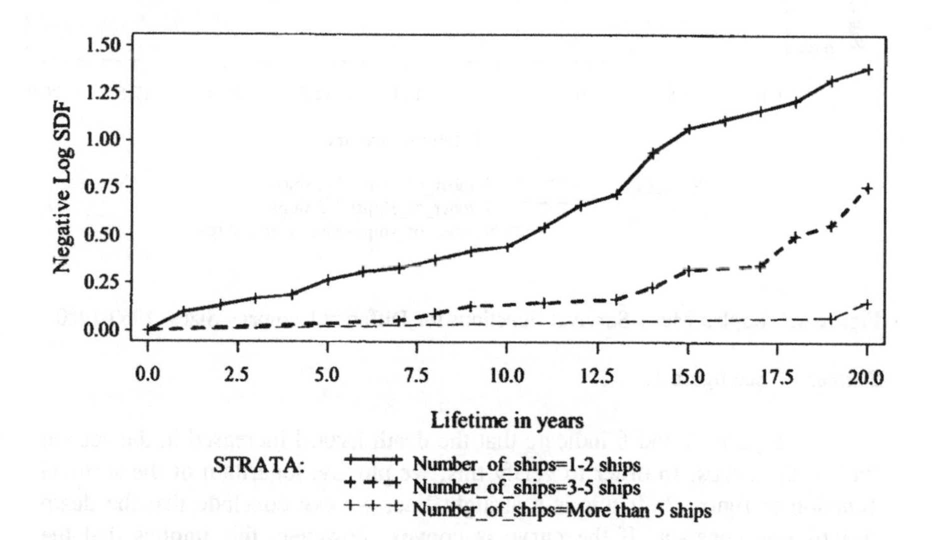

Figure 7: Logarithm of survival functions (Kaplan-Meier) for different company sizes, 1960-1980

Source: See figure 1.

---

[14]On the Weibull survival model used in studies such as this, see Glenn R. Carroll and Michael T. Hannan, *The Demography of Corporations and Industries* (Princeton, 2000), 283.

[15]We have also tried to estimate the model with dummies for all ports. Since this does not alter the main results, we therefore prefer the simpler model presented here.

We also estimated the model with tonnage as the size criterion. The first variant describes companies as small if tonnage was less than 17,500 grt (25th percentile); medium if tonnage was above 17,500 grt but less than 62,800 grt (75th percentile); and large otherwise. In the second variant, we included tonnage as a continuous variable. Tables 5-7 show the parameter estimates, as well as the standard errors and the probability value. A probability value lower than ten percent means that the estimate is significant at the ten-percent level of confidence.

Table 5
Number of Ships as Size Measure

Parameter	Estimate	Standard Error	Pr > ChiSq
Intercept	4.2337	0.3995	<.0001
Small (1-2 ships)	-1.3483	0.2730	<.0001
Medium (3-5 ships)	-0.8560	0.2646	0.0012
GC (General cargo)	-0.2858	0.2261	0.2062
Average size	-0.0000	0.0000	0.9319
Average age	-0.0006	0.0134	0.9643
Oslo	-0.2136	0.1382	0.1224
Bergen	-0.0253	0.2039	0.9011
Weibull Shape	1.7713	0.1740	
Log likelihood	-147.24		
Pseudo-R^2	0.199		

Source: See figure 1.

Table 6
Tonnage as Size Measure, Category Dummies for Tonnage

Parameter	Estimate	Standard Error	Pr > ChiSq
Intercept	4.6259	0.4193	<.0001
Small (less than 17,500 tons)	-1.4023	0.2873	<.0001
Medium (less than 62,800 tons)	-0.9752	0.2636	0.0002
GC (General cargo)	-0.3690	0.2262	0.1029
Average size	-0.0000	0.0000	0.0955
Average age	-0.0089	0.0136	0.5143
Oslo	-0.1749	0.1386	0.2070
Bergen	0.0833	0.2070	0.6873
Weibull Shape	1.7480	0.1725	
Log likelihood	-149.98		
Pseudo-R^2	0.177		

Source: See figure 1.

Table 7
Tonnage as Size Measure, Continuous

Parameter	Estimate	Standard Error	Pr > ChiSq
Intercept	3.0438	0.3061	<.0001
Tonnage (1000 tons)	0.0174	0.0035	<.0001
Average size (1000 tons)	-0.0362	0.0177	0.0415
GC	-0.2759	0.2208	0.2115
Average age	-0.0045	0.0125	0.7185
Oslo	-0.2459	0.1373	0.0732
Bergen	-0.0111	0.2004	0.9559
Weibull Shape	1.7965	0.1758	
Log likelihood	-141.17		
Pseudo-R^2	0.221		

Source: See figure 1.

Tables 5-7 confirm the strong association between the size of a company in 1960 and its expected lifetime. This association is clear, regardless of whether tonnage or number of ships is used as the size criterion. If we concentrate on the number of ships, the estimate for the indicator variable "small" (recall that this variable is coded 1 for companies with only one or two ships) tells us that the expected lifetime for this group is around one-quarter of the expected lifetime of the largest companies. The medium-sized companies have an expected lifetime slightly more than forty percent as long as for the reference group (the large companies).[16] Furthermore, we also find a very weak indication of a shorter lifetime for companies based in Oslo. The strategy variable indicates that companies using the GC strategy had a lower probability of survival. Again, however, the association is weak. Finally, the model confirms that the death hazard increases slightly over time, as the estimate for the Weibull shape is larger than one. This confirms that a Weibull model is an appropriate specification for these data.

How well do our models describe the actual development? We have included a measure of model fit which we call the "pseudo-R^2" in tables 5-7.[17]

---

[16]The lifetime of the small-sized group compared to the reference group is calculated as exp (-1.34) = 0.26. Using the same method, we find that the lifetime for the medium-sized companies compared to the reference group is exp (-0.85) = 0.42.

[17]We use the McFadden Adjusted pseudo-R^2 to compare with the standard R^2 from an ordinary least-squares procedure (OLS) which minimizes the variance in the data; the R^2 from an OLS measures how much of the total variance is explained by the model. The maximum likelihood procedure (MLP) employed in the models shown in tables 5-7 is not designed to minimize the variance but rather to select parameter values that maximize the probability for observing the data.

This compares the likelihood of the estimated full model to one without any explanatory variables (called the "Intercept Model"). Thus, it tells us whether the inclusion of covariates leads to an "informational gain" over a model without any covariates at all. The pseudo-R^2 ranges from 0.177 to 0.221, which tells us that the covariate models are superior to the "Intercept Model" as they all lead to substantial information gains. The model that best explains the data is the tonnage model in table 7, where the continuous measure of tonnage is employed (this model has the highest log-likelihood).

The specification in table 7 tells us that tonnage increases the expected lifetime of a company, while the average size of ships in a particular fleet actually leads to a decrease in expected lifetime. The parameter estimates indicate that for each increase in total tonnage of 1000 grt, the company's life expectancy increases by 1.7 percent. On the other hand, a 1000-grt increase in the average size of the ships reduces the lifetime by approximately 3.6 percent. Both estimates are statistically precise. In this model, we also find a significantly shorter lifetime for companies based in Oslo (the probability value is 0.07). In fact, there is a significant difference between Oslo and the rest of the country regarding the structure of company survival. In unreported regressions, we found that if the dummy for Oslo was removed from the model, average vessel size no longer was a significant predictor. Thus, the association between the average size of the ships and the lifetime of the company was much weaker in Oslo than elsewhere in the country.

Finally, we will briefly judge how well the model fits the data. There are several methods that can be used to evaluate this, but the preferred method is one that utilizes the residuals from the survival regression.[18] By using residuals in judging the model fit, the covariates in the regression are taken into account.[19] If the model adequately fits the data, these residuals will have an exponential distribution. Graphically, this means that if we plot these residuals against the negative log of the estimated survival function, the resulting plotted line should be at a forty-five-degree slope. In figure 8, the forty-five-degree line is shown as the dotted line, while the Cox-Snell residual is solid. Since the latter is close to the forty-five-degree line, this indicates an adequate model fit.

---

[18]Allison, *Survival Analysis Using SAS.*

[19]There are several ways to define the residuals; see, for example, David Collett, *Modelling Survival Data in Medical Research* (London, 1994; 2nd ed., London, 2003). We use the recommended approach for a Weibull-model, the Cox-Snell residuals; see Allison, *Survival Analysis*, 94.

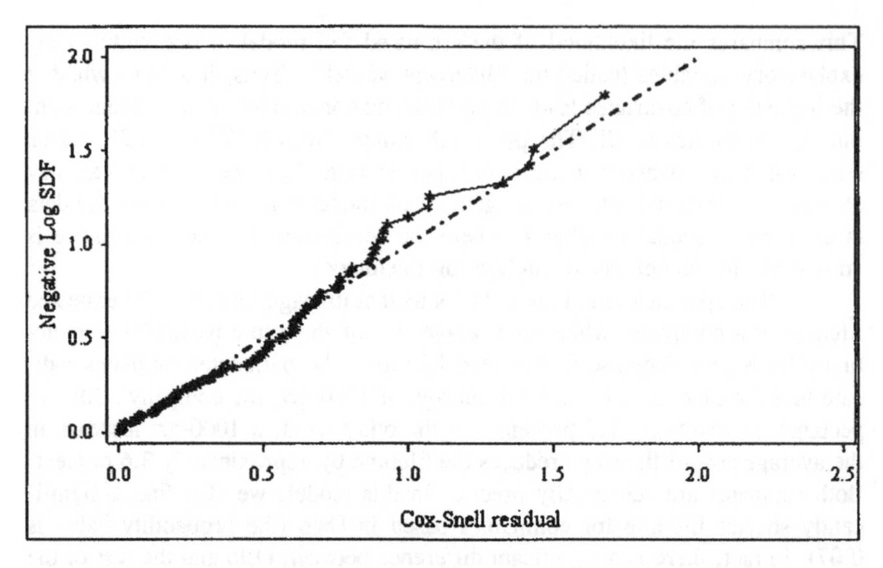

Figure 8: Goodness of Fit Measure Cox-Snell Residual Plotted against the Logarithm of the Estimated Survival Function

Source: See figure 1 and table 7.

Concluding Remarks

In the first part of this essay, we suggested that problems related to the replacement of tonnage might explain the disappearance of small companies (one or two ships) in the period when the market was good. In addition to explaining the high death rates among small companies, it is likely that this problem also affected some of the smaller medium-sized companies (three to five ships). We also suggested that over-investment, rather than lack of investment, could be a potential explanation for the demise of the medium-sized companies during the latter part of the 1970s. Specifically, there could have been firms that over-stretched their resources by committing to new investments just before the freight market crashed.

The fourteen medium-sized companies that disappeared in the period 1978-1980 can be used to consider this hypothesis. Eleven of the fourteen, or almost eighty percent, had signed contracts for new vessels when the market collapsed in 1974.[20] This can be compared with the medium-sized companies that survived: only fourteen of the twenty-seven medium-sized companies that

[20]To perform this analysis, the data set has been linked to the lists of "Norwegian Newbuilding Contracts by Owner," *Norwegian Shipping News*, 1974 and 1975, various issues.

survived after 1980, or fifty-two percent, had newbuilding obligations in 1974/1975.[21]

The econometric analysis has confirmed the importance of company size in explaining the survival - and, implicitly, the "deaths" - of the 1960 population of Norwegian shipping companies. At the same time, we were surprised that the average size and age of the vessels the companies owned in 1960 had practically no effect on their probability of survival. This could, however, be a result of the strength of the size effect - the handicap of the "little men."

Our analysis has looked at the development of Norwegian shipping companies in a period marked by both the "boom" and "bust" for which shipping is known. There are several possible extensions of the analysis. One possibility would be to follow the development of the survivors in the years after 1980, although the quality of the data for this period is not as good as for the years covered in this paper. Another possible extension would be to include the year of the establishment of the companies in the model. We treat all companies as "new-borns" in 1960. Yet we know that their histories at this point differed significantly - some had been involved in shipping since the previous century, while others had much shorter histories. It is likely that this is another element that might influence survival rates; some of the companies had already proven themselves to be "survivors" in previous periods.

Finally, we are fully aware that we present an unrealistically negative picture of Norwegian shipping in the period 1960-1980. More than half of the companies we tracked disappeared, while we totally disregard those entrepreneurs who established new ventures. The companies that disappeared during the 1960s were all replaced; indeed, there were 176 companies with vessels above 5000 grt in 1970, a net increase of more than seven percent relative to 1960. In the subsequent decade, the picture was bleaker - hardly any of the companies that disappeared were replaced, and by 1980 the number of shipping companies in Norway had fallen to 128.

---

[21]Moreover, all of the six large companies that disappeared in 1979 and 1980 (figure 4) had ordered new tonnage before the market collapsed.

The Growth of the Deep-Sea Car-Carrying Industry, 1960-2008

Espen Ekberg

Introduction

During the latter half of the twentieth century, the structure of international shipping was transformed drastically. Among the most important new trends was the growth of a substantial fleet of specialized vessels carrying specific cargoes such as chemicals, liquid gas, cars, forest products, refrigerated goods and passengers.[1] By 2008, the share of specialized tonnage in world shipping had reached forty percent. Yet only thirty-three years earlier, in 1975, it had been a mere three percent.[2] While this fundamental structural transformation of the international shipping market has been increasingly recognized in the literature, our understanding of how the process came about is still limited.[3] This article is an attempt to improve the situation by investigating the growth of car carrying as a specialized segment within international shipping, with a particu-

[1]See Martin Stopford, *Maritime Economics* (London, 1988; 3rd ed., London, 2009).

[2]Figures estimated on the basis of Lloyd's Register of Shipping, *Statistical Tables*; and Lloyd's, *World Fleet Statistics*, various years.

[3]For a general account, see Stig Tenold, "So Nice in Niches: Specialization Strategies in Norwegian Shipping, 1960-1977," *International Journal of Maritime History*, XXII, No. 1 (2010), 63-82. The only niche that has been studied extensively is the chemical segment; see Tenold, "Steaming Ahead with Stainless Steel: Oddfjell's Entry and Expansion in the Chemical Tanker Market, 1960-1974," *International Journal of Maritime History*, XVIII, No. 1 (2006), 179-198; Atle Thowsen and Tenold, *Oddfjell: The History of a Shipping Company* (Bergen, 2006); Hugh Murphy and Tenold, "Strategies, Market Concentration and Hegemony in Chemical Parcel Tanker Shipping, 1960-1985," *Business History*, L, No. 3 (2008), 291-309; and Tenold, "Vernon's Product Life Cycle and Maritime Innovation: Specialised Shipping in Bergen, Norway, 1970-1987," *Business History*, LI, No. 5 (2009), 770-786. A large research project on the contemporary development of Norwegian shipping also produced case studies of several of the niches developing in international shipping from the 1960s, focusing on the participation of Norwegian owners. A summary is provided in Tor Wergeland, *Norsk skipsfarts konkurranseevne* (Bergen, 1992).

lar focus on the role played by some selected Norwegian shipowners in the establishment and early growth of the industry.

Car carrying developed as a specialized segment in international shipping from the 1960s onwards. The growth coincided with the massive increase in the world trade in cars visible first in the expansion of European exports from the early 1960s and later with the development of Japan as the world's largest producer and exporter of cars. Gradually, the car carriers would also handle - and facilitate - the increasing world trade in larger vehicles, such as buses, tractors and harvesters, as well as in heavy cargoes, including machine parts, generators and forest equipment. By 2008, RoRo/car carriers constituted the second largest specialized segment in world shipping in terms of tonnage.[4] The market was more or less controlled by five companies. Three of these - NYK, MOL and K-Line - were Japanese-owned, while the remaining two - WalleniusWilhelmsen and Höegh Autoliners - were owned by Scandinavian interests, with a dominant share held by Norwegian shipowners.[5]

The essay traces the establishment and growth of seaborne car carrying through a two-part analysis. First, it provides a general overview of the industry, focusing on the increasing demand for seaborne car transport stemming from the expanding car manufacturing industry, the gradual development of the car-carrying ship, the evolution of the main trading patterns and the ownership structure of the fleet. The overall ambition is to understand how deep-sea car-carrying as a specialized segment evolved historically. What characterized the expansion of the international car trade from the 1960s onwards? What kinds of ships were employed in the trade? How did a fleet of specialized car carriers develop? Who were the major participants and how did ownership patterns change over time?[6] The second part looks in more detail at the experiences of the three most successful Norwegian car-carrying firms. Through these case studies, I seek to provide a more detailed view into how the car-carrying industry was established and evolved. In investigating the

---

[4]Figures from Lloyd's, *World Fleet Statistics* (London, 2008). The largest specialized segment was chemical tankers.

[5]By 2011, WalleniusWilhelmsen was owned equally by the Swedish firm Wallenius and the Norwegian company Wilh. Wilhelmsen. The majority of Höegh Autoliners was owned by the Norwegian firm Leif Höegh and Co. Holdings A/S (62.5 percent), while the Danish company A.P. Møller-Mærsk A/S owned the remainder. A sixth large company in operation was the Korean-based Eukor, the former car division of Hyundai Merchant Marine. From 2002, eighty percent of this company was owned by WalleniusWilhelmsen, and the market share held by this company was typically registered under its control.

[6]The essay deals exclusively with the deep-sea, car-carrying industry and does not analyze the development of the substantial fleet of short-sea, feeder ships that evolved parallel to its growth.

cases I ask three basic questions: How and why did these firms become engaged in car carrying? How did they develop the necessary competence to succeed in the trade? What were their main strategies for growth? To research these questions, I draw on a diverse set of both primary and secondary sources, including archival records, extensive interviews with industry participants as well as statistics, market reports and company studies.

The Expansion of Car-Carrier Shipping as a Specialized Segment

In the postwar years, automobile production became one of the largest industries in the world, and cars were among the fastest growing exports in world trade. According to figures from the General Agreement on Tariffs and Trade (GATT), the total value of car exports increased from 3.3 billion US dollars in 1955 to 456 billion US dollars in 1995. In relative terms, the share of car exports in total exports rose from 3.5 to 9.3 percent.[7] This made cars the third largest export item in world trade in terms of value. The growth in volume was also substantial. In 1960, the total number of cars exported was just above two million. By 1995 the figure had risen to nineteen million, and ten years later it was more than twenty-seven million.[8] The growth had been fairly linear, albeit with some temporary dips caused by tariff increases, the introduction of branch-plant factories and general economic downturns.

About half the cars exported are transported by sea, a figure that has remained fairly stable throughout the postwar years. The increase in car exports led to increased demand for seaborne transport, and a fleet of specialized car carriers gradually developed to provide it (see figure 1). In 1955, the Swedish shipowner Wallenius launched what are regarded as the first purpose-built ships to transport cars on transoceanic routes. *Rigoletto* and *Traviata* were two medium-sized vessels capable of holding 290 cars. Both were constructed, however, to carry various bulk cargoes as well.[9] Most of the vessels used in the growing, tramp-based car trade of the late 1950s and early 1960s were similar. Often traditional ships of the "Liberty class" were used, taking 300-400 cars in a single shipment. Gradually, "shelterdeckers" refitted with provisional car-deck systems and capable of taking up to 1000 cars were employed.

---

[7]Figures adopted from Nigel Grimwade, *International Trade: New Patterns of Trade, Production and Investment* (London, 1989; 2nd ed., London, 2000), 14.

[8]Figures from Drewry Shipping Consultants, *Car-Bulk Carriers: Their Impact on the Freight Market* (London, 1971); and Drewry, *Car Carriers: The Fast Lane of International Shipping* (London, 2006).

[9]Robert Gardiner (ed.), *The Shipping Revolution: The Modern Merchant Ship* (London, 1992), 124-125.

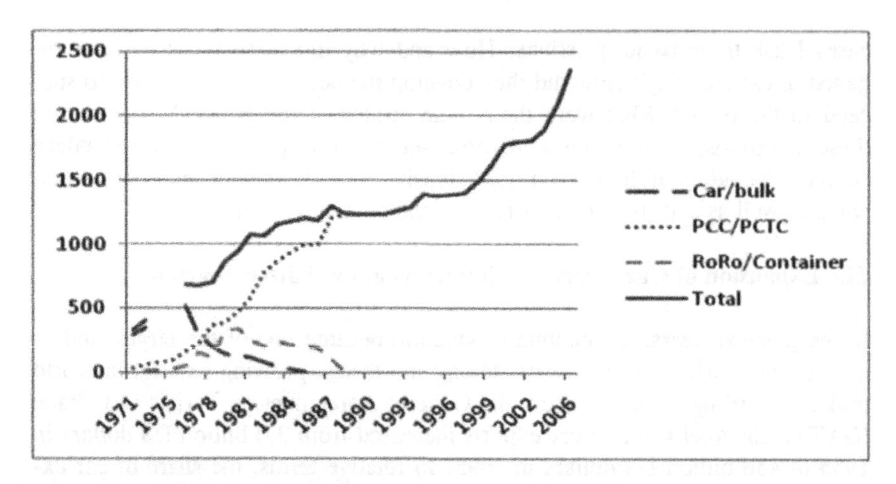

Figure 1: Capacity of the Car-Carrying Fleet by Ship Type, 1971-2006 ('000 Car Equivalent Units [CEUs])

Source: Estimated from RS Platou, *Report* (Oslo, various years); Drewry, *Car-Bulk Carriers*; Drewry, *Growth of the Car-Carrying Fleet*; Drewry, *Car Carriers: The Fleet and Global Vehicle Trade* (London, 1995); and Drewry, *Car Carriers: The Fast Lane of International Shipping* (London, 2006).

As trade volumes increased even further, shipowners began to convert single-deck bulk carriers into car carriers. The ships were rebuilt with a series of hoistable car decks and specialized loading gear. The first of these so-called "car/bulk carriers" was launched in the late 1950s, and the number of conversions peaked in the early 1970s. By then, ships of 30,000-40,000 deadweight tons (dwt) with capacities of more than 2500 cars were in operation.[10] Most of these ships were operating with so-called "LoLo technology" where cars were lifted on and off using cranes and slings. Some of them did, however, experiment with alternative loading and unloading techniques. In 1963, Wallenius launched *Anaria*, where cars could be rolled on and off through a bow door, although the actual stowage still used cranes.[11] Later, some bulk ships disposed of the loading gear altogether, replacing it with side ports and ramps.

The car/bulkers exploited two advantages. First, their sheer size implied obvious economies of scale. More important, since the car decks could be dismantled or erected easily, the ships could combine the transport of cars with conventional bulk cargoes. This was a very important feature, since seaborne car exports in the 1950s and 1960s essentially remained a one-way trade. While a rapidly increasing number of cars were exported from Europe

[10]Drewry, *Car-Bulk Carriers*.

[11]*Gallois Genootschap*, 3 May 2006.

to North America, the number going the opposite way was minuscule and was even decreasing. Of a total transatlantic car export in 1965 of 618,000 cars, only about three percent went from North America to Europe. Two years later, the share fell to two percent.[12] Moreover, before the expansion of the car trade, most European exports consisted of manufactured goods that were not suitable for bulk transport. As a consequence, the growth in the European car trade became an opportunity for bulk operators to radically decrease voyages made in ballast. Employing flexible car/bulk carriers meant that shipowners could carry full loads of cars from Europe while taking bulk cargoes, such as coal or grain, on the return leg. As a result, the growth of the car/bulk fleet was a major step in the development of car carrying as a specialized segment of shipping, and the main motivation for the early innovators was the prospect of improving the earning potential in the traditional dry-bulk trade from North America to Europe. It is no coincidence that the large majority of shipowners operating car/bulkers had long experience in the dry-bulk trade.[13]

The early growth in the international car trade was dominated by German exports, particularly by the Volkswagen group.[14] By the early 1970s, however, the dominance of German car producers was increasingly challenged by the Japanese, most prominently by Toyota and Nissan. Japanese car exports grew dramatically during the 1960s and early 1970s (see table 1).

Table 1
World Export of Passenger Cars, 1961-1975 (percent)

	1961	1963	1965	1967	1969	1971	1973	1975
West Germany	43	42	45	41	39	33	33	23
UK	20	22	21	17	17	11	11	8
France	18	18	15	17	16	17	17	19
Italy	12	10	10	12	12	10	10	10
Japan	1	1	3	7	11	20	20	28
Sweden	2	2	3	4	3	3	3	2
US/Canada	5	5	3	2	2	6	6	10
Total	100	100	100	100	100	100	100	100

Source: Drewry Shipping Consultants, *Car-Bulk Carriers: Their Impact of the Freight Market* (London, 1971); and Drewry, *The Growth of the Car-Carrying Fleet* (London, 1977), 52-56.

---

[12]Estimated from Svein-Gustav Steimler and Sverre Stavseth, *Car Transport by Sea* (Bergen, 1970), 16.

[13]*Ibid.*

[14]*Ibid.*, 13. About sixty percent of all car imports to the US in 1968 were Volkswagens.

Japanese trade accounted for less than one percent of total world exports in 1961. By 1969, its share had increased to more than eleven percent. During the same period, the shares of most European countries, excluding Sweden and Italy, declined. By 1975, Japan had passed Germany to become the world's largest exporter of cars, controlling a quarter of total world exports. Its share of the seaborne car trade was even larger, standing at about forty-five percent in 1975.[15] The great majority of Japanese exports went to North America, but Japanese exports to Western Europe also grew strongly during the last half of the 1960s. By 1975, Europe was the destination for more than one-quarter of total Japanese car exports.

The increasing volume and spatial dispersion of the car trade made it economically viable to employ fully specialized carriers. In 1964, the Norwegian shipowner Jan Erik Dyvi launched *Dyvi Anglia*, a specialized carrier designed to transport cars on short-sea routes within Europe.[16] Built at the Norwegian yard Torsvik Aker, the ship was constructed with several fixed decks and was fully based on the Roll-on/Roll-off (RoRo) principle. It was the word's first ship built to transport only automobiles.[17] While *Dyvi Anglia* could carry only 450 cars and was constructed solely for short-sea shipping, Dyvi soon launched two more vessels, *Dyvi Atlantic* (1965) and *Dyvi Oceanic* (1968), capable of carrying 1400 and 2500 cars, respectively. Both were employed in transatlantic operations carrying Volkswagen-built cars. By this time, many other shipowners were considering building pure car carriers, and by 1971, sixteen such ships were in operation. Together, these vessels could carry about 40,000 cars, or eleven percent of the total carrying capacity of the world fleet.[18]

The PCC (Pure Car Carrier) fleet gradually outgrew the car/bulk carriers. As long as ballasting could be minimized, these specialized vessels had a number of cost advantages over the car/bulker. Since the ships were constructed with several decks, they had a much greater carrying capacity relative to the gross tonnage of the ship. Because port fees were charged on the basis of gross tonnage, this gave the PCCs a substantial cost saving. The use of

---

[15]Drewry, *The Growth of the Car-Carrying Fleet* (London, 1977).

[16]A detailed description is provided by Dag Bakka, Jr., *Livsseilas I umerket farvann: Dyvi A/S; hovedtrekk I rederiets historie* (Oslo, 2007).

[17]The RoRo principle was not new. As we have seen, Wallenius had launched a car/bulker with RoRo facilities in 1963. Combined passenger/car ferries operating in the North Sea and on cross-Channel services in the 1950s were also designed with RoRo facilities. For details, see Drewry, *The Status of Deep-sea RoRo Services* (London, 1980), 1-2.

[18]Estimated from Drewry, *Growth of the Car-Carrying Fleet*.

RoRo techniques further minimized costs since loading and unloading times were greatly reduced and the potential for damage was reduced significantly. Since the ships had no loading gear, maintenance costs were also lower. Moreover, with a hull design that was better adapted to the cargo actually carried, the PCCs could operate at much higher speeds with relatively lower fuel consumption. By 1976, PCCs comprised one-quarter of the total world capacity of 688,650 cars.[19] The trend toward PCCs was clear. In its 1976 *Report*, the Norwegian shipbroker RS Platou noted that "despite fair prospects for the car trade in 1977, Lift on/Lift off tonnage is now on its way out in favour of RoRo ships, with orders for a number of new pure car carriers as a result."[20]

The car/bulker was also soon challenged by a third type of ship.[21] The deep-sea RoRo/containership was first operated in the North Atlantic trade by the Swedish company Transoceanic, which along with Wallenius and a group of other European shipowning companies from 1965 launched the Atlantic Container Line.[22] These ships - the first two of which, *Atlantic Song* and *Atlantic Span*, were launched in 1967 - were typically designed for specific liner trades where full containerization was not yet deemed feasible. The ships combined RoRo technology with a system for loading containers as well as breakbulk cargo shipped on pallets or in barges. In addition to cars, they could also transport other wheeled cargoes that were either driven or towed onto the ship. By the early 1980s, the total car-carrying capacity of the RoRo fleet was twice that of the car/bulk fleet.[23] In contrast to the development of the car/bulkers, which were dominated by former tramp ship operators, the development of the RoRo/Containership was pushed forward by liner companies. In other words, the development of car carrying as a specialized niche involved a broad and diverse group of participants from the shipping community.

---

[19]Estimated from *ibid.*, 29 and 37.

[20]RS Platou, *Report* (Oslo, 1976), 5.

[21]The following paragraph is based on Drewry, *Status of Deep-sea RoRo Services*; and Drewry, *The Market Role of Large Container RoRo Vessels* (London, 1985).

[22]Transoceanic was a cooperative venture between the Swedish companies Broström and Transatlantic. In addition to Transocean and Wallenius, the participants were the Swedish America Line, Holland-America Line (Incotrans) and later the British liner company Cunard and the French Cie Genereale Transatlantique. See http://www.walleniuslines.com; and Bård Kolltveit and Hans Christian Bangsmoen, *Wilh. Wilhelmsen 150 år: Historien or historier* (Oslo, 2011), 320.

[23]Platou, *Report* (Oslo, 1984), 25.

Both the RoRo/containership and the car/bulk carrier were designed to provide flexibility in cargo handling. The ships could - and did - take a variety of cargo in addition to cars. It therefore was with the introduction of the PCC that car carrying truly became a specialized niche. In fact, the PCC soon turned out to be too specialized. With its fixed decks, set at a standard intermediate height of 1.65 metres, about the only cargo it could take was standard passenger cars. By the late 1970s, though, a more flexible type of car carrier - the so-called Pure Car and Truck Carrier (PCTC) - was launched.[24] The PCTC was designed with adjustable decks which made it possible to combine the transport of regular cars with larger vehicles like buses, trucks and trailers, tractors, harvesters, dump trucks and bulldozers. Several of the decks and loading ramps were strengthened and widened to accommodate static, voluminous and/or heavy cargo, such as machine parts, generators, turbines, windmill parts, paper rolls and other forestry products that could be rolled onto the ship using plates and trucks.

By the late 1980s, the PCTCs and PCCs dominated car-carrying shipping. All of the car/bulkers had been phased out, while only a few multipurpose RoRo vessels still handled cars for selected markets.[25] Throughout the 1990s and 2000s, most PCCs gradually left the industry, leaving the majority of the market to the flexible PCTCs, or the enlarged LCTC (Large Car and Truck Carrier).[26] As can be seen, since its scant beginnings in the early 1960s, the capacity of the car- carrying fleet has grown substantially. The shift in the dominant technology is also clearly visible, from the dominance of car/bulkers, through a period when there were a diverse set of ship types, to the full dominance of the PCTCs.

Among the most active participants in the early development of the car-carrying fleet were the Swedish owner Wallenius and the Norwegian Jan Erik Dyvi. As German automobile exports expanded rapidly during the 1960s, a substantial share of the transport needs was provided by established Norwegian tramp shipping companies, taking Volkswagens on long-term time charters. According to some estimates, by 1969 two-thirds of the vessels transport-

---

[24]See Drewry, *Car Carriers: The Fast Lane of International Shipping*.

[25]According to Platou, *Report* (Oslo, 1990), by 1989 PCCs and PCTCs handled all the car-carrying capacity of the world's fleet. In truth, some vehicles, particularly second-hand cars, continued to be transported in non-specialized general cargo ships, lumber carriers and even reefers. Some new cars were also transported in containers; see Drewry, *Car Carriers*.

[26]In addition, the operators of car carriers typically also operate a fleet of large RoRo vessels to compete specifically for high-and-heavy and break-bulk cargoes.

ing Volkswagen cars were owned by Norwegians (see table 2).[27] This dominant position was also reflected in the ownership of the world fleet. Of a total car/bulk capacity in 1971 of 294,000 cars, Norwegian owners owned forty-one percent. In addition, they owned seventy percent of the still rather small PCC fleet. Together, forty-five percent of the world's car-carrying capacity was in the hands of Norwegians.

Table 2
Ownership and Control of World Car-Carrying Fleet, 1971-2006 (percent)

	1971	**1976**	**1995**	**2006a**	**2006b**
Japaneese	22	25	54	27	45
Norwegian	45	25	13.7	12	21
Swedish	10	7	11	6	12
Other European	16	16	4.6		
Other	7	27	16.7	55	22

Notes: Estimated by car-carrying capacity. Includes both car/bulk carriers and PCCs. Figures for 1971, 1976 and 2006a are based on ownership, while those for 1995 and 2006b are based on the capacity of the fleet actually operated.

Source: Drewry, *Car-Bulk Carriers*; Drewry, *Growth of the Car-Carrying Fleet*; Drewry, *Car Carriers: The Fast Lane of International Shipping*; and Drewry, *Car Carriers: The Fleet and Global Vehicle Trade*.

With a few notable exemptions, the majority of the companies owning these ships were rather small. By 1973, some twenty-five Norwegian shipowning companies owned a total of sixty-six car/bulkers.[28] Most of these firms had also owned part of the large dry-bulk fleet owned and operated from Norway in the 1950s and 1960s, and cars were treated primarily as a valuable additional cargo. Rather than a step towards a specialization in transporting cars, these companies saw the car/bulk carrier as a way of diversifying their dry-bulk operations.

By the early 1970s, Japanese car exports were booming, and Japanese shipowners were gradually entering the car transport market. Japanese shipping had traditionally developed in close concert with domestic manufacturing,

---

[27]Steimler and Stavseth, *Car Transport by Sea*, 43.

[28]Anders Martin Fon, "Et stormakt I Tørrbulk: en økonomisk-historisk analyse av norsk tørrbulkfart, 1950-1973" (Unpublished PhD thesis, Norwegian School of Economics and Business Administration, 1995), 211.

and the development of car-carrying was no exception.[29] All the large shipping companies operating car-carrier tonnage were somehow related to the large *keiretsus* that dominated Japanese business, and most would come to be closely associated with one or a few automobile manufacturers. Although for the largest of these companies - especially the K-line (Kawasaki Kisen Kaisha), MOL (Mitsui-OSK Lines) and NYK (Nippon Yusen Kaisa) - the carriage of cars was part of a broader diversification programme which also included other types of specialized transport, such as container shipping, the growth of Japanese car-carrying capacity was substantial. By 1971, twenty-two percent of the world's car-carrying capacity was in the hands of Japanese owners, making it the second largest such fleet in the world.

In addition to the fleet they owned, the Japanese also controlled a substantial amount of additional tonnage through time charters. In 1971, thirty-five car/bulk carriers with a capacity of more than 55,000 cars were controlled by Japanese owners through such arrangements.[30] Looking more closely at the fleet owned and operated by the three largest Japanese car-carrier companies in 1971, almost half the tonnage was in fact chartered from abroad, a substantial proportion of which came from Norwegians.[31] Since Norwegian owners did not charter in foreign tonnage to the same extent as the Japanese, the actual control of the world fleet of car carriers in 1971 was therefore probably spread more evenly between Norwegian and Japanese interests than the ownership figures suggest. The third largest fleet in terms of ownership at this point was Swedish; about ten percent of the world fleet of car carriers was owned by Swedes.

The large share of Norwegian-owned car carriers in the world fleet gradually declined. By the end of 1976, the Norwegian-owned fleet had decreased to twenty-five percent. This was partly due to disinvestments by the original owners. Many of the smaller tramp operators who invested in car/bulkers in the 1960s left the industry in the mid-1970s as their long-term contracts expired and their vessels became less profitable in competition with the more efficient PCCs. As Drewry noted in 1977, "Scandinavian interests have been disposing of older tonnage and now control fewer car-bulk carriers than they did."[32] Moreover, some of the early innovators moved on. Jan Erik

---

[29]For an overview, see Tomohei Chida and Peter N. Davies, *The Japanese Shipping and Shipbuilding Industries: A History of Their Modern Growth* (London, 1990).

[30]This suggests that about one-fifth of the total fleet of car/bulk carriers operated on time charters for Japanese shipowners.

[31]Drewry, *Car-Bulk Carriers*.

[32]Drewry, *Growth of the Car-Carrying Fleet*, 37.

Dyvi, who had launched the first PCC, sold off his fleet of car carriers and shifted much of his investments to offshore industries.[33]

One important reason for the declining Norwegian position, of course, was the continued expansion by Japanese shipowners. Until 1976, this expansion might seem quite modest, but since the figures in table 2 are based on ownership, they underestimate the size of the fleet effectively controlled by Japanese interests. In 1976, a large share of the fleet owned by others was in fact operated on time charter by Japanese owners. This was also true for many of the Norwegian-owned vessels. As a result, it should also be recognized that by this point Japanese owners, together with the Norwegians, completely dominated the market for modern pure care carriers. Indeed, more than ninety percent of the capacity of this fleet (fifty out of fifty-six ships) was in the hands of Japanese or Norwegian owners; the remaining six were owned by either Swedish (Wallenius) or Italian (Grimaldi) companies.[34] Hence, in terms of the investments made and the possibilities for future expansion, the Japanese and Norwegians were by far the best placed.

Table 3
Leading Car-Carrier Operators, 2006 ('000 CEU)

	Capacity Owned	Capacity Controlled	Share of Total Capacity
NYK	264	393	17
MOL	235	320	14
K-Line	145	344	15
Höegh Autoliners	142	220	9
Wallenius Wilhelmsen	195	264	11
Eukor (WW)	124	350	15
Total			80

Note: Since many of the figures are based on estimates, they may not accurately reflect actual ownership arrangements.

Source: Adopted from Drewry, *Car Carriers: The Fast Lane of International Shipping*, 12.

During the 1980s and 1990s, Japanese owners maintained their dominant position. By 1995, half of the entire car-carrying fleet was effectively in their control. The Norwegian and Swedish presence also remained substantial: at that point, owners from these two countries operated close to a quarter of the fleet. Developments over the following eleven years largely confirmed this

[33]Bakka, *Livsseilas I umerket farvann*.

[34]Drewry, *Growth of the Car-Carrying Fleet*.

pattern (see table 3). In ownership terms, the Japanese fleet remained stable, and Japanese owners continued effectively to control about half of the world's total capacity of car carriers. The Scandinavian ownership share was reduced, but in terms of actual control the fleet was in fact strengthened after 1995. By 2006, Norwegian owners alone controlled a fifth of the world's car-carrying capacity.

Parallel to this development, the overall concentration of ownership was increasing. In 1973, twenty-five Norwegian companies had owned ocean-going, car-carrier tonnage, but by 2006, only two firms were effectively in control of the large majority of the Norwegian fleet. Similarly, while at least eight Japanese companies operated car-carrier tonnage at the beginning of the 1970s, by 2006 the Japanese fleet was primarily controlled by the three majors, NYK, MOL and K-Line. In Sweden, Wallenius had always been the dominant player, but by 2006 all of the smaller owners had left the industry. Hence, as table 3 reveals, by that time four-fifths of the world's ocean-going car-carrying capacity was in fact controlled by only six companies.

To grasp in more detail how the car-carrying industry developed from the perspective of these dominant companies, the following section examines the establishment and growth of the three major Norwegian car-carrier operators. Two of these – Wilhelmsen and Höegh – were still operating in the sector in 2011, while the third, Ugland, left the industry in 2000. The case studies investigate why these companies became involved in the car-carrying industry, how they gained experience and the various strategic approaches each adopted.

Case I: Ugland

We can trace the history of the shipowning company A/S Uglands Rederi (Ugland) back to 1930, when Johan Milmar Ugland bought the sixteen-year-old Anglo-Saxon tanker *Melina* (renamed *Sarita*), which was taken back on a time charter for Anglo-Saxon Petroleum Co., the transport arm of Royal Dutch Shell.[35] After a difficult start, the Ugland fleet was enlarged by the acquisition of more tankers and, after World War II, also by dry-bulk carriers. During the 1950s and 1960s, large bulk ships operated in the iron ore and grain trades became the main focus of expansion. By the mid-1960s, Ugland was Norway's third largest operator of bulk carriers and was the largest in the ore trade. By

[35]The Ugland family, however, traces its history in shipping much further back. For a detailed study, see Gunnar Nerheim and Kristin Øye Gjerde, *Uglandrederiene: verdensvirksomhet med locale røtter* (Grimstad, 1996). The following section draws heavily on this study. In addition, it draws on some selected primary sources, including Andreas K.L. Uglands Private Archive (AKLUPA), "Starten for store bilskip," unpublished memo, 2005; AKLUPA, "Special Developments in Shipping and Offshore," unpublished lecture notes, 2005; and Andreas K.L. Ugland, interview, 23 November 2010.

now, Johan Milmar had stepped down and his two sons, Johan Jørgen and Andreas, were in charge of the company.

Andreas soon became the driving force in the company's expansion into car carriers. During the expansion of their bulk fleet, the Ugland brothers had developed a special relationship with the Swedish shipyard Öresundsvarvet AB. Of the eight bulk ships ordered during the 1950s and 1960s, five were built at this yard. In the early 1960s, however, the yard ran into difficulties: it was about to finish building the last of a series of five bulk carriers for Ugland - the 29,000 dwt *Angelita* - and no further ships were on order. To assist the yard, Andreas Ugland orchestrated a deal whereby he and the yard would finance and own a ship similar to *Angelita*. It was to be launched as a traditional bulk carrier in December 1964; Ugland's plan was to operate it on the spot market.

During the building of the ship, though, the prospective owners had contact with the Swedish company Wallenius, which needed tonnage for round-the-world trade in pig iron, cars and containers. Two months before the ship was launched, Ugland and Öresundsvarvet concluded a ten-year time charter with Wallenius. Soon thereafter, the ship was modified from a pure bulk vessel to a combined car/bulk carrier. With the ability to take cars and heavy cargoes in alternate holds, the ship became more flexible and better suited to Wallenius' trades. The ship was also rebuilt with RoRo facilities so that cars could be driven onto the vessel via side ramps. When the ship left the yard on 20 September 1965, it had become one of the first RoRo-based, car/bulk carriers.

The mid-1960s was a period of growth for Wallenius, and between 1964 and 1966, Ugland organized the construction of six more ships to be put out on time charter to the Swedish firm. In addition to cars and heavy bulk cargoes, these ships could also carry containers on deck. Altogether, the ships could transport 1450 cars, 23,000 tons of heavy cargo and 650 containers. On a typical voyage, the vessels would take pig iron and cars from Europe; drop off the cars at a port on the US east coast; continue to Japan with pig iron (or in some instances, South American ore or American coke); and return to Europe with Japanese cars.

Operating the car/bulk carriers in this round-the-world trade provided Ugland with substantial knowledge of the car trade. Educated as a marine engineer, Andreas Ugland was particularly interested in efficient ship design, and he soon saw many possibilities for improving the car/bulk technology. As he wrote in an internal memo,

> We in UMC learned a lot from this development and one of the conclusions we soon made was that in car transport ships should be built specifically for this light cargo, where we thereby could build a hull that was much sharper, with less

use of bunkers, better transport systems onboard and a better stability to transport cars than what was the case with bulk carriers.[36]

In 1967, the first experiments with the development of such a ship were made when Ugland bought a second-hand shelterdecker from Anders Jahre and rebuilt it into a pure RoRo vehicle carrier. The modifications were made at Ugland's own shipyard, A/S Nymo, and supervised by the newly hired engineer, Tor Arne Thorsen. The rebuilding was made possible by a deal made directly with Saab to take its cars to the US east coast, returning with Chrysler cars as well as trucks, tractors and some break-bulk cargo. The ship was renamed *M/S Saab*. In January 1968, it left Sweden with its first cargo of 993 cars, and by year's end a total of 9500 Saabs had been carried from Sweden to the US. By then, Andreas Ugland had decided to expand his engagement in car transport dramatically by developing ships specifically designed to carry automboiles.

In July 1968, Ugland signed a contract with the German shipyard AG Blom and Voss to build three specialized PCCs. Andreas Ugland and Thorsen worked closely with the yard to construct a ship that could operate more efficiently while also decreasing the amount of damage sustained by the cars. The first ship - *Laurita* - was launched in January 1970. It had a capacity of more than 3000 cars and a maximum speed of twenty-one knots, five knots faster than a typical car/bulk carrier.[37] According to Drewry, it was the fastest and largest PCC in the world when launched.[38] At 5300 gross registered tons (grt), and with the capacity to carry 3200 cars, the capacity-to-volume ratio was substantially improved. By comparison, the car/bulk carriers developed for Wallenius' trade had been registered at about 18,000 grt and could carry only 1500 cars. It soon became apparent that the new design also reduced the damage to the cargo. According to Ugland, during the first trip, damages were reduced from an average of twelve dollars to between two and three dollars per car.[39]

To employ the new PCCs, Ugland Management Co. (UMC), a subsidiary of the Ugland firm, negotiated a three-year contract with Fiat to transport its autos to the US and Australia. The deal was made directly with the Italian manufacturer. Andreas Ugland considered shipbrokers to be unneces-

[36]AKLUPA, "Starten for store bilskip," unpublished memo, 2005.

[37]According to Nerheim and Gjerde, *Uglandrederiene*, the capacity was 2800 cars, but Drewry, *Growth of the Car-Carrying Fleet*, put it at 3200 cars.

[38]See Drewry, *Growth of the Car-Carrying Fleet*, 66-67.

[39]AKLUPA, "Starten for store bilskip."

sary and obstructive, and he considered direct contact with manufacturers the way to provide the best possible service.[40] In addition, making deals directly increased profits. As Ugland wrote, "the contract was made directly with Fiat Transport's managers Mr. Manera and Dr. Maspoli, without brokers in between, which probably saved us 1¼ to 2½ percent of the gross freight."[41]

By 1971, UMC operated a fleet of seven car carriers, four of which were PCCs. The total car-carrying capacity was about 15,000, or 4.5 percent of the world total, and UMC had become one of the largest car-carrier operators in the world.[42] Still, to maximise fleet utilization, more volume was needed, so in the autumn of 1970, Ugland therefore negotiated a deal with the Norwegian shipowner Höegh to organize a car-carrying pool. It was named Höegh Ugland Auto Carriers (HUAL). At the time, Höegh operated a fleet of eight purpose-built car/bulk carriers and was in the process of converting two old turbine tankers into large PCCs. Höegh's ships were engaged in the Volkwsagen trade, but more important, the company had recently signed a contract with Nissan to transport its cars to Europe. Later, the two companies also managed to take a share in the increasing transport of cars to the Middle East. The cooperation provided the two firms a good deal of flexibility in the use of their ships and led to much higher rates of vessel utilization.

Cooperation within HUAL was a substantial success. In 1977, a separate organization was established in Oslo to organize the business; a year later, the pool was formally established as a jointly owned, limited-liability company. During the crisis in the international oil and dry-bulk markets, earnings from transporting autos were substantial. According to Andreas Ugland, "in 1975 and 1976 it was only the car transport market that gave good results."[43] Indeed, to meet all its obligations the pool actually had to charter in tonnage. In the period from 1974 to 1978, the number of ships on time charter for HUAL increased from three to fourteen.[44]

By this time, the partners were ready to order more ships themselves. Ugland ordered its first newbuilding since the three German-built PCCs in

---

[40]Ugland, interview, 23 November 2010.

[41]AKLUPA, "Starten for store bilskip." This point is also noted by Nerheim and Gjerde, *Uglandrederiene*, 182-190.

[42]Estimated from Drewry, *Growth of the Car-Carrying Fleet*.

[43]AKLUPA, "Starten for store bilskip."

[44]Dag Bakka, Jr., *Shipping through Cycles: Leif Höegh & Co., 1927-1997* (Oslo, 1997), 199.

August 1978.[45] The order went to the Japanese yard Mitsui Engineering and Shipbuilding Co. Three months later, two more ships were ordered from the Japanese Tsuneishi yard.[46] The ships had several novel features. Most prominently, they were much more flexible than the original PCCs in terms of cargo handling. While the PCCs were mostly designed for small cars, the new ships were constructed with several hoistable decks and strengthened ramps which enabled them to carry not only cars but also high-and-heavy cargoes. When the ships were delivered in 1980, they were among the first Pure Car and Truck Carriers (PCTSs) in operation.

HUAL continued to be successful throughout the 1980s and 1990s. A new PCTS was delivered by Tsuneishi in 1983, and by the end of the 1980s two additional large PCTS ships with a capacity of more than 6000 cars were delivered from the South Korean yard Daewoo. For UMC and the Ugland group, HUAL became the most important contributor to earnings. As an example, half of the company's total income in 1992 stemmed from HUAL alone. Concluding their study of the company's car-carrying operations in 1996, Gunnar Nerheim and Kristin Øye Gjerde noted that "the car carriers had been a goldmine for the Ugland group for 25 years and they still were."[47]

Much the same story can be told about the other partner in the HUAL pool, Leif Höegh and Co. While Ugland and Höegh cooperated closely through HUAL – and reaped similar economic benefits – the way that Höegh initially entered the car-carrying trade and developed its fleet and market position differed significantly from the experience of Ugland.

Case II: Höegh

Leif Höegh and Co. first entered shipping in 1927 when Höegh established the company Atlantica and signed a contract with a Danish shipyard in Odense for the delivery of an 8000-dwt motor tanker. The ship, named *Varg*, was delivered in 1928.[48] The tanker fleet expanded quickly, and by 1932 Leif Höegh managed a fleet of six vessels. Höegh then went on to buy several dry-cargo vessels to carry break-bulk and general cargoes. In 1936, he bought an 8000-dwt cargo liner to be operated on the Silver-Java Pacific Line between the US west coast and the Middle East, via the Philippines, Indonesia, Singapore, Malaya and India. By 1939, it was operating four cargo liners.

---

[45]Since then, two second-hand ships had been converted and added to the fleet: the liner *Akarita* and the passenger ferry *Cilanos*.

[46]A year later, a third ship was ordered by Ugland (not by UMC).

[47]Nerheim and Gjerde, *Uglandrederiene*, 466.

[48]The following is based largely on Bakka, *Shipping through Cycles*.

During the early postwar years, fleet renewal and expansion were based on tankers and liners. A substantial number of new tankers were delivered in the 1950s, most of which were operated on five- or ten-year time charters. The liner service was expanded by using conventional vessels on routes from the US to the Arabian Gulf and East Asia. Through a joint venture with the French shipowner Francois de Luubersac, a Norwegian–French West Africa Line was also established. A third, but less important, segment was the dry-bulk market. During the late 1950s and early 1960s, Höegh operated three dry-bulk vessels in the 20,000-dwt range. At the time, they were among the largest bulk carriers in the Norwegian-registered fleet.

From the mid-1960s, a purposeful strategy of diversification was adopted. Instead of participating in the rush to order larger tankers and dry-bulk carriers, Höegh sold a large part of its existing fleet and invested the profits in a variety of new ships. One of the trades which attracted Höegh's interest was cars. The first cars were carried on Höegh's ships in 1961, when the West Africa Line signed a contract to transport Volkswagens to the area. More important, Höegh became one of the first Norwegian shipowners to take part in the expanding trade in Volkswagen cars to North America. Through the Norwegian brokers RS Platou, a deal was signed in 1964 to transport Volkswagens to the US east coast and Japan. The return cargo was forest products from Vancouver and Tacoma to Great Britain. To handle the trade, four purpose-built car/bulk carriers were ordered from Japanese shipyards, all of the traditional LoLo type. Three years later, a further three ships were ordered. This time the Norwegian yard Kaldnes in Tönsberg, who had built a series of car/bulk carriers for other Norwegian owners, received the contract. Again, the vessels were destined to transport Volkswagens to the US east coast, returning with forest products from Tacoma.

In 1969, an important three-year contract was signed with Nissan, again with the intermediation of RS Platou, to carry Nissan cars to Europe. An important requirement for Nissan was that its cars were transported in modern PCCs. To meet this obligation, Höegh bought two older turbine tankers and had them converted to PCCs at the Victor Lenak yard in Yugoslavia. The ships were launched in the autumn of 1970 and immediately went to work for the HUAL pool. Less than half a year later, three old passenger/cargo liners were bought and converted into PCCs. Two of these went to Höegh, while Ugland took the third. In the course of only a few years, Höegh had become a large, specialized car-carrying company operating four large PCCs and eight car/bulk carriers.

As with the Ugland group, the HUAL venture was an instant success for Höegh, and it remained so for the next thirty years. The decision to enter the car-carrying trade had been part of a diversified strategy in which conventional tanker and liner tonnage was sold off to finance diversification into new segments. As Dag Bakka wrote in his company history:

> The profits from the operation and sale of 18 ships in 1968/69, with the financial contribution from foreign investors, were injected into a large-scale diversification programme which entailed orders for some 20 vessels. The company abstained from the VLCC-contracting rush...aiming instead at combined carriers, car/bulk vessels, car carriers, gas tankers and factory trawlers.[49]

This purposive strategic shift towards specialized tonnage, including car carriers, contrasts sharply with how Ugland had entered the car trade - primarily by accident. Still, it was Ugland and not Höegh which became the prime mover in developing new and more efficient tonnage. This was not because Höegh lacked a staff of well-educated engineers and naval architects. In fact, as Bakka noted, alongside the strategy shift in the mid-1960s, "some 40 highly skilled professionals were recruited over the next 5-6 years." But Ugland still seems to have been more far-sighted. As late as December 1967, Höegh ordered the conventional, LoLo-based car/bulk carriers, while UMC already operated all its car/bulkers on a RoRo basis. UMC also ordered its first PCCs without having found proper engagements for the ships - it was convinced that the future lay in specially designed car carriers. Höegh's move into PCCs, by contrast, was the result of the deal with Nissan who demanded that the ships be based on the RoRo principle. Finally, while Ugland's first PCCs were purpose-built, with a radically improved car/tonnage ratio, higher speeds and better fuel economy, Höegh's ships were all conversions. The registered volume of Höegh's first PCCs was above 20,000 grt, and the ships could take 3400 cars and operate at a maximum speed of about sixteen knots; this compared with Ugland's first new-built 5000-grt PCCs, which could carry about 3000 cars and steam at twenty-one knots.[50] With rising fuel costs in the 1970s, the converted tankers soon proved unprofitable and were replaced in 1975 by Höegh's first two purpose-built PCCs. The two ships, *Höegh Target* and *Höegh Trigger*, were ordered initially by Jan Erik Dyvi, but they were taken over by Höegh before they left the yard. With a carrying capacity of close to 4000 cars, these vessels were among the world's largest PCCs in terms of capacity. Their registered volume, however, was just above 7000 gross tons, and they could reach a maximum speed of about eighteen knots.

A further difference between the two companies in their approach to the car-carrying trade can be seen in the ways they approached the shippers. Höegh's first experiences with carrying cars were mostly through deals orchestrated by RS Platou. Ugland, by contrast, operated more independently, build-

---

[49]*Ibid.*, 73.

[50]Drewry, *Growth of the Car-Carrying Fleet*, 66-67.

ing his network and arranging contracts on its own. As the two firms cooperated closely throughout the 1980s and 1990s, their strategies and contracting principles tended to become more similar. Both contracted for PCTSs in the early 1980s. Still, while Ugland ordered most of his newbuildings at Tsuneushi, Höegh chose to build at various yards. The company even opted for a new conversion project. A contract for the construction of a Liquified Petroleum Gas (LPG) tanker at the Polish Gdynia yard - the fourth in a series - was converted into two large PCTSs. With a capacity of more than 5000 cars, *HUAL Trader* and *HUAL Transporter*, delivered in 1982, became the largest ships in the HUAL pool. Being conversions, however, the ships suffered some of the same problems as the first rebuilt PCCs, and in 1992 they were sold to make way for new, purpose-built tonnage.

By the mid-1980s, HUAL used its fleet in a complex trading pattern involving a variety of different types of cars as well as larger vehicles, trucks, mobile cranes, agricultural equipment and other high-and-heavy cargoes.[51] The basic pattern consisted of carrying Nissans from Yokohama to Europe, then Volkswagen, Saab, Renault and Fiat cars to the US east or west coasts. Some European cars and heavy vehicles were also taken to the Middle East and Latin America. From the US, the ships took Chrysler and General Motors cars to the Middle East, and then went in ballast back to Japan to pick up more cars. Finally, some Nissans were also carried directly to the US west coast. As the demand for cars expanded into new regions, HUAL opened services directly from Japan to South America and from Europe to West, South and Southeast Africa. As the Korean car industry expanded, HUAL also started to load in several Korean ports. These contract-based transport routes gradually developed into scheduled services. Hence, instead of making long-term contracts independently with the car manufacturers, HUAL gradually developed a fixed set of sailing routes and marketed these to the manufacturers and other companies which needed to ship various types of rolling cargoes. From the tramp-based car/bulk operations in the 1960s, car-carrying thus developed into something resembling a regular liner service.

To service this trade, by the early 1990s the HUAL fleet comprised fourteen ships, seven of which were owned by Ugland and seven by Höegh. In addition, the pool chartered a substantial amount of tonnage.[52] By 1995, HUAL was the world's fifth largest operator of car carriers and the largest of the two Norwegian "majors." With a total carrying capacity of 104,000 CEUs, it controlled about 7.5 percent of the world fleet.

---

[51]The following paragraph is based on Bakka, *Shipping through Cycles*, 199-201 and 230-231.

[52]Nerheim and Gjerde, *Uglandrederiene*, 466.

In 2000, Ugland decided to sell its share in HUAL, and the entire fleet was taken over by Höegh. Sailing under the new name Höegh Autoliners (HA), the fleet continued to grow substantially, and by 2006, it consisted of twenty-six ships with a total capacity of 142,000 cars. In addition, a total of twenty-three vessels were chartered in; hence, the total number of ships actually controlled by Höegh had reached fifty. The total estimated capacity was 220,000 CEUs, or more than double the capacity eleven years earlier. As table three above showed, this growth kept HA among the world's largest operator of car carriers, controlling a nine-percent market share.

In short, even if Höegh and Ugland cooperated closely from the early 1970s in developing their car-carrying businesses, their strategies varied significantly. Most prominently, while the car-carrying operations owned by Andreas Ugland were developed largely on the basis of strong technical and innovative capacities, Höegh's fleet development seems to have relied more on financial considerations and broad market knowledge. Compared to Ugland, Høegh was clearly a follower rather than an innovator in the employment of ships for the car-carrying trade. Still, the company managed to develop a sound operation through its strong managerial and financial competence. A somewhat similar story may be told about the third large Norwegian company which operated successfully in the car-carrying trade. Wilh Wilhelmsen entered this sector in much the same way as Höegh, but its recipe for growth differed significantly, and the way the company became one of the world's largest operators of car carriers exhibited many distinctive features. We turn to this story in the final case presentation.

Case III: Wilh. Wilhelmsen (WW)

With an unbroken history dating back to 1861, Wilh.Wilhelmsen is among the most renowned firms in Norwegian shipping.[53] After operating in both the traditional tramp trade and the early growth of the oil tanker business, the mainstay of WWs operations from the 1920s became liners, especially the scheduled service between Europe and Australia.[54] By 1961, WW operated a fleet of seventy-two vessels, sixty-three of which were cargo liners; the remaining nine were oil tankers. After leaving the tanker industry in the early 1920s, WW re-entered it at the beginning of the 1950s. Tankers gradually became the

---

[53]For two overviews of the company, see Bård Kolltveit and Michael Crowdy, *Wilh. Wilhelmsen, 1861-1994: A Brief History and a Fleet List* (Kendal, 1994); and Kolltveit and Bangsmoen, *Wilh. Wilhelmsen 150 år*.

[54]For details, see Dag Bakka, Jr., *Speed and Service: Wilhelmsen's First Century in Australia* (Broadway, NSW, 2004).

second main part of the company's operations, and by the mid-1970s it operated a total of twenty-five tankers.[55]

Like Höegh, WW's main operations in the 1950s and 1960s were in the liner and the tanker businesses. A third concentration of the Höegh fleet had been the dry-bulk trades. Some dry-bulk ships had also been added to the Wilhelmsen fleet in the 1960s, but as Bård Kolltveit has noted, "involvement in the general tramp and bulk trade had remained modest."[56] From the early 1970s, however, massive investments in bulk tonnage began; between 1970 and 1977, a total of fifteen dry-bulk vessels were ordered.

WW's first experience in carrying cars came through one of its dry-bulk operations. In 1970, in cooperation with what was then Canada's second largest shipowning company, Upper Lakes Shipping (ULS), WW took delivery of five ships designed for bulk, car and paper transport.[57] The ships were to be operated by a new pool - Open Bulk Carriers, marketed as Troll Carriers - established jointly by the two firms. They were specially designed to carry forest products, but could also take up to 2000 Volkswagen cars on removable decks. The ships operated on a LoLo basis. Like the deal which initiated Höegh's decision to order a large number of car/bulk carriers, Troll's project was orchestrated by the Norwegian broker RS Platou. The basic idea was to transport paper products from Canadian and US east coast ports (and later also from the US Gulf) to Europe and to carry cars on the return leg.

Eventually, however, only two of the ships delivered operated in the combined forest products/car pool. The remaining three vessels, all owned by WW, were soon placed on time charters to NYK, MOSK and other Japanese freighters to carry only cars. In 1977 and 1978, WW added two more ships to this trade by converting two conventional bulk ships into PCCs. According to the recent Wilhelmsen company history, while the economic achievements of the "open bulk carrier project" were rather meagre, it gave the firm some "practical experience" in handling cars. More important, perhaps, the time charter deals provided the company with "good relations with the Japanese freighters."[58]

A second route into the carriage of cars came through the company's traditional liner operations to Australia and New Zealand. Again, this bears some resemblance to Höegh, which had taken its first load of cars on its liners

---

[55]Kolltveit and Crowdy, *Wilh. Wilhelmsen*, 24.

[56]*Ibid.*, 32.

[57]Eventually, four of the ships were owned by WW while the fifth was owned by ULS. The following largely follows Kolltveit and Bangsmoen, *Wilh. Wilhelmsen 150 år. Historien og historier*, 313-314.

[58]*Ibid.*, 314 and 397.

going to West Africa. But the scale of these operations had remained limited. By the mid-1970s, Höegh's West Africa line was still operated exclusively using conventional cargo liners with traditional cargo-handling gear, and cars were hardly an important cargo. The operation of WW's Australia and New Zealand lines turned out rather differently.

The Australia and New Zealand lines were a traditional stronghold for WW. By the late 1960s, however, these markets were in transition due to the introduction of the container and the increasing use of cellular container ships on a growing number of routes. WW's response to these changes was to strengthen its ties with other Scandinavian companies and to consider ordering new ships. In July 1969, WW, in collaboration with the Danish East Asiatic Company (EAC) and the Swedish company Transatlantic, decided to establish a common operating company, ScanAustral, for the three companies' Australian trade. To carry on the trade, the three partners ordered five combined RoRo/container vessels, a ship type with which the Swedish partner Transatlantic already had some experience. As we recall, the Ro-Ro/container ship had first been used by Wallenius and Transocean - of which Transatlantic was one of the main partners - in the Atlantic Container Line, established in 1965.

A major advantage of RoRo/container ships in competing with cellular container vessels was that it was able to carry rolling cargoes, including cars, harvesters and large machinery, efficiently. This advantage was well exploited by ScanAustral. After tense negotiations, the company managed to gain acceptance from the Europe-Australia conference that since rolling cargoes could not be carried by its competitors, which by now primarily were operating cellular container ships, they were to remain outside the regulated pool. The result was that for a time ScanAustral was the sole carrier of cars from Europe to Australia.

The carriage of cars soon became quite important to ScanAustral. At the same time, it became more and more difficult to defend the Australian market from the operations of the specialized car carriers. In 1979, ScanAustral's administration suggested to the board that the company should "consider the possibilities" of developing a "liner-type" car-carrying service to increase its frequency and total coverage by catering to the car trade to areas located between Europe and Australia, such as Africa, the Arabian Gulf and East Asia. It was believed that this would make it "more difficult for the car carrier operators to combine such cars with the Australian cars."[59] The suggestion came to nothing, however, and the ScanAustral venture remained a combined operation.

The parallel operation of car/bulk carriers and rebuilt PCCs for Japanese freighters, as well as the ScanAustral venture, developed a growing interest in the Wilhelmsen group for the car-carrying business. But despite the im-

[59]Cited in *ibid.*, 399.

portant experience gained, it was evident that the company lacked both the necessary tonnage and the specific competence required to organize and operate such a business efficiently. To solve the first of these problems, WW ordered a purpose-built car carrier, *Takayama*, for delivery in May 1983. More important, when *Takayama* was delivered it made a deal with Norwegian Specialised Auto Carriers (NOSAC) to buy a share in the company and provide ships for a common NOSAC pool. The deal in many ways marked Wilhelmsen's first step into car carrying as a specialized business.

Soon, however, it seemed that this move into specialized car-carrying operations would be a short-lived affair. After the 1983 deal with NOSAC had been agreed, WW ordered three more ships on its own. But two of these were sold only a year after delivery due to major economic difficulties in the Wilhelmsen group. The company also had to sell major parts of its share in NOSAC. By 1988, seventy percent of NOSAC was owned by the Norwegian America Line (NAL), while Wilhelmsen owned the remainder. As part of a major restructuring, Wilhelmsen also disposed of a series of other activities, such as offshore service ships and mobile rigs. At the same time, it restructured its liner business. Ownership was concentrated in ScanCarriers (former ScanAustral), with Barber Blue Sea as second liner consortia. In 1991, WW took control of Open Bulk carriers, and from April, all lines were operated under the common Wilhemsen Lines profile. New RoRo/container tonnage had been added throughout the 1980s, and the fleet continued to be enlarged in the early 1990s. In 1994, WW contracted for a 44,000-dwt RoRo/container ship – at the time, the world's largest such vessel – at the Mitsubishi Yard in Nagasaki. It seemed clear that transoceanic liner shipping using RoRo/container ships would remain WW's core business, while specialized car carrying at best was to be regarded a subordinate activity.

Only a year later, though, there was a major shift when WW took full control over the shares of NAL, including the entire fleet of car carriers operating under the NOSAC banner. Suddenly, WW was in full control of eleven large and modern specialized car carriers, each with a capacity of about 6000 cars. Within the next few years, two more large PCTSs originally ordered by NOSAC were added.[60] Luckily, since the firm had never been responsible for such a large fleet of car carriers, much of NOSAC's staff and competence were successfully transferred to Wilhelmsen. The strategic rationale behind the move was clearly to decrease the reliance on containers, and particularly on ships carrying combined cargos, in order to focus specifically on cars and other rolling cargoes carried in fully specialized ships. After the purchase of NAL, much of the liner traffic which had been a mainstay of the company's operations since the interwar years, was gradually ended. No more combined

---

[60]Bakka, *Speed and Service*, 167.

RoRo/container ships were ordered, and by 2004, nine of these vessels had been converted to pure RoRo ships.

The acquisition of NAL paved the way for yet another major structural shift. In March 1999, WW and Wallenius agreed to establish a common operating company for their entire fleets of car carriers and RoRo ships. With the acquisition of NAL, the size of Wilhelmsen's car-carrier fleet had suddenly reached the size of that owned by Wallenius. The annual revenues of the two fleets were also virtually identical, and hence this was a merger of equals. The new company, WalleniusWilhelmsen Lines, immediately became one of the market leaders in international car transport, controlling twenty-one percent of the trade.[61] The launch of the new company was followed by an unprecedented fleet expansion. Within about ten years, Wilhelmsen took possession of sixteen large, purpose-built RoRo ships, PCTCs and Large Car Truck Carriers (LCTCs).[62] In addition, another major structural move was made in 2002, when Wallenius and Wilhelmsen jointly acquired the majority of the shares in the car-carrying division of Hyundai Merchant Marine, itself one of the world's largest car-carrying companies. The unit was re-launched as a standalone company named EUKOR, managed by a Korean staff and owned forty percent by Wallenius, forty percent by Wilhelmsen and twenty percent by Hyundai Motor Company and Kia Motors Corporation. Together, the fleets of WalleniusWilhelmsen and EUKOR constituted the largest specialized car-carrying fleet in the world.

Within thirty years, Wilhelmsen had gone from having no experience in handling cars to becoming part of the world's largest car-carrying company. The firm had hardly been a first mover in the trade. Instead, it gained its first experience in handling cars through its car/bulk operations in the early 1970s, by which time other companies already had started to operate purpose-built tonnage that was fully specialized for the transport of cars. For a long period, Wilhelmsen also continued to carry cars in combination with other cargoes. It developed one of the largest and most advanced fleets of combined RoRo/container ships, and even its first specialized car carriers had facilities to carry containers on deck. The overall commercial strategy and types of ships operated by Wilhelmsen therefore differed substantially from the strategies and fleets of its two main Norwegian competitors, Höegh and Ugland. Its overall growth strategy also differed markedly from the other two. While both Höegh and Ugland developed their fleets, as well as their expertise in the handling of cars, gradually and organically, Wilhelmsen expanded its fleet in spurts, pri-

---

[61]It should be noted that the establishment of WalleniusWilhelmsen Lines was not a full merger of Wallenius and Wilhelmsen. WalleniusWilhelmsen was only a common operating company, and the ships continued to be owned separately by the two companies.

[62]Kolltveit and Bangsmoen, *Wilh. Wilhelmsen 150 år*, 443-445.

marily through mergers and acquisitions. Competence in the operation of specialized car carriers was largely brought in from outside. The acquisition of a share in NOSAC in the early 1980s was the first step, followed by the takeover of NAL in 1995, which included the transfer of a large and well-trained staff. The establishment of WalleniusWilhelmsen in 1999 and the acquisition of Hyundai Merchant Marine's car division in 2002 were the final last steps in this strategy. It was thus no coincidence that the British shipping consultants Drewry, in commenting on WallniusWilhelmsen's purchase of Hyundai Merchant Marine's car division, concluded that this "was but the latest move in a clear line of industry consolidation, *in which Wilhelmsen has been the prime mover.*"[63]

Conclusion and Further Research

The growth of specialized shipping was one of the main trends in the post-WWII international maritime industry. Increasing specialization meant that cargoes which traditionally had been transported in tramp ships or cargo liners - or not traded at all due to the difficulties of transporting them over long distances - were now handled by ships purposely built to carry them. From the 1960s, a series of ship types never before seen in international shipping entered the market. Together with the more commonly acknowledged bulk and container revolutions, the development of specialized shipping fundamentally transformed the international shipping market. From the traditional two-tier structure of liners and tramps, the market for seaborne transport diversified into a number of separate sectors, each operating according to its own industrial logic.

This "specialization revolution" has increasingly been recognized in the international literature. Our understanding of how it actually came about, however, remains limited. The present essay has tried to fill some of these lacunae by investigating the establishment and growth of the seaborne car-carrying industry. It has explored the technological history of the specialized car carrier and shown how the PCTCs which dominate the industry today were preceded by a series of alternative ship types. The article has also investigated the development of the ownership pattern and identified the major companies involved in the establishment and subsequent growth of the industry. The organizational histories of some of these companies were explored through three detailed case studies.

While the specialization process characterizing international shipping from the 1960s onwards is often described as a "revolution," the development of the specialized, deep-sea car-carrying industry was essentially an evolution-

[63]Drewry, *Car Carriers: The Fast Lane of International Shipping*, 81 (emphasis added).

ary process. Although overseas trade in cars started to develop from the 1960s, seaborne car transport long remained a combined trade in which automobiles were taken by conventional bulk operators to replace ballast voyages or were transported together with other manufactured goods, various types of break-bulk cargoes or with containers. It was not until the early 1980s that the capacity of the specialized car carrier fleet exceeded the capacity of the combined car/bulk and RoRo/container fleets. The technological development of the specialized car-carrying ship similarly turned out to be a gradual process. A large variety of ship types, stowing arrangements and loading and unloading techniques were employed before operators in the early 1980s finally settled on the PCTC, a ship that in fact was less specialized than the PCCs launched in the early 1970s. This protracted process contrasted with the development of one of the other major specialized segments in world shipping; chemical tankers. The breakthrough for this trade came with the introduction of the parcel tanker in the early 1950s.[64] The parcel tanker made overseas trade in a large variety of chemicals economically viable since it solved the basic problem of how to transport simultaneously many different types of chemicals in bulk. While the parcel tanker went through major technological improvements in the following years – the introduction of stainless steel tanks being one of the most important – the basic technology remained essentially the same. Not so for car carriers, however, which went through a series of fundamental technological shifts before operators settled on a common ship design. Similar to the chemical trade, though, the ownership structure of the car-carrying industry remained stable. While Norwegian and British owners came to dominate chemical shipping, Japanese and Scandinavian owners controlled the car-carrying industry from the beginning and remain dominant today. As the case studies showed, this does not mean that the recipes for success and the strategies for growth within the car-carrying industry were similar for all the firms involved. Rather, the company studies showed that the firms operating car carriers became involved in the industry for very different reasons. Moreover, they drew their competitive strength from different types of organizational capabilities and adopted markedly different strategies for growth. In sum, then, the growth of the deep-sea car-carrying industry, from its beginnings in the early 1960s until the first decade of the twenty-first century, was a complex, evolutionary process. Technologically, it involved much trial and error. At the company level, it was driven by a variety of organization-specific capabilities and strategic responses.

While hopefully providing some valuable insights, the analysis above leaves many important questions unanswered. More research is needed if we are to understand fully the complex forces that shaped the growth of the car-carrying industry. The relationship between the seaborne car-carrying industry

---

[64]For an overview, see Murphy and Tenold, "Strategies, Market Concentration and Hegemony," 291-309.

and automobile manufacturing remains largely unexplored. Moreover, we still know little about how the introduction of the car/bulk carrier, and later PCC and PCTC, affected the price of overseas car transport and hence the substantial growth in the international car trade. The phenomenal growth of the Japanese car-carrier fleets and their role in the development of new technology has also been ignored by scholars. Scandinavian sources tend to claim that shipowners from the Nordic nations were the pioneers in introducing new technology and that the Japanese simply followed their technological lead.[65] But these claims rest on a biased set of sources and need to be examined critically. More research, therefore, is still needed on the development of car transport as a specialized niche in international shipping. This work should proceed alongside studies on the development of other niches, as well as on the process of specialization more generally.

---

[65]This view was propounded in most of my interviews and has also resonated in much of the Scandinavian literature.

Printed and bound by CPI Group (UK) Ltd, Croydon, CR0 4YY

16/04/2025

14658576-0003